The Languages of the Jews

Historical sociolinguistics is a comparatively new area of research, investigating difficult questions about language varieties and choices in speech and writing. Jewish historical sociolinguistics is rich in unanswered questions: when does a language become "Jewish"? What was the origin of Yiddish? How much Hebrew did the average Jew know over the centuries? How was Hebrew re-established as a vernacular and a dominant language? This book explores these and other questions, and shows the extent of scholarly disagreement over the answers. It shows the value of adding a sociolinguistic perspective to issues commonly ignored in standard histories. This is a vivid commentary on Jewish survival and Jewish speech communities, and is essential reading for students and researchers interested in the study of Middle Eastern languages, Jewish Studies, and sociolinguistics.

BERNARD SPOLSKY is Professor Emeritus of the English Department at Bar-Ilan University and editor of *The Cambridge Handbook of Language Policy* (2012).

The Languages of the Jews

A Sociolinguistic History

Bernard Spolsky

CAMBRIDGE
UNIVERSITY PRESS

CAMBRIDGE
UNIVERSITY PRESS

University Printing House, Cambridge CB2 8BS, United Kingdom

Published in the United States of America by Cambridge University Press, New York

Cambridge University Press is part of the University of Cambridge.

It furthers the University's mission by disseminating knowledge in the pursuit of education, learning, and research at the highest international levels of excellence.

www.cambridge.org
Information on this title: www.cambridge.org/9781107699953

First published 2014

Printed in the United Kingdom by Clays, St Ives plc

A catalogue record for this publication is available from the British Library

Library of Congress Cataloguing in Publication data
Spolsky, Bernard.
The languages of the Jews : a sociolinguistic history / Bernard Spolsky.
   pages cm
Includes bibliographical references.
ISBN 978-1-107-05544-5
1. Jews – Languages – History.   2. Sociolinguistics.   3. Jews – History.
I. Title.
PJ5061.S66   2014
408.9924–dc23

                                                                    2013043052

ISBN 978-1-107-05544-5 Hardback
ISBN 978-1-107-69995-3 Paperback

For Ellen

Contents

Contents

Maps

Preface and acknowledgments

I started working on the topic of this book thirty years ago, shortly after I returned to Israel and began to think about the multilingual society I was again living in. A first paper[1] broached the field for me, and exposed me to the challenge of studying the sociolinguistic ecology of no longer existing communities. That was my first attempt at historical sociolinguistics; there were further essays in the genre within two later books, *The Languages of Jerusalem*[2] and *The Languages of Israel*.[3] The present book seems to me a natural next step, filling in the gaps between the history in the former and the contemporary survey in the latter.

The title should make it clear that I am going beyond the concern with Jewish languages (such as Yiddish and Ladino), the study of which was opened seriously by Max Weinreich and has been continued by a large group of scholars (they appear on the website www.jewish-languages.org), to ask about any of the "co-territorial" varieties – as Weinreich called them – that have become the vernacular or standard languages used by Jewish communities. This perspective will challenge me to consider when a variety adopted and used by Jews has been sufficiently modified to justify calling it a "Jewish language".

The book sets out to combine a brief history of the Jewish people with a history of the sociolinguistic ecologies that resulted from this history, and thus forms a continuing study of language loyalty, as Joshua Fishman called it in his pioneering work on language shift, loss, maintenance, death, and revival.[4] By force of circumstances, ever since the Babylonian exile in the sixth century before the Common Era, and even more since the destruction of the Temple and the Jewish state by the Romans and the dispersion of Jews throughout the ancient world, exacerbated by regular expulsions by Christians and Muslims alike, resulting in even wider geographical spread and contact with even more languages, Jews have been individually plurilingual and collectively multilingual, held together over these three millennia by their devotion to and use of the original Jewish language: Hebrew.

Hebrew having been limited to liturgy, scholarship, and literacy for centuries, the story of its revernacularization and revitalization as the dominant language of the renewed Jewish state of Israel is seen as a model for many groups threatened with the loss of their own heritage languages. This book, focused as it is on Jewish language use, provides an opportunity to explore many of the most significant issues and processes in the theory of language policy and the practice of language management as relevant to endangered languages.

I began these studies in conversations and collaboration with the late Robert Cooper and with Elana Shohamy, and was encouraged to persevere with historical sociolinguistics by Christina Bratt Paulston. As will become apparent to anyone who glances at the endnotes and the references, this book is built on the research and scholarship of a large number of others, to whom I must offer my deepest gratitude. While I sometimes take issue with their opinions, I cannot ignore their findings, and depend on the data they have published. Of these, Fishman has obviously been the first and most important. There are others whose names crop up regularly and whose leadership has been critical. Weinreich was clearly the major scholar in the field, and the new edition of his classic study, more than doubled in size to include the notes, has been invaluable.

Although I wrote most of this book in Jerusalem, some of the revision was done in quiet moments looking out over the hills of Tuscany, where I was spending a fortnight with the family. Several days were devoted to trips to some of the walled cities, and twice we visited Lucca, an obviously prosperous town with a wall that can be comfortably walked or biked around. There is no trace of the Kalonymus family, whose ancestor moved from Lucca to help establish the Ashkenazi community in Metz, playing a key role in the development of Loter. The only trace we noted of Jewish presence was a *gelateria* whose ice cream was reputed to be kosher. Only in Rome and Milan are there still large and active Jewish Italian communities. Even Rome, the largest and oldest community, turns out to have had a very embittered history. Jews in Rome were crowded into a tiny area on the banks of the river Tiber. When the synagogue was rebuilt at the end of the nineteenth century, it was modeled on a church building, for there were no Jews in Italy who had been allowed to study or practice architecture or engineering. After a brief period of emancipation at the beginning of the twentieth century, the Fascist regime lowered the civil status of Jews. Since the end of Fascism, there have been brief moments of glory (the visit of a Pope to the synagogue) and horror (the bombing of the synagogue), confirming the fragility of Jewish life there.

What this trip reminded me of is the virtual absence of Jews from many of the sites described in this book. The Jews of central and eastern Europe were finally exterminated by the Nazis with the help of local anti-Semites, many Jews who survived the Holocaust and Stalinist oppression in the Soviet Union have now emigrated to Israel, and almost all Jews in Arab and Muslim lands have also been driven out. Only in western Europe do Jewish communities survive, dealing with new restrictions on Jewish observance, such as a ban on the kosher killing of animals and on circumcision. And liberal democratic western Europe, after a brief period of regret at its share in the Holocaust, now resumes anti-Jewish activities disguised as defense of freedom fighters. So, too, have the Jewish varieties of language that grew in Europe and the Middle East disappeared, with the destruction of their speakers or the assimilation of survivors.

This is an appropriate place to thank Andrew Winnard and his colleagues at Cambridge University Press, who have guided the publication of this and my three preceding books. I thank also the three anonymous scholars who read and approved the proposal, making a number of useful suggestions, which I have incorporated. I thank Judith Baskin and Kenneth Seeskin for permission to use their maps. I want also to pay tribute to the search engines (especially Google and Google Scholar) that helped me find sources and the digital records of books and articles, which saved me hours of library work and yards of home shelf space. With the aid of a computer and the internet, I have been able to accomplish in fifteen months what would have taken a lifetime when I first started academic work.

I want also to acknowledge the love, devotion, patience, and questions of my wife, Ellen Spolsky, over the half-century we have shared, especially as she has been distracted from her own writings by my regular demands for her attention. Given the pressures of publication and the continuing developments of the field, additional information and updates can be found at www.cambridge.org/spolsky.

Glossary

Ashkenazim (singular *Ashkenazi*)	Jews from Europe
Beta Israel	Jews from Ethiopia
Halacha	Jewish religious law and practice
Haredim (singular *Haredi*)	fundamentalist or ultra-orthodox Jews
Hasidim (singular *Hasid*)	members of one of the sects of orthodox Judaism following a movement founded in the eighteenth century; sects are usually named after the town of their first leader, such as Lubavitcher, Satmar, or Belz
Heder	traditional Jewish elementary school
Leshon hakodesh (Hebrew; *loshn koydesh*, Yiddish)	Hebrew or Hebrew–Aramaic, sacred language
Mishnah	early (third century CE) compilation of commentaries and interpretation of the Torah
Mizrahim (singular *Mizrahi*)	Jews from north Africa and Arab countries
Sephardim (singular *Sephardi*)	Jews originating from Spain or Portugal
Teiku	Talmudic term meaning "The question has not been resolved"

1   Is Hebrew an endangered language?

Two questions

When people learn that I am a linguist, the first question they ask me is: how many languages do you know? Once I have successfully dodged an answer, the next question depends on where I am. At conferences dealing with language policy, one of the first questions people ask me is about the revitalization of Hebrew, and what I can tell them about it so that they can use the information to deal with the problem of the endangerment of their heritage languages.

Once you judge a language not by how many speakers it still has but by the age of the youngest speaker, you know it is in trouble. Joshua Fishman, one of the leading experts in the field of the sociology of language, defines the lowest stage of language maintenance as when it is known only by old isolated individuals without anyone to speak to.[1] This was the situation with Eyak, a language once spoken by natives of Alaska; Michael Krauss, a linguist who studied it, said he knew only two old women who could speak it, and they hadn't talked to each for many years; both have since died. Eyak had started to disappear when members of the tribe began to switch to Tlingit, a language that now has about 400 speakers in the United States and Canada, most of whom are now bilingual in English. All over the world, speakers of the many languages that are endangered are trying to restore their use, which is why they ask about what they call the miracle of the rebirth of Hebrew. I tell them about the special conditions that made this possible and warn them how hard a task they are facing.

At home in Israel, I am asked a different question: is Hebrew itself in danger? Has the immigration of 1 million Russian speakers made it less likely to survive? Do all the English words we hear in Hebrew mean that it is threatened? And what about English-language TV, and computers, and the way that children slip English words and phrases into their conversations? And how, the president of the Academy of the Hebrew Language has recently asked, can we prevent the universities from using so much English and forcing the students to use it?[2] And might the fact that Arabic is legally recognized as an official language detract from Hebrew's status? After all, didn't we lose Hebrew once, during the

Babylonian exile, and again, more seriously, after the destruction of the Temple by the Romans and in the Diaspora?

My first simple answer is that Hebrew is alive and well, and no more threatened than any other language of a small, vital nation. In the rest of this chapter, I flesh out this answer by describing what I call the *sociolinguistic ecology* of Israel, the complex network of communication that Hebrew dominates while sharing it in part with many other language varieties. To do this, I use a model that helps us understand the way that language varieties divide up a communication habitat.

First, I need to give two preliminary definitions. To start, I take the most obvious and common meaning of a *language* to include all the varieties to which the name may be attached; thus, *English* includes all the varieties,[3] including the historical and obsolete, such as the languages of *Beowulf* and Chaucer, and the modern dialects (Texan and Irish and Australian and Indian[4]), which may or may not be mutually intelligible. In this approach *Hebrew* includes the classical biblical language (as it changed over the epochs when it was spoken and written) and its later descendants: Mishnaic Hebrew (which I accept represents a later, more colloquial variety and not an artificial language of the rabbis), and the various medieval and Enlightenment versions, and all the varieties of Modern Israeli Hebrew (General or Ashkenazi, Sephardi, Mizrahi, Yemenite, or whatever), with all their lexical and grammatical changes and ethnic and social dialects and accents. I will be more precise when it seems relevant, and make clear when I am talking about the kinds of mixed varieties that occur as when, for instance, English- or Spanish-speaking immigrants to Israel use the language, or when their children switch between Hebrew and their heritage language.

Second, I start by assuming the widest possible meaning for *Jews*, leaving for others the difficult question of whether we are referring to a people, a religion, a nation, a culture, or a civilization, or whatever other label seems appropriate.[5] As you read, you will come to realize that I have much more elaborate and complex definitions for these basic terms, but they shouldn't hold us up.

Sociolinguistic ecology

Although my first jobs were as a language teacher, my academic research was in applied linguistics and language testing. As time went on, I developed an interest in sociolinguistics, a field that deals with the uses of the varieties of language in a social setting, finishing up with my current preoccupation with language policy. I have published two recent books on the topic, *Language Policy*[6] and *Language Management*,[7] and I have also just edited *The Cambridge Handbook of Language Policy*,[8] with thirty-two chapters written by colleagues who are experts in the many parts of the field. This focus explains my lack of expertise in formal linguistics, such as grammar and historical language change, and my need to rely on experts in those areas.

I will be more confident in standing by my own judgment applying generalizations I have developed studying specific language situations and dealing with language policy. The model I am finding most useful for this is a *sociolinguistic ecology*; Einar Haugen[9] introduced the term and the biological evolutionary metaphor, with language varieties seen as competing for dominance in the many habitats of language use in a society.

It is hard to define the limits of the objects of study. What do we mean by "the Jewish world", which includes Israel?[10] In this chapter, I am dealing specifically with Israel. But how do we treat non-Jews in Israel and Jews in the Diaspora? Perhaps the fact that there is now a state in which Hebrew is one of the official languages as well as the dominant variety changes the picture considerably and means we do not need to worry about its survival in a diaspora community. But diaspora communities can be important, especially when they are all that is left, as Cook Island Māori is now spoken mainly in New Zealand. For a sociolinguist, the loss of language use in a diaspora community may be as relevant as in the homeland, for our interest is in a community of speakers. For a linguist worried about Russian language endangerment, the fact that Russian-speaking immigrants to Israel are slowly moving to Hebrew is irrelevant, as the language continues in the Russian Federation. So what happens to Hebrew in the United States is important, but not vital for the survival of the language.

There are two different linguistic approaches to defining communities. The classic approach in the work of the structural linguists was to talk about a *language* community, such as the English-speaking world, or *la francophonie*, or all the speakers of a language whether or not they were ever in contact. For sociolinguists, the more useful unit has been the *speech* community, a term invented by John Gumperz[11] and quickly picked up by his colleagues[12] and exploited by William Labov in his study of New York City as a speech community.[13] Labov suggests, and others agree, that it is not important that all the members of a speech community use the same language varieties but, rather, that they share the same values for the varieties: New Yorkers don't need to be able to imitate a Brooklyn accent, but to be able to recognize one. Dell Hymes, who has defined speech community as the "concurrence of rules of grammar and rules of use",[14] emphasizes its social nature: one should start with the community and its means of expression rather than with a language.[15]

Communities and demographics

When we are interested in language maintenance and loss, the first question is: who uses it? To answer the question about the current stability of Hebrew, it helps to distinguish between Israel (where it is the official and dominant language and is passed on to babies) and the Diaspora (where it is associated with Israel and with Jewish education and religious practice, but depends for its survival on schools and immigrants from Israel).

Within Israel there are a number of distinct communities, each including smaller ones. A first division might be made between Jews, Arabs, and foreigners. Jews in Israel can be divided sociolinguistically between native-born and immigrants. They also divide between a general group (secular and modern orthodox) and *Haredim* (ultra-orthodox), although modern orthodox and *Haredim* share education in older varieties of Hebrew and use of religious terms.[16]

Another division, cutting across the first, is between *Ashkenazim* (those whose ancestors came via Europe), *Sephardim* (descended from the Jews expelled from Spain in 1492 who moved to the Ottoman Empire or north Africa), and *Mizrahim* (north African or Middle Eastern Jews whose ancestors lived in Arabic-speaking countries until they escaped or were expelled). Immigrants divide up linguistically between those who have been here for long enough to learn Hebrew and those whose immigration is more recent; among their children, a critical difference is between those who have been in Israel for six or seven years and more recent arrivals. They also divide up according to country of origin, with major groupings from Russia, Ethiopia, France, the United States and England, and South America added to the earlier groups from eastern Europe and Arab countries.

Israeli Arabs too need to be more finely defined; one useful division is between city dwellers, in regular contact with Jews or working in Jewish businesses, and villagers or those living in Arab towns. Another relevant division is between the Muslim majority and the Christian minorities, who add other languages (Armenian, Turkish, Syriac, or Aramaic, for instance). Two important groups are Bedouin and Druze, both of whom may serve in the army and therefore know more Hebrew.

There are also foreigners; not just large numbers of tourists and pilgrims, but also many workers from Africa or Asia, who may be documented or not. Foreign workers are commonly employed either in agriculture or the building industry, or as caregivers.[17]

The language practices of these communities are not hard to guess (which is just as well, because, in the absence of a language question on the Israeli census, it can only be guessed or derived from small focused studies or from the language questions included in the 2011 Social Survey, which I discuss later).

Native-born Jews and their children are most likely to have Hebrew as their mother tongue (the language in which their parents spoke to them when they were growing up) and to use it regularly. Most *Haredim* now know and use Hebrew, but some sects of *Hasidim*[18] still use or favor the use of Yiddish as a way of keeping separate from the Hebrew-speaking Zionists who serve in the army and whose taxes and charity subsidize their large and largely unemployed families. Many older immigrants still use their heritage languages, such as Polish or Yiddish and various forms of Judeo-Arabic; most are bilingual in Hebrew, and their heritage languages incorporate many Hebraisms. More recent immigrants are likely to be proficient in their heritage languages, such as English, French, Russian, Spanish, or Amharic, but their children are becoming increasingly proficient in Hebrew, and after six or seven years in Israel are similar to native-born (the Beta Israel are an exception). Palestinian Arabs from the Arab towns and villages tend to speak Palestinian Arabic, but, with increasing education or with employment in the general sector, are likely to develop proficiency in Hebrew; those from the mixed towns are commonly bilingual in Palestinian Arabic and Hebrew; their schooling has included classical or Qur'anic Arabic.

Foreign workers in agriculture have minimal Hebrew (their foremen act as interpreters) and continue to use their native languages, whether Thai or an African language. Those employed as caregivers (many from the Philippines) or in hotels and restaurants will have learned some Hebrew or picked up the language of their employers.

Cutting across these divisions are some general tendencies. Arab women and *Haredi* men are less likely to be employed in the workforce, and so less likely to be proficient in spoken Hebrew. Druze and those Bedouin who serve in the army will be more proficient in Hebrew than other Palestinian Arabs. Immigrants who live in closer contact with their compatriots (in Russian neighborhoods such as Ashkelon, or French neighborhoods such as Netanya, or English neighborhoods such as Raanana, Bet Shemesh, or Efrat) are more likely to keep using their heritage language in public as well as private, and some of their children will still speak a heritage language.

But Modern Israeli Hebrew remains the dominant, normal, and unmarked language of Israel. If we had a language census, it would still be by far the most common language, as it was in 1983, when there were estimated to be 2,166,973 people speaking it, compared to 667,810 speakers of Palestinian Arabic, 199,780 speakers of English, 189,220 speakers of Yiddish, 116,690 speakers of Romanian, 107,335 speakers of French, and 101,065 speakers of Russian (an extra 1 million or so arrived in the 1990s, making it the second largest language), listing only those over 100,000. If we are worrying about numbers alone, with the current 6 to 7 million estimated speakers and a higher proportion of younger than older speakers, the Hebrew language seems relatively safe in Israel. The 2011 Social Survey supports this view.

2011 Social Survey

There are at last some data available on native languages and language use in Israel.[19] Since 2002 the Israel Central Bureau of Statistics has conducted the annual Social Survey on a sample of Israelis aged twenty years and over. Each year the questions have included 100 items covering the main areas of life, and each year an additional module has been added dealing with one or two specific topics. In 2011 the two added topics were studies during a lifetime and the use of language. This second topic provides the first survey data since the language question in the 1983 census, although the questions and the population were not comparable: the 1983 question asked about language knowledge and dealt with people over fifteen, while the 2011 survey focused on native language and language use in a population over the age of twenty.[20]

The questionnaire named eight languages: Hebrew, Arabic, English, Russian, Amharic, French, Spanish, and Yiddish. There are a number of interesting changes in the ranking of the languages from the 1983 census. Hebrew remains first, though the number calling it their native tongue now stands at 49 percent (but 61 percent among Jews, compared to 59 percent in the 1983 census), and Russian[21] native speakers are now 15 percent, compared to a total of 5 percent in the census. Arabic remains unchanged at 18 percent, and Yiddish has dropped to 2 percent, while English and French have risen to 2 percent. Among Jews, about 75 percent report very good proficiency in Hebrew. Filling out forms in Hebrew is a problem for 27 percent of the sample and for 45 percent of the Arabs.

As well as the native speakers counts, there were questions on language use. Among Arabs, 98 percent speak Arabic at home, but 4 percent also speak Hebrew there. Of those who are employed, 79 percent use Hebrew at work, but only 20 percent use only Hebrew; 79 percent use Arabic at work, but only 16 percent use only Arabic.

Among those born in the former Soviet Union, 88 percent speak Russian at home, and 48 percent speak only Russian at home; 48 percent speak Hebrew at home, and 8 percent speak only Hebrew at home. Of those former Soviet Jews[22] who are employed, 93 percent speak Hebrew at work, and 32 percent speak only Hebrew at work, but 57 percent speak Russian at work, and 6 percent speak only Russian at work. Employment and knowledge of Hebrew are closely connected. Most former Soviet Jews (87 percent) continue to speak Russian with their friends, but 38 percent speak only Russian with friends; 9 percent speak only Hebrew with friends.

Age is also correlated with native language: only 18 percent of the respondents over sixty-five have Hebrew as a native language, 44 percent of those between forty-five and sixty-four, and 60 percent of those between twenty and forty-four. Jews generally claim stronger proficiency in Hebrew than Arabs, as do immigrants who arrived before 1990 than those who arrived later.

Proficiency in Hebrew is related to income, as shown in earlier studies of immigrants in many countries.[23] Among Arabs, the level of academic success is also related to proficiency in Hebrew; while Arab schools in Israel use Arabic as the language of instruction, they also emphasize developing Hebrew-language skills. Ability in language is also related to employment; 82 percent of those Arabs with high levels of Hebrew proficiency are employed.

These new data clearly confirm the dominance of Hebrew in Israel. It is understandable that the addition of over 1 million immigrants from the Soviet Union in the 1990s changed the language balance towards Russian, but, remembering that setting the lowest age for the survey at twenty means that most of the Russian speakers included were born in the Soviet Union and that all Israeli schools teach in Hebrew only, we can see the shift of this population too towards Hebrew, with education and employment accounting for much of the change. With all the evidence showing that younger speakers are becoming Hebrew speakers, it seems reasonable to suggest that, without the continuing immigration of Russian speakers, the language will continue to decline over the next generations. The data also reveal the incursion of Hebrew into the Israeli Arab population: its relation to education and employment demonstrates the pragmatic pressures on the language practices of the community.

Domains

The numbers, then, are positive, but another way to estimate a language's stability is to list the domains in which it is used. Joshua Fishman introduced this concept in his major study of the Jersey City *barrio*.[24] A sociolinguistic domain, he suggests, has typical participants (defined by their roles), topics of conversation, and locations. For the New Jersey Spanish-speaking population, he identifies five significant domains. The first is family, in which typical participants are family members; the second is friendship; the third is religion, in which participants are priests and congregants; the next is education, with teachers and students; and the last is employment.[25] There turned out to be regularities of language choice in these situations, with Spanish most used for family and religion, and English for education and employment. This pattern, he argues, produces stable *diglossia*, a term he uses for the division of functions for language use equivalent to the cases of the stable contrast between the uses of standard German and Swiss German in Switzerland, or Classical Arabic and the regional varieties, or French and Creole in Haiti. That is to say, people are not just bilingual, but live in a speech community where there are defined rules for choosing a language.[26] When I go into a post office in my Jerusalem suburb, I expect to use Hebrew; when I meet a tourist, I expect to be addressed in English.

Applying the domain model to Israel, we find that the most common language for home and neighborhood use among Jews (except for recent and elderly immigrants and some Hasidim) is Hebrew. In new immigrant families that still use heritage languages, the children increasingly use Hebrew with each other, and even with their parents. Russian immigrant parents prefer to use

Russian with their children, but the majority permit switching. The children report that they use Russian with their parents half the time and with their grandparents all the time; only 10 percent use Hebrew with their parents. Over 40 percent use Hebrew with siblings, and 70 percent use Hebrew with the Russian-speaking peers who are their main friends.[27] Shulamit Kopeliovich has studied the families in one community of former Soviet Jews as their children bring Hebrew into the family and as the parents attempt (with varying degrees of success) to persuade the children to maintain their Russian.[28] Earlier studies confirmed this, reporting that children of Soviet immigrants were learning Hebrew rapidly.[29] Another study of the children of former Soviet immigrants found that it took six or seven years in Israel for Russian children to catch up with native-born children in Hebrew and mathematics scores.[30] The same study showed Beta Israel (Ethiopian) immigrant children took longer, as confirmed in evidence that the language of the home and the language used with children remains Amharic or Tigrinya.[31] In *Haredi* families most spoke Hebrew; mothers generally spoke to their children in Hebrew, but in some Hasidic groups there is encouragement of Yiddish. Boys start to learn Yiddish when they go to *heder* (ultra-orthodox state-funded but independent elementary schools, usually not following state curricula) and their sisters may be taught Yiddish as a subject when they go to school.[32] While French remains important to immigrants from north Africa, many of whom speak it, the children of these immigrants grow up speaking Hebrew but may be encouraged to learn French in school.[33]

For most Jewish immigrant children, the first outside pressure to speak Hebrew comes from peers who live in the neighborhood. The government policy of concentrating Ethiopian immigrants helps account for the slowness of assimilation of this group. The second outside pressure is the school, with pre-school programs having a major effect too. "The second generation of Russian-speaking immigrants are generally exposed to the L2 (Hebrew) as soon as they enter a kindergarten at ages two to three, with the result that Hebrew inevitably appears to be the socially and educationally dominant language."[34]

The rapid urbanization of so many communities throughout the world is a key factor in language endangerment and loss; in 1950 70 percent of the world's population was estimated to be rural, and 30 percent urban, but by 2050 these figures will probably be reversed. There are urban neighborhoods in Israel where languages other than Hebrew are heard in public, such as the Arab-speaking towns and villages of the Triangle and parts of Jaffa and Haifa, the centers of intensive Russian and Beta Israel settlement, the English or French immigrant suburbs, or the Haredi Yiddish enclaves.

Early studies[35] showed the use of English in some neighborhoods of Jerusalem, and, in a shopping street close to the center of the city, 14 percent of the conversations overheard were in English. Most of those using English were native speakers, but only a half of those using Hebrew had grown up speaking it.[36] While these studies attest to the high status of English – something noted earlier in a study of the attitudes of high school students[37] – and its value as a second language among non-speakers of Hebrew,[38] they also make clear the public dominance of Hebrew, especially taking into account that most of the shopkeepers in the study were native speakers of Yiddish or Arabic. There are middle-class neighborhoods where French is heard in public (Netanya is an example), but the bulk of French speakers are of north African origin; in their neighborhoods, a north African variety of French and Moroccan Judeo-Arabic can be heard, especially from the elderly.[39] There are neighborhoods in Tel Aviv where one hears Yiddish from the elderly, but they are commonly bilingual and use Hebrew with their younger relatives. Varieties of Judeo-Arabic continue to be heard from older people, but the numbers are declining rapidly, as their children commonly speak an unmarked variety of Hebrew.[40] Other languages too will be heard, including the Spanish of the Latin American immigrants, and the Amharic and Tigrinya of Beta Israel and the African languages of non-Jewish economic refugees.

Palestinian Arabic is, of course, the unmarked language in Arab villages and towns and Arab neighborhoods of mixed cities, but in them there is gradual increase in the influence, and even use, of Hebrew. Israeli Palestinians are rapidly becoming bilingual, first borrowing Hebrew words and then code switching and developing bilingual proficiency.[41] There is not an analogical learning of Arabic by Hebrew-speakers, but a continuing loss of the Judeo-Arabic varieties brought by Jews from Iraq, north Africa and Egypt, and only a limited learning of school Arabic in many, but not all, schools.[42]

Public signage (commonly labeled "linguistic landscape", though it usually refers to cityscape) often provides a clue to the sociolinguistic make-up of a neighborhood; it is strongly influenced, however, by the state of literacy in the language and the community, the existence of government (national or local) rules, and the advertising preferences of large national and international firms. As early as the 1960s scholars noted the intrusion of English into commercial signs in a West Jerusalem shopping street.[43] A study of signs in the Old City of Jerusalem showed the complexity of this phenomenon, with changes in language (dropping Hebrew from street signs in the Jordanian period, adding it to Arabic and English after the reunification of the city in 1967) and in the ordering of the languages (English, Arabic, and Hebrew under the Mandate; Hebrew, Arabic, and English under Israeli rule).[44] There were disputes over Arabic in signs in Upper Nazareth, considered a Jewish (therefore Hebrew) neighborhood by the local government but a mixed Arab–Jewish city by local Arabs and their organizations.[45] But Israeli neighborhoods are predominantly Hebrew, with marked exceptions of speaking and signs in other languages.

Education as a factor

Schooling is one of the most significant domains for language loss and maintenance, and the decision on a language of instruction as well as of other languages to teach is a crucial one. Commonly ignoring the logical and simple policy of using the language of the children, most national language education policies use this decision to manage language practices and beliefs.[46] The most significant step in the revitalization of Hebrew was the decision of some Yiddish-speaking immigrants to Ottoman Palestine in the late nineteenth century who had settled in small agricultural towns to replace French with Hebrew. The teachers, Yiddish speakers but literate in Hebrew, were called on to use Hebrew to talk about everyday life and to encourage their pupils to speak it all the time. This was adopted as school policy also in the kibbutzim founded in the early twentieth century and in the Jewish towns growing up at the time and in the Hebrew city of Tel Aviv. In particular, the schools of the *Hilfsverein der Deutschen Juden*, an organization supported by German Jews to help Jewish communities, became the new centers for the restoration of the language and its modernization. While the schools of the *Haredim* continued to use Yiddish to teach their pupils, the Zionist schools taught all subjects in Hebrew at all levels.

A crisis came in 1913 when a plan was announced to start a tertiary institution, keeping Hebrew for humanities and Jewish studies but teaching science in the then current language of science, German. It was students and teachers from the high schools who led the demonstrations that are now known as the Language War. During World War I the German consul is reported to have encouraged teaching in German, but the British troops soon put a stop to that, enforcing under military government a decision to recognize Hebrew officially for the Jewish schools.[47]

Under the British Mandate, the government (underfunded, as were most aspects of the British Empire apart from military forces) left it to the Arab and Jewish communities to set up and pay for their own schools, though they required both systems to teach English as a second language. When in the 1920s, after the war, the Jewish tertiary institutions were established, both the Hebrew University of Jerusalem (note "Hebrew" in the name!) and the Haifa Technion adopted rules requiring teaching, examinations, and student writing to be in Hebrew. The result was that, at the time of the foundation of the state in 1948, when a decision (echoing Treaty of Versailles and League of Nations policies) was made to use Arabic or Hebrew in a school according to the make-up of the pupils, Israel already had an established policy of using Hebrew from pre-school level to university.

In the main, this continues to be the practice, with minor exceptions. Whereas many nations with larger and longer-established modern languages find it necessary to carry on advanced education in other languages (e.g. French is still the language of secondary schools in north Africa, and many universities in Europe now teach in English,[48] almost all lecturing and student work in Israeli universities (except in the English and some other foreign-language departments) is in Hebrew, although, in the social sciences and sciences, more advanced courses require students to read material in English.[49] Lecturers are expected to publish and participate in conferences in international languages, and students to develop reading proficiency in them, but all levels of Jewish education (apart from Haredi schools, some of which favor Yiddish, and a few programs for foreign students) use Hebrew.

Other domains

Hebrew is, of course, firmly entrenched in Israeli Jewish religious life, not just as the sacred language of worship and study but also as the public language of most sermons, lessons, and announcements. There are a few exceptions, such as when sermons might be given in an immigrant language such as Russian, English, or French, but this is a rare phenomenon. In the Haredi community, the language of worship is also Hebrew (though with a different pronunciation), but, in many cases, the language of teaching for males is still – but decreasingly – likely to be Yiddish. Most ultra-orthodox schools for girls teach them Yiddish as a subject, but teach in Hebrew.

Thus, within the Jewish community, secular as well as religious, the sacred and traditional status of Hebrew reinforces its hegemonic position and its maintenance. For Muslims, worship and sermons are in Qur'anic Arabic. Palestinian Christians too are likely to use Arabic, especially now that the Catholic Church has permitted the vernacular. The tiny Armenian and Syrian Christian communities maintain Armenian and Syriac (a variety of Aramaic) as their heritage languages. Arab schools teach in Arabic. Two Circassian villages have language revival programs, but now use Hebrew in schools.[50]

After completing high school and before employment or university study, about a half of Israelis (men and women alike) serve for two or three years in the Israel Defense Forces (IDF); the main exceptions are Palestinian Israelis (except Druze and some Bedouin) and Haredim, most of whom continue to resist responsibilities to the state.[51] Although in the early days, after the mass immigrations, the sergeant's problem was the many languages spoken by his platoon, by now almost all recruits can be assumed to speak Hebrew, which is the regular language of the army, air force, navy, and border police in which they will serve. The IDF does test recruits for Hebrew proficiency, making a minimal level a prerequisite for promotion and professional training; it also provides Hebrew instruction for new immigrants and for others with low literacy, aiming that all will have achieved at least the level of high school graduation by the end of their service. The IDF encourages some other language training: it provides Arabic instruction for its intelligence branch (supporting Arabic in Jewish schools as well), and English instruction for pilots and officers who will go overseas for training. Just as it played a major role in the teaching of Hebrew to immigrants in the early days of the state, so the army clearly continues to bolster the maintenance of the language.

Modern Israeli Hebrew is also firmly established as the language of the workplace. In stores, restaurants, factories, hospitals, and offices, it is the unmarked language, the one in which you normally address a stranger, and the first language offered by a telephone answering service.[52] There are exceptions: just as stores and restaurants throughout the world advertise that "English is spoken here" to encourage the tourist trade, so in a multilingual society such as Israel there are adjustments. Storekeepers try to match the languages of their customers: in the *shuk* (market) in the Old City of Jerusalem,[53] just as in the Ethiopian markets,[54] it is the seller who learns the language of the prospective buyer. Waiters and waitresses, and sales staff too, are often chosen for their ability to deal with the languages of their patrons. Hospitals exploit the plurilingualism of nurses and doctors to accommodate patients who do not know Hebrew, or rely on the Hebrew-speaking relatives who accompany them; in the wards, one hears Arabic and Russian regularly from the medical staff.

Although Hebrew remains the dominant language of business, there are some obvious exceptions. Lawyers, for instance, are expected to learn English while at university, but it is mainly those who practice international law and handle real estate transactions for non-Israelis who actually use it in their professional life.[55] In the many start-up computer businesses, English is valued for its usefulness in selling and in collaborating with firms overseas, but Hebrew remains the common language of daily work. Agriculture is another exception, as it involves hiring Arab and foreign workers, but they too pick up some Hebrew from their employers and foremen.

All this is clearly reflected in the media. Although Israel has a remarkable number of foreign-language newspapers for new immigrants and tourists (five in Russian, three in English, one each in French and German), the high-circulation daily newspapers are in Hebrew (ten altogether; there are also four in Arabic). Radio stations too broadcast in the main in Hebrew, though there are short regular news broadcasts in other languages, and an Arabic language program. Israeli television channels are in Hebrew, with a Russian-language channel and Arabic broadcasts. Cable stations provide programs in many other languages, but they are regularly subtitled in Hebrew.

There is a strong Israeli film industry; foreign films are generally subtitled in Hebrew. Plays in Hebrew (original, classic, and translated) are regularly staged in Hebrew throughout the country. Now that computers can handle Hebrew script as well as Latin, the internet is no longer a force weakening Hebrew, although it adds to the appeal of English. While experimental apps are starting to appear for Hebrew script for cellphones and iPads, there remain major problems, but young users have found ways to work around them. The publication of books in Hebrew continues to flourish, and popular works, translations from major languages as well as original Israeli literature, provide significant support for the language. There is thus a rich Israeli Hebrew culture, providing firm support for the language and also allowing access in translation to international literature and cultures.

All levels of government too are conducted in Hebrew. Members of local and city councils as well as legislators in the Knesset conduct their business in Hebrew, although there is a policy that permits Arab members of the Knesset to use Arabic if they give advance notice so that an interpreter can be provided. Citizens contact government agencies in Hebrew, but most provide telephone and computer services also in Arabic and Russian, and occasionally English. The police and the law courts operate in Hebrew, but provide interpreters when necessary. Laws and regulations are published first in Hebrew, but English, and later Arabic, translated versions are also available.

Hebrew is not endangered

Hebrew is firmly embedded in the Israeli sociolinguistic ecology, appearing to be healthy in all the domains we have looked at. Applying Fishman's *graded intergenerational disruption scale*,[56] Hebrew in Israel is to be rated beyond the highest level (stage 1), for it is designated by the national government as an *official language* and is politically independent. It does not need to be recreated from earlier writings (such as Cornish) or from socially isolated adults (as is the case with a large number of endangered languages). Its speakers are "socially integrated and ethnolinguistically active" and not beyond the childbearing age (as with the speakers of Māori in 1960 and most secular speakers of Yiddish and Judezmo and other Jewish languages today); rather, there is intergenerational oracy, as the majority are still brought up speaking the language even if their parents are immigrants or Haredim. There is Hebrew literacy in the home, the school, and the community (with a strong tradition of Hebrew literature, both popular and intellectual); it is required in compulsory elementary education (for Arabs as well as Jews); it is the most common language of the workplace; and it is used in governmental services and the mass media, including higher education. These considerations move it well beyond the level of threatened languages.

But what about its official status, and the fact that it shares this status with Arabic? The British government was persuaded in 1919 when establishing its rule over Ottoman Palestine (where Turkish had been the language of government) to add Arabic and Hebrew to its imperial English as official languages. Clearly, this did not mean that British officials under the Mandate were required to work in either or both, but that, wherever the local population warranted, laws and regulations were to be published in one or both of the languages, and interpreters were to be provided for law courts and official contact with Arabic- and Hebrew-speaking citizens. The newly independent government of Israel dropped English from the list of official languages, but in practice English continued to be used in publishing translations of laws and regulations. The maintenance of Arabic as an official language did not change the status of Hebrew, which continues as the dominant, even hegemonic, language of the government. Arabic is not used in the Knesset (except with advance notice to the Speaker); its formal requirement as a second language in schools is widely ignored or weakly implemented; its inclusion on public signs depends on local decisions or on legal enforcement on highways where there is evidence of need, and on street signs in centers of Arab population. It appears symbolically on stamps and currency, but less than Hebrew and English.[57] There is no apparent threat to Hebrew, then, from continuing to list Arabic as the second official language.

This is not strange if one considers the use of the term "official" for languages. The Wikipedia definition is a good start: "An *official language* is a *language* that is given a special legal status in a particular country, state, or other jurisdiction. Typically a nation's official language will be the one used in that nation's courts, parliament, and administration." It goes on to point out that, in New Zealand, Māori, though a minority language spoken by 5 percent of the population, and Sign language, used by the Deaf community, are the only "official" languages; English is just taken for granted, as it is in England, the United States, and Australia. In Ireland, the fact that Irish has been the official language since independence has not moved it beyond minority status, and increasing immigration means that it will soon be passed by immigrant languages such as Chinese and Polish. Inclusion in a list of official languages does not guarantee widespread public use: Urdu, while the official language of Pakistan, has fewer native speakers than several non-official languages. Nor does listing two languages as official depend on or encourage national bilingualism. Nations such as Switzerland and Belgium turn out, on closer analysis, to be territorially divided. Each canton in Switzerland decides its own language policy, while Belgium is divided into a complex patchwork of regions where either French, Dutch, or German are required or permitted; only Brussels (actually a French-speaking enclave within a Flemish region) is officially bilingual. Finland remains officially bilingual, but Swedish (historically dominant) is now mainly regional. Canada's official bilingualism has been successful in persuading Québec, increasingly francophone after the departure of many English speakers, to remain in the confederation but not in successfully establishing French–English bilingualism all across the country: "les deux solitudes" continue. South Africa's listing of nine African languages alongside Afrikaans and English in its constitution does not guarantee their use in higher functions. Tunisia's listing of Arabic as the only official language does not lead to its use in higher education.

There is thus no reason, other than the same nationalist mistrust that motivates the Official English movement in the United States to fear unofficial Spanish, to worry that the official status of Arabic is in any way a threat to Hebrew, which appears to be easily overcoming the potentially more serious challenges of global English and a million Russian-speaking immigrants.

My regular answer, then, to those who ask me is that Hebrew is not endangered or even threatened in any way, and its inclusion by Fishman in a book on "threatened languages" is related not to its current situation but to its success in "reversing language shift" and restoring language vitality, daily vernacular use, modernization, and cultivation, as befits a modern standard language of a small multilingual country, and providing a model for others.

There are, of course, language problems. One is the need for Israelis – like most other residents of non-English-speaking countries – to learn English in order to maintain external commercial ties, to allow access to advanced science and technology, to conduct a successful tourist industry and to travel abroad, and in order to keep up connections with a non-Hebrew-speaking Jewish Diaspora. A second is a regrettable failure to develop the strength in proficiency in Arabic consistent with geographical location in the Middle East. A third is that the ideological strength of Hebrew has worked and continues to work against the rich plurilingualism in Jewish, immigrant, and international languages of the Jewish population. But, in spite of the universal tendency of Hebrew to be influenced by a global language such as English, and in spite of its generally benign tolerance of multilingualism, there are no real signs of a threat to the continued existence of reborn Hebrew.

At the same time, while deprecating the pessimism of the normativists and language activists and their anxiety for the survival and purity of the language, one cannot ignore the reasons for their concern, which will emerge in the rest of the book, or discount the value of their efforts to constantly draw attention to what they see as errors and impurities – efforts that help to encourage Hebrew language use and the maintenance of standard forms, or to defend the language. The Hebrew Language Academy seems to be doing a good job in making available the new terminology needed to keep the language up to date (I say "seems" because we have no hard evidence, since the studies in the 1970s, of the effect of their efforts).[58] Hebrew, like all other living languages, will continue to change, and, like all other languages of small states, will continue to be influenced by developments of the large international languages. But it is in no more danger than Czech, or Danish, or Hungarian.

That is a sketch of the current state of Hebrew within the Israeli sociolinguistic ecology. In the rest of the book, I explore how this situation developed, answering finally the other question: how was Hebrew so success-fully "revived"? As this is not a mystery novel, perhaps I should give away the solution, which will be that Hebrew was never really "dead"; with rare excep-tions, it always played a central role among the many languages of the Jews. While it was not a spoken vernacular for about 1,900 years, it continued as a sacred and literary language throughout most of this period, and so was easily available for the renewed vernacular use that followed the return to Zion.

The emergence of Hebrew

Teach your tongue to say "I do not know" lest you be caught in a falsehood.
Tractate *Derech Eretz Zuta* (chapter 3)

Historical sociolinguistics and the puzzle of origins

A number of years ago two of the founders of the field of sociolinguistics,[1] Joshua Fishman and John Gumperz, were working together on a pioneering study of Spanish–English bilingualism in a Jersey City barrio.[2] From time to time they would argue over their findings. When challenged for evidence, Fishman (trained in statistics and sociology) would go to his office and bring back a ream of computer printout with analyses of multiple questionnaires. On other days, when Fishman challenged Gumperz (a field linguist and ethnographer), Gumperz would reply: "Last night at a party I heard someone say it."[3] The claims in the last chapter about the current state of languages in Israel can be tested by either of these two methods of handling data: by statistical analysis of the results of surveys or questionnaires, or by ethnographic observation and interviews.

But, unfortunately, we do not have the data. At the end of Chapter 1, I was probably more certain than I should have been, for Israel has had no language question on the census since 1983. Israeli Hebrew language departments continue to discourage studies of Hebrew later than the Mishnaic period; Modern Hebrew, they assert, has not yet jelled.[4] So my personal assessment of the present sociolinguistic situation is open to debate, and my guess about the future can also be questioned, accounting for the nervousness of the president of the Hebrew Language Academy. But that is talking about something that could be checked, were there resources available for surveys or interviews. Neither of these methods is even conceivable for historical studies, especially in trying to reconstruct the sociolinguistic ecology of communities thousands of years ago.

Even when we move to periods when we assume humans had started to use language (and when this happened is still debated),[5] we face many difficulties. Our problem is the lack of evidence; we have no tape recordings of the spoken language and so must rely on the evidence (when it exists) of the written records, which in alphabetical scripts are assumed to be related to the spoken form, but may largely misrepresent it. A related fallacy of many who study "linguistic landscape", which normally means public signs in the city, is to ignore the state of literacy of the population, so that they might easily misinterpret the language of signs. We will see this when we ask about how to interpret the languages of inscriptions of ancient Jewish communities: did the use of Greek on so many tombstones mean that this was the language people were speaking or was it, rather, the language preferred by engravers? Clearly, the further we go back in time, the more doubts we should have. We have to depend on the scholarly but debated reconstructions of historical linguists or our own sense of the probable sociolinguistic behavior of communities very different from our own, much smaller and with their own language attitudes. So, if I seem certain at times, feel free to doubt and question my version, and, if I seem doubtful, please forgive my hesitancy.

The question of how and when human language originated led in the nineteenth century to such exhausting debate that, in 1866, the Linguistic Society of Paris forbade further discussion of the issue; only towards the end of the twentieth century did the topic become a respectable one for speculation and study. Current views work within evolutionary theory, with the majority holding that it was a gradual process. A recent collected volume includes sixty-five chapters by experts in various fields – linguists, biologists, archeologists, ethologists, neuroscientists, anthropologists, psychologists, geneticists, paleontologists, and others.[6] While the details remain controversial, the weight of opinion seems to be that language, with its distinctive differences from animal communication systems, such as the various systems of combination (sounds into words, and words into sentences), first emerged over 200,000 years ago. But we have no hard evidence of language before the first Sumerian examples of writing, with pictographs emerging in Mesopotamia in the thirty-fifth century BCE (before the Common Era) and the first cuneiform writing found on clay tablets at Jemdet Nasr in the late 1920s. This kind of archeological evidence gives one picture; a second approach, established by the work of historical linguistics, has since the early nineteenth century endeavored to establish language histories by comparing existing languages and working backwards to determine early forms.[7] Our current views of language families and relationships come from this comparativist approach, checked with historical inscriptions and texts (see Map 1).

Traditionally, there were various theories of the original or Adamic language. The Bible assumed that it was Hebrew, with the creation of other languages a punishment at the incident of the Tower of Babel. The sixteenth-century Dutch humanist Johannes Goropius Becanos proposed that Antwerpian Brabantic, a Dutch dialect, was the original language.[8] Other seventeenth-century Dutch scholars argued that one people (the Germanic) did not come down from the

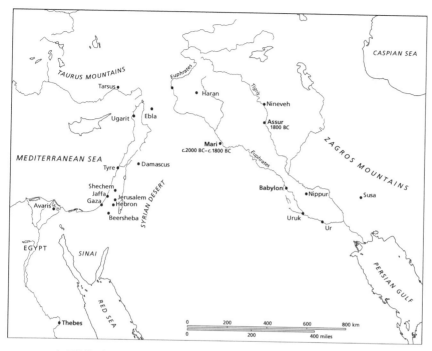

1 Biblical Israel in the ancient Middle East
Source: Brettler (2010).

Ark on Mount Ararat to Babel but chose a different route, so that the original language of the Garden of Eden stayed unchanged. The Turkish language reformer Mustafa Kemal was, for a time at least, convinced by the speculations of an Austrian linguist, Hermann F. Kvergić, that Turkish was the first language.[9] There is no agreement among linguists about the issue: Roger Lass[10] and other linguists are critical of the methods used to establish language super-families, and no one goes so far as proposing the form of a Proto-Sapiens (or Proto-Human) language; there is even disagreement as to whether there was one origin (monogenesis) or several (polygenesis).[11] In any event, our question is not the origin of language but the origin of Hebrew, just over three millennia ago.

What evidence, hard or soft, do we have of the languages being spoken in Canaan when Hebrew was born? To start, we depend on the work of archeologists, who find traces of written material in their excavations. There is written evidence, in tablets found at Amarna and elsewhere, that enables us to identify some of the languages being written by scribes at the time, over a thirty-year span around 1380 BCE; they are mainly in cuneiform in Akkadian.[12] Seeing that Semitic scripts did not generally record vowels, we can only guess at pronunciation, or use comparative linguistic methods to try to reconstruct earlier versions of the languages that survived. The limitations of these data are clear: first, the remnants we have are preserved by chance. Another chance discovery, such as the fabulous troves found in the Cairo Genizah or the caves at Qumran, may one day lead to a revolutionary rewriting of major portions of linguistic history.

There is also the evidence of the Bible, the earliest manuscripts of which were found in the Dead Sea Scrolls at Qumran and date perhaps from the second century BCE; there is an important Greek translation that dates from the fourth century CE, and other translations (such as one in Ge'ez, from Ethiopia) that seem to show reliable early variants. There is good reason to believe that there were various texts of the Bible as late as the Second Temple period: the texts at Qumran include multiple variants, and the Septuagint translation and the Samaritan Pentateuch show considerable differences from what was later the basis for the Masoretic text now accepted.[13] These differences suggest oral transmission, like the explanation now accepted for the composition of the works of Homer, and which we know to have been the case with the Talmud. Composed much earlier than the time they were written down, these texts were normalized by the Pharisees, so that after the destruction of Jerusalem a single text was preserved. Some argue that the decisions about which texts were preserved, and in which versions, reflect the ideologies of the two "orthodox" groups, Pharisaic Rabbinic Judaism and Christianity.[14]

There are also major disputes among Bible scholars and archeologists over the date of the composition of the texts. The traditional religious view dates the Torah (the Pentateuch, the "Five Books of Moses") from the time of Moses in the fourteenth century BCE, and other books from then until 400 BCE. The documentary or Wellhausen theory[15] developed by nineteenth-century Bible scholars claims that it was combined from four (or more) separate sources, composed between 950 BCE and 500 BCE and edited later. Other views suggest that the Torah is made up of combinations of earlier fragments edited sometime between 900 BCE and 450 BCE. The other books of the Bible are assumed to have been composed between the eighth and fifth centuries BCE. In an intriguing analysis of the Book of Leviticus, the anthropologist Mary Douglas takes the position of "the largest scholarly consensus"[16] in accepting that Leviticus, like Deuteronomy, must have been redacted at a time of attempting to rebuild solidarity after the disasters of war, and accepts the fifth century BCE as the appropriate date.[17]

Obviously, each of these positions leads to different evaluations of the historical value of the written texts. Eyewitness accounts of incidents have been shown by psychologists to be questionable and often untrustworthy in

2 Divided monarchy
Source: Brettler (2010).

court;[18] if these stories were written many years after the event, they represent ideological interpretations of the past, with contemporary significance.

Dealing with the earlier periods, there are conflicting approaches to the agreement or otherwise between archeological and biblical accounts. Some scholars hold the view that the archeology confirms the Bible, while the "minimalists" build their theories on archeology and non-biblical sources alone: others take a more "centralist" position.[19] The detailed record keeping and editing and building of national scriptures such as the Bible are most likely to have occurred during a period of state building, and in the case of the Bible this happened not during the time of David but, rather, during the days of Josiah as king of Judah (see Map 2). The accounts that we have, in this view, are reflections of ideas of religious reform and the territorial ambitions of the kingdom of Judah at the end the seventh century BCE.[20]

Early Hebrew and language in the two kingdoms

From extant texts, linguists have attempted to reconstruct the existence and form of Hebrew as it developed over a period of many hundreds of years. But there are only a few rare references to the languages spoken at the time, and those refer to the language of Canaan and "Yehudit" (Jewish, or the language of Judah), but do not use the term "Hebrew". One needs to build a sociolinguistic description on the basis of minimal evidence.

Even at the more recent date of Roman Palestine, constructing a reasonable picture out of literary, epigraphic, and archeological sources proves a major challenge, though the sources are richer.[21] Here we find a mixture of Rabbinic texts in the Mishnah and Talmud, and accounts of life in the New Testament and by the Jewish historian Josephus. There are also papyri from the Judean desert and later synagogue and burial inscriptions. Especially important are the Dead Sea Scrolls and other writings such as the Apocrypha (in the Greek Bible) and Pseudepigrapha, preserved in Greek but not Hebrew or Aramaic originals, and even texts such as the Book of Enoch, preserved mainly in a Ge'ez version of the probably Aramaic original.[22] There has also been extensive archeology of major sites as well as evidence of daily life. But 1,000 years earlier, when we take the first shaping of Hebrew to have occurred, the evidence is much sparser.

We have archeology-based estimates of the population density. In the Late Bronze Age (1550 BCE to 1200 BCE) there was a drastic decrease in population in the region, which took place over a century as a result of military invasions, civil strife, and social breakdowns.[23] In the Early Iron Age, which followed, there was a dramatic increase in the number of settlements, as a consequence of clearing forests by fire, the building of terraces to provide better soil, and the solution of irrigation problems.[24] Based on the assumed ability of the land to support population, the region would support a maximum population of 60,000 by about 1200–1000 BCE, rising to 400,000 a few hundred years later.

Hebrew emerged in "a matrix of closely related tongues in Syria–Palestine".[25] Northwest Semitic is believed to have formed a dialect continuum, from Phoenician at one end to Aramaic at the other. Within this was the Canaanite group, out of which Hebrew seems to have developed. Hebrew, halfway between Phoenician and Old Aramaic, with its earliest inscriptions in the tenth century BCE, was probably used in some early Bible texts.[26]

All this adds up to a fairly murky picture, with no solid scholarly consensus about the language situation, and leading to a need to interpret different kinds of evidence with care. We do have a story dealing with Hebrew dialect variation at the time of the Judges, the often cited "shibboleth" example, which is based on differences in pronunciation between tribes on either side of the Jordan; there is other evidence of dialect variation, but exactly how these dialects were formed or later merged remains an open question.

There were other language varieties in the region. Living in the south, with five major cities forming the Pentapolis, and identified as Israel's worst enemy, were the Philistines, who may have originally spoken an Indo-European language and flourished more or less from the eleventh to the seventh century BCE. The Egyptians had blocked their attempted invasion, but could not prevent their settling the Gaza Strip. Their culture was similar to Mycenaean, and they were part of the Greek Sea Peoples, who occupied some parts of Canaan. There, they adopted Canaanite language, culture, and religion, and in time shifted to Aramaic.[27] North of Gaza were the coastal city states (Sidon and Tyre in what is now Lebanon were the two main cities) that constituted Phoenicia, also occupied by Sea People who had come from Greece and spoke Phoenician, a Semitic language close to Hebrew;[28] a seafaring people, they also established colonies in the southwestern Mediterranean. They developed the Phoenician script, which was the source of the Greek and, later, Roman alphabets, starting later to write vowels as well.

Comparative linguists generally place Hebrew in the Afro-Asiatic macro-family (previously known as Hamito-Semitic), with close to 100 member languages. The family is usually broken into several major subgroups: Semitic, Berber, Egyptian, Chadic, and Cushitic groups.[29] Common features include a two-gender system, emphatic (glottalized or implosive) consonants, a tendency to organize sentences verb–subject–object, words inflected by vowel changes as well as prefixes and suffixes, and a causative affix. Hebrew descends from the Semitic group, within its older subgroup (Akkadian, Ugaritic, Hebrew, and Phoenician), rather than the younger group (Aramaic, Arabic, and Sabean). There is no agreement on their origin: one theory holds that Semitic came from Arabia, with Arabic close to Proto-Semitic. Others believe it came from Africa, and a third theory is that it developed in the Levant. The group is marked by the formation of words from tri-consonantal roots to which prefixes, suffixes, and vocalizations are added.

By the second millennium BCE Akkadian had become the dominant written language of the Fertile Crescent, replacing Sumerian in the cuneiform texts, and by 1500 BCE alphabetic writing of Proto-Canaanite appeared in Ugaritic texts. French archeologists discovered Ugaritic in 1928 in excavations in Syria. A number of archives have been found in Ugaritic[30] and Akkadian, and some in other languages, and it is assumed that Ugarit was a center for scribal schools.[31] The city was a trading center, with evidence of Syrian, Canaanite, Egyptian, Mesopotamian, and Mediterranean cultures.

The cuneiform alphabetic writing of the tablets dates from the fourteenth century BCE until about 1180 BCE. The texts are in a scribal written language rather than a local dialect; tablets in Ugaritic have been found widely dispersed in the region. Most texts are of an administrative and economic nature, but there are a number of legal texts, and a group of religious and literary texts that illustrate Semitic culture of the period. Many common words are the same as in Hebrew, such as the word for "father", "man", "right hand", "cup", and "God". In addition, many texts are similar to Bible texts, especially Psalms, and they give details of Baal worship, condemned in the Bible. The Ugaritic sources assist in interpreting some uncertainties in the Bible. What this makes clear is the multilingualism of the region, with widespread trade establishing close relations and encouraging lexical borrowing, a factor that makes it more difficult to decide what is the result of historical development and what is influence from contact. The comparative method uses the similarity of two words in different languages as possible evidence of relationship between the languages, but it might well simply be the result of borrowing.

Starting in the first millennium, written texts have been preserved in Aramaic, Old South Arabian, and Ge'ez. Canaanite was spread by Phoenician colonies, and Hebrew as a sacred language was developing its influential literature. But where did Hebrew come from? The Hebrew linguist Chaim Rabin notes that the biblical account has the Patriarchs coming to Canaan from Mesopotamia, where their language would have been different, and wonders if the account in Genesis (31: 47) of Laban naming a cairn in Aramaic and Jacob naming it in Hebrew suggested the change of language as early as this. But it is hard to determine, Rabin says, the extent to which the Israelites adopted Canaanite or kept original features of the Mesopotamian variety, because there is no hard evidence of the earlier language, nor are there enough words borrowed from Egyptian to support the period of residence there.[32]

What this suggests is that, when Hebrew emerged, it was in the context of a multilingual Semitic Canaan with established scribal literacy and a developed literary tradition. But there are serious differences of opinion as to how Israel first appeared in the record. Each view has a different implication for the development of Hebrew. The traditional view follows the biblical account. William Chomsky believes that Abraham and his clan came to Canaan speaking a Semitic language close to the varieties spoken there, and easily adopted their variety, in much the same way, he argues, that the Normans who occupied England after 1066 adopted a French-influenced variety of Anglo-Saxon.[33]

According to the biblical account, the Israelites returned to Canaan after an exile in Egypt. The Book of Joshua gives details of the conquest, although archeology has not produced evidence of the number of Canaanite cities claimed to have been destroyed in the process. In fact, many archeologists argue that there is no solid evidence to support the biblical accounts of the Patriarchs, the Exodus, or the Conquest, which can be best read as later ideological versions of orally transmitted myths.[34] One alternative account is of peaceful infiltration by a "mixed multitude" of semi-nomadic tribes who settled the more or less deserted hill country. For this to be accepted, one needs to account for the unification of these tribes and their agreeing a common sanctuary. A third approach is the theory of the revolt of Canaanite peasants, either a violent revolt against oppressive landowners or an escape into the hills, where they were not threatened by chariots.[35]

Each of these views is partially supported by the growth of an oral and later written literature, paralleling other Near Eastern literatures, but in Hebrew. What this language was like is hard to establish, but there is evidence in the shibboleth story (Judges 12: 5–6) of dialect differences, at least between the Ephraimites (settled in Samaria) and Gileadites (living east of the Jordan river).[36] The oldest literary records, such as the Song of Moses at the Exodus (Deuteronomy 32: 1–43), and the Song of Deborah (in the Book of Judges 5: 2–31), which some date as early as the twelfth century BCE, are written in pure Hebrew without traces of Aramaic. The written texts include borrowings from Akkadian, the Assyro-Babylonian language and the international diplomatic language of the Middle East until the eighth century BCE, when it was replaced by Aramaic; there is also some evidence of borrowings from Egyptian and from the language of the Sea Peoples – variously known as Philistines and Phoenicians – coming from the west, who invaded Egypt and Canaan from the twelfth century and were finally defeated by David.

The language that emerged, known as the language of Canaan (*sfat Knaan*) in Isaiah 19: 18 and as the language of Yehudah (*yehudit*) in 2 Kings 18: 26, Isaiah 36: 11, and Nehemiah 13: 24), was not called Hebrew (*ivrit*) before the Hellenistic and Roman period. It developed among the other Canaanite varieties, with some of which it may have been mutually intelligible; in any case, the varieties were close enough to permit speakers of one to learn the others easily and rapidly in the prevailing situation of mixed populations and trade.[37]

Whatever its origin, Israel appears to have developed into a political unit under David and Solomon (there are some scholars who consider this too a myth), and to continue as a united monarchy for some time. This is presented in the traditional sources as a golden age, with the building of the Temple in Jerusalem and the centralization of power. While Solomon is portrayed in legend as knowing seventy languages and being able to speak to the animals, the United Monarchy was presumably monolingual in Hebrew.[38]

After the death of Solomon (traditionally assumed to be 928 BCE), the United Monarchy of David was split into two separate states, with the border probably permeable. The northern state continued to exist until a conflict with the growing Assyrian empire, the dominant power from 925 BCE to 605 BCE. In 738 BCE Tiglath-Pilezer invaded. The kingdoms continued to struggle with each other and with Damascus, and in about 730 BCE, after renewed problems, the king of Judah, Ahaz, appealed to Assyria (where Eastern Aramaic had replaced Akkadian as the dominant language) for help. Tiglath-Pilezer accepted tribute, and sacked both Damascus and Samaria. Some of the population was deported, and in about 720 BCE the remainder were scattered (these are the Ten Lost Tribes),[39] although some moved to Judah, increasing its population considerably. The deportees were replaced by others, in the kind of forced population exchange that Stalin later perfected: "The king of Assyria brought [people] from Babylon, Cuthah [these are the Cuthim or later Samaritans], Avva, Hamath, and Sepharvaim [who maybe spoke Babylonian] and he settled them in Samaria in place of the Israelites. . . [E]ach nation continued to make its own gods. . ." (2 Kings 17: 23–4).

Hezekiah, who was king of Judah and who is praised in the Bible for his major religious reforms, joined with other states in 701 to revolt against Sennacherib of Assyria. It was during the ensuing siege of Jerusalem that Sennacherib sent Rab-shakeh to Jerusalem; the biblical account suggests that, while court officials knew Aramaic, the common people didn't.

Isaiah 36: 11–12 and 2 Kings 18: 26–8 both have an account of the visit of Rab-Shakeh, the emissary of the king of Ashur, sent to warn Hezekiah and the people that they would be invaded and destroyed if they continued to trust in Egyptian protection. After the emissary's opening speech, "Eliakim [who was in charge of the palace], Shebna [the scribe] and Joah [the recorder] replied: 'Please, speak to your servants in Aramaic, for we understand it; do not speak to us in Yehudit in the hearing of the people on the wall.'" Rab-shakeh replied and "cried with a loud voice in the language of Judah [Yehudit]: 'It was precisely to the men sitting on the wall – who will have to eat their dung and drink their urine with you – that I was sent to speak.'" This is a key text in trying to trace sociolinguistic history, as it suggests that only the court officials knew Aramaic and not the "men sitting on the wall", which could mean the soldiers or all the inhabitants. But it could perhaps mean that these officials knew diplomatic formal Aramaic, which the general population did not, though they may have had limited proficiency in informal colloquial Aramaic. One might guess, however, that the population movements increased the likelihood of contact with Aramaic speakers.

Hezekiah surrendered, but was permitted to continue to rule as a vassal. He was succeeded by his son Menasseh, who reigned until 643 BCE. Conditions appeared to have been stable. The archeological evidence suggests that he was a strong ruler who saved Judah from destruction by developing a modus vivendi with Assyria; Judah became a major source of olives, and seems to have had a high level of literacy.[40] The Bible account says, however (2 Kings 21), that "he did what was displeasing to the Lord", building idolatrous altars, worshipping Baal, placing an Asherah (a Semitic mother goddess) in the Temple, and putting innocent people to death, so that he was held responsible for the fall of Jerusalem. According to 2 Chronicles 33, Manasseh was taken into captivity to Assyria, but returned to Judah after he repented; he was succeeded by Amon, who reigned for two years before Josiah became king.

It was probably about this time that a number of Jewish soldiers were sent to Elephantine (close to Aswan in Egypt) to provide support for the Persian control of Egypt. The members of the colony built a temple modeled on the Temple in Jerusalem, perhaps as a reaction to Manasseh's introduction of pagan ceremonies there.[41] The Elephantine temple was destroyed by Egyptians in 410 BCE. For 100 years the Jewish community at Elephantine observed many aspects of Jewish law and maintained Hebrew names, but adopted common Aramaic patterns with some Egyptian influence in their legal documents. Intermarriage with non-Jews occurred. The Aramaic documents have no Hebraic elements, suggesting that the community was established and existed at a time when Aramaic was well established, or that the soldiers may have been in service elsewhere before coming to Elephantine.[42] An alternative theory proposes an earlier date for the foundation of the community, with mercenaries coming from the kingdom of Israel rather than Judah.[43] There is no evidence of the fate of the community after 399 BCE, but this early Diaspora is the first evidence of the adoption of Aramaic outside Palestine, and might suggest its use as a vernacular in Judea.

Josiah, like his great-grandfather Hezekiah, was considered a great reformer; one important event attributed to his reign was the discovery (or redaction) of the Book of Deuteronomy. With the rise of Egyptian power, Assyria had withdrawn, and the major religious reforms were accompanied by hope of political triumph. There are scholars who assume that the stories of the triumphs of David and Solomon and the glories of the United Kingdom paint the hopes and aspirations of the time of Josiah.[44] Josiah was killed in battle with the Egyptians at Megiddo in 609, however, and the situation grew worse under his successors.

The king of Judah, Ahaz, accepted Assyrian vassaldom under Tiglath-Pilezer, a ruler known to have foreign soldiers in his army. According to various sources – the Book of Kings (late seventh century BCE) and also Chronicles (fourth century BCE), Isaiah and other prophets, and the highly propagandistic Annals from Nineveh – Judah after the destruction of Israel continued as a vassal kingdom, but prospered, so that the son of Ahaz, Hezekiah, became wealthy. There was demographic growth, Jerusalem expanding with refugees from north and west. Hezekiah shut the high places, the altars in Samaria where temple worship had been performed, established Jerusalem as the only accepted central site for sacrifice, destroyed idols, and instituted major religious reforms.

There was considerable literary output: the Books of Elijah, Hosea, and Isaiah may have been composed about this time; Deuteronomy was discovered, according to the traditional view, or written, according to those who follow the documentary hypothesis.

Hezekiah was succeeded by his son Manasseh, who ruled for the next forty years, reversing all his father's religious reforms and permitting the return of idolatry. The upper classes adopted foreign customs and perhaps language. Business transactions followed Assyrian legal practice and contracts may have begun to be written in Aramaic, a custom that continues in contemporary Jewish practice for marriage and divorce documents. But Manasseh made economic and political progress. His son Amon followed what the Bible considered his evil ways, and he was overthrown after two years, and replaced in turn by his son, Josiah, who adopted a reforming religious policy, like his grandfather, for thirty-one years.[45] Josiah was seen as a successor of Moses, Joshua, and David: "Before him, there was no king like him who turned to the Lord with all his heart and all his soul and all his might, according to all the Law of Moses, nor did any like him arise after him" (2 Kings 23: 25). Josiah too destroyed the altars used for idolatry and killed the priests.

Babylonian exile

In 605 the Babylonian king Nebuchadnezzar defeated the Egyptians, and set out to gain control of the Middle East. The Babylonians conquered the coastal cities, and besieged Jerusalem, capturing it in 597 and taking King Jehoiachin, princes, the aristocracy, and the priests captive into Babylon – "[N]one remained except the poorest people of the land" (2 Kings 24). Zedekiah was appointed puppet king, but he plotted with other states to rebel, so that the Babylonians returned in 588 BCE, destroyed the cities of Judah, and finally, in 587, devastated Jerusalem and the Temple, carrying a second group into exile. Gedaliah was appointed governor of the province, but after his assassination, in about 582, many of the remaining population fled to Egypt; others may have gone into captivity in Babylonia.

The exiles joined the countless émigré communities throughout Near East. Jehoiachin (the former king) and the elite were transferred to Babylon, where they received food rations. The main body of deportees settled on the border between Assyria and Babylonia. In Babylon, self-governing communities were organized ethnically. There, Aramaic, the lingua franca of the region, eventually replaced Hebrew as the vernacular; Hebrew was kept as a literary language. There was other evidence of assimilation: Babylonian names for the months and Aramaic (square) script were adopted, as were Babylonian personal names.

But a critical question is: how many went into exile, and how rapidly did they lose Hebrew? Jeremiah (52: 28–30) gives a total of 4,600, but it is not clear whether these were only heads of families. In any case, it seems that no more than a quarter of the population of Judah went into Babylonian exile, and the rest continued their agricultural life and included skilled workers, priests, and prophets.[46]

The prophet Ezekiel gives a picture of the beginning of the exile, describing the dark visions of one who was himself taken into captivity, while the so-called Deutero-Isaiah (chapters 40–55) prophesies the return, detailing the roles of Cyrus, the Persian king who defeated the Babylonian empire in 540 BCE and authorized the return, and presents visions of future glory.[47]

There are few details of life in Babylonia, although it can be assumed from indirect statements that the exiles from Judah lived in the city and in undeveloped sites in the country.[48] A letter from Jeremiah, in Jerusalem, to the exiles gave them advice for a long stay: "Build houses and live in them, plant gardens and eat their fruit. Take wives and beget sons and daughters; and take wives for your sons, and give your daughters to husbands, that they might bear sons and daughters. Multiply there, do not decrease. And seek the welfare of the city to which I have exiled you, and pray to the Lord on its behalf, for in its prosperity you shall prosper" (Jeremiah 29: 4–7). These arguments for assimilation no doubt encouraged the exiles to adopt Aramaic eventually. It has been suggested that the exiles, as forced migrants, would have undergone the normal three-generational shift, with the first generation lamenting the exile, the second hoping for a new adjustment, and the third accepting the new homeland.[49] One assumes that this three-generational pattern suggested by Fishman also applied, with the immigrant generation adding the new language, their children being bilingual, and the third generation moving to the new language. But forty years is too short a time for the complete shift, so it is not unreasonable to assume that those who returned so soon were still bilingually proficient.

Hebrew in a multilingual context

Our current view of Classical Hebrew is, of course, as the majestic language of the Bible, the source of the three major religions that emerged from the small land marking the focus of three continents. What we have there is a written and literary language, forming the sacred texts of Judaism and the inspiration for the sacred texts of Christianity and Islam. It echoes many of the features of

Canaanite and Ugaritic texts, and one can only assume that it was the H or High version of a diglossia written by people whose daily vernacular was less formal and possibly closer to Aramaic. The oldest Hebrew alphabet, dated as early as the fourteenth century, came to replace the elaborate cuneiform of Akkadian and the simpler cuneiform of Ugarit; it was to be replaced by the square Aramaic characters (called *Suri*, Syrian, in the Talmud) around the fourth century.

The traditional view is of Hebrew monolingualism up to the Babylonian exile and Aramaic vernacular monolingualism plus sacred Hebrew after the return. This picture is heavily biased by the assumptions of monolingualism in traditional Jewish and modern Anglo-Saxon views (many Christian scholars wondered which language Jesus spoke, not accepting the multilingualism of the period). Such a view is linguistically naïve: an Aramaic-speaking clan moves to Canaan; becomes Hebrew-speaking by the time it goes to Egypt; keeps its language intact (for which it is praised) over several hundred years; returns and lives among Canaanite dialects, in contact with Philistines and Phoenicians; remains monolingual in Hebrew until the time of Hezekiah, when the Northern Kingdom is destroyed (about 710 BCE); is conquered by Nebuchadnezzar 100 years later, and some of its leaders and perhaps a quarter of the population are deported to Babylon; those who return fifty years later are surprised to find that those left behind intermarried with local non-Jews and speak "Ashdodese"; but (if we accept a later Talmudic view) everyone now requires an Aramaic translation to accompany the weekly Torah reading; and the rabbis produce an artificial Hebrew for their commentaries in the Mishnah.

Much more likely than this traditional view is a multilingual pattern, with varying levels of individual plurilingualism, and an overall triglossia of the sort that emerged later, with use of Hebrew for higher and sacred functions and as a continuing internal spoken vernacular (though a slowly changing variety under the pressure of Aramaic and other varieties, as shown in Mishnaic Hebrew), and changing varieties of Aramaic serving both as the co-territorial variety for contact with non-Jews,[50] with whom there was regular trade, and in many cases (such as among those with the major external contact or with the higher status associated with wealth and trade) as a regular vernacular.

Accurate terms help. The European Commission scholars responsible for the foreign language curriculum[51] make a useful contrast between *multilingualism*, by which they mean a speech community with many languages functioning in it, and *plurilingualism*, which they use to refer to the proficiency of individuals controlling more than one language. In point of fact, the language varieties in each case are always unevenly divided: a multilingual society has different languages favored for different tasks, so that one might be the language of government, another the language of business, and others might be used in various neighborhoods. Often the distinction is in fact territorial: in Belgium and Switzerland the territorialism is legally recognized, as is starting to happen with devolution in Spain and the United Kingdom; in others, such as India and South Africa, it forms a complex myriad of levels and localities; in others, such as immigrant communities, it depends on settlement patterns and intensity; this latter was the pattern we recognized in contemporary Israel in Chapter 1.

Plurilingualism (like bilingualism) is also commonly uneven: there are certain tasks that one can perform in one language better than another (I speak and read Hebrew and read French easily, but am weak on writing both and speaking French). And there are certain domains that individual plurilinguals can handle better than others: we have our kitchen languages, and our work languages, and our shopping languages, so that the whole forms a very complex profile, to match more or less the complex sociolinguistic ecology in which we live. Going more deeply, we probably mix our varieties in use: there are many terms that I use in Hebrew when I am speaking English to a fellow bilingual, and I need to make a special effort to find the English word(s) for *lul* (chicken coop), or *aliya* (immigration to Israel), or *minyan* (ten adult Jewish males). In multilingual societies (and most large urban areas are now becoming multilingual), such mixtures make a nonsense of the common belief that we speak (or should speak) pure labeled languages.

That this kind of model fits ancient cities, such as Rome, with its regular use of Greek alongside Latin, and the Aramaic and Gallic varieties of slaves and soldiers and traders, and such as Jerusalem at the time of Jesus, with Aramaic and Greek and Hebrew and a little Latin, seems well established. But how early can we assume it to be true? In other words, how monolingual were the Israelites and the other Canaanites, and how monolingual were their communities?

Evidence is provided by small villages with their own languages, such as the linguistically distinct pueblos of New Mexico and Arizona, and the linguistically isolated villages of Papua New Guinea. The Rio Grande pueblos were small villages that spoke a number of languages, Hopi, Zuni, Keresan, and three Tanoan languages (Tewa, Towa, and Tiwa). The classic bilingual community was Hano, one of the nine villages of Hopi, whose inhabitants all knew Tewa as well as Hopi, and who served as interpreters with outsiders, including the American government;[52] another was Santo Domingo, a village renowned for trading and multilingualism. For Papua New Guinea, with 850 languages for its 6 million population, there are many isolated villages with their own languages. Gapun is one, a village in East Sepik province of Papua New Guinea with a population of under 100 speaking, until recently (no one under ten was still speaking it in 1990), an isolate language, Taiap. The first European to do fieldwork in the village traced how the young men of the village who went away to the plantations to work brought back Tok Pisin, the language of Papua New Guinea, with them, which was passed in due course to all the children.[53] Plurilingualism is commonly produced by taking slaves, by intermarriage (and, with women captives, the two are related), and by trade, even without settling in the same town.

While the Bible stories do not make claims for multilingualism, they include many stories of intermarriage, such as among the Patriarchs. Jacob's sons, apart from Joseph, who married an Egyptian, were reported to have had Canaanite wives; Moses married a Midianite; and the Children of Israel came out from Egypt with a "mixed multitude" (Exodus 12: 38). And, as we noted, the Canaanite pattern was part of a dialect continuum.

The traditional history with conquest by Joshua does not contradict the existence of Hebrew as a component of plurilingualism and multilingualism. The other theories of origin are also consistent with this suggestion. Both the peacefully infiltrating semi-nomads and the revolting peasants moving into the hill country can easily be assumed to have established contact with the existing speakers of Semitic varieties, just as their elite later were shown to have picked up the Aramaic of diplomacy and as a trading lingua franca. Hebrew was certainly maintained as the language of ritual and literature, and probably continued to be spoken as a vernacular until the destruction of the Temple and even later, but it was used, I suspect, in a multilingual pattern.

Language shift

Max Weinreich, the leading scholar of the history of Yiddish,[54] had a clear sociolinguistic understanding of language shift. The switch to Aramaic, which he dates after the return from Babylon, was not rapid (as believed by nineteenth-century scholars) but a long process that may have lasted until the fourth century CE. It was part, he argues, of the spread of Aramaic varieties throughout the Middle East, lasting 1,000 years or so until the Arab conquest (and persisting in some mountainous Christian and Jewish communities after that).[55] The process of shift could have taken a few hundred years, spreading from one section of the community to another and from one functional domain to others. At times, a situation of what Weinreich calls "co-territorial multilingualism" was probable, with most people knowing each language to a certain extent.[56] For some, Hebrew remained the language of everyday life; for others, Aramaic became the most used language. For the Aramaic speakers too, Hebrew remained the language of prayer, and the language to speak to the elderly and to villagers. Weinreich further argues that the first adopters were probably the upper classes, such as the court officers who claimed to know it before the Babylonian exile, while the last to change would be those without contact with strangers, such as "the elderly, women of the lower strata, villagers in remote districts".[57]

In a book on language spread, Robert Cooper poses the question: "What characteristics (e.g., position within the communication network, need-achievement, openness to change) distinguish adopters from nonadopters and early adopters from late adopters?"[58] In another chapter in the same collection, Herbert Paper deals with a puzzling case – a "basic conundrum", as he calls it: the spread of Aramaic. It seems to have been widespread among different groups even before the appearance of Aramaic texts, and to have spread without some major political development, unlike the later spread of Arabic as a result of "religious-cultural-political conquest". Its script spread, as did its use as "an international common second official language", and it was written not just officially but also in private letters and literature.[59] Paper cites as one example the case of the Jews who did not go into Babylonian captivity but took Gentile wives, so that their children spoke the language of Ashdod and did not understand Hebrew (Nehemiah 13: 23–4).

We need to understand this phenomenon more clearly, since I will be talking about language shift through much of this book. Language contact, a topic best explained by Max Weinreich's son, Uriel, occurs in the mind of the bilingual speaker, but depends on a situation in which the speech community includes bilinguals and two sets at least of monolinguals.[60] In Gapun in Papua New Guinea, young men had gone away to work in the plantations, bringing back with them proficiency in Tok Pisin (the lingua franca of New Guinea) along with much-admired material objects representing the *cargo*, the basis of the Cargo cult that developed in New Guinea and elsewhere in the nineteenth century but increased during World War II, with the Americans and Japanese forces seen bringing in large quantities of goods and materials. To assert their status, Don Kulick suggests, these young men would speak Tok Pisin to each other; then other members of the village, noted for their interest in learning languages (a person leaving the village would be farewelled in the language of his or her destination), picked it up and used it when speaking to their children, who grew up knowing no Taiap.[61] Max Weinreich suggests a similar model for co-territorial languages moving into the Jewish community: the men who traded or did business outside the community, where they learned the languages of their customers, would return and show their status by using the new language. Others would imitate them. In our study of the *shuk* of the Old City, we would sometimes hear Arab merchants sitting outside their booths and speaking the Hebrew they had learned for business with Israeli tourists.[62] In a study of an Israeli Palestinian village, we found that children whose fathers worked in construction or agriculture in the Jewish sector were the most likely to know Hebrew words.[63] Unless there is active isolation, contact in the neighborhood as well as at school will usually produce a socially desirable knowledge of the dominant local language. So we can understand both why the Jews remaining behind in what became mainly Gentile communities picked up Aramaic and why those who went into exile where Aramaic was established would also start to learn and use it.

But the timing of this shift will be the topic for the next chapter. To sum up, there is evidence that members of the royal court of Judah started to acquire proficiency in formal diplomatic Aramaic before the Babylonian exile, and there are some reasons to suspect that contacts with refugees and trade had made some degree of multilingualism even more common. If this were so, one can easily imagine Jewish plurilingualism to be of an earlier origin than the exile, and to have been a continuation of the multidialectal situation of Canaan. Even if we take the common view that the kingdoms of Israel and Judah were monolingual in Hebrew, there is good reason to believe that the language pattern was built on earlier multilingualism, and we will see later that the dominance of Hebrew was weakened with the destruction of the First Temple.

But a final word of caution. The smaller and less developed communities of the ancient world were unlike the modern urban speech communities we have been using as analogies. One should think rather of the small interrelated settlements of Papua New Guinea, supporting in mountainous jungles tiny villages with unrelated languages, and producing individual plurilingualism by conquest, warfare, taking slaves, and trade, seldom developing the neat multilingual and diglossic patterns of the Pueblo villages in New Mexico or the towns of the Pale of Settlement in Russia. This is a problem of the sort that the Talmud concluded with the word *Teiku*. We just do not know.

3   Hebrew–Aramaic bilingualism and competition

What is the evidence?

My tracing of Jewish multilingualism back to the period of settling in Canaan may well be wrong, and my assumption of knowledge of Aramaic in pre-exilic Judah is also based more on sociolinguistic than biblical or archeological evidence, but all scholars agree that the surrender to Sennacherib and the deportations that followed Nebuchadnezzar's destruction of Jerusalem in 597 BCE had a major influence in adding Aramaic to the languages of the Jewish people. In one simple view, favored by nineteenth-century scholars, we start with a period of Hebrew monolingualism, then enter, after the Babylonian exile, an Aramaic period, and next have Greek added after Alexander's conquests; Hebrew lingers as Latin did in the Middle Ages: an artificial variety for writing sacred text. Or, perhaps, we go from a period when Jews lived in a multilingual region, and chose individually to be plurilingual, to a period when the Jewish nation shifted from speaking only Hebrew, with appropriate roles for each of its languages. The big questions that remain undecided are how fast these transitions were and what happened to Hebrew.

There are two major schools of thought, which I might label the multilingualist Hebraists,[1] who believe and argue that Hebrew continued to be spoken until the destruction of the Second Temple or later, albeit in a bilingual or diglossic pattern with Aramaic enriched later by the addition of Greek; and the monolingualists, who assume that Hebrew became a limited artificial religio-literary language, like Latin in the medieval Church. It was this second group, raised in Anglo-Saxon monolingualism, who would ask what language Jesus spoke, ignoring the probability of plurilingualism. My own prejudice, as a sociolinguist happy to watch his grandchildren growing up as comfortable bilinguals, tends to be with the first school, but at the outset I admit it seems hard to reach a conclusion. Many Talmudic discussions end with the simple word *Teiku*, translated in bilingual editions as "The question remains undecided", and used in Modern Israeli Hebrew to report a draw in a football match. This will be the only reasonable answer, in the meantime, to many of the questions raised in this book.

To explain the reason for doubt, one must take into account the nature of the sources. In studies of the language policy of existing nations, we usually depend on the results of language questions on national censuses.[2] Of course, there are problems at times with censuses, such as the questions asked,[3] the language names used,[4] the use of samples rather than full populations, and the long gap between language censuses.[5]

This is bad enough for contemporary sociolinguistic studies, but when we are doing historical sociolinguistics we have a vastly more difficult task. Sometimes there are archeological remains: ostraca, such as the sixty-four legible pieces of pottery written in Hebrew found in the treasury of the palace of Ahab in Samaria and dated before 750 BCE;[6] or stele, such as the Menephtah stele found by Flinders Petrie in 1896 at Thebes[7] and dated to about 1200 BCE with the first mention of Israelites; or the Akkadian clay tablets, which range from 2500 BCE to 100 CE. We also have documents written on papyrus, including the Dead Sea Scrolls found at Qumran, which revolutionized scholarly ability to study the biblical period. Each of these gives evidence of written language but few offer any clues to the spoken language. We know that, in many speech communities, there is a disjunction between speech and writing, such as with the Navajo Nation, where written records such as Tribal Council minutes and laws, court proceedings, and the tribal newspaper used English even when most oral speech was in Navajo.[8] In the contemporary Arab world, writing is in Classical or Standard Arabic, while people speak a regional variety that is lexically and grammatically different, so that written evidence is misleading.

Of course we have the Bible, a large collection of material written in Hebrew mainly, but with portions in Aramaic and other parts preserved in Greek and Ge'ez, and the New Testament books in Greek recording what was presumably an Aramaic original.[9] The difficulty we face in using this large collection as a source for sociolinguistic history is twofold: first, as with other written sources, we have no way to be sure that what was written was the spoken language; second, we have no hard evidence of authorship and dating.

As I explained in Chapter 2, there are different opinions. The traditional Jewish view holds that the Torah (the Pentateuch, the first five books of the Bible) was written by Moses in the fourteenth century BCE, and the other books by their named authors from then until 400 BCE. Bible scholars in the nineteenth century such as Julius Wellhausen[10] developed the documentary theory, claiming that the Torah was combined from four (or more) separate sources, composed between 950 BCE and 500 BCE and later edited. In this view, the biblical accounts are not factual accounts but have been selected and shaped to present positions being argued for by later redactors.[11]

The Deuteronomic historical writings are particularly a problem, with various approaches to their composition. A recent book by Raymond Person tries to summarize current views and presents his own hypothesis.[12] He cites a book that first presents the consensus model set out by Avi Hurvitz, who recognizes three historical periods of Hebrew, which he calls Archaic Biblical Hebrew, Early Biblical Hebrew, and Late Biblical Hebrew.[13] Robert Polzin has proposed adding to this a transitional style, between early and late, for Chronicles. Frank Polak suggests the criterion of oral rhythm to distinguish early and late. This analysis gives us four periods: Classical, Transitional Classical, Late Pre-exilic, and Post-exilic. One is inevitably reminded of Polonius with his listing of kinds of dramas.

Oral composition and scribal redaction of the Hebrew Bible

In their own theory, Young and his colleagues torpedo these neat patterns, suggesting that the various writers and editors chose a style according to personal preference or reflecting their geographical dialects, which they consider to have shown considerable variation.[14] Person too is skeptical about the possibility of identifying and dating the many layers. He assumes, as most scholars do nowadays, that there was a period of oral transmission, such as that proposed for Homer by the scholar Milman Parry and his student Alfred Lord, who observed and recorded the long epics sung during Ramadan by Balkan singers. Homer, they then argued, represented the transcribed collective poems of a tradition of singers.[15] Applying such a model to the Bible, Person argues that the texts were redacted by different scribal schools that existed (one at a time) in exilic Babylon and post-exilic Judah.

What do we know about scribal schools? Those in ancient Sumeria have been described in some detail. Instruction was in Sumerian, a language isolate about whose ancestry and relationships there is no consensus that had been replaced by Akkadian as a spoken language in Mesopotamia about the second millennium BCE, but that was maintained as a written language. This scribal conservatism helps justify those who argue that Hebrew was still being written long after it was replaced by Aramaic as a vernacular, just as Latin was written for long after it was no longer spoken. The cuneiform tablets found in the school buildings were originally believed to be in a Semitic language, but were recognized as Sumerian and partially deciphered in the middle of the nineteenth century; only in the early twentieth century were a complete dictionary[16] and grammar[17] published.

Scribal training in Sumer started young. The excavated archeological remains at Nippur and Ur are of quite small private houses, probably run by educated priests for two or three students. The tablets they left tell of an earlier period, in the twenty-first century BCE, when the kings of Ur set up academies of learning to train bureaucrats. The *eduba*, as they were called, started with basic training in writing the letters, moved on to learning Sumerian and memorizing literary texts, and added instruction in mathematics and writing letters and contracts. At more advanced stages, scribes would specialize in types of literary text including epics and hymns. It appears they were expected to sing as well as write.[18]

Did such formal scribal education exist in the two kingdoms of Israel and Judah? Some believe that there was a place of prestige for scribal skills in early Israel.[19] Because of the time it took to acquire control of the writing system, formal training would have been needed.[20] There is no reference to such schools in the Bible; the earliest is in Ben Sirah (Ecclesiasticus) 51: 23, written probably in the second century BCE by a Jerusalem scribe who moved to Egypt, where he established a school: "Draw near unto me, you unlearned, and dwell in the house of learning [*bet midrash*]." It would not have been easy to learn the writing system, considering that it takes several years to achieve proficiency in writing Modern Hebrew, with its complex grammatical vowel system (and it takes even longer for native speakers to learn to write Arabic, with the gap between spoken and written language).

Although there is no evidence for public education, an innovation in Talmudic Judaism, there were schools. There is sufficient paleographic evidence of written Hebrew to support the idea of "diachronic development with systematic consistency" at datable times; this points to formal standardized scribal education. Orthography also shows diachronic development and systematic consistency. There are dialectal differences between north and south. The use of complex hieratic numerals (the Egyptian system) also suggests scribal training. There is some similarity in the structure of letters. While there are no building sites, there is good reason to suppose that the scribal education system was under royal command.

The smudging of the date and composition of the Bible has a double effect: it permits greater freedom of interpretation, but leaves us in final uncertainty – *Teiku*. In what follows, I accept two positions and offer what seem to me to be two reasonable alternatives (my own major contribution being in sociolinguistic likelihood), but avoid rigid conclusions. But you will note that a great deal is built on very little evidence. My favorite example of this is from the later writing of Josephus. Speaking at the siege of Jerusalem, by which time he was with the Roman army, Josephus in his *Wars of the Jews* (Book VI) refers to a message from Titus "in the Hebrew language". The footnote by the later, Christian, editor does not accept this evidence of language use, but says: "The same that was in the New Testament so called and was then in the common language of the Jews of Judea which was Syriac."[21] It is not uncommon to interpret what evidence there is in accordance with one's opinions.[22]

Did Hebrew survive the return?

Whether or not the exiles were prepared for a long stay, the situation changed drastically in 539 BCE, when the Persians defeated the Neo-Babylonian

Empire. One of the first acts of the new ruler, Cyrus, was to order the restoration of the Jewish state and the rebuilding of the Temple (Ezra 1: 2). A first group (numbered about 50,000 and listed by town and family name) is said to have returned and started to rebuild the Temple. There was trouble with the "people of the land", who presumably included the intermarried Jews who had remained, but the Persian governor was instructed by the new king, Darius, to allow and provide funds for the building, which was completed in 516 BCE. About fifty years later Ezra, the scribe and a priest, was authorized by King Artaxerxes (the letter of authority in Aramaic is quoted in Ezra 7: 13–28) to lead a second group back and report on the state of affairs in Judea. His complaints about intermarriage and a shift from Hebrew were to be echoed by Nehemiah, who was cupbearer or butler to the king and was appointed governor of Judea in about 445 BCE. Again, there was opposition by neighboring groups to the rebuilding of the walls of Jerusalem, but the work was completed. Nehemiah carried out social reforms and banned intermarriage.[23]

For the next 200 years Judea was under Persian rule. Known as Yahud medinata (the province of Judea in Aramaic), it was a part of the Achaemenid or Persian Empire, which lasted until Alexander's conquest of the Middle East. The empire had a centralized bureaucracy and a professional army and navy, and conducted its official business in Elamite (another language isolate), used alongside Old Persian and Akkadian until the conquest of Babylon, when Aramaic became the lingua franca. Some scholars believe that this post-exilic period was the time of the redaction of much of the Bible, arguing that it reflects the ideology of the time in its presentation of earlier history.

And it was during this period that Aramaic became a language of the Jews. Nehemiah (13: 24) describes the return of a party of Jews from Babylonian exile, and notes in particular the fact that many Jews who had remained in Israel had married wives "of Ashdod, of Ammon, and of Moab; and their children spake half in the speech of Ashdod and could not speak in the Jews' language [Yehudit], but according to the language of each people". These accounts written before and after the Babylonian exile (which lasted from about 587 to 538 BCE) suggest that Hebrew and not Aramaic was spoken by the common people in the earlier time, but that it was known by courtiers, and that Hebrew (Yehudit) was still the common language after the return from Babylonia, although Jews who had remained there were speaking other varieties after the return and could not understand the Hebrew of the returning exiles.

This perhaps showed the tension of Jewish communities that had to adopt features of the cultures and languages among which they lived and the simultaneous need to maintain linguistic identity.[24] What is significant is that the concern about intermarriage is expressed in terms of a loss of knowledge of Hebrew, meaning, effectively, a loss of identity. While it is not clear whether the other language was Aramaic, or a foreign language, or a foreign-influenced variety of Hebrew (all have been suggested), the important statement is about the growing inability of the children of such foreign wives to understand "Yehudit" – Hebrew. Nehemiah was dealing with the difficulties faced by those returning from exile to maintain identity and language. But what is clear is the assumption that Hebrew was still alive and well after the return from exile, though threatened by the tendency to assimilation of those who had not gone to Babylon.[25]

There are two biblical references commonly cited as recording the shift from Hebrew to Aramaic, which is widely assumed to have taken place (or, as Weinreich and other Hebraists suggest instead, to have started to take place) after the Babylonian exile. The first is the passage in which Nehemiah criticized those who stayed behind in Judea for their intermarriage and assimilation with non-Jews:

When they had heard the law, they separated from Israel all the mixed multitude... In those days also saw I Jews that had married wives of Ashdod, of Ammon, and of Moab: and their children spake half in the speech of Ashdod, and could not speak in the Jews' language [Yehudit], but according to the language of each people. And I contended with them, and cursed them, and smote certain of them, and plucked off their hair, and made them swear by God, saying, Ye shall not give your daughters unto their sons, nor take their daughters unto your sons, or for yourselves. (Nehemiah 13: 3, 23–5)

Ashdod was one of the principal cities of the Philistines, originally inhabited perhaps by speakers of non-Semitic languages, but by this time assumed to be speaking a variety of Aramaic. The Jews who had gone into captivity left behind a remnant, large as it may have been, that was committed neither to traditional religious observance nor to national identity,[26] and likely to have become readily assimilated to the mixed culture produced by the population exchanges that were being implemented. There are differing opinions as to whether Nehemiah was objecting to loss of Hebrew or to an impure Hebrew, but it is clear he was objecting to intermarriage as a loss of ethnic identity, which he associated with language loss.[27]

It is taken for granted by many scholars that those who went into exile in Babylonia picked up Aramaic, which some believe replaced their Hebrew. This also was the view of the Talmud, although the biblical account in Nehemiah seems to blame those who had remained in Judea more than the returnees with Ezra. The traditional view holds that the Jews in Babylonia, like their forefathers in Egypt, maintained their identity by keeping their names, their dress, and their language, but this may be a later argument for Hebrew rather than a historical account.

But, given the view that those who did not go into captivity also lost their Hebrew, the Babylonian Talmud (Nedarim 37b) cites and then interprets the account of the institution of the public reading of the Torah as evidence for shift.[28] Here is Nehemiah's account:

Ezra the scribe stood upon a wooden tower made for the purpose. . . And Ezra opened the book in the sight of all the people, for he was above all the people; as he opened it, all the people stood up. Ezra blessed the Lord, the great God, and all the people answered, Amen, Amen, with hands upraised. Then they bowed their heads and prostrated themselves before the Lord with their faces to the ground. Jeshua, Bani, Sherebiah, Jamin, Akkub, Shabbethai, Hodiah, Maaseiah, Kelita, Azariah, Jozabad, Hanan, Pelaiah, and the Levites explained the Torah to the people, while the people stood in their places. They read from the scroll of the Teaching of God, translating it and giving the sense; so they understood the reading. (Nehemiah 8: 4–8)

That is taken from the new translation of the Jewish Publication Society (JPS).[29] The King James Bible (1611 version) is different: the last verse there is: "So they read in the booke, in the Law of God distinctly, and gaue the sense, and caused them to vnderstand the reading." The key word, translated "distinctly" in the Authorized version (and kept by Harold Fish in his modified version for the Koren Bible), is the Hebrew word *meforash*. The JPS translation follows the Talmudic interpretation (Tractate *Nedarim* 37b):

For Rav Ika Bar Avin said in the name of Rav Chananel, who said in the name of Rav: "That which is written 'They read in the scroll, in God's Torah, elucidated, heeding the sense, and they understood the reading' is interpreted exegetically as follows … *meforash* – elucidated – this refers to Targum [the traditional Aramaic translation] which elucidates Scripture."

The Jewish traditional commentators identify this as the Aramaic translation of Onkelos, which they believed existed in the time of Ezra, but must then have been lost until about 110 CE, several hundred years later. "Rav" is a reference to Abba Arika, the second-century CE rabbi who lived in Babylonia and established the school at Sura that began the Talmudic age. By his time, several hundred years, the custom of following the reading in Hebrew of each sentence of the weekly Torah portion by an oral translation into Aramaic had become established.[30] It was certainly appropriate in Babylon, where the spoken Jewish vernacular was a variety of Aramaic, but is it an accurate account of a situation in Judea several hundred years earlier?

Some scholars see the possible need for interpretation into Aramaic for both those who had gone to Babylon and started to lose Hebrew and those who remained behind and had no experience with formal Hebrew. They also point out that a translation into Aramaic, a high-status language, would add a touch of "high culture" to the occasion. Further, they argue that the spoken language must have changed more quickly than the written. There could then be a reason for interpretation other than a language change. Therefore, building on this single reference and a much later Talmudic opinion, the theory that those who returned with Ezra and Nehemiah had suddenly and completely switched to Aramaic is, many scholars believe, an extreme and doubtful view.[31] On the contrary, Nehemiah's complaint about children of mixed marriages who did not understand

Hebrew seems to be evidence that it was still being spoken by those who returned from Babylon.

We may compare this to the more recent return to Israel of Jews from Western emancipated countries, who have done so as a matter of choice and not forced by being refugees from post-Holocaust Europe or Islamic nations. As was the case with the return from Babylonia, only a portion of the exiled population returned, and many (including religiously observant Jews who prayed daily for the restoration of the Temple and its services) chose to remain in exile. Thus we can reasonably assume that those who voluntarily moved back to Israel did so because of a strong commitment to identity, land, and presumably also language. The notion that Hebrew had been lost by the return is thus very doubtful.

When did Aramaic replace Hebrew?

But there are in fact a number of scholars who argue for early loss of Hebrew as a vernacular and reinterpret or deny the arguments put forward for the continuity of spoken Hebrew. These scholars hold that Judea was bilingual at the end of the sixth century BCE or the beginning of the fifth; that Aramaic began to supersede Hebrew by the middle of the fifth century BCE, a process completed during the fourth century, so that interpretation and translation of Hebrew texts was needed by the end of the fourth century and during the third century. I now present the arguments of members of this school, which attempts to explain away all the evidence of Hebrew being used as a vernacular until the destruction of the Second Temple, and even later.

First, they hold that the Jews who went into exile in Babylonia rapidly switched there to Aramaic, which was to be expected, because they had come from a tiny town of a few thousand to a huge metropolis. Here, we need to consider the speed with which immigrants lose their language. Modern studies suggest that the third generation no longer controls the language of their immigrant grandparents. But there are clearly cases in which externally or internally imposed isolation from the new linguistic environment slows the process down. It would be strange if the Jews going into exile did not maintain some kind of distance: the picture of Jewish society in Talmudic Babylon clearly includes features such as kosher food and Shabbat observance that call for a good deal of isolation from others. Even without this, the time between the exile and the return is rather short to suggest that a complete language shift had taken place.

Those who argue for rapid complete shift claim that any maintenance of Hebrew was restricted to use by the educated priests and leaders as a "religious lingo". The term shows prejudice; one doubts whether they would have used it for medieval or Church Latin, which was the probable model for their argument. They also seem to assume that all who remained in Judah during the exile also switched to Aramaic. In their view, the reference to intermarriage is a later addition; by the time of the return, they believe that all the children and not just the offspring of intermarriage were speaking Aramaic, called in Ezra *leshon Ashdod*. This they consider a dialect of Aramaic different from the Imperial Aramaic or the Babylonian Aramaic the returnees were assumed to speak. Only educated returnees still knew Hebrew, but those who had stayed behind neither spoke nor cared to speak it. If this is true, Nehemiah was trying to persuade people to speak Hebrew again, as he tried to persuade them to send their Gentile wives away, but, failing that, introduced interpretation and translation.[32] Again, these are arguments that support a view rather than evidence.

It is true that the limited epigraphic evidence is mainly in Aramaic. The fact that personal documents such as marriage and divorce papers were in Aramaic might furnish evidence that Aramaic was the common language, rather than an acceptance of the common use of Aramaic for commercial and legal documents, as others hold. Coins were in Hebrew script, but use the Aramaic name Yahud (sometimes written in Hebrew letters) rather than the Hebrew Yehudah.

Any use of Hebrew after the Persian period in this theory was literary or religious "lingo". The priests in the Temple and the members of the Dead Sea sects used their own varieties of Hebrew, but they were two different "religious lingos", each like Church Latin. The requirement that the Inspector of the Camp in the Dead Sea document *4QMMT* (the *Halakhic* letter) had to be "master of every secret of men in every language" argues that Hebrew was no longer spoken, as all Hebrew dialects must have been mutually intelligible, and must have meant the Aramaic and Greek assumed to be spoken by new recruits.[33]

Perhaps the reference was to a gap between vernacular Hebrew and the Hebrew of the Camp.[34] The letters in Hebrew in the Dead Sea documents date from the Bar Kokhba revolt, and represent the language revival ideology of the rebels. Except in the leases written by Simeon, there is Aramaic influence in the Hebrew. That "Hebrew was the language of the priests in the Temple, in particular, and the tongue used to describe religious rites, in general"[35] reflected their ideology rather than current vernacular usage. One is reminded of the stories of Diaspora Jews who would speak Hebrew at the table on the Sabbath.

The Hebrew of the Dead Sea Scrolls shows Aramaic influence in syntax and morphology, while the Aramaic documents of the period only show borrowing of Hebrew lexicon. True, there is Hebrew influence in the Aramaic of the Palestinian Christians and the Samaritans too, but the Christian influences were earlier, and the Samaritans can be accounted for by their also using Hebrew as a religious lingo.[36]

For those who argued that spoken Hebrew was dead, the fact that the rabbis wrote in Mishnaic Hebrew then simply showed that they too developed their own non-priestly religious lingo; the statement that fathers had to teach their children Hebrew provides undated evidence that it was no longer being spoken to babies by mothers. The statement of Rabbi Yehuda Hanasi (second century CE), "Why speak *leshon sursi* [Aramaic]? Either *leshon hakodesh* [Hebrew] or Greek" (Baba Qama 83a), showed that Aramaic was the common language, but in their theory says nothing about the other two languages. The statement of Rabbi Yosi in the same place, "In Babylonia why speak *leshon Arami*? Either *leshon hakodesh* or *Parsi* [Persian]", can also be explained away as presenting an argument that, in Babylonia, Hebrew had remained the religious lingo. Sanhedrin 22a, which discusses the introduction of the *Ashuri* (Aramaic) script to replace the Old Hebrew, may be misdated, for if language and script never changed why was Daniel the only one who could read the writing on Nebuchadnezzar's wall; the answer is because it was in *gematria*, meaning a code.

Finally, these scholars reinterpret the story of Rabbi Yehuda Hanasi's maid, who his students heard using a number of Hebrew words they did not know, such as *serugin* (a few at a time), *chaloglos* (purslane, a succulent plant still used in salads), *salseleha* (to delve into and turn over), *yechavcha* (your burden, a word that occurs in a psalm that Rabba bar Chana also heard used by an Arab caravan merchant), and *matateh* (broom). Their explanation is that his maid was exceptional in speaking archaic Hebrew, rejecting the interpretation of Hebraists such as Rabin, who believe it was because she came from a Judean village where Hebrew was still spoken.[37]

There is thus a case to be made for the Talmudic assertion 1,000 years later that, after the return from Babylon, Hebrew was lost rapidly, but the arguments seem forced, and there is an equally strong case to be made that it continued to be spoken. *Teiku*, again.

Did they speak Hebrew at Qumran?

Echoing and extending the notion that Hebrew at Qumran was a "religious lingo", William Schniedewind even calls it an "anti-language", a term he takes from Michael Halliday,[38] referring to a variety of language used ideologically to separate its speakers from others.[39] He considers Mishnaic Hebrew to be a "literarization of a colloquial linguistic register", itself a development of Late Biblical Hebrew, but Qumran Hebrew, the language of the sectarian documents, is sufficiently different to need explanation.

To understand the continuity of Hebrew, we have looked at evidence towards the end of the period it was spoken, for, unless we assume an early language revival, any evidence for Hebrew use in the late Second Temple period and later in the Mishnaic period would make it clear that it survived the return from Babylonia 500 years earlier. Whatever its status as a spoken vernacular so late, no one doubts its continuation in the religious and literary domains, and many scholars see it not as an artificial religious lingo or anti-language but as a written version of a language that continued to be spoken by many.

In this chapter, then, we have seen the end of Hebrew monolingual hegemony, although, as I have argued, I am more comfortable with the idea of earlier plurilingualism and multilingualism, and the development of a period of bilingualism to which a third language was soon to be added. But we have also seen (and will see again) a reluctance of many scholars to accept the survival of the Hebrew language. This is not surprising, considering the almost unbelievable survival of the Jewish people, remnants of a tiny kingdom that grew up surrounded by the mighty Babylonian, Egyptian and Persian Empires (which no longer exist), that lost its larger neighbor with the scattering of the Ten Tribes, and that survived an exile, a period without sovereignty, and a second even greater exile. No wonder many European intellectuals are discomfited by the modern restoration of Israeli statehood and puzzled by the rebirth of Hebrew as the dominant language of that state.

4   Three languages in Hellenistic and Roman Palestine

Linguistic effects of Alexander's conquests

The defeat of Persia by Alexander the Great and the resulting Greek-speaking empires produced a major change in the sociolinguistic repertoire of the Jewish people living within them, adding Greek to the Hebrew–Aramaic bilingualism that had begun with the Babylonian exile. Aramaic was by this time firmly fixed in the Jewish sociolinguistic profile, although, as I argued in the last chapter, its exact role as a vernacular alongside or replacing Hebrew remains open to question. Hebrew remained the preferred language for religious and literary composition, but it was a combination of Hebrew and Aramaic that was later to be entrenched as the language of the Babylonian Talmud, recognized in combination as *loshn koydesh* (the sacred tongue, Yiddish) in Ashkenaz.[1] Now, in the latter part of the fourth century BCE, Greek was added as a third component, producing a trilingual pattern that was to be a template among Jews living in Palestine or elsewhere in the eastern Mediterranean throughout Roman rule during the later Second Temple period, and more or less until the Islamic conquest.

A complex process of cultural merger produced a version of Jewish Hellenism that survived the Maccabean revolt.[2] For a second time the Jewish sociolinguistic ecology was revolutionized by external pressure, a military success of the Macedonian warrior whose surviving nation is still disputed between Greek and Slavic speakers. Alexander conquered the known world, spreading his power as far as India and establishing a rule over the Middle East that entrenched Greek there for several hundred years. Jews remaining in the tiny state and those who emigrated from it were exposed to the new language and culture, setting off a struggle between Judaism and the dominant non-Jewish culture surrounding it that came to typify Jewish history.

Alexander himself died young, and his empire was divided between his generals. Ptolemy became satrap (governor) of Egypt after the partition of 320 BCE, and Seleucus took over Babylonia and the eastern part of the Empire, as far east as the Indus, and including the Levant. They and their successors struggled for territory and power. Part of this struggle took place in the geographic center, Palestine, where the Maccabean revolt aiming at independence erupted about 175 BCE.

Before the revolt there had been acceptance by many in Judea of various aspects of Greek civilization, including language. A possible early reference to a Greek-speaking Jew appears in the work of the Jewish historian Josephus, who cites Clearchus of Soli, a third-century philosopher of the Aristotelian school, who told of meeting a Jew who was proficient in Greek.[34]

Whether Clearchus is to believed or not, under the Greek rule of the Levant, Hellenism and the Greek language subsequently spread into sections of the Judean population. The Maccabean revolt was a reaction, according to Jewish sources, to excessive persecution and the banning of traditional Jewish practices by Antiochus IV, who had changed the Temple in Jerusalem into a pagan place of worship, burned copies of the Torah, and forbade circumcision. The victory of the Hasmoneans in 165 BCE permitted the cleansing and rededication of the Temple and the restoration of traditional practices.

But the two written accounts, I Maccabees, composed originally in Hebrew by a "pious Palestinian Jew, steeped in the Bible", and II Maccabees, written by a Diaspora Jew "in an elegant, occasionally florid, Greek", do not emphasize a conflict with Hellenism and Hellenizers.[5] While they note the Maccabees' commitment to Judaism, the enemies are not so much the Greeks or even the Jewish Hellenizers but the co-territorial Gentiles, the "surrounding nations" or "peoples of a different race".[6] After the Maccabean victory there were negotiations with the Seleucids that showed that a political and cultural compromise had been reached. The rulers of Judea had regular dealings with Greek kings, adopted Greek names, wore Greek clothes, minted coins modeled on Greek coins, and presumably learned the Greek language. With the weakening of Seleucid power, Judean independence grew, but it did not mean a rejection of many aspects of Hellenism but, rather, "an enrichment of Judaism".[7]

By the end of the fourth century BCE, therefore, some Jews were beginning to speak Greek, starting in the growing Diaspora communities in the eastern Mediterranean and spreading to Judea, but not replacing Aramaic in Babylonia.[8] The earliest Jewish book in Greek was the Septuagint, produced in Alexandria, a translation of the Torah into *koine* Greek, the "common" language that became the lingua franca of the Western world until Latin replaced it in the Western Roman Empire. Begun in the third century BCE and completed in 135 BCE, the translation was produced for Greek-speaking Jews in Egypt; it was later rejected by the rabbis,[9] but preserved by the Christians and used as the basis for many translations into other languages.

But here too there are uncertainties: we are not sure of the translators, who presumably were scholarly Jews knowing Hebrew and Greek (they were spread over time, and perhaps space); some parts may have been translated elsewhere than in Alexandria.[10] The translation of the Septuagint recognized the significance of Greek as the dominant language in much of the Jewish world; it also represented a compromise between cultures. The translation, which was more or less literal, showed the marked influence of the Hebrew original in the frequent calques.[11] This was a choice of the translators, who could have written a more "acceptable" Greek. Septuagint Greek is different, capturing as much as possible the structure and style of the Hebrew original.

A related question is: how well was knowledge of Hebrew preserved in Alexandria?[12] In the case of the Aramaic Targumim used in post-exilic Judea, there are arguments that the audience still knew Hebrew; was this the case in Alexandria?[13] The very style of translation might well have been a method of resistance and of maintaining the Hebrew nature of the original. On the other hand, there are those who argue that the translation showed the loss of Hebrew in the Greek-dominated Diaspora. Clearly, we are again faced with an ideological dispute between those scholars who argue for and those who argue against belief in the maintenance of Hebrew until the second century BCE.[14]

Greek was used everywhere for inscriptions on Jewish tombstones and honorary plaques; in fact, 75 percent of the inscriptions found in Judea are in Greek (and 85 percent of those in the Diaspora). Many were written in poor Greek and appeared on the tombs of rabbis, officials, merchants, and craftsmen, providing strong support for the argument that Greek proficiency was not restricted to the elite.[15] Saul Lieberman was the first scholar to present a strong case for the extensive knowledge of Greek by the rabbis and others; he found around a thousand borrowed words, and puns that depended on knowledge of the language.

There is additional evidence of Jewish proficiency in Greek. In 150 BCE Judah Maccabee sent two emissaries to Rome to negotiate on his behalf; they addressed the Senate, presumably in the Greek that educated Romans knew (1 Mac 8). At Qumran, most documents are in Hebrew (750 texts) or Aramaic (150 texts), but twenty-seven texts are in Greek; most of them are literary, but the existence of a few documentary texts in Greek suggests that, in spite of their ideological preference for Hebrew and Aramaic, Jews were using Greek for economic and commercial purposes.[16] The Bar Kokhba archive (about 134 CE) includes three letters in Greek, with evidence that the writer, a fighter in the Second Revolt (which restored archaic Hebrew script to its coins), preferred it to Hebrew or Aramaic.[17] But the Greek inscriptions are mainly found in cities and not the countryside, and the proportion of inscriptions increased greatly after 70 CE, reflecting the fact that Greek had probably by then become the vernacular language of most Jews in the Mediterranean Diaspora. Perhaps writing inscriptions in Greek was a matter of custom not related to spoken language use, or the result of the limited writing skills of those who made the inscriptions. Again, we need to be reminded that public signs do not necessarily provide evidence of the spoken language of the community.

Josephus describes his own learning of Greek:

Afterward I got leisure at Rome; and when all my materials were prepared for that work, I made use of some persons to assist me in learning the Greek tongue, and by these means I composed the history of those transactions.[18]

We need to seek an explanation of the Talmud's ban on the learning of "Greek wisdom".[19] The Talmud in *Sotah* says that *hochmat yevanit* (Greek wisdom) was not to be studied, explained by the medieval commentator Rashi to be a set of cryptic expressions or gestures known only by the Greco-Roman aristocracy and not the common people. The Talmud asks if it was forbidden to teach the Greek language. "But Rabbi said, 'In Eretz Yisrael, why speak the Syriac language [a western dialect of Aramaic, according to Rashi]? Rather speak *leshon hakodesh* [Hebrew] or *leshon yevanit* [Greek]. *Leshon yevanit* is one thing, and *hochmat yevanit* is another.'" The ban did not cover the Greek language, then, or probably even general Greek philosophy.[20]

By the middle of the first century CE even the study of Greek philosophy as we know it was acceptable:

But is Greek philosophy forbidden? Behold Rab Yehudah declared that Samuel said in the name of Rabban Simeon ben Gamaliel, . . . there were a thousand pupils in my father's house; five hundred studied Torah and five hundred studied Greek wisdom.[21]

But the Talmud adds: "It was different with the house of Rabban Gamaliel because they had close associations with the government."

It is true that there were 1,000 Greek words in rabbinic literature, but this is not enough by itself to prove that people spoke Greek.[22] Greek was better known in the cities among the upper classes than in the countryside, and certainly in the partially Hellenized cities such as Tiberius and Caesarea, which were centers of Roman administration. There are many cases in the Talmud of rabbis showing their knowledge of Greek by puns or other wordplay. There are also many Greek inscriptions and trilingual inscriptions with Greek alongside Hebrew and Aramaic. Nonetheless, the answer to the question of how much Greek was known in Talmudic Palestine remains open: *Teiku*. "We do not know *exactly* how much Greek the Rabbis knew."[23]

Jewish beliefs about multilingualism

Of the three aspects of language policy – practices, beliefs, management[24] – we have so far been concerned mainly with the first, language practices, as we struggle to reconstruct what people actually did, but these Talmudic citations remind us of the second aspect of language policy, language beliefs or ideology. They provide evidence of the beliefs that lay behind the practices. Greek, the rabbis said, is valuable for those who deal with the government; this can be good or bad, for, while it is useful to have government contacts, you can't trust people who speak Greek because they may be government agents. Quite another aspect of the issue is presented in the Palestinian Talmud (*Peah* I.1 15c): "A man may teach his daughter Greek because it is an ornament." These arguments are carried further into the third component of language policy, language management, when they are used to persuade people to learn and use Greek rather than Aramaic:

Rabbi said, why use the Syriac [*sursi*, also "clipped"] language in Palestine? Either *leshon hakodesh* [Hebrew] or Greek.[25]

This statement encouraged a later Babylonian rabbi to speak up for Persian, the language of the ruling empire there:

Similarly, Rav Yosef [a third-generation *Amora* living in Babylonia about 300 CE] said, "In Babylonia why speak the Aramaic language [probably Eastern Aramaic]? Rather either *leshon hakodesh* [Hebrew] or Persian."

Rashi suggests that this was because of the closeness of Aramaic and Hebrew. The *Shita Mekubetzet* (a sixteenth-century collection of commentaries), citing a Gaon – a tenth-century commentator – interprets these two sayings as arguing that Jews should learn the language of the government for dealing with external power, but otherwise speak their own language, Hebrew, within the community.

These examples of language beliefs also demonstrate language management, as the rabbis were arguing for the maintenance of Hebrew at a time that it was no longer a mother tongue. This echoes sentiments expressed by Nehemiah on the return from Babylon, criticizing the people who had intermarried and whose children no longer knew Hebrew. It is reaffirmed in the opinion of Rabbi Meir (a fourth-generation *Tanna*)[26] that one who speaks with his son in *leshon hakodesh* is guaranteed a place in the world to come.[27]

There are five passages in Palestinian rabbinic sources, four from *Tannaim* and one from a *barayta* (an oral law tradition not included in the Mishnah but of similar antiquity), that express this obligation.[28] For instance, the *Sifrei* (a collection of commentaries believed to have originated in the school of Rabbi Akiva) in *Eikev* (piska 10; Deuteronomy, piska 46) states that, when a child first begins to talk, his father should speak to him in Hebrew and teach him the Torah, implying that this will guarantee the child a long life, and that failure to do so will, unfortunately, ensure the opposite. The same idea is found in *Tosefta* (a compilation of Midrashic commentaries compiled about 200 CE) in *Chagigah* (perek 1, halacha 3), though with a slight variation: this source states that, when a child knows how to talk, his father should teach him Hebrew. The emphasis, in mid-second-century Galilee, was not just on teaching Hebrew but on speaking to one's son in it. Another persuasive statement is one by Rabbi Yehuda the Prince praising the Jews in exile in Egypt for keeping four commandments: remaining chaste, avoiding tale bearing, not changing their names, and keeping their language.[29]

The rabbis held that the Torah was given in Hebrew, which was also the language of creation. A passage from *Genesis Rabbah*, a rabbinic commentary on the Book of Genesis, derives this from the sentence "She shall be called *isha* [woman] because she was taken out of *ish* [man]"; this shows that the Torah was written in *leshon hakodesh*. "Rabbi Pinchas and Rabbi Helkiah, in the name of Rabbi Shim'on [about 300 CE], said, 'Just as it was given in *leshon hakodesh*, so was the world created with *leshon hakodesh*.'" In the Babylonian Talmud, however, an opinion is noted in Rab's name (a disciple of Rabbi Judah the Prince about 220 CE) that Adam spoke Aramaic, because Psalm 139: 17 contains what may be an Aramaicism. Resh Laqish (an *Amora* living in Palestine around 250 CE) considered the word to be Hebrew.[30]

There are other discussions of multilingualism. In the Jerusalem Talmud *Megilla* (1: 11 71b), Rabbi Eleazar (about 300 CE) is cited as saying that there were multiple languages spoken before the Tower of Babel, and that God's punishment for the attempt to build the tower was to stop people understanding each other's language. Rabbi Yochanan (about 280 CE) disagrees, arguing that everyone spoke Hebrew before Babel, and that the single language was then divided there into seventy. Bar Qappara (about 350 CE) suggests an intermediate position, with Greek existing alongside Hebrew before Babel.

The Book of Zephaniah (a minor prophet writing, according to tradition, about the time of Jeremiah)[31] declares that, in the world to come, everyone will speak a "pure language", a restored universal Hebrew (3: 9). Providing further evidence of Jewish support for multilingualism, there is an account in the Mishnah (*Sotah* 7: 5) describing the building of an altar after the entry into the Promised Land, and writing on the stones "all the words of this Torah in seventy languages". There are two interpretations offered: in one, only the seventy-language version will express the full meanings of the Torah; in the other, the translations make the text available to the seventy nations of the world. Knowing seventy languages is an advantage, but not common: only two or three members of the Sanhedrin were expected to have this skill, for which Joseph in Egypt was famed.

How did rabbinic support for Hebrew fit in with the other languages of Judea? There is a specific source supporting my argument for multilingualism. The Jerusalem Talmud recognizes four languages, each with its own domain: "Four languages are of value: Greek for song, Latin for war, Aramaic for dirges, and Hebrew for speaking" (Palestinian Talmud, *Sotah* VII). The assertion about Hebrew is variously interpreted, some using it to prove that Hebrew was still spoken in the south (Beit Guvrin) as well as Galilee.[32] The reference to Aramaic dirges has been supported by the recent discovery of Aramaic *piyyutim* (liturgical poems) written for eulogies.[33]

Developing trilingualism or triglossia

In practice, Greek became the main language of government and commerce in the Near East, but varieties of Aramaic continued to be widely used as a vernacular.[34] In Judea, by the time of the Roman conquest in 63 BCE, "Greek, Aramaic, and Hebrew were all used in various spheres of life and among various ethnic groups".[35]

During the Hellenistic period (332–165 BCE) there continued to be ostraca (pieces of pottery) written in Aramaic, and there are Aramaicisms in the Septuagint. There were texts composed in Aramaic during this period, such as Tobit, some parts of Daniel, and some of the Enoch literature, Aramaic segments of which have been found at Qumran. Aramaic (together with Greek and Hebrew) is found on coins of the Hasmonean period (165–63 BCE); and many Qumran texts, including the Genesis Apochryphon and the Targum to Job, are in Aramaic, although "poetry, theology, religious law, and biblical commentary" continued to be written in Hebrew.[36] The First Book of Enoch was probably composed in Aramaic; the existing version is an Ethiopian translation derived from Greek; portions have been found at Qumran and it is extensively quoted in the New Testament. The Second Book, also a translation from Greek of a Hebrew or Aramaic original, is known as the Slavonic version, and written in Old Church Slavonic, the language of the Eastern Orthodox Church. The Third Book is written in Hebrew, with a few Latin and Greek borrowings; it claims to have been written about 100 CE, but the oldest fragments are from 400 CE.[37] The Book of Enoch clearly illustrates the multilingualism of Judaism and early Christianity.

With the introduction of Roman power in 63 BCE, Greek and Latin became important, but Aramaic remained the vernacular of many Jews (and Hebrew of some) and was used in inscriptions and legal documents. New Testament documents include many Aramaic words. Some later archives, up to and including the Second Revolt in 135 BCE, include items in all three languages. This suggests a double diglossia,[38] Hebrew as the H language and Aramaic as the L within Palestine, and Greek as an H language in Gentile–Jewish interaction. Paul demonstrated this: he spoke Hebrew in Jerusalem (Acts 22: 2) but wrote to Diaspora churches in Greek.[39]

Timothy Lim[40] sums up the case for recognizing multilingualism in the ancient world, emphasizing the difficulty of interpreting the evidence of writing as showing the contemporary spoken patterns. He points out that the Aramaic texts of Elephantine include borrowings from Old Persian, Egyptian, Akkadian, and Greek, suggesting a multilingual society. He interprets a reference in the *Letter of Aristeas* (a Greek account of the Septuagint translation) to the community's acceptance of the accuracy of the translation as showing their bilingual proficiency. He cites the qualification for the guardian of all the camps at

Qumran as having mastered the secrets of men "and the languages of all their clans", wondering if this individual plurilingual proficiency was common. But he finds evidence of plurilingualism in Paul's knowledge of Greek, Hebrew, and Aramaic. The Bar Kokhba and the Baath archives (two caches from the Second Revolt, the first with letters in Greek, Hebrew, and Aramaic, the latter a cache of thirty-seven documents in Nabatean, Aramaic, and Greek) showed multilingualism, the former with evidence of nationalist reasons for selecting Hebrew.

Seth Schwartz[41] has suggested that Hebrew was a common spoken language until 300 BCE but with no role in "identity construction", replaced by Aramaic but respected as the language of the Temple and the Torah, which became "symbols of corporate identity" for those who controlled these institutions and used Hebrew, and after 70 CE, with the loss of "a curatorial class", lost political importance but maintained "evocative power". Schwartz claims that neither the unique Tower of Babel story nor the occasional mockery of foreign speech in Psalm 81: 6,[42] Ezekiel 3: 5,[43] or Psalm 120:2[44] shows the existence of nationalist attitudes to languages. He argues that the languages of the Near East were so similar as to mean that language was not considered a means of identity; Nehemiah, in his view, was complaining about intermarriage and not about linguistic impurity. The Greeks, he argues, who identified strangers as people who didn't speak Greek, had an elaborate metalanguage to deal with style, but the Hebrews didn't. Hebrew texts such as Daniel and Ezra-Nehemiah could switch from Aramaic to Hebrew and back.

Thus the existence of contemporary multilingualism is accepted even by those who do not think that Hebrew was still a vernacular but, rather, a language limited to religious and literary functions.

The survival of Hebrew

As time went on, the whole of the Middle East became Aramaized. Nineteenth-century scholars agreed that Judea too underwent this switch, with Aramaic replacing Hebrew except as a limited religious language, until Moses Hirsch Segal[45] made the case that Mishnaic Hebrew was not an Aramaic calque language[46] but a formal version of a vernacular Hebrew. Segal's argument was accepted only by "Zionistically inclined Hebraists" until the new evidence of the Dead Sea Scrolls showed other use of contemporary vernacular Hebrew.

Schwartz is impressed but not convinced: there is no evidence, he says, that the common people used Hebrew after 300 BCE, and the evidence of the inscriptions favors widespread knowledge of Aramaic.[47] Nor does he accept Edward Kutscher's suggestion that Aramaic was common in Jerusalem and Hebrew was maintained in the countryside.[48] He doesn't think the notion of diglossia fits, and he doubts the argument for widespread multilingualism,[49] assuming that it would be restricted to "some male members of the upper class".[50] Arguments for continued proficiency in Hebrew among the common people ignore, he argues, the ideologies that developed from the third century BCE on, with Hebrew and its association with Temple and Torah as centralizing institutions. This ideology was picked up later in the two revolts, with the coins both during the Great Revolt and the Bar Kokhba Revolt using not just Hebrew but archaic Paleo-Hebrew script. He cites a passage from the Book of Jubilees (assumed to be second century BCE, and available in full only in Ge'ez), written originally in Hebrew, that gives an example of this ideology: the angel is instructed to open Abraham's mouth, in Hebrew, "the tongue of creation", which had been lost at the Tower of Babel. From the third century, he argues, it was only the "curatorial class" that wrote and spoke in a glorified Hebrew. After the destruction of the Temple, in 70 CE, it was the rabbis who constituted the curatorial class and became responsible for Hebrew and its ideology. They begin to speak of *leshon hakodesh*, which Schwartz suggests means "language of the Temple", as *shekel hakodesh* meant the shekel of the Temple. But later, he suggests, Hebrew lost its importance even in the synagogue.

The "Zionistically inclined Hebraists" are perhaps best represented by Moshe Bar-Asher,[51] who simply asserts that "Jews in Palestine during the Hellenistic period were clearly bilingual and perhaps even trilingual . . . [I]t is certain that in Palestine Hebrew was a living language. Beyond this understanding, it is hard to suggest any sociological or geographical criteria according to which Hebrew was used." Willem Smelik[52] agrees that there was a "popular linguistic basis" for Mishnaic Hebrew. But there is much dispute about its nature.

There are those who argue that historical development of Hebrew cannot be traced because of the editing of the texts at different times, and that the different varieties identified as Late Biblical Hebrew and Mishnaic Hebrew constitute, instead, separate dialects. Miguel Perez Fernandez[53] suggests that the rabbis elevated a continuing spoken dialect of Hebrew into a literary language. He distinguishes between Rabbinic Hebrew of the Tannaim[54] and of the Amoraim, the second having a great deal of Aramaic influence, as spoken Hebrew was being replaced. He does face up to the question of the domain of spoken Hebrew in the period; it could, he recognizes, have been restricted to "academic circles, for teaching or in court – in the same way that Latin was used in mediaeval scholarship and, until quite recently, in the Roman Catholic church – but not in everyday life".[55] But he notes the arguments for its continued use as a "popular, spoken language" such as its use in the Dead Sea Scrolls, and the care with which the Oral Tradition required that the words of a teacher be transmitted "in the language of his teacher".[56] He recognizes territorial differences: Aramaic in Galilee and Samaria and Rabbinic Hebrew in a smaller area of Judea; Greek in the Hellenistic cities and Latin in administration; north Arabic dialects in the south of Palestine; and some towns in the north with continuing Phoenician. He believes Mishnaic Hebrew developed even before the exile, and coexisted for a while with Biblical Hebrew. It was also the language of the Pharisees, and of the oral law they developed, and was attacked by the Qumran community as "a blasphemous uncircumcised language", though they developed their own version. There were also, he accepts, following Rabin, different kinds of plurilingualism: Hebrew–Aramaic bilinguals, the use of a lingua franca (probably Greek) for communication between groups, and a kind of diglossia within Hebrew speakers. It was the suppression of the Bar Kokhba revolt in 135 CE and the forced transfer of population to Aramaic-dominant Galilee that would have led to the loss of Tannaitic Hebrew.

While there is no easy way to test the theory, it is worth considering that in fact one had the kind of multilingual intercomprehensibility and variety mixture that is now starting to be recognized in the speech communities of multilingual cities.[57] In a recent conference talk, Ray Jackendoff has suggested that his theory of parallel architecture, which includes lexical and grammatical units as learnable items, can be modified to add stylistic and variety features.[58] This model handles code switching, multilingual intercomprehensibility, and language shift, and avoids the need to set strict borders between labeled varieties. In this approach, we can easily assume that Hebrew and Aramaic and Greek operated together in the Jewish speech community, with differences in proportion of knowledge and use depending on demographic and domain and functional situations. Rather than dealing with "either/or", we might look for the socially acceptable mixtures.

The language situation in Roman Palestine

Roman Palestine was multilingual, with regional and territorial differences and functional variation. Although Aramaic may have been the common vernacular, there were people who spoke Greek or Hebrew as colloquial varieties. For the Dead Sea sect, a variety of Hebrew was a mark of identity, and perhaps a secret language that served as a gatekeeping mechanism.

Without the Dead Sea Scrolls and Qumran, the story we are telling would be thinner and vaguer, but, with the discovery and ensuing publication of the cache of documents in the caves of Qumran, our picture is enhanced not only by additional and earlier texts and versions (as the Dead Sea Scrolls provide support for the differences between the Masoretic and the Septuagint texts, and provide Hebrew originals for what was until then known only in medieval Ge'ez) but also by one model of a curatorial group, fleshing out one example of the puzzling class of scribes and even more uncertain view of scribalism. I described in Chapter 3 the nature of Mesopotamian scribal schools, and the fact that the only schools in Palestine with similar roles as training scribes were, according to the archeological evidence, small and private rather than large institutions attached to royal courts.

Pre-exilic scribes in the Bible appear to have been diplomats and court officials rather than scholarly preservers or creators of sacred literature. This continued into the Persian period, when Ezra was described as a scribe, priest, scholar, and teacher of the Torah.[59] In the Hellenistic period there was an increase in the number of scribes employed in bureaucratic functions. There were a number of "scribes of the temple" who, like priests and singers, were exempt from tax under Antiochus III. The references to scribes in Ben Sirach and I Maccabees do not give a clear picture of their role and responsibilities.

There is also no clarity about scribes in the Roman period. Josephus describes scribes as high bureaucratic officials, as temple officials, and as low-level village officials. The New Testament describes scribes as a distinct group, but does not explain their functions. Nor are there detailed explanations of the role of scribes within the Qumran community. Scribal activity can be deduced from the results of their work, however – not just copying, but glosses and corrections as well as "higher level editorial and compositional activity".[60] Many scribes went beyond copying (with varying degrees of freedom) and enriched the text, taking part in the creative process.[61] Two clear examples of "rewritten scripture" among the Dead Sea Scrolls are the Book of Jubilees and the Temple Scroll, which both paraphrase and add new sections to the Torah originals.[62]

Perhaps in the early stages of composition (say about 500 BCE), "authors and copyists were not clearly separable classes of literary practitioners. One rather may presume that a *unio personalis* was the rule: an author often served, when the need or the occasion arose, also as the editor, transmitter, scribe or copyist of his own works or the works of others."[63] Two examples are Ezra the Scribe (fifth century BCE) and the Tanna Rabbi Meir (second century CE), who were recognized not just as scribes but also as creative teachers. There appear to have been creative scribes at work at Qumran. In ancient Israel and the Near East, the professional scribe was not a "slavish copyist" but a "minor partner in the creative literary practice".[64]

It can be argued that the four separate biblical sources recognized by the documentary hypothesis were put together by a redactor, such as Ezra the Scribe, an "Aaronid priest" who was authorized by the Persian emperor Artaxerxes to re-establish the law of God in Judah and Jerusalem (Nehemiah 7: 11–26). Ezra combined the existing portions, adding, perhaps, some extra priestly sections, and producing a combined work that included all the parts by then generally attributed to Moses.[65]

James Kugel has a more basic explanation of the existence of various versions, arguing that the Bible texts were for a long time "malleable". Up until the fifth century BCE this meant that it was permissible and even appropriate to change the wording of the text, abbreviating or expanding it to make the interpretation clearer. There were, for example, two different versions of Jeremiah: a Septuagint version, also found at Qumran, that is one-eighth shorter than the Masoretic text, which was also found there, in five manuscripts. In addition, an Exodus fragment at Qumran has a different version of the Song of Miriam at the crossing of the Red Sea. Later, this malleability was maintained in interpretive writing, such as the Book of Jubilees and *Ben Sirach* and other non-canonical texts preserved in various languages by Christians and forming the Apocrypha and Pseudoepigraphica. They were also the basis for the *Midrashim* in Jewish traditional interpretations.[66]

We might want to add to this non-fundamentalist, non-literalist approach to the Jewish sacred texts the rabbinic principle (*Temurah* 16a and elsewhere) that problems (such as the missing *halakhot* or the dispute between Beit Hillel and Bet Shammai) are not to be answered directly by God but through analysis by man: "It is not in heaven." True, the source of the Torah is divine, but, once it was given on Mt. Sinai, the working out of details is a matter of authoritative interpretation. Following Kugel, for a long time these interpretations even permitted changing the texts; then they involved composing additional texts, including the Talmud; later, they had to be expressed in commentaries and decisions by authorized interpreters. The process continues, with teaching and sermons in synagogues.

This is an appropriate place to go into a little more detail about Qumran and its scribal activities. One large room in the excavated site overlooking the Dead Sea was identified as the "scriptorium" by Father Roland Guerin de Vaux, the French Dominican priest who led the team excavating the site, on the basis of some furniture and inkwells. It was de Vaux who insisted that there was a link between the site at Khirbet Qumran and the caves containing the scrolls, and who proposed that the site was inhabited by a community of Essenes – a view now widely accepted.[67]

A visitor to the site of the dig at Qumran nowadays is welcomed by a movie depicting the life of the community, with its three major activities: bathing for purification in the many *mikvahs* (ritual baths), eating in the dining hall, and writing on papyrus scrolls in the scriptorium. There have been many disputes and alternative proposals since the discovery of the site in 1947; one such argument held that the buildings were a private villa and the scrolls had been brought from Jerusalem to escape the Roman destruction of the city. This is essentially the theory espoused by Norman Golb, who finds a number of anomalies in the Essene hypothesis, such as the celibacy rule of the community and the absence of business documents produced over the 200 years of occupation. In his view, then, the variety in the documents is explained by their multiple authorship.[68] His approach does not account for the large number of autograph manuscripts, however, or their basic agreement with Essene doctrines. Most scholars now agree with de Vaux that the scrolls were produced by this community.[69]

The Essenes were a group that broke away from the Zadokites over the appointment of Jonathan as High Priest in 152 BCE. The site at Qumran on the shore of the Dead Sea was settled about 100 BCE by a schismatic group of Essenes, deserted after an earthquake in 31 BCE, and resettled about 2 BCE by another group, who remained there until its destruction by Roman troops, probably in 68 CE. The small Essene community at Qumran (its numbers seem to have varied between about 2,000 and 3,000) was mentioned by the Roman geographer Pliny the Elder as including no women, with the men having renounced sexual desire and money, and living with "only palm trees for company". New recruits kept up the numbers.[70] Their beliefs and practices, detailed in their writings, agree with Josephus' description of the beliefs and practices of the Essenes. I have also mentioned their multilingualism and the notion that they developed their own "religious lingo" or "anti-language" as a symbol of their separateness.

Clearly, the Qumran scribes fitted the model of creative copyists and interpreters, as they did more than maintain the texts of the many scrolls they had collected; they also modified and wrote living additions to the established texts. Their use of Hebrew was one way to claim authority; the modifications they made to the language were a way of asserting their independence and separation. There is evidence that they could write in a more standard Hebrew style, so they provide evidence of the continuation of at least one group using Hebrew as a vernacular up to the destruction of the Second Temple.

Synagogues in Roman Palestine and the Diaspora

Synagogues played an important role in the multilingualism of Palestine, just as, later, they account for the preservation of Hebrew in the Diaspora. Synagogues or *proseuche* (a term sometimes meaning the open space of a gateway used before synagogues were built, but sometimes used as a synonym) developed in the Jewish world as community centers with religious functions from the first to the seventh century CE.[71] Josephus reports the existence of synagogues in Judea and Asia Minor. Philo describes Alexandrian synagogues. The New Testament gives a number of reports of synagogue activities. There are a number of archeological remains in Palestine from the era prior to 70 CE, but an even great number after that.

A dozen building have been identified as synagogues in the Diaspora in this period, and 100 in Roman-Byzantine Palestine. There is considerable variation in the design. While the Torah-reading ceremony may have taken place originally in the city gate, the best evidence suggests that it developed in synagogues in the first century, both in Palestine and the Diaspora. Just as nowadays Jews try to form congregations of others from the same country or city, so this effort to form a synagogue consisting of Jews from a common Diaspora origin is already noted in pre-70 CE Palestine. The New Testament records the presence in Jerusalem of Greek- and Aramaic-speaking Jews, and of synagogues established by Jews from Cyrene (a Greek city in Libya), Alexandria, and Cilicia (the southwest corner of Asia Minor, which included Tarsus). A Greek inscription in Jerusalem describes a synagogue for a community, perhaps from Rome, for reading the Torah, studying, and accommodating pilgrims, and built by Theodotus, the son of Vettenos and a third-generation *archisynagogos*. Some of these synagogues had permission from the rabbis to pray in their Diaspora language. Just as we will see in seventeenth-century Venice and elsewhere, Jewish multilingualism encouraged the establishment of language-identified synagogues.

What about Latin?

Roman Palestine was multilingual, with Aramaic, Greek, and Hebrew playing significant roles, but what about Latin? The Roman government in the Near East neither insisted on the use of Latin nor used the local native languages, so Greek was the language of communication between Roman rulers and their subjects. Documents addressed to the government, and proclamations, were in Greek. Only a few rare cases provide exceptions.[72]

There are many inscriptions that use Latin, however: 190 from Caesarea, which was the center of Roman power, and 530 (including 150 milestones) from the rest of Israel. There are, Werner Eck assumes, many more still to be found. There are only four in Jerusalem that include the name of an emperor. Those that have been found are associated with military or administrative activities. Even in the second and third centuries CE, when most of the Roman soldiers would have been Greek or Aramaic speakers recruited locally, the use of Latin in public signs remained an assertion of Roman power rather than evidence of the spoken language situation. Latin, then, was the language of Roman administration, but there is no evidence of widespread knowledge of it among the common people or the rabbis.[73]

Mishnaic Hebrew

Composing orally and, later, writing in Hebrew was a mark of the Palestine-based rabbis, who initially kept a strict distinction between what was written (the Torah) and the commentaries and laws derived from it (the oral law). Mishnaic Hebrew was based on a spoken variety, a descendant probably of biblical Hebrew, that was a vernacular from the second century BCE until the third century CE, after which it persisted only as a written language "used for juridical, intellectual, philosophical, poetic, and liturgical purposes".[74] Mishnaic Hebrew literature covers a period from 70 CE to 500 CE, starting with the writings of the

Tannaim (the early rabbis) for the first half of this period, including the *Mishnah*, the *Toseftah* (a supplement to the Mishnah), the Halachic *Midrashim*,[75] and the *Seder Olam Rabbah* (a chronological history probably written about 160 CE but further edited). In the second half of the period there is the work of the *Amoraim* (rabbis of the later period), including the Jerusalem Talmud, a number of aggadic *Midrashim*, and the Babylonian Talmud.

The Tannaitic texts were redacted by Rabbi Judah the Prince about 200 CE. During the Tannaitic period Hebrew continued as a spoken language, but by the Amoraitic period the common spoken language was Galilean, or Jewish Palestinian Aramaic in Palestine and Babylonian Aramaic in Babylon. The Amoraitic texts include Hebrew–Aramaic switching. But, offering support for arguments for continued spoken Hebrew, there is evidence of transition from Biblical to Mishnaic Hebrew, with early appearances of words that appear in Mishnaic Hebrew. By then many features of Biblical Hebrew had disappeared and new features had emerged. There had been semantic change too, so that Biblical Hebrew *mezuzah* meant a doorpost, while in Mishnaic Hebrew it meant an encased scroll nailed to a doorpost. There is also evidence of dialectal differences, with Biblical Hebrew forms lasting longer in some dialects. This all supports the argument for Mishnaic Hebrew as reflecting a natural change over time in the spoken language.[76]

Nor is Mishnaic Hebrew uniform, but it shows diachronic and dialectal variation, with, of course, major differences between Tannaitic and Amoraic Hebrew, and in the latter between Palestinian and Babylonian varieties. Hebrew was in close contact with Aramaic during these periods, testifying, Bar-Asher points out, to the bilingualism of the speakers. There are Akkadian and Persian borrowings through Aramaic. Many lexical items in Mishnaic Hebrew are borrowings from Greek and some are from Latin. While there are no contemporary manuscripts, there are other sources, such as Qumran documents, the Hebrew of the Samaritans, evidence from the Septuagint, and Hebrew words transcribed into early Church documents. The language of the *piyyutim* and other liturgy also reflects Mishnaic Hebrew.

What, then, was the extent of Hebrew knowledge in the first two centuries of the Common Era? The rabbis provided for people who did not know it, by prompting those making a declaration required during the ritual of the first fruits in the Temple, and requiring that the priest explain to a wife accused of adultery the details of the ceremony; both of these applied to the period before the destruction of the Second Temple. There was also a provision in the Mishnah citing Rabban Simon ben Gamaliel: "The scrolls of scripture may be written in Greek" (M. Megillah 1: 8). During this time the composition of new works in Hebrew continued, though there were already translations into Greek.

There were a number of different dialects of Aramaic: Jewish literary Aramaic, Qumran Aramaic, the Aramaic of Targum Onkelos (the official

Babylonian translation of the Torah, which may have originally been composed in Palestine), the Aramaic of Targum Jonathan (the rabbinically recognized Babylonian translation of the Books of Prophets), and perhaps later Targums of the Books of Writings; there were also Palestinian Targums and the Palestinian Talmud. There were also Christian, Samaritan, and Nabatean dialects of Aramaic. The variety of written versions suggests that spoken Aramaic showed similar variety.[77]

There is good reason to assume that Aramaic was adopted in the northern regions of Palestine – Galilee and the Golan – but no hard evidence that it replaced all local vernaculars. For example, the Nabateans, living in Jordan, adopted Aramaic, and their inscriptions are in Aramaic, with Arabic borrowings, until the Arab conquest.[78] Greek, in fact, became common, with about as many inscriptions as in Hebrew and Aramaic. There were Jews in Palestine who knew Greek better than Hebrew.[79]

Smelik is critical of the triglossic model I proposed, pointing out the absence of detailed evidence of functional and regional differentiation. He argues for a more complex model of individual differences, depending on social context and geographical environment. Hebrew, he proposes, "served as the principal language for the written transmission of religiously relevant information".[80] Greek works were preserved by Christians rather than Jews. Hebrew was also used for legal and liturgical purposes. But Aramaic was used for exegesis, for narratives, for legal rabbinic discussions, and for translation. He is arguing, then, for individual plurilingualism rather than the more socially established multilingualism that I am proposing. Lacking the possibility of sociolinguistic surveys, we must accept this as another open question. *Teiku.*

The three language varieties

To sum up, Alexander's conquests and rule by his Seleucid (Babylonian) and Ptolemaic (Egyptian) successors introduced Greek in a significant role in the Jewish sociolinguistic ecology. In the Diaspora communities, a variety either of Aramaic or of Greek came to be the common language, but Hebrew was maintained as a sacred language and probably as a vernacular (Alexandria at the time of Philo may be the exception). In Roman Palestine, with regional variations, the three languages filled different functions for different people, but there does not seem to be enough evidence to map domains more precisely. We have evidence of inscriptions in all the languages (and also in Latin in government centers); of the composition of religious texts in Hebrew and probably Aramaic among Jews, and in Greek among Christians; of translation into Greek and Aramaic of Hebrew originals; and of letters and other documents in all the languages.

If we accept that the early Israelites were multilingual in the various Canaanite dialects during the period of combined and separate kingdoms, they may well have moved during the United Monarchy to a period of Hebrew hegemonic monolingualism, with some convenient plurilingual individuals enabling contact with surrounding peoples. After the destruction of the First Temple and the return from Babylonian exile, however, Hebrew–Aramaic bilingualism began, succeeded in the Hellenistic-Roman period by a trilingual Hebrew–Aramaic–Greek pattern that laid the foundation for Diaspora Jewish multilingualism.

5 From statehood to Diaspora

The loss of statehood

The Hellenization of Judea (which from a language point of view meant adding Greek to the Jewish sociolinguistic ecology after the conquest of Alexander the Great) bled almost unnoticeably into the period of Roman rule, which, as noted earlier, did not mean a substantive addition of Latin except in government use and on official inscriptions. This period marks the beginning of Jewish trilingualism (or perhaps even triglossia),[1] which we will find, with occasional exceptions, to be the dominant model at least until the eighteenth century, when western European emancipation started to weaken the role of Jewish varieties. A first question is where to start our chapter, and how to label the period it describes.

Without doubt, the destruction of the Second Temple in 70 CE was a major turning point, when centralized Temple rituals were replaced by synagogue worship and priestly leadership gave way to rabbinic. But was this a major linguistic transition? Synagogue worship was already under way and Diaspora communities were already in existence before 70 CE. Indeed, by 100 CE there were 5 million Jews in the Diaspora, five times the estimated 1 million who remained in Palestine.[2] Perhaps one should, rather, select as a starting point the Bar Kokhba revolt in 136 CE, one of the last attempts to restore Jewish sovereignty; its failure marked the beginning of nearly 2,000 years of dispersion. But there were other revolts later, up to the Arab conquest. Or should we label it a Hellenistic-Roman period, which in Palestinian archeological terms included Byzantine rule until the Arab conquest?[3]

Sociolinguistically, one might set a boundary at 300 CE, the end of Hebrew as a vernacular. This was the time when the rabbis called on fathers to teach the language to their children, and when the synagogues spread through Palestine and the Diaspora included what developed into Hebrew schools, permitting the educational maintenance of the language until natural intergenerational transmission was restored at the end of the nineteenth century.[4]

Or perhaps there is no neat boundary but, rather, a bleeding of periods, a gradual loss of central focus and the growth of separate Jewish communities in Palestine and beyond, with associated modifications in sociolinguistic ecology.

Perhaps there were no abrupt language shifts but stages of modified multi-lingualism, as in modern cities with growing immigration. Accepting this as the best compromise, we will look in this chapter at the linguistic patterns of post-revolt Byzantine Palestine and in the various Diasporas. I use two useful guides to the linguistic environment of this period: a consideration of rabbinic attitudes to Targum (the translation of sacred texts into Aramaic) and multilingualism in Galilee,[5] and the evidence – archeological and written – of Jewish synagogues.[6]

Syria Palestina under Roman and Byzantine rule

Politically, in 132 CE the Roman emperor Hadrian combined Judea and Galilee into Syria Palestina, with Jerusalem rebuilt as a Roman city and renamed Aelia Capitolina and temples to the Roman gods built there. Three years later the Bar Kokhba revolt was put down and half a million Jews killed, according to a history of Rome written by Cassius Dio about 220 CE.[7] Many Jews and Christians left the country by choice, and others were taken into slavery, those later liberated producing the nucleus for Italian Jewish communities. New pagan cities were established in Judea; for instance, Beit Guvrin, demolished by the Romans during the Bar Kokhba revolt, was rebuilt and renamed Eleutheropolis in 200 CE; Lydda, destroyed during the earlier Kitos War,[8] was rebuilt in 200 CE; Emmaus, destroyed by the Romans in 4 CE, was settled about 200 CE by Romans and Samaritans.

It was during this period that rabbinic (Pharisaic) Judaism separated from Christianity, as the new religion dropped Jewish practices and accepted as converts an increasing number of Gentiles. After the destruction of the Temple, three of the major Jewish groups that had been identified by Josephus disappeared: the Sadducees, who had been closely associated with the Priesthood and the Temple; the Zealots, who had led and been crushed in the revolt; and the Essenes. This left the Pharisees and the Christians, who, Daniel Boyarin argues, were very close and overlapping until "heresiologists" in each group defined orthodoxy to exclude the other.[9] It was during this period that the use of Hebrew as a spoken vernacular in Jewish communities is commonly agreed to have come to an end, though it remained a sacred and literary language.

In the partition of the Roman Empire into Western and Eastern Empires, which took place starting in 330 CE, Palestine came under Byzantine rule, with Greek as its major language; Latin was the language of the Western Empire. By this time Jewish presence in Palestine was strongest in Galilee, especially the east. Constantine became eastern emperor and was converted to Christianity; his mother identified the important sites from the New Testament story in Jerusalem. A further Jewish revolt in the early years of Byzantine rule (351–352 CE) followed Christian persecution and the destruction of synagogues. The revolt was firmly put down, many Jews were killed, and Galilee was garrisoned by Byzantine troops.

Towards the end of the Byzantine period another Jewish revolt occurred, when, in 613 CE, a Jewish army recruited in Persia joined with the Sassanid Empire (which lasted from 224 CE to 664 CE) to attack Byzantium. Palestinian cities were captured, and Jerusalem was taken in 614. When the Persian army moved on to Egypt, the Jerusalemite Byzantine Christians revolted, but the Persian-Jewish forces returned, and stormed the city "in great fury, like infuriated wild beasts".[10] Thousands of Christians were massacred. Briefly there was Jewish rule again, under a leader named Nehemiah ben Hushiel, but in 617 CE Nehemiah was killed, Christian rule was re-established, and the Jews were again expelled from Jerusalem.[11]

Persian rule was short-lived: ten years later a Byzantine army reconquered Jerusalem, and the emperor Heraclius entered the city and ordered the Jews there to convert or be slaughtered. Heraclius is credited with making Greek the official language of the Eastern Empire in place of Latin, and also with changing the titles of rulers accordingly, so that the head of state became *Basileus* instead of *Imperator*.[12] Ten years later, in 638, the Byzantine Empire lost control of Judea to Caliph Umar and the Arabic Islamic Empire, which soon imposed its language and religion on the Near East and north Africa.

Aramaic and Hebrew after the destruction of the Temple

How long did Hebrew last alongside Aramaic as a vernacular spoken language? A useful source is the rabbinic discussion of the practice of Targum (translation), the custom of accompanying Hebrew Torah reading in synagogue services with a sentence-by-sentence translation into Aramaic. There are no earlier sources, and no discussion by Philo, Josephus, or the New Testament of this practice, but there is a rich array of sources from Mishnaic and Talmudic texts.[13] Galilee from the third to the sixth century CE was the main concentration of Jewish inhabitants and was most probably a trilingual region.[14]

Stephen Fraade notes the intermediate Halachic status of written Targumim, which, according to the Mishnah and *Toseftah* (additional material from the time of the Mishnah but not included in it), did not defile the hands of anyone touching them (which made it easier to have them copied without all the special purification that a scribe of a sacred scroll had to follow) but could be rescued from a burning building on the Sabbath (Mishnah *Shabbat* 16:1) "in whatever language they may be written"; in addition, they should be *genizah*, "withdrawn from circulation", if they contained mistakes that made them unfit for use.[15]

At this time, synagogue reading of the Torah was expected to consist of alternate recitation of a verse read from a scroll in Hebrew followed by an oral interpretation (not reading from a text) by a different person. The Aramaic, Fraade says, could not substitute for the Hebrew. Not until medieval times (by Rashi, for instance) was it suggested that the translation was for the unlearned (women and uneducated men). The Mishnah allowed a reading of the translation of the Book of Esther in Greek for congregations that did not know Hebrew. The Aramaic version of the regular Torah portion had defined constraints, so that certain modifications were condemned, and some "embarrassing" sections, such as the Golden Calf incident, were to be read in Hebrew and not translated. These rules, Fraade points out, applied to public reading and not to teaching in schools. The task of a *meturgeman* or translator was not defined as a professional role, however (unlike a *hazzan* or synagogue supervisor[16]), but could be given to anyone, including a minor. In the Tannaitic curriculum for Jewish education, Targum (Aramaic translation) comes after *Miqra'* (reciting the Torah in Hebrew) but is followed by *Mishnah* (oral teaching in Hebrew and Aramaic) and *Talmud* (advanced study also in both languages). Fraade emphasizes that the individual in his private studies was also expected to be able to move from one language to the other.[17]

Later traditions interpret this use of the Targum to mediate the Torah reading as equivalent to the giving of the Torah at Mt. Sinai, where God's word was mediated by Moses. There is indeed a tradition (in *Sifrei* Deuteronomy 343) that the Torah was given in four languages – Hebrew, Aramaic, Arabic, and Latin – and, in other texts, in seventy languages. The different languages were a way of giving different meanings. But Aramaic had a special status, providing "a medium of interpretive reception . . . in dialogic accompaniment to the Hebrew original" and intended for a bilingual audience.[18]

While admitting there can be no certainty, Fraade believes there is a "presumption" that Hebrew, Aramaic, and Greek functioned "at different times in different places among different classes and under different circumstances" and occurred in various mixtures.[19] The rabbinic literature showed this kind of mixture, moving from Hebrew to Aramaic and back and including Greek words, sayings, and – as noted earlier – even puns. There were also synagogue inscriptions in Aramaic (mainly), Hebrew, and Greek in Galilee from this period, including many that switch languages. Fraade draws attention to the *piyyutim* (liturgical poems) found in the Cairo Genizah dating from around 400 CE and written in a variety of Hebrew that involved knowledge of Galilean Aramaic; also in the Genizah there were found eulogies written in Aramaic.

Summing up, Fraade argues that the Targumim provide evidence of continuing multilingualism.[20] The Aramaic Targumim did not replace Hebrew, as the Septuagint did in Greek-speaking synagogues and in the Christian Church, but continued alongside it as a complementary medium of interpretation and teaching. Aramaic was preserved as a Jewish sacred language when it, in turn, was later replaced by Arabic as a spoken language.

Hebrew was still being spoken up to 300 CE.[21] Aramaic was increasingly becoming the vernacular, and was also being used in written texts. Hebrew and Aramaic were close enough for speakers of Greek to consider them the same language, but Hebrew had the higher status as the sacred language. The Qumran scrolls include many written in the Aramaic of the period; the Targum Onkelos and Jonathan (the two major Aramaic translations of the Bible) too appear to have been composed in Palestine at this time. Passages in Aramaic appear in the Tannaitic texts[22] in the Talmud. The Galilean Aramaic of the Talmud (Babylonian and Palestinian) is later, however. The other Targumim include Babylonian features. The Babylonian Talmud uses Eastern Aramaic, marked, for instance, by the use of a final *aleph* rather than *he* marking the feminine, and the elision of final vowels and consonants; the later Gaonim (heads of the major Yeshivot – academies) use archaic forms, and there are insertions in the Babylonian Talmud in Palestinian Aramaic. Although Aramaic largely[23] ceased to be a spoken language of the Jews after the Arab conquest, it was until then firmly established as a major Jewish language.

Demographics

What was the size and nature of the Jewish population at this time? It is hard to answer the question with any degree of certainty, for there are no surviving census data; there had been a census conducted by the Roman legate in 6/7 CE, as mentioned by Josephus (*Antiquities of the Jews* 18: 1–3) and Luke (2: 1–3), but no results survive.[24] An Israeli archeologist has estimated the maximum population based on the "carrying capacity" of the area, which he calculates to have been 1 million Jews and non-Jews by 600 CE,[25] but others question these calculations, believing that "it is impossible to determine how many people lived in the Land of Israel during the Mishnah and Talmud periods".[26] Most scholars believe that there was an increase in population around this time, with more settlements and growing cities, although there are arguments for a demographic downturn in the fifth century.[27]

Assuming that cities were mixed but villages had religiously homogeneous populations (and this too is disputed), Claudine Dauphin believes that Jews were becoming a minority by the end of the fourth century CE, when there were forty Jewish sites, forty-eight Christian, five Samaritan, and three mixed. A century later there were 157 Jewish, 161 Christian, twenty-two Samaritan, and forty-five mixed. For the sixth century she lists a reduction in Jewish sites to sixty-three and an increase in Christian sites to 191, and she puts Samaritan and mixed-stable villages at twenty and forty-two, respectively. At the close of the period, in the sixth century, she lists only fifty-four Jewish sites but 454 Christian, eighteen Samaritan, and thirty-one mixed. This change she blames on a policy of the Church and the Byzantine state to reduce the Jewish

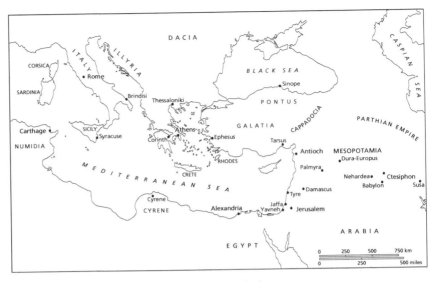

3 The Mediterranean world in late antiquity
Source: Lapin (2010).

population.[28] More recently, David Goodblatt has disagreed, arguing that Dauphin underestimates the Jewish population, which he sets at closer to 15 percent, or as much as a quarter if you compare the number of Jewish synagogues and Christian churches. But, as we lack information on the size of settlements, these figures are very rough guesses.[29]

There is also evidence of regional concentrations, with eastern Galilee predominantly Jewish and western predominantly Christian. Of course, this all assumes evidence of religious identification – something questioned for the period before the fourth century by Boyarin's arguments.[30] The evidence of mixed populations and of trade and commerce throughout the area supports, of course, the probability of continuing multilingualism.

Palestine was increasingly urbanized under Hellenistic, Maccabean, and Roman rule, but, as time went on, the cities were in the main non-Jewish; the rabbis were opposed to the pagan aspects of urban life. Some Jews were attracted to the city, but maintained separation from the urban elite. But there is evidence that they acquired Greek and even some Latin in the city.[31] While the cities were mixed, it is widely assumed that villages were likely to be religiously homogeneous. Only rarely (such as in the case of Capernaum) does one find a village with both a synagogue and a church, or either alongside a pagan temple.[32]

After 70 CE, and even more after the failure of the Bar Kokhba revolt, most Jews remaining in Palestine moved north to Galilean villages. Josephus distinguished between cities and villages. The rabbis referred to cities with a wall (*kerakh*), towns and large villages (*'ir*), and villages (*kfar*). An *'ir*, probably the most common, was a regional center, often with a synagogue but no other institutional buildings. The Romans built a network of roads, and, although seafaring was dangerous, it was a common method of travel; migration too was common (see Map 3). The rabbis appear to have traveled a great deal to visit colleagues: Paul's travels are not an exception. Rabbis occasionally traveled by sea. Jewish pilgrimage to Jerusalem probably ceased after the destruction of the Temple; Christian pilgrimages started in the fourth and fifth centuries CE.[33]

The role of Greek and the growth of the Diaspora

Public education in Roman times was limited, though those people wealthy enough would hire Greek-speaking teachers to ensure that their children became bilingual. While earlier scholars argued for the existence of universal Jewish primary education for boys, this depends on a mixing of sources and dates. Most references to Jewish schools are late or amoraic. Schools developed alongside synagogues, and concentrated on the teaching of the Torah, including the ability to read in public. Individuals could go on to study with a rabbi, and a few *batei midrash* are reported.

Some Jews – Josephus is a prime example – may have obtained education in Greek and Latin in non-Jewish schools.[34] Contact with the government required education in Greek; the household of Rabbi Gamaliel was cited earlier as having permission to do this. In cities such as Caesarea, middle-class Jews may have been educated in Greek, and even may have prayed in it (Palestinian Talmud Sotah 7: 1 21b). In Roman Palestine, only "members of the upper class and the intellectual elite" would have used writing, a task made more complex by the number of languages. Professional scribes were widely employed. Letters, probably dictated to a scribe, were used by political, military, and rebel leaders, and by rabbis for Halachic communication.[35] There is controversy over the transition from oral to written transmission of the Mishnah. There was a complex interplay about the oral performance of memorized written texts as a method of maintaining authority for rabbinic interpretation.[36]

The liturgy

Reconstructing the development of Jewish liturgy in the period is a complex task, as the existing texts, such as those found in the Cairo Genizah, are late, perhaps preserving forms that had been written down closer to the tenth century and later. The synagogues before the destruction of the Temple had social and educational rather than liturgical functions, but there was a development of liturgical customs at Qumran and later.[37] Tannaitic rabbis set about standardizing some prayers, and, recognizing multilingualism, debated the appropriateness of Greek, Aramaic, and Hebrew for prayer. Tractate *Berakhot* of the Mishnah and Toseftah gives rules on the language to be used for the *Shema*, *Amidah*, and *Birkhat Hamazon* (grace after meals). Another early liturgy is the Passover *Haggadah*; other private early prayers are the *Kiddush* for the beginning of the Sabbath and *Havdalah* for the end.

The rabbinic presentations of standard rules such as the requirement for Hebrew were most probably efforts at language management, aiming to influence what people did, rather than descriptions of normal practice. Permitting the liturgical use of Greek, a language recognized as great by many rabbis, and the use of Aramaic for private prayer reflected a multilingual situation, but one in which Hebrew remained primary. As time went on, more strict guidelines for liturgy developed, psalms were added to the ritual, and the *Kedushah* (in Hebrew) and *Kaddish* (in Aramaic) were developed late in or after the Talmudic period. Hebrew *Piyyutim* (liturgical poems) started to be composed in pre-Islamic times, and, later, even threatened to swamp the established traditional liturgy.[38]

Synagogues

The existence of synagogues provides a way of tracing the location of Jewish settlements in Palestine and the growth of Diaspora communities. A Greek inscription in Jerusalem describes a synagogue for a community, perhaps from Rome, using Greek for reading the Torah and for study, that accommodated pilgrims and had been built by Theodotus, the son of Vettenos and a third-generation *archisynagogos* (a rich man who functioned as head of the community).

By the first century there were between 3 and 5 million Jews in the Diaspora, each community probably with its own synagogue or *proseuche* (synagogue or space outside a synagogue). There is limited evidence apart from inscriptions. But epigraphical, literary, or archeological evidence remains for synagogues in Egypt,[39] Bosphorus,[40] Rome, Syria, Cyrene, Asia Minor, Delos, and Greece.

Synagogues served as community centers. There was an *archisynagogos*. Public meetings were held in the synagogue, and there were communal meals. Judicial matters were dealt with. Synagogues contained schools; this was probably the first development of public Jewish education.[41] Worship was probably limited to the Sabbath and holidays, with Torah reading on a three-year cycle as a central part of worship. Readings from the prophets were added later. The reading was accompanied by study and instruction, including a sermon and reading from the Targum in Aramaic. There may have been some communal prayer after the destruction of the Temple.

After the destruction of the Temple, in 70 CE, the role of the synagogue increased in importance, replacing the Temple as the appropriate place for prayer. Further changes took place in the fourth century CE with the Christianization of the Roman Empire and the close of the Talmudic period in Palestine. There is surprisingly little in the Mishnah and the Talmud about this period, when, after 200 years, many more synagogues were built in Palestine. The growing conflict with Christianity, especially after Judaism had been attacked by Christian preachers and the mobs they encouraged, and restricted by imperial rulings, had an impact on synagogues. In a number of Diaspora cities – Stobi in Roman Macedonia, Gerasa (Jerash) in north Jordan, Apamea in Syria – archeology shows evidence of synagogues that were converted to churches, and literary sources list similar examples in Italy, Mauretania, Spain, Gaul, Syria, and Minorca. In Byzantine Palestine, however, synagogues continued to be built in Merot, Capernaum, Bet Alpha, and Qatzrin and to be repaired in Chorazin, Hammat Tiberias, Ein Gedi, and Nevoraya. Surprisingly, in the light of a ban by Hadrian on Jews living in the Jerusalem area, a number of synagogues have also been found in south Judea. Twenty-five Byzantine synagogues have also been identified in the Golan, all adding up to over 100 sites.[42]

The synagogue at Capernaum, finished in the fifth century, was "monumental in size and ornate in decoration"; it dwarfed the church of St. Peter, built in Rome about the same time.[43] Also at this time there was an increase in the writing of *piyyutim* and apocalyptic works and the editing of amoraic *Midrashim* and of Targumim. There was variation in the design of synagogues, a diversity of mosaic floors, and inscriptions in Hebrew, Aramaic, and Greek. Some were highly Jewish; others (as at Bet Alpha) were markedly Hellenized. This was matched by regional variation in synagogue liturgy.[44] By this time, too, synagogues were commonly oriented towards Jerusalem.

While this gives a rich picture of Jewish life in Byzantine Palestine, there are only a dozen archeological remains of Diaspora synagogues, in Dura Europus (Syria), Gerasa (Jordan), Apamea (Syria), Sardis and Priene (Asia Minor), Aegina (Greece), Stobi (Macedonia), Plovdiv (Bulgaria), Ostia and Bova Marina in Italy, Hammam Lif (north Africa), and Elche (Spain). But they show the extent of Jewish settlement from east to west. Dura has nineteen Greek and twenty-two Aramaic inscriptions, but its paintings also include texts in Middle Persian and Parthian, and there is a Hebrew text close by, making this "the largest number of languages yet discovered within a single monument of this modest size";[45] Gerasa has a Greek and a Hebrew inscription; those at Apamea are all in Greek, as are those in Sardis; Aegina has two in Greek; Stobi has a large Greek inscription with Latin words; Ostia has an inscription with one line in Latin and four in Greek; Naro (Hammam Lif) has inscriptions in Latin. There are references in inscriptions in the catacombs to about a dozen otherwise unknown synagogues scattered through Rome, which appear in Greek and Latin.[46] Again, this evidence shows the extent of Jewish multilingualism.

What is a Jewish language variety?

At this point, before I deal with one of the earliest language varieties that includes "Judeo-" in its name, I need to take a little space to discuss the sociolinguistic implications of what I will be talking about. In common lay talk, and in the writing of many professional scholars, the term "language" is regularly taken for granted, and it is commonly assumed that a name such as "Hebrew", or "Aramaic", or "English" represents an accepted and delimited object of study, with defined lexicon, grammar, and pronunciation. We do normally allow for the existence of what we call "dialects", which we differentiate from the "languages" to which they are agreed to belong, by a number of specific features: differences of lexicon, such as "footpath" and "pavement" distinguishing British from American English: or of grammar – British writers tend to treat "committee" as plural while Americans prefer it to be singular; or of pronunciation – I learned to replace the "t" in "butter" with the "d" my New-York-born wife uses. When faced with a question such as whether to label "Yiddish" as a language or a dialect, we happily cite the definition quoted by Max Weinreich from a student in one of his classes (he never revealed his name, but said he was an older man): "A language is a dialect with an army and a flag." Because of this confusion (and how else did Serbo-Croatian suddenly become Serbian, Croatian, Macedonian, and Kosovan?), I prefer to talk about "varieties" rather than "languages".

But this too is an overgeneralization, increasingly true as more and more people live in multingual cities, where their speech mixes words and grammar and pronunciations from more than one language variety at a time. There are older, more cautious speakers who try not to mix, but, if you are a plurilingual and live in a multilingual environment, it is hard not to exploit the additional expressive power this gives you. I recall hearing two young Israeli army officers at the university saying goodbye to each other using Hebrew, English, and Italian: "*Lehit!*", "Bye!", "*Ciao!*". And the "English" I use in Jerusalem includes such words as *shuk* (Arabic for "market") and *shul* (Yiddish for "synagogue") and *kupat holim* (Hebrew for "health fund").

Now, we can deal with this linguistic phenomenon as borrowing or code switching or as individual language shift, but when we look at "real" language use we find there are sufficient regularities to want to recognize this mixed speech as a "variety", with consistency in a speech community and with regional and social variations, as with any language. Some sociolinguists today argue that these chaotic mixtures are in fact the objects we should be studying, rather than the grammar-book and dictionary-standardized versions we generally assume. Jan Blommaert uses the term "super-diversity" for the multilingualism of the modern globalized city,[47] but there are many earlier cases[48] revealed by the receptive multilingualism of speakers of the Scandinavian[49] or Slavic varieties, who maintain their own national language varieties but can understand people speaking other varieties.[50] Thus, whenever I talk about a language or a variety, you need to imagine that it has these murky boundaries – a blending of features, a mixing of lexicon, and the imprecision of pronunciation – that you hear in a bus or a café in a modern city, rather than the neat boundaries assumed by grammarians, purists, and teachers.

This makes it both harder and easier to deal with Jewish varieties, for they are the paradigmatic case of the results of language contact, as Jews chose or were forced to move from one linguistic environment to another, and to add to their sociolinguistic proficiency while maintaining as much as they reasonably could their accustomed speech patterns within their own community. Weinreich in his classic account of Yiddish, the prime example of a Jewish language variety, has proposed a model of what happens. Jews, with their traditional knowledge of Hebrew and Aramaic, speaking an established Jewish variety (say the Judeo-Romance that Rashi used), move into a new linguistic environment where a variety of German is spoken, and come into business contact with the local population. Assuming more or less open relations and no virulent anti-Jewish activities,[51] they develop a degree of proficiency in the new language, but when they speak it to each other, as they may do to demonstrate their status[52] or simply to show their skill,[53] they add words from their existing languages, modify the grammar, insert sentences when they are blocked otherwise, and speak in a way that is largely influenced by their old language patterns and pronunciation.

In time, other members of the community, and especially the children, imitate them,[54] and show their assimilation by using the new variety both in contacts with the Gentile community and with each other. Over time, a new Jewish variety[55] is developed, with elements from each of the varieties that contributed to its creation. If there is free and easy contact with the Gentile world, as happened in Europe after the emancipation, the variety might disappear, as did Western Yiddish in the German-speaking areas; if there is isolation (internally or externally imposed), as when Yiddish-speaking Jews moved into less hospitable Slavic areas, the variety may become stable and last for many generations, until a major change in situation (renewed persecution and expulsion) sets the process off again.

We will look more closely at the theory and evidence when we deal with the creation of Yiddish, but I suggest that some such process produced each of the Jewish varieties, each Judeo-X, that we will be talking about. Of course there is variation, depending especially on the development and availability of written evidence of the variety (always later than the spoken), its length of existence, the size of the Jewish community, and the nature of the relationships with other Jewish communities and with the Gentile world.

Aramaic as we described its role as a Jewish vernacular and as the language of the Targum, with all its regional difference, is reasonably considered a Jewish variety[56] on this basis: a variety spoken within the community that had been picked up by Hebrew speakers in contact with Gentile speakers in Palestine and Babylonia, and transferred into major functions in many domains of Jewish life. In the Babylonian Talmud, one sees how it was interspersed with Hebrew, but the Targumim and other texts showed a clearer, purer picture of the variety. It lasted until the Muslim conquest spread Arabic over the Near East, preserved only in some peripheral Jewish and Christian mountain communities.

This leaves open the question of when we should identify a language spoken by Jews as a Jewish language. Is it a percentage of words from Hebrew? Is it a recognizable pronunciation difference? Is it the fact the non-Jews do not understand it? Does it need some formal recognition by the publication of books using the variety written in Hebrew letters? Or is it enough that some scholar has identified and described it? Jewish languages are a subset of the languages of the Jews, but how to distinguish them remains an unanswered question. And an intriguing related question is whether to consider Hebrew – in any of its many versions, from the language of the Bible through the Mishnaic and Medieval and Haskalah versions to the revernacularized Israeli language – a Jewish language, or simply as the main language of the Jews. This is a good question for the last chapter.

Judeo-Greek – a Jewish variety

There are scholars who claim that Judeo-Greek[57] has existed since the first meetings between Jews and Greeks. Because of its long history, it has lexical and morphological characteristics of the Greek language of various periods.[58] During the Hellenistic period in Egypt, Jews translated the Bible into a Judaized dialect of Attic and Ptolemaic *koine*, producing the Septuagint. Later, under Roman rule, Christian Jews wrote three of the gospels and most of the epistles of the New Testament in a Jewish dialect of *koine*; the variety shows an Aramaic basis.

The Septuagint version and other Hellenistic Jewish and Christian writing influenced the language of the Greek Orthodox Church, which, in turn, influenced the Greek vernacular called *demotiki*. The ninth-century Byzantine patriarch Photius took Josephus and Philo as models of style. Eusebius (fourth century) preserves most of the Greek fragments of Hellenistic Jewish writers. The Talmud includes 1,000 words and expressions from Greek, showing the knowledge of Greek of the Palestinian rabbis.[59] Judeo-Greek was the community language of the Jews in the Roman world throughout the Byzantine period.[60]

Rhomaioi (Greek) or *Romani* (Latin) was the term used for the Byzantines; Jews in the Balkans under the Orthodox Church were *Romaniot* (Hebrew), and a minority were permitted to exist, albeit regularly persecuted or forced to convert. Their vernacular was a version of Judeo-Greek. Fragments of texts written in Hebrew script were found in the Cairo Genizah, including a translation of the Book of Jonah. A small Romaniot community survived in Constantinople.

The *Machzor Romania* codified the Romaniot synagogue rite in the early sixteenth century and preserves an extensive body of *piyyutim* written over the past fifteen hundred years either in Hebrew interspersed with Greek vocabulary or completely in Greek (e.g., a prayer for the New Moon). In addition to lexical examples in Romaniot Bible commentaries, Greek-speaking *payyatanim* [composers of *piyyutim*] continued to produce sacred poetry through the nineteenth century. Judeo-Greek flourished in the Romaniot areas of Greece (e.g., Epiros, Peloponnesos, and Crete), reflecting local dialects and containing admixtures of Hebrew with loan words from Turkish and Italian. The Romaniot Jews of Istanbul and the Karaites maintained their Judeo-Greek until recent times. Some examples of spoken Judeo-Greek (testimony of witnesses to a dispute) are available in rabbinic responsa of the Ottoman period; it is still a living language among descendants of Romaniot Jews in diaspora and a handful in Greece itself.[61]

There is, then, a good case for recognizing Judeo-Greek as an early Jewish language. What about Judeo-Aramaic?

Babylonia and Judeo-Aramaic

In a recent study, Steven Fine discusses the kind of multilingualism and multiculturalism that can be inferred from the synagogue at Dura Europus, on the border between the Byzantine and Persian Empires, a Jewish community that was made up – he believes – of Greek, Aramaic, and Persian speakers from both empires. The inscriptions, in Greek and Aramaic but not Hebrew, refer to people with biblical names, although he assumes that Hebrew was the liturgical language, and it appears on some pieces of parchment found nearby. The Persian and Parthian inscriptions may have been added by later visitors, commenting on the paintings. Perhaps they were made by non-Jews or proselytes, but there is no way of knowing.[62]

The Babylonian Diaspora was different in many ways. The only information we have is from the Babylonian Talmud, slanted by the rabbis' views. The rabbis' status was raised by their association with the Exilarchate, the head of the Jewish community. The grant of a degree of autonomy to the head of the Jewish community (*Rosh galut* in Hebrew, or *Reish Galuta* in Aramaic) dates from the beginning of the exile until the sixth century CE, and was restored under Arab rule from the seventh to eleventh centuries CE. Rabbis and scholars

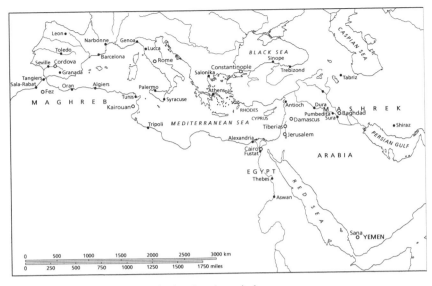

4 Jewish Diasporas in the Geonic period
Source: Stillman (2010b).

formed part of the retinue of the Exilarch and were often appointed as judges. Although the rabbis were involved in the synagogues, they had their own institutions, such as the Yeshivot, and were not directly involved in synagogue administration.[63] Some scholars believe that the Babylonian synagogue had only liturgical functions, but this is not clear from the sources.

The two major religious educational institutions in Babylonia were Yeshivot (academies): one at Sura, established by Rav (Abba Arika, who had studied in Palestine and returned to Babylonia in 219 CE); and the second, headed by Samuel, at Nehardea, which moved to Pumbedita in 259 CE (see Map 4).[64] These two academies played the major role in the development of the Babylonian Talmud. Twice a year, in the months of Adar and Ellul, scholars from all over Babylonia would gather at the Kallah (assembly) of one of the academies, and spend a month debating and studying a selected treatise, at the end of the time agreeing on the answers to the questions raised.

While there were a good number of differences between the liturgy in Palestine and Babylonia, such as sitting or standing for the *Shema*, reciting the *Amidah* silently or aloud, reciting the *Kedushah* daily or on the Sabbath only, or the number of times the priestly blessing was recited on a fast day and the Day of Atonement,[65] prayers in both countries were usually in Hebrew, though Rabbi Yochanan in third-century Palestine took a stringent position on this (Babylonian Talmud, *Sotah* 33a, *Shabbat* 12b). There were regular Torah readings in both countries, with an Aramaic Targum accompanying the Hebrew reading in both. A clue to the language of the synagogue is given in the account in Tractate *Soferim* (a non-canonical minor treatise redacted probably about the eighth century CE in Palestine) of a reading of the Book of Lamentations on *Tish'a b'Av*,[66] calling for a translation by the reader or someone skilled to translate it so that the audience – men, women, and children – could understand an obligatory reading. The tractate goes on to say that women are required to read the *Shema* and recite the *Amidah* and the grace after meals, and, "if they do not know Hebrew, we teach them in any language so that they can hear and learn".[67]

Sermons were a regular part of the synagogue service, particularly on the Sabbath. The Book of Luke (4: 20–1) reports Jesus preaching at Capernaum, and the Book of Acts (13: 15) Paul preaching at Antioch. Philo (*Hypothetica* 7: 13) reports that it was customary to gather on the Sabbath:

And then some priest who is present, or some one of the elders, reads the sacred laws to them, and interprets each of them separately till eventide; and then when separate they depart, having gained some skill in the sacred laws, and having made great advances towards piety.

There are many references in later years to sermons, given by rabbis or by itinerant preachers. The Mishnah in *Eruvin* describes how to redefine the area permitted for Sabbath travel to be able to hear a visiting preacher. The *Darshanim*, whose role was to *doresh* (explain and comment on) a biblical text, sometimes prepared their sermons but might also be expected to extemporize; they were sometimes accompanied by a *meturgeman*, who was not (as the word suggests) a translator but a "loudspeaker", who would repeat their quiet words in a louder voice.[68] Much of the Midrashic material in the Talmud may have originated in sermons, but there is no reason to assume that the text that is preserved was that given in a sermon, nor that it represents the language used; just as in the nineteenth century we find sermons given orally in Yiddish being published in Hebrew, so we may assume that sermons were delivered in the mixed Hebrew–Aramaic of the Talmud, or in a similar mixture with Greek in those synagogues where it was used.

A third aspect of the liturgy in this period was the *piyyut*, a word derived from the Greek ποιητής but referring to liturgical poems composed mainly in Hebrew and inserted in various parts of the service. It is now generally agreed that *piyyutim* first appeared in Byzantine Palestine, where the composers (*payyatanim*) would have been proficient enough in Hebrew.[69] There are disputes about the origin: some medieval commentators argue they were written to deal with Justinian's Novella 146 criticizing the Jewish practice of praying only in Hebrew, and requiring prayer that included prophecies announcing Jesus in

Greek and "any other tongue", or during periods of Sassanian persecution; others assume they were an internal development.[70]

Jewish Babylonian Aramaic

From the third century to the eleventh, Jews in the area of present-day Iraq and Iran spoke and wrote a variety of Aramaic. Evidence for this is preserved in the surviving texts of the Babylonian Talmud, in common phrases and other material written by the heads of the Babylonian Yeshivot, in writings by Karaites found in the Cairo Genizah, in a large number of magical texts, and in some Masoretic treatises. There have been a number of dictionaries published.[71]

One unsolved puzzle is the difficulty of the language of *piyyut*: how much of the audience, which was assumed to need a Targum for the more straightforward Hebrew of the Bible, could have understood the difficult poetic language of the *piyyut*? There are about fifty *piyyutim* written in Palestinian Jewish Aramaic, many of which would have been easily understood by worshippers. All remaining *piyyutim* are Palestinian in origin, and later Babylonian *geonim* appear to have disapproved of them.[72]

By the reign of Justinian (527–565 CE), the last Byzantine emperor to have been a native speaker of Latin, Jews were already widely scattered, but the largest concentration in the empire was in northern Palestine and Syria.[73] There were also large communities in southern Italy, and smaller ones in Spain, Africa, Egypt, Arabia (there were Jews in Yemen among the Himyarites converted to Judaism,), northern Italy, Sicily, Sardinia, Crete, Cyprus, and the Aegean. Some Jews lived in Jerusalem, but Tiberias was the main Jewish center in Palestine. There were Jews among the Berbers in north Africa, and of course in the Sassanian Empire.

Most of these Jews mingled freely with non-Jews, distinguished by neither clothing nor language. In some synagogues, Greek was used for readings and liturgy. Jewish life continued, but was becoming precarious after Christianity became official, with regular imperial restrictions, persecution, and pogroms. Aramaic was still strong, but Jews were excluded from Greek and Latin schools, producing a growing rift, and encouraging internal education in Aramaic and Hebrew. Greek was no longer a language of high culture for them.[74]

The evidence of Jewish language use at this period is confusing: we know some communities used Greek in the liturgy, but the details are unclear. And the use of Latin, Greek, and Hebrew in inscriptions does not answer the question of what languages were spoken.[75] Some generalizations are safe, such as that there was no evidence of Hebrew being spoken in Europe, except perhaps by immigrants or travelers as a lingua franca. European Jews were mainly Judeo-Greek speakers, but probably spoke local languages too. But, from the eleventh century on, Hebrew was the language of liturgy, and it was the high language of

Jewish literacy starting in the ninth century. Early Christian sources (including Gregory of Tours in the sixth century) do not mention language problems in contacts with Jews. Possibly, the Jews of Orleans greeted King Gontrand in 585 in Hebrew. Sermons were presumably given in the local language, and pagan slaves of Jews in Lyon in 822 CE wishing to be baptized had learned the local language. By this time, too, there was evidence that Christian scholars had access to Hebrew sources, showing the presence of Jews who could translate into Latin or the local language. There is other evidence from south Italy, and from the Crimea (in Cyril's mission to the Khazars), of ninth-century use of Hebrew.

Very few of the hundreds of inscriptions in Europe include Hebrew (80 percent are in Greek, others in Latin), and any Hebrew is usually formulaic. There are, however, a number of multilingual inscriptions in southern Italy that include Hebrew, perhaps attesting to migration from Egypt or elsewhere, at a period of forced baptism in the Byzantine Empire, where Hebrew was still the language of liturgy and learning.[76]

Apart from Babylonia, where Jewish learning remained strong in the Yeshivot, and Palestine, Jews in the growing Diaspora appear to have adopted Greek or Latin or the local language, with some communities perhaps maintaining Hebrew for the liturgy. The dominant multilingual pattern was Hebrew–Aramaic in Babylonia and Palestine, with Greek added in Palestine; Judeo-Greek with some Hebrew–Aramaic elsewhere in the Near East; and local languages such as Judeo-Romance starting to be used by Jews in the rest of the Diaspora. There were Jews (or converts to Judaism) in Yemen and Arabia who would have acquired Arabic, but the full pressure of that language was still to come. And growing anti-Jewish feeling and action was pressing further migration and exile, adding to the number of languages used by Jews and to their spread throughout the sociolinguistic profile. As Jews spread, so they added additional languages. The next major addition was to be Arabic, which became a major language of the Jews and from which Judeo-Arabic emerged.

Adding another major language

This book has so far traced the adoption and development of the first three major languages of the Jews: Hebrew, from its misty origins until its loss as a spoken language about the second or third century CE; Aramaic, added as a vernacular language and becoming semi-sacred during the years after the Babylonian captivity; and Greek, which was introduced during the period of Hellenization and greatly strengthened under Roman and Byzantine rule. It has also noted the change of balance in population from Palestine to the Diaspora, as, starting with the Babylonian Diaspora, many Jews fled to other places that seemed safer or economically more desirable.

These developing Diaspora communities were in place and waiting, as it were, for the Muslim conquest; in fact, Josephus reported that Jews lived everywhere in the world as he knew it. It was migration and conversion, however, that first added Arabic to the Jewish sociolinguistic ecology, as some Jews moved as traders and settlers through the Nabatean lands in the south and on into the Arabian Peninsula. The number of migrants is not clear, and may not have been large; indeed, with the evidence of the conversion of local pagans, it seems at times that it was Judaism rather than Jews that moved to the Arabian Peninsula and crossed into Ethiopia, the two forming – according to some – the Land of Cush.[1] There, Arabic was adopted as a language of the Jews by migration and linguistic assimilation into Arabic-speaking regions, and by the conversion of indigenous peoples; later it was spread, as a result of the Muslim conquest, by the diffusion of Arabic throughout the rapidly growing Arab Empire, from the Indus in the east to Andalusia in the west. Other languages were added too as a number of African groups adopted Judaism, although the dating is in doubt: while their traditions claim early conversion, the African groups emerge as Jewish only in the nineteenth century and later.

The importance of the long contact of Jews with Arabic, dating from the pre-Islamic migrations to the current sharing of territories, cannot be overestimated. The relationship between the two peoples has seldom been even; once in power, Islam accepted followers of other religions only as of lower social, political, and economic status, who were granted "protection" without any claim to rights except those conceded by the Muslim rulers.[2] Only in comparison with the continual persecutions and expulsions of Jews in medieval Christian Europe does the experience of regular extortions, murders, expulsions, restrictions, segregation, and massacres under Islam[3] seem less harsh, and the occasional examples of tolerance show the possibility of happier integration.

The early period is marked by increasing dispersal of the Jewish people after the destruction of the Second Temple by the Romans, the loss of Jewish political autonomy, and the failures of the many revolts against the Roman rulers in Palestine and the Diaspora. The first and best known of these revolts lasted from 66 to 74 CE. It was described by Josephus, who helped lead the unsuccessful defense of Galilee, and ended when the Roman general and future emperor Titus captured Jerusalem. The second revolt started outside Palestine, in 115 CE, in Cyrenaica in Libya, but moved to Palestine, where it was crushed by the Roman general Lucius Quietus in 117 (it was known after him as the Kitos War). The third is the better-known Bar Kokhba revolt, starting in 132 CE and led by Simon Bar Kokhba, who was proclaimed Messiah. For a while Judea was independent again, but the uprising, which was crushed by a large Roman army commanded by Hadrian, ended with many casualties on both sides, the destruction of Jerusalem, and its rebuilding as a Roman city, Aelia Capitolina, banned to Jews.[4] There were later revolts, in 351 CE against Constantine, in the fifth and sixth centuries by the Samaritans against Byzantine rule, and in 614 CE by Jews against the Byzantine emperor Heraclius, which succeeded for a while when they were allied with the Persians, but was put down when the Persians later threw their support to the Christians.

We shall in later chapters follow up on the earlier Diasporas in the Persian Empire, where the Babylonian Talmud was being developed in Hebrew and Aramaic, and in the Greek-speaking regions of north Africa and the Mediterranean (see Map 5). We will also trace developments in Palestine after Hebrew was no longer spoken. But, to try to simplify a complex picture, it seems best to concentrate on one additional language at a time, and follow the developments up until the creation of the State of Israel, with its in-gathering of the exiles and marginalization of the rich languages that made up their multilingualism. Arabic is the next language to consider, although it is important to note the other languages that Jews were learning at the same time, such as Latin in the Vandal kingdom of north Africa, and Persian in the east, where Islam later came to rule.

Jews in Arabia before the rise of Islam

Many will be surprised to learn (as I was) that Jewish knowledge of Arabic preceded the Muslim conquest. According to the biblical account, the earliest Jewish contact with Arabia was the visit of the Queen of Sheba to Solomon.

5 Middle East, Arabia, Ethiopia
Source: Based on http://d-maps.com/m/africa/nil/nil07.pdf.

Sheba may have been Ethiopian – the Ethiopians indeed claim her as an ancestor – or she may have been, as some Muslim sources and archeological findings suggest, from southern Arabia or Yemen.[5]

There is evidence of early Jewish trade relations with Arabic speakers. The Nabateans, originally Aramaic speakers who were influenced by the language of the people whose land they occupied and who became Arabic speakers, were southern neighbors of the Jewish state, and were incorporated into the Roman Empire in 106 CE. They competed as traders with Jews,[6] and Jews settled in Nabatea and along the trade routes as far as Arabia.[7]

There are a number of accounts of Jewish migration southwards in Islamic legends, expanding on the Bible story. At Rephidim, the Children of Israel fought with the Amalekites, who attacked them as they came out of Egypt (Exodus 17: 8) and were instructed (Deuteronomy 25: 17) to "blot out their memory". Later, Saul is said to have lost his kingdom to David because of his failure to carry out this command (1 Samuel 28: 18). A Muslim addition to this account reports that the Israelite warriors who spared an Amalekite when told by Moses to kill them all at Rephidim were banished to Arabia, where they settled. Young priests who fled after the destruction of the Second Temple joined them, also according to the Muslim legends. This Muslim tradition is paralleled by an account in the Palestinian Talmud of 80,000 young priests who fled to the Ishmaelites (the normal Talmudic term for Arabs) and were given water by the Bedouin.[8] There were two Arabian tribes, Banu Qurayza and Banu an-Nadi, that claimed to be descendants of priests who left Palestine after 70 CE.[9] They lived at Yathrib (Medina), and in 627 were defeated by Muhammad as he gained control of Arabia; the men were beheaded and the women and children enslaved.[10]

There are Christian hints too of the early presence of Jews in Arabia. Paul (Galatians 1: 17) reports a visit to Arabia that may have been to preach to Jews there.[11] Another New Testament source, Acts (2: 11), mentions Arabians among the many Jews from abroad who came up to Jerusalem for Pentecost during the time of the Second Temple. These accounts show that there were Jewish immigrants to Arabia, presumably Hebrew and Aramaic speakers who acquired Arabic in their new land.

A second major source of Jewish population of the Arabian Peninsula was conversion. Jews and Christians of various sects are reported to have come to pre-Islamic Arabia to convert the polytheistic Arabs. Islamic tradition suggests that conversion from paganism was conducted by two rabbis. By the time of the birth of Muhammad, there were reported to be strong Jewish communities in the Hejaz (in western Arabia), of all classes (merchants, warriors, farmers, and even poets), speaking Arabic, Aramaic, and Hebrew.[12] There were Jewish clans among the Arabic tribes, and conversion and intermarriage were common. Samaw'al [Samuel] ibn 'Adiya, who was born in Arabia into a clan that had converted to Judaism in Yemen, was famous as a poet and warrior in the sixth century CE, and was said to have been captured and poisoned by Justinian. His Arabic writing shows no trace of his Jewishness.[13] These converted Jews were presumably Arabic speakers, who may have learned some Hebrew or Aramaic. Ethiopia too appears to have been a place where conversion was more significant than migration; while there are traditions of descent from the Queen of Sheba and King Solomon, there is little evidence of Jewish presence to account for the fact that at one time half Ethiopia was considered a Jewish kingdom.

Epigraphic evidence supports the existence of early Jewish settlement. Ancient Southern Arabic had four main dialects, the best attested of which was Sabaic, with inscriptions appearing from the eighth century BCE on. These inscriptions include Greek and Jewish Aramaic expressions.[14] The extensive graffiti in the western two-thirds of the Arabian Peninsula show a widespread literacy among settled people and nomads. There were a number of varieties, distinct by using h- (as in Hebrew) or zero in place of 'al for the definite article, forming Ancient North Arabic, which coexisted with Old (proto-) Arabic, itself only a spoken language until it adopted the Nabatean Aramaic alphabet in the sixth century CE. All the evidence supports the notion that there were some Jews in Arabia before Muhammad, speaking Hebrew and Aramaic and learning Arabic, and many local Arabs, converted to Judaism, perhaps learning Hebrew.

Can we trust the sources?

Many scholars challenge the reliability of the Bible as a historical source. Starting in the seventeenth century with questioning of the sources of the Bible, and reaching a high point with the approaches of the German scholar Julius Wellhausen,[15] they assume the Bible to be a collection of edited compositions from different authors and periods. There has been similar recent questioning of the trustworthiness of Islamic sources, as a result of the beginning of the application of the higher criticism method to the Qur'an by German scholars.[16] This has even gone so far as a statement of doubt of the existence of Muhammad by Sven Muhammad Kalisch, professor of Islamic Studies at the University of Münster.[17] He points out the absence of contemporary references and the gap of 100 years before any detailed biography is written.[18]

This questioning of the very existence of Muhammad, not dissimilar to that of scholars who question the existence not only of Moses but also of David and Solomon, suggests we need to be very careful in using the Qur'an as a source of history. When it is subjected to the same scrutiny that the Hebrew Bible and the New Testament have received, the Qur'an may turn out to be a misleading source of reconstruction. Further, the Arab historians' preference for stories of individual glory and bravery makes them hard to accept as evidence of real events. While there is little real doubt that Muhammad lived between 620 and

630, and that he fought in wars, the precise details cannot be recovered from the available texts. Most medieval Islamic historians were writing a long time after the events they describe, and were committed to strong ideological stances.[19] I shall be cautious, then, when I cite their versions of history.

The Jewish tribes of Arabia

There were Jews in Arabia before Muhammad, and, just as Christianity grew up with an attempt to persuade Jews of the coming of the Messiah, so Islam had a similar history centuries later. Whether migrants or, more likely, proselytes, there were said to be fifteen Jewish tribes in Arabia. Many were listed in Muhammad's ordinance for Medina, a "pact and covenant with the Jews, confirming their religion and their possessions", and setting conditions starting with the payment of the "bloodwit" (a fine for shedding blood).[20] The ordinance stated that "any Jew who follows us shall have aid and comfort; the Jews have their religion and the Muslims have theirs; each side is responsible for its expense". The tribes were reported to have migrated from Palestine at various periods or to have been converted in Arabia by Jewish travelers, rabbis, and traders.

According to the Qur'anic account, Muhammad was initially hopeful that the Jews would accept him as the Messiah, but most refused. Abu Muhammad 'Abd al-Malik bin Hisham, who wrote a biography of Muhammad in the ninth century CE, describes how Jewish rabbis began to question Muhammad and harass him. When the Prophet Muhammad was born, around 571, there were many Jews living in the northern Hejaz, especially in the environs of Yathrib (Medina). There has been considerable controversy over the origin of this Hejaz Jewish community, with scholars from the nineteenth century disagreeing as to whether they were converts or migrants; after summarizing the dispute, Moshe Gil tends to favor the Muslim sources that believe most were proselytes.[21] In this city, Jews were organized in three tribes: the Banu Nadir, the Banu Qaynuqa, and the Banu Qurayza. There was also a Jewish community in nearby Khaybar.

These Arabian Jews (or Jewish Arabians) made their living from date plantations, from the caravan trade, and by working in various crafts. Integrated into the life and society of the Arabian Peninsula, they spoke Arabic, although, among themselves, the immigrants and their descendants were reported also to use a mixture of Hebrew and Aramaic, and they adopted many of the values of the desert society. Their language variety, sometimes called *al-Yahūdiyya*, Judeo-Arabic, developed over time and was written in Hebrew script.[22] There is some dispute about the variety called *kana yartūnu al-yahūdiyyati*, however, and others argue that it was more likely to be Aramaic.[23] There is no direct evidence of the existence or nature of Judeo-Arabic before the tenth century, although Jews are said to have been writing

Arabic in Hebrew script. Jewish migrants probably learned Arabic quite quickly, taking advantage of the closeness of the two related Semitic languages.

One of Muhammad's earliest reactions to the rejection of his claim to be the Messiah by the Jews was to attack and defeat the Jewish tribes of Medina;[24] a few Jews remained there after the Muslim victory, but they too were later driven out.[25] In 628 CE Muhammad went on to conquer the town of Khaybar. After some negotiations, Khaybar was finally persuaded to surrender; the remaining members of the Banu Nadir were killed, but the Khaybaris were allowed to remain on condition that they paid half their date harvest to the Muslim ummah. These and other Jewish oasis tribes of the northern Hejaz were allowed to remain for a few years until the caliph Umar (who ruled from 634 to 644 CE after the death of Muhammad) ordered their expulsion; they were no longer needed for labor, as this was now supplied by slaves brought to Arabia from ongoing Islamic conquests.[26] The town of Mecca soon fell to Muhammad as well, and the Jews and Christians of Yemen also began to pay tribute.

Towards the end of his life Muhammad instituted a poll tax, to be paid by any Jews or Christians who did not accept Islam. This formed the basis for the *dhimma*, the special status of Jews and Christians and, later, of Samaritans, Sabaeans (a south Arabian people), and Zoroastrians (in Iran) under Muslim rule. *Dhimma* (obligation or treaty) refers to the obligation of Muslims and especially Muslim rulers to protect non-Muslims. Being protected depended on acceptance of the higher status of Islam, the payment of a special tax, and the observance of Islamic law. *Dhimmi* (minorities) had the right to observe their own religion anywhere except in Saudi Arabia, where additional religions were not permitted.[27]

The rules of *dhimmitude* were later refined in the Pact of Umar, set out at the end of the seventh century CE and varying in details and enforcement over the next twelve centuries, and still widely preached by Muslim religious and political leaders. Basically, the various versions of the pact allowed members of monotheistic religious groups to continue to live and practice their religion in Islamic states, but only as second-class citizens. Their stigmatized status was marked by the fact that they were not permitted to build new churches or synagogues, or to ride on saddled animals, which would make them higher than Muslims walking by. Their women might not use the same bathhouses as Muslims. *Dhimmi* could not wear or sign their names with Arabic signet rings. They had to pay a special tax. A provision enforced in Yemen until quite recently was that they could not ride on camels. *Dhimma* status was maintained in north Africa until European colonization, and in Yemen and Persia into the twentieth century.[28] Apart from restrictions preventing Jews and Christians from assimilating unless they converted to Islam, there were commonly clauses forbidding them to have Muslim servants or marry Muslim women, or to hold official positions in a Muslim state. All this had obvious sociolinguistic consequences.

There were also specifically linguistic rules imposed on the *Dhimmi*. They were not to teach their children the Qur'an, nor to speak as Muslims do, nor to follow the Muslim custom of naming a man after his son (for example, Abu Musa). The effect of this policy, variously enforced as it was, was to impose social isolation, which discouraged the adoption of Standard Arabic and led to the development of what Joseph Blau has called "Middle Arabic", a variety used by Christians and Jews based on the vernacular, and distinct from the Classical Arabic of the Qur'an, which was written in Arabic script. Middle Arabic was written by Jews in Hebrew script, and was the language of much Jewish religious literature.[29]

Having successfully conquered Medina, Muhammad is reported to have drawn up an agreement with the Jews that recognized the religions of the Banu Awf and the other Jewish tribes. Gil accepts the authenticity of what is called the Ordinance of Medina, and agrees that it was written soon after the capture of the city by Muhammad. In a close reading of the document, he suspects that it was drawn up to justify the expulsion of the Jews from Medina for their failure to meet the conditions it describes.[30]

The Jewish presence in Arabia had an influence on Islam and on Arabic, but was effectively ended soon after the death of Muhammad. There is evidence in the Cairo Genizah, however, that a small number of Jews continued to live in Arabia until the Saudi tribe took over the country in the eighteenth century.[31] A Muslim tradition speaks of a Jewish community in Tayma in northwestern Saudi Arabia. Benjamin of Tudela, the twelfth-century Jewish traveler, gave an account of Khaybar, the seat of government of which is Thema (or Tehama);[32] the warrior Jews there, he wrote, had many fortified cities, raided the surrounding districts, and included a group of pious men who studied the Torah and fasted all week praying for the population. In Khaybar he said there were 50,000 Jews. But Benjamin's numbers were often highly exaggerated, and he did not visit Arabia, nor did he claim to have visited it.

Later travelers did not find Jews in Khaybar.[33] The English explorer Charles Montagu Doughty, seeking evidence of the fabled *Yahud Khaibar* (Khaybar Jewry), spent some time there in 1875, but found no evidence of Jewish residence; nor did the merchants of Baghdad know of any descendants.[34] The inhabitants of Telma had moved there 200 years beforehand, and had a tradition that "Old Telma of the Jews" had twice been destroyed by floods. Benjamin also mentions Katifa, a town on the Persian Gulf in the east of Arabia, where he says there were 5,000 Jews and pearl fishery was said to be controlled by a Jewish official.[35]

There were again Jews living in Arabia for a while after 1934, when Saudi Arabia conquered a border Yemenite city, Najran, absorbing its Jewish community; in 1949 these Jews were permitted to leave for Aden, where they joined the Yemenite Jews who were migrating to Israel. With these uncertain exceptions, then, there is no significant Jewish history in what is now Saudi Arabia after the expulsion by Umar in the seventh century CE, and so the history of Arabic as a Jewish language has to be sought elsewhere.

Yemen and Yemanic

Yemen, to the south, was different, as the Arabian ban on additional religions did not apply there. The Jews of Yemen claimed to be descended from Jews who had left Palestine before the destruction of the Temple and refused a request from Ezra to return.[36] There were trading connections as early as the first century BCE.[37] But conversion was probably the main source of the large Jewish population in Yemen too. Jews constituted the largest religious community in Yemen at the beginning of Islam, largely as a result of mass conversion. According to the ninth-century Arab historian Ya'qubi, they had been converted by two rabbis.[38]

There are ossuaries in Bet Shearim in Judea showing that Jews from Yemen brought their dead to be buried in Palestine in Mishnaic times. In Greek, the inscription on one reads "Of the people of Himyar", and in Southern Arabic script "A prince of Himyar".[39] "Himyarite inscriptions found in Yemen prove that some pre-Islamic kings of that country had embraced Judaism, as was asserted by Muslim historians."[40]

Current studies record the development of the Jewish kingdom of Himyar in Yemen.[41] In the late fourth century CE many people converted to Judaism, and the kingdom was established by 425 CE "explicitly dedicated to Judaism and the persecution of its Christian population". Recent epigraphic evidence and internal and external sources establish that Himyar rejected polytheism and probably converted to Judaism in 380 CE.[42] Reforms establishing Judaism as the dominant religion prefigured and inspired the policy of Muhammad 250 years later.

But it is not clear whether the whole population did convert, or just the elite.[43] And there is no evidence of how deep the influence was, or how observant the community was. In any case, the Jewish Himyarite kingdom was overthrown in 525 CE, when an army from Christian Ethiopia assisted by forces from the Byzantine emperor in Constantinople replaced Jewish rule with Christian; Christian rule survived until 570 CE, when the Persians, with Jewish support, expelled the Christian rulers.

Sixty years later, in 630, Yemen was conquered by Islamic forces that had arrived from the north. Jews remained in Yemen, but under severely restricted conditions. Initially they were protected as *Dhimmi* in exchange for paying the *Jizya* (poll tax), but in the tenth century, under the Shiite-Zaydi clan, which had seized power, their conditions worsened; they were forbidden to touch, or be higher than, a Muslim, or to build tall houses, or to ride on camels. Under the

Orphans Decree, any Jewish child whose parents died was to be taken under state control to become a Muslim. But Jews stayed on, working in trades that were needed, as silversmiths, weavers, and tailors, for instance. There were a number of cities with a significant Jewish population, including Sana, Sada, and Beda.

From the start of the Islamic period and until the mass emigration to the newly founded State of Israel in the mid-twentieth century, the Jews of Yemen were in regular communication with other Jewish centers in the Diaspora – in Babylonia, in Palestine, in Egypt, in Spain, and in the countries of Europe. In the third century CE bodies were sent to Bet Shearim for burial; at the beginning of the sixth century there was correspondence with the Jews of Tiberias; later, the Jews of Yemen accepted the authority of the Yeshiva at Pumbeditha.[44] In the twelfth century there were business connections with the Jews of Egypt. The Cairo Genizah contained letters from Mediterranean merchants stopping at the port of Aden on their way to and from India. Yemenite Jewish scholars corresponded with Maimonides in Egypt, and it was to them that Maimonides addressed his famous "Epistle to Yemen" during a period of persecution.

The epistle to the Jews of Yemen opens and closes in Hebrew, but the main text is in Judeo-Arabic "so that everyone – men women and children – may read it with ease".[45] The Yemenite Jews developed their own traditions, but kept up to date with Jewish religious observance elsewhere. They still expect any adult male called to the Torah to be able to chant his own passage, and maintain the custom of having the Aramaic Targum recited by young boys after every Hebrew verse. From the tenth to twelfth centuries there were works composed in Yemen in Judeo-Arabic that form a significant part of the Islamic Jewish cultural world.[46]

Jews in Yemen were discriminated against in many ways, and conditions grew worse under the Bani Tahir dynasty, which started in 1454. There was some protection under the Ottomans (1536–1635), who were generally tolerant of minorities, but with the victory of the Zaydis there were persecutions and expulsions, with a brief respite in the second half of the eighteenth century. The nineteenth century produced continued persecution, with some improvement under renewed Ottoman rule from 1872 to 1918.[47]

In the nineteenth century depressing conditions stimulated three messianic movements among Yemenite Jews; this messianic activity paralleled several similar movements among Muslims.[48] Traditional Jewish education continued in the nineteenth century, but some modern subjects were introduced into one school. Once Jews were allowed to leave Yemen, there was steady *aliya* (immigration) to Ottoman Palestine from 1881 to 1918, although it was a while before Yemenites were recognized as Jews by some orthodox residents of Jerusalem. In the early twentieth century there was a major dispute between a group that supported Maimonides and another that followed the Zohar.

Emigration from Yemen was not permitted after 1922, and there were no certificates for Palestine available once the British White Paper of 1939 was in force. After the creation of the state, permission to leave was finally granted in 1948, and many took advantage of the opportunity: Operation Magic Carpet, between 1949 and 1950, brought 50,000 Yemenites to Israel, and most of those remaining in Yemen left in 2009.[49]

Over the centuries the Yemenite Jews maintained knowledge of Hebrew, developing different pronunciations influenced by Arabic. There are three major traditions in the pronunciation of Hebrew: the Yemenite, the Sephardi, and the Ashkenazi. Because of geographical isolation, the Yemenites have retained a traditional pronunciation, though it is influenced by Yemenite Arabic vernaculars. For example, the Hebrew *gimmel* is realized as an affricate (dž), as in the English "John", a velar (g), as in the English "go", or a palatalized sound (g'), corresponding to the pronunciations in three parts of Yemen. Present-day vowels are similar to Babylonian pronunciation, with both *segol* and *patach* the same, and with *holem* realized as *sere* in Aden and the southwest. Yemenites have also preserved other features of Babylonian traditions from the days of the Gaonim, proving the maintenance of a connection. Five regional varieties of Yemenite Hebrew pronunciation have been described.[50]

There are Yemenite Bible manuscripts from the ninth century, and manuscripts of medieval Jewish writings. There are also a number of commentaries and other books composed in Yemen from the fifteenth century. Most of the material from Yemen was written in Middle Arabic, but poetry was entirely in Hebrew. Judeo-Yemenite (Yemanic) is a variety of Judeo-Arabic, and *Ethnologue: Languages of the World*[51] recognizes four dialects, Sana, Aden, Beda, and Habban, each derived from the local varieties of Yemenite Arabic.

When the first Jews from Yemen came to Jerusalem in the nineteenth century they were mistrusted and not accepted by either Ashkenazi or Sephardi communities, but, as time went on, their high level of biblical scholarship proved their deep connection to Judaism. Suspicion and discrimination continued even after the establishment of the State of Israel, for they are dark-skinned, but as they moved into the army and other institutions, and as their traditional culture was glamorized, they gradually won acceptance as another variety of Israeli. They brought with them Judeo-Arabic and knowledge of Hebrew, serving as a rare case of continuity dating back many centuries.

Beta Israel: Judaism in Ethiopia

Judaism and, according to one theory, some Jews crossed from the Arabian Peninsula into Ethiopia, an incursion into Africa. The result was the addition of Ethiopian languages (Ge'ez, Amharic, Tigrinya) to the Jewish sociolinguistic ecology. The area, referred to in the Bible some fifty times as the Land of Cush, was known to the Jews, although there is no archeological evidence for their presence.[52]

Known as Aksum, the area of northern Ethiopia was a major kingdom by the third century CE. There is evidence of Southern Arabian influence, but the language of inscriptions was already becoming different. A distinctive Ethiopic script appears in the second century CE, and from the fourth century, when the king was converted to Christianity, until the sixth century Ge'ez became the language of the Christian Church, alongside Greek and South Arabian. There was by this time also a tradition of Jewish influence, with some beliefs that one-half of Ethiopia was Jewish. In any case, many biblical traditional practices continued – circumcision on the eighth day, Sabbath observance on Saturday, church architecture, the observance of dietary laws – and there was a tradition of descent from the Queen of Sheba and King Solomon. There is debate as to whether this was the result of biblical influence or of the presence of Jews; if weight is given to the inclusion of Aramaic words in the Ge'ez translation of the Greek Bible,[53] one might suspect the presence of a small number of Aramaic-speaking Jewish mission-aries. There is some evidence of influence from Jews in Arabia. A cautious view leaves open the question of whether we are talking about Beta Israel[54] as descendants of Jews or as the result of Jewish influence.[55]

There are three distinct theories about the origin of Ethiopian Jews. One (the acceptance of which by the Israeli Rabbinate and government has made the immigration of Ethiopian Jews to Israel possible, so that they now form a community of over 120,000) is that they are descendants of the Lost Tribes. A second, long the dominant scholarly view, is that they are the descendants of Agaw people who chose to be converted by Jewish missionaries (a small number of whom were believed to have come from south Arabia or through Egypt). There is no hard evidence to support either of these theories. There is increasing support for a third theory, that they were descendants of a rebel group that did not accept Abyssinian feudalism or the developing Ethiopian Christianity. Thus, their Jewish practices were adopted from Christianity, strengthened by reading of the Bible. The absence of any Hebrew influence adds weight to this theory.[56] Even so, *Teiku*: the question remains open.

From the sixth century to the twelfth century CE there are many legends but little hard evidence about the Jews in Ethiopia after the collapse of the Aksum empire. According to tradition, Beta Israel or Gondar formed a separate Jewish state, which fought the Ethiopian kingdom and was later involved on both sides in the latter's struggles with invading Muslims in the early sixteenth century. The Jewish kingdom was defeated and became subject to the Christian after 1627. Many Jews were forced to convert, and Jewish culture and practice were seriously damaged. But Beta Israel continued to exist in the Gondar area.

A visiting Portuguese traveler claimed in the seventeenth century that they were still speaking corrupt Hebrew and using it in synagogue services.[57] During the troubled eighteenth and nineteenth centuries the Beta Israel suffered a further decline. In the nineteenth century they were discovered by Christian missionaries and explorers, who were finding Jewish traces throughout Africa, and, in reaction, some Jewish authorities visited them, calling for their recognition as Jews.

In 1904 a Polish-born Jew who had studied Ethiopian languages at the Sorbonne, Joseph Faitlovitch, visited the Beta Israel and established an international committee; as a result, many rabbis recognized them as Jews, as did the Ashkenazi Chief Rabbi of Israel in 1921. But Emperor Haile Selassie, the Italian colonial government that ruled from 1936 to 1941, and the Soviet-backed military junta that overthrew the emperor in 1974 did not permit emigration. In 1975 the State of Israel finally recognized Beta Israel as Jews, and various waves of emigration to Israel began in 1979, up to 1985 via the Sudan with US support, and in 1991 in an airlift from Addis Ababa of over 46,000 in thirty-six hours. Currently there are about 120,000 Beta Israel in Israel. Most adults and many children speak Amharic or Tigrinya, depending on where they lived in Ethiopia, and use Ge'ez as their liturgical language as they slowly acquire Hebrew. Integration has been slow, partly as a result of the village origins of many, partly as a result of a government policy of concentrated settlement and an educational policy that refuses to recognize their home language.

Here, we have the case of languages added as their speakers become or are recognized as Jewish[58] rather than as the result of Jewish migration to areas speaking the language.

Black Jews and their languages

Yemenites and Beta Israel constitute two major recognized groups of Jews, the latter black Jews and of uncertain origin. Having included Beta Israel in this survey, this is an appropriate place to consider the whole issue of the relationship between Jews and blacks and its sociolinguistic relevance.[59] Strictly speaking, the recognition externally and internally of blacks as Jews is a modern phenomenon, starting seriously in the eighteenth century and peaking in the nineteenth, but, as it refers to the fate of the Lost Tribes and the hypotheses of Jewish settlement in Africa 2,000 years ago, I will deal here also with the various African and Afro-American groups that adopted Judaism.

It turns out to be a large and complex issue, with various examples at different times and places. One theme is the fate of the Lost Tribes. Particularly in the nineteenth century, Christian missionaries in Africa discovered what they considered to be Jewish characteristics (such as large noses) or Jewish practices (especially circumcision) among the African tribes they were working with.

Some claimed to have found Semitic words in the languages they were starting to learn; in extreme cases, they believed that the tribe was speaking pure Hebrew.

Confusing the issue was a traditional Gentile notion that Jews were black, either because they were in fact darker or, according to one opinion, because they did not have intercourse with their wives while they were menstruating, believed to be a requirement for white skin. Additionally, the general Christian view included both Jews and blacks in the category of "others". At various stages in history, especially in former Islamic territory, where slavery continued to be accepted until quite recently, Jews owned black slaves, who, by Halacha, they were required to set free and convert. With the increase in the number of such converts, many communities whose members had picked up the general non-Jewish prejudice against blacks stopped according full Jewish rights to these former slaves. Encouraged by the opinions of Christian missionaries and explorers, many African groups began to claim that they were Jews.

One such group, the Lemba, in Zimbabwe, have a tradition of coming from outside Africa and have for many years been considered by some to be of Jewish or Semitic origin.[60] Originally, in the middle of the nineteenth century, a German explorer was told by missionaries that the ruins found in what is today Mozambique were the work of ancient Phoenicians or King Solomon, being beyond the capacity of blacks,[61] and perhaps evidence of the presence of white Jews, from whom the Lemba descended. There was no solid evidence of Jewish origin for the Lemba, however, although some genetic studies did seem to support a south Arabian origin. The Lemba leadership was happy with this result, but it has not yet led to official recognition by rabbinical or Israeli authorities.

Some nineteenth-century explorers and missionaries also proposed a Jewish origin for the Yoruba in Nigeria, but an even stronger case had been made a century earlier for the Igbo,[62] and in the middle of the nineteenth century a British expedition took with it a letter written in Hebrew in the hope that people who could read it would be found.[63] There were claims for Jewish origin in Ghana as well, especially in connection with the Ashanti, whose language and culture were assumed to be Semitic or Hebrew in genesis.[64]

Tudor Parfitt remarks: "The spread of the ideology connecting Africa and black people in general with the Jews has been spectacular." It was, he argues, "an *innate* feature of western colonialism throughout the world" to construct Jewish connections not just in Africa but also in Britain (the Anglo-Israelite movement).[65] The hypothesis was influential in the United States also, where the Native Americans were reported by many to be descended from the Lost Tribes. In the nineteenth century, under the influence of Anglo-Israelite beliefs, Afro-Americans were added to the picture, and black slaves found it attractive to consider themselves to be descended from the ancient Hebrews who had escaped from slavery in Egypt. From this developed a number of Afro-American Jewish groups, including the Black Hebrews, who now live in Dimona in Israel.[66]

Parfitt concludes that "in the United States, Israel, Africa, and elsewhere, including Papua New Guinea where there are altogether millions of adherents to some or other aspects of black Israelism, groups that exist increasingly consider themselves and may be considered by others as a completely legitimate, trans-national, black Hebrew/Israelite community".[67]

This section has perhaps made clearer my hesitation about defining the Jewish people: if these groups are to be added, there are many more languages also to be included. Cautiously, I so far count only those groups recognized by the State of Israel as Jewish. But, as there is perhaps as much evidence for the Lemba as for the Beta Israel, one would be foolish to assume any finality.

The Arabian link added Arabic to the languages of the Jews even before Islam, and provided the connection to Africa and blacks that developed later. Although the community was not continuous except in Yemen, it set a precedent for the development of Arabic as a language of the Jews and of Judeo-Arabic as a major Jewish language.

The spread of Islam

The Muslim conquest of Syria Palestina

Yemen is part of the Arabian Peninsula, so its rapid conquest by Islam was not surprising. But what is more in need of explanation is the rapidity with which the Muslims conquered such a large portion of the ancient world (see Map 6). At his death, in 632 CE, Muhammad controlled the Arabian Peninsula, but eighty years later the Umayyad caliphs ruled over the Middle East, from the river Indus in the east, and were starting to conquer Spain in the west. Muhammad's successors, the Umayyads and the Abbasids, ruled over that territory until 945, and Islam and Arabic have remained dominant after that in all of it, except Spain, until this day.[1] What accounts for the speed with which these territories fell to Muslim rule?

Hugh Kennedy, who has one of the most convincing explanations of this, and whose account[2] I will follow, asks how small armies (never larger than 20,000 men and often smaller) were able to conquer major empires so rapidly and to maintain their identity while persuading the conquered peoples to adopt Islam and later Arabic. Within a century Greek- and Aramaic-speaking Syria, Aramaic- and Persian-speaking Iraq, Greek- and Coptic-speaking Egypt, Pahlavi-speaking Persia, and Latin-, Greek-, and Berber-speaking north Africa had all come under Islamic rule, and were in the process of conversion to Islam and becoming Arabic-speaking.

Part of the problem of finding an answer, Kennedy suggests, is that modern historians who study the question are divided between those who know Latin and Greek and those who know Arabic and Persian; there are few who know both. Moreover, exact facts and dates are uncertain and controversial, as both Muslim and non-Muslim sources are generally not contemporary and tend to be anecdotal and biased.

The main explanation that Kennedy proposes for the speed and success of military conquest was the weakness of the opposing empires. Bubonic plagues starting in 540 had reduced population in the region, so that the Arabian warriors were often moving into comparatively empty territory. The long and bitter wars between the Byzantine Empire, based in Constantinople, and the

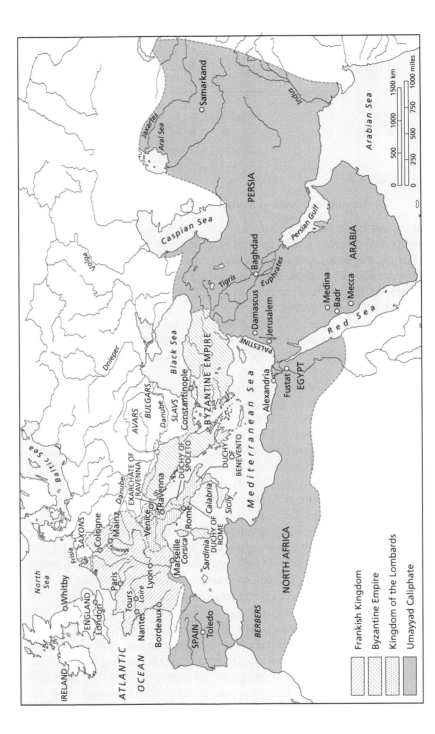

6 The Islamic conquests, 632–750 CE, both during and after the lifetime of Muhammad

Source: Based on map from www.studenthandouts.com.

Map labels:

Frankish Kingdom
Byzantine Empire
Kingdom of the Lombards
Umayyad Caliphate

Arabian Sea

1500 km
1000 miles
1000
750
500
250

Samarkand

Jaxartes
Aral Sea

Indus

PERSIA

Caspian Sea

Volga

Baghdad
Tigris
Euphrates

Persian Gulf

ARABIA

Medina
Badr
Mecca

Red Sea

Damascus
Jerusalem

PALESTINE

Alexandria
Fustat
EGYPT

Dnieper

Black Sea

BULGARS
AVARS
SLAVS

Constantinople

BYZANTINE EMPIRE

Danube

Mediterranean Sea

NORTH AFRICA

BERBERS

EXARCHATE OF RAVENNA
DUCHY OF SPOLETO
DUCHY OF BENEVENTO
Ravenna
Venice
Rome
DUCHY OF ROME
Calabria
Sicily

Baltic Sea

SAXONS
Frisia
Cologne
Mainz
Moselle

Paris
Loire
Tours
Nantes
Lyon
Bordeaux
Marseille
Corsica
Sardinia

SPAIN
Toledo

North Sea

Whitby
ENGLAND
London

IRELAND

ATLANTIC OCEAN

Sassanid Empire, which was centered in Persia and ruled as far east as Pakistan, had left both these major powers weak. The existence of religious schisms among the Christians in the Roman world meant that Christians who opposed Byzantine orthodoxy sometimes supported the Muslim invaders. Additionally, the comparatively lenient conditions set by the Islamic conquerors (there was a poll tax – *Jizya* – to be paid by non-Muslims, but a degree of tolerance for monotheists) made surrender less of a problem than fighting.

Military conquest, then, was quite fast, as the efficient Arab warriors moved rapidly, often leaving large sections unconquered, but conversion to Islam took 300 years, and the change of language was also much more gradual. In fact, there were close cultural ties between Byzantium and Islam for several hundred years, and an amalgam of Christian, Islamic, and Jewish cultures.[3]

The language of the new elite was Arabic, but the existing languages of administration — Greek in Syria and Egypt, Middle Persian (Pahlavi) in Iraq and Iran, Latin in Spain – were still used at least until about 700 CE, when Abd al-Malik decreed that Arabic alone was to be used. Anybody seeking a bureaucratic position after that was expected to be able to read and write Arabic; coins, inscriptions, and milestones were in Arabic. But the other languages continued in community use.

There are very few contemporary accounts of the conquest from Muslim or non-Muslim sources, and the vast number of later and often contradictory accounts need careful interpretation. A large historical literature began to appear, but it is multi-layered, edited at the end of the period of conquest, in the ninth and tenth centuries.

Once the Arabian Peninsula had been conquered, a war against non-Arabs and non-Muslims was needed, Kennedy says, to "direct the frenetic military energies of the Bedouin", which otherwise would have reverted to intertribal warfare. Comparatively small forces of fighting men were sent out. Each Bedouin soldier provided his own weapons (a broad two-edged sword, a spear, and bows) and food. The resulting force was highly mobile, motivated by the rewards of Paradise for martyrs (*shuhad*).[4]

The prospective enemy had been weakened by plague, war, and religious schism. In 632 Syria/Palestine, the first logical target, was ruled by the Byzantine[5] Empire. The province had Greek-speaking elites; Syria (like Egypt) was mainly Christian, with some important Jewish communities and some paganism. Only Christians could hold office, but there was a serious schismatic split between Diophysites (Chalcedonians) – who were the orthodoxy of the Byzantine government – and the Monophysites (the heretics). Up to 540 the Byzantine Empire had been prosperous and successful, but bubonic plagues broke out and continued into the seventh century: the Plague of Justinian started in Constantinople, and resulted in the death of a quarter of the population of the eastern Mediterranean.

The plague also contributed to the failure of Justinian's wars with the Western Roman Empire. The Byzantines had other enemies too in the northeast when, in the middle of the sixth century, the Sassanian emperors started to invade their territory. The major invasion, in 611 CE, resulted in the capture of Jerusalem in 614 and of Alexandria in 619. A decade later the Byzantine emperor Heraclius turned the tables, and in 630 he recaptured Syria, Egypt, and Jerusalem. But these wars left their mark. Additionally, the doctrinal struggles meant that many Syrian Christians were supportive of the invading Muslim armies.

The Bedouins had long known Syria from trade and visits. Their first attacks in 629 were unsuccessful. New campaigns were launched in 632, and soon succeeded. Some Jewish communities were happy at the defeat of the Byzantines. The Byzantine forces at the battle for Damascus probably spoke Greek, Armenian, and Arabic, leading to communication problems. The battle of Yarmuk, which lasted a month, resulted in a Muslim victory, and Heraclius withdrew his army. The city of Caesarea, a major center under Roman rule and still flourishing, continued to resist, but soon it too fell. Other cities of Palestine were taken.

Eventually Jerusalem, the Byzantine city rebuilt by the Romans, was besieged.[6] The patriarch Sophronius finally negotiated with Umar, and surrendered. The Covenant of Umar was purported to have been signed by Caliph Umar with Sophronius.[7]

The people of the city were required to expel all "Romans", which meant Byzantine soldiers; anyone who wanted to leave was free to go with them, and those who remained and did not convert were to pay the *Jizya*. All churches and crosses were protected, as was other Christian property. There is a clause stating "None of the Jews shall reside with them in *Ilia* [Aelia Capitolina, the Roman name for rebuilt Jerusalem]", but this was probably a later addition, as Umar invited the leader of the Jewish community of Tiberias and seventy Jewish families to return to Jerusalem and to pray on the Temple Mount.

No new towns were established and there was no extensive settlement of Bedouins in Syria or Palestine. Thus, neither conversion nor, even more so, Arabicization was perhaps as fast as Kennedy seems to believe; Christians and Jews continued to be important contributors to the developing culture.[8]

From 634 to 1099, under the Muslim rule of Palestine, there were eight different caliphates, each with a different policy to the Jews. Jews of the time recognized four different institutions of authority: in Babylonia, there was the Exilarch, the secular leader, and the two Yeshivot, Surah and Pumbeditha; in the Byzantine Empire, there was the Palestinian Yeshiva in Tiberias.[9] These four institutions and the leadership of the three Gaonim or heads of the Yeshivot continued throughout the period of Muslim rule. When Jews migrated from one country to another (and the spread of unified Muslim rule made this possible), they formed communities loyal to their original Yeshiva; there were thus Babylonian Rabbanite communities in Palestine.

Some Jews continued to live in Muslim Palestine. Evidence of the transition from Byzantine to Muslim rule for the Jews is the synagogue discovered at Na'aran (also known as Naarah and now called Ayn Duq), a Jewish village in the time of Eusebius (fourth century CE) built on a bluff overlooking Jericho.[10] It was a typical basilica, much like churches of the time, with two mosaics and a synagogue floor decorated with Judeo-Aramaic inscriptions with Hebrew loan-words and in Hebrew script. It was built at a time when such building was not permitted by Roman law and when synagogues were being attacked by Christians. The Muslim conquest was probably welcomed by these Jews, who modified the mosaic by removing human and animal images, as required by Muslim iconoclasm. There were other influences of Islam: rabbinic literary work, which flourished in Tiberias, Jerusalem, Cairo, and Baghdad, was produced in codices rather than in the scroll form that had previously been followed. As Aramaic was replaced by Arabic, new versions were produced, and books began to be written in a variety of Biblical Hebrew and later in Arabic. Jews and Samaritans began to use Arabic for secular and religious works.

Under Muslim rule, Jews were permitted to return to Jerusalem. There followed a renewed interest in priesthood and an outburst of messianic claims and move-ments, such as the Karaite *Avilei Zion* (mourners of Zion), who criticized the Rabbanites for placing "illicit" arks in their synagogues and remaining in the Diaspora.[11] According to an eleventh-century Jewish source, Jews were permitted to live on the Mount of Olives and were exempted from the poll tax.

There are only fragmentary records in the Cairo Genizah of the heads of the Palestine Yeshiva, which had seventy members and remained in Tiberias until the tenth century. *Piyyutim* were written there until the eighth century. Inscriptions (often dedicatory) in the synagogues of the period were in Judeo-Aramaic and Greek: a start was made translating the Bible into Arabic. Emissaries were sent to north Africa and Spain. In the eleventh century the Yeshiva moved to Jerusalem, where it was in contention with a growing Karaite community and with the Babylonian Yeshivot, which asserted the superior authority of the Babylonian Talmud whenever it disagreed with the Palestinian. In the late eleventh century there was a leadership struggle, with the government and the Karaites involved too. Under the Turkomans, who gained control in 1071, conditions for Christians and Jews worsened, and the Karaite leaders moved to Egypt and the Yeshiva leaders to Tyre.

There is very little evidence on the nature of the Jewish communities before the eleventh century.[12] Rabbanite communities were scattered throughout, and there is no archeological evidence of destruction by the invading Muslims. From time to time there were complaints of excessive tax burdens to fund the Muslim wars, and Jews were commonly the victims. In addition, there were struggles with the Christians and attempts by Christians to expel Jews. In Jerusalem in the eleventh century there was a major conflict between Rabbanites and Karaites who had come to Jerusalem expecting the Messiah. The Rabbanite and Karaite population[13] remained in Jerusalem until both were slaughtered by the crusaders.

In the eleventh century the Gaon of the Jerusalem Yeshiva wrote to the Egyptian and other Diaspora heads in Hebrew, showing that, after the end of Aramaic as a Jewish vernacular and before Judeo-Arabic was fully established by, say, 1050, Hebrew was still considered appropriate.[14] The process of adding Arabic and switching to it from Aramaic was not as fast as Kennedy implies, but, by the millennium, we can assume it had taken place in Palestine and Syria.

A note of caution is suggested by recent scholarship, including radiocarbon dating showing that the transition from Byzantium to Islam was in fact slower than commonly assumed. A recent exhibition at the Metropolitan Museum of Art in New York and its accompanying catalog[15] reveal how gradual the process of change was. A review summarizes the events: the Arab armies did not wipe out the existing Christian and Jewish communities, which were allowed to continue their traditions with little change: "[T]he spread of Islam did not happen overnight."[16] Thus, in spite of the rapidity of military conquest, the period was one of gradual cultural, religious, and – we assume – linguistic transition, so that Jews could continue to use their earlier languages as they gradually acquired proficiency in Arabic.

The Karaites: a Jewish counter-movement

While traditional Judaism followed the ideas of the rabbis, by the Middle Ages a significant second stream had grown, known as Karaitism. There are many ideas on the origin of the Karaite movement, but no hard evidence or agreement. Their legal system, based on a close reading of the written Torah and using techniques similar to Islamic practices to determine interpretation, and many of their customs (for instance, not wearing shoes when praying and sitting on the floor in the synagogue, and using observation rather than calculation for the calendar) demonstrate strong Islamic influence.

The Karaites were fundamentalists, in that they followed the written Torah "literally", rejecting the Rabbanite tradition of interpretation. Originally called Ananites, they followed the eclectic views of Anan ben David, who accepted many traditional Jewish views but combined them with extreme asceticism, which drove many away. In the ninth century the movement was reduced to a small number of hermits praying for Zion, with strict observance of rules, but in the tenth century a more moderate version of Karaitism emerged. Karaitism and its writers continued to flourish in the tenth and eleventh centuries, being brought to Europe in the twelfth century, and existing peacefully alongside Rabbanism in Byzantium in the fourteenth and fifteenth centuries. As time went on, however, many Karaites converted to Islam or became Rabbanites, especially in Egypt under the leadership of Moses Maimonides.

A third period of Karaitism took place in eastern Europe, with strong seventeenth- and eighteenth-century activity in Lithuania and Russia. There was much publication in the nineteenth century, and official recognition in the latter part of the century, including a renunciation of association with Judaism and support from the anti-Semitic Russian government. There continue to be Karaites in the United States, Turkey, and Israel, where they are recognized as Jews.

Some of the early Karaite works are written in Hebrew or Aramaic, but most are in Judeo-Arabic, sometimes in Arabic script. Karaite grammarians maintained good knowledge of Hebrew. Only the Karaites transliterated the Bible into Arabic script.[17]

The Karaite movement emerged in Iran, Iraq, and Palestine in the eighth and ninth centuries CE, and had its golden age in tenth-century Jerusalem. After the crusader conquest, communities were found in Byzantium, Crimea, and Lithuania; some remained in Egypt and the Ottoman Empire.[18] The Karaim language developed as a Jewish variety of Turkic origin in dialects in Lithuania, where it is maintained in a small community in Troki, and in a Crimean dialect, with a few remaining speakers.[19]

The Islamic conquest of Babylonia and Talmudic Hebrew–Aramaic

Having conquered Syria and Palestine, Islam now faced Persia. The Sassanian Empire, founded in the third century CE, and ruled by a warrior aristocracy, included Iran, Iraq, Afghanistan, and Turkmenistan.[20] In Iraq, there were large Christian and Jewish populations; most of the Christians were Nestorians, heretics in the orthodox Byzantine view; and the Jews had three major institutions, the Exilarch (the secular ruler) and the Yeshivot of Sura and Pumbeditha, each headed by a Gaon. The Sassanian aristocracy owned large agricultural estates worked by serf-like peasants, who formed a distinctly lower tax-paying class; there was an intermediate group of lesser landowners. The aristocracy spoke Pahlavi, a prestigious Middle Persian variety, while the majority of the population spoke Aramaic; the Jews spoke a Jewish variety of Aramaic and knew Hebrew.

The Sassanian army was reported to be defensive and cautious, not suited to fighting the highly mobile Arabs; it was weakened too, as it had been severely defeated by the Byzantine emperor Heraclius at Nineveh in 627. A number of short-lived rulers reigned, leading to political chaos, which was quickly exploited by the invading Muslims. A number of towns were taken, and slaves were captured. Some years later Umar again sent a small force to invade, which met the Persian army commanded by Rustam, who inflicted a major defeat on the invaders. Not discouraged, Umar recruited a new army. At the battle of Qadisiya, in 636 or thereabouts, the Persians were defeated, and negotiations began with Rustam. Fighting resumed, and the Persians were defeated and

Rustam killed. The Arabs pursued the fleeing Persian armies to Babil (Babylon) and defeated them there. The Persian capital, Ctesiphon, was captured in 637 and the city looted. Other parts of the empire were also conquered, including Khuzestan, in present-day Iran, and Susa, famous as the town of Daniel.

After the conquest, Umar ordered the Muslims to settle in two new towns, Kufa and Basra. First soldiers, and then settlers from Arabia, moved in and built up the towns, which became military and administrative centers. Another town the Muslims settled was Mosul. Easy terms were set for the population: they paid taxes, but there was no interference with their religion, and no Arabs settled among them.

Before the Muslim conquest, Jews were well established in the Parthian and Sassanian Empires; after the destruction of the Temple, two Babylonian Yeshivot were founded, one at Nehardea (it later moved to Pumbeditha) headed by Samuel, and the second founded at Sura by Rav in 530 CE. These two Yeshivot were responsible for the formulation of the Babylonian Talmud, the huge compendium of oral law that had taken final shape by 700 CE; they remained central authorities for Rabbinic Judaism until the middle of the eleventh century. The Jews were relatively free under the Sassanids, and were spared the persecution suffered by the Christians. They seem to have found favor with the invading Muslims, and in about 641 were joined by Arabic-speaking Jews expelled from Arabia, probably speeding up the adoption of Arabic by an Aramaic-speaking community.

Jews continued to be privileged, but rivalry among the Jewish leadership weakened their position, which deteriorated under the Umayyads in the eighth century, when the ban on building new synagogues was enforced and Jews and Christians were required to wear a yellow badge and both were heavily taxed. Communication was maintained with the Jews of Europe. Jewish interest in science developed, and Jews participated in the translation of Greek and Latin authors into Arabic. In the ninth century persecution increased: synagogues and churches were converted to mosques. In the wars that followed the Mongol invasions in the thirteenth century, the existing Jewish community was killed or emigrated, and was replaced by immigrants from Aleppo. Thus, while there was no continuity in the Judeo-Aramaic of Babylonia, the use of the language for the Babylonian Talmud established its place as a semi-sacred language, so that there is good reason to replace "Hebrew" in the triglossic relationship with "Hebrew–Aramaic".

The conquest of Egypt

Egypt was a quite different story from Syria and Palestine, for there were few Arab contacts before the invasion.[21] By the time of the Arab invasion, Egypt had long been ruled by the Ptolemies (successors of Alexander the Great), and later it became a Roman province. While the origin of Christianity in Egypt is unclear – perhaps Mark visited – there are fragments of the Gospels written about 200 CE, and Gnostic writings produced shortly afterwards.[22] The Edict of Milan, issued by Constantine in 313, legalized Christianity, and, with his conversion, it became the majority and dominant religion.

The Christian patriarchs in Alexandria were powerful and rich. The pagans had lost power, and Jews were the largest minority. Greek was the dominant language, but the general population spoke Coptic.[23] Later, Byzantine rule of Egypt weakened: the plagues and the Byzantine–Sassanian wars had a significant effect, and a Persian army entered Egypt in 617, causing great destruction. The Persians withdrew a decade later after the defeat by Heraclius. In the restored Roman country, there was a struggle between the majority Monophysite Coptic Church, which believed that Jesus had a single nature (divine, or combined divine and human), and the minority Chalcedonians (Diophysites, who believed that Jesus had dual natures, divine and human), who were supported by Heraclius in Constantinople. There was also a rift between the Greek-speaking ruling and military class and the Coptic-speaking majority, and persecution of the Copts.

It was during this period that the Muslim threat appeared, staved off for a little by paying tribute, but finally given reality by an invasion of a small army of tribes from Yemen led by Amr. After much fighting, in 640 the Byzantine army was defeated and retreated to Cairo, where Trajan had built a fortress in response to the Jewish rebellion around 100 CE. The fortress and city were finally taken by the Muslim invaders in 641. The Treaty of Mis, which perhaps was either not authentic or signed at a different time,[24] set out conditions similar to the Covenant of Jerusalem, only this time it was the Nubians who were not permitted to stay in the city. The city of Alexandria also fell to the Muslims in 641, and Egypt came under Arab rule.

The governors were now Arabic-speaking Muslims and not Greek-speaking Christians, but, showing the gradualness of change, Greek remained the language of administration for half a century. Egyptian grain was now sent to Medina and Mecca and not Rome or Constantinople. The capital was established at Cairo. Arabic immigration was limited to about 100,000 in all, and restricted for some time to Fustat, Alexandria, and Aswan, leaving the Coptic Christians the majority in the rest of Egypt. There was continual migration from Arabia, however, changing the demographic and linguistic balance. By the tenth century the Coptic patriarch was complaining that Copts no longer spoke Greek or Coptic and were communicating in Arabic.[25] At the same time, Judeo-Arabic replaced Judeo-Greek as the language of the Jews of Egypt. But, without further evidence, we can only surmise the nature of the transition: was it language shift or the result of changing demographics?

There was a large Jewish community in Alexandria at the time of the Muslim conquest, and many Jews are assumed to have moved from there to the new

Muslim city of Fustat. There is very little known, however, about the community during the first three centuries of Muslim rule. With the start of Fatimid rule in 969 CE, a converted Jew, Yaqub Ibn Killis, became vizier, and he recruited practicing Jews to his service. Many Jews from the Maghreb moved to the new capital, Cairo, and traded as merchants. There was persecution under Caliph al-Hakim, but calm was restored under his successor in 1021. All remained peaceful, and Jews were prosperous in their *Dhimmi* roles until the end of Fatimid rule in 1171.

The Jewish community at Fustat, which included both Rabbanites and Karaites, probably reached 4,000. The Rabbanites were divided between supporters of the Babylonian and the Palestinian Yeshivot, each with their own synagogues in Egypt. There were Jews from Maghreb in both. The Jews spoke Arabic and knew Hebrew.[26] The Karaite community included Jews who had come from Persia and Iraq; there was intermarriage between the communities and evidence of cooperation. The communities were well organized, each with its communal chest. For a while the head of the Palestinian Yeshiva was recognized as Gaon, and his representative as *Rav Rosh* (Chief Rabbi); around 1065 the Fatimid government appointed a *rais al yehud* (head of the Jews, known in Hebrew as *Nagid* – prince); under the Mamluks this office became even more important, and from the twelfth century it was held by Moses Maimonides and his descendants, until the Ottoman conquest in 1517.[27]

Maimonides had been born in Muslim Spain; his family emigrated during the reign of the Almohads, who were forcing Jews to convert, and after spending some years in Morocco and Palestine settled in Fustat and later Cairo, where in 1171 Maimonides was appointed *Nagid*. From then until his death in 1204 (his body was re-interred in Tiberias) he composed works on Judaism and philosophy (usually in Judeo-Arabic, but the *Mishne Torah* was in Hebrew), and medical works in Arabic.

During the Mamluk[28] period in Egypt (1250–1517) the position of *Dhimmi* worsened, and they were required to dress differently (Jews wore red clothes and Christians yellow). Jews could not hold official positions, nor could Jewish physicians treat Muslim patients. Many Jews converted to Islam, some trying to continue Jewish practices in secret. At the end of the fifteenth century many Sephardic Jews arrived in Egypt after their expulsion from Spain.[29] The Cairo Genizah, which contains fragments and writings from the ninth century to the nineteenth, gives evidence of the linguistic richness of the Jewish community of Egypt, as it moved from its pre-Conquest Judeo-Greek to Judeo-Aramaic and Judeo-Arabic, maintaining all the time a special position for Hebrew.

After the conquest of Egypt, Islam continued to spread to the east as far as Persia and to the west as far as Spain, with significant results for the languages of the Jews in the conquered territories.

The Islamic conquest of Spain

The movement west, leading to the conquest of al-Andalus, Spain, and Portugal, was fast, taking from 711 to 716, the Muslim forces being led by the Berber commander, Tariq ibn Ziyad. The area had been the Visigothic kingdom of Hispania, but at this time was divided by a struggle for succession. There were already Jews in Spain, and the Visigoths had just made laws under King Sisebul in 612–621, cancelled in 654 but renewed by the seventeenth Church council in 694, requiring all Jews to convert to Christianity. There are scholars who argue that the Visigothic kings were not opposed to the Jews;[30] only a few took anti-Jewish positions for political reasons, and the legislation was not effective and provoked opposition.[31] But the "growing Arab menace and the apparently paranoid fear of Jewish conspiracies" produced a "citadel mentality" among the Visigothic rulers, which may have resulted in Jewish support for the Muslim invaders.[32]

The details of the first years of Arab rule are scant. The conquest of Spain was followed by a series of invasions of France, which climaxed in 732 (probably) with the battle of Poitiers, also know as the battle of Tours, at which Charles Martel halted the Arab advance into Europe.

The story of Islamic and Christian Spain and its Jewish communities we will pick up in Chapter 9, after we have looked at the spread of Islam to the east. In this chapter we have seen the addition of Arabic as a language of the Jews and the start of the development of Judeo-Arabic. There were three significant processes: Jewish immigration to lands where Arabic was spoken, the conversion of Arabic speakers to Judaism, and Islamic conquest of countries where Jews were living. The processes of adding Arabic and the formation of a Jewish variety were different in each case, but the ultimate effect was establishing spoken Judeo-Arabic varieties and Middle Arabic as a written language.

The conquest of Persia

By the start of the Islamic conquest the Jewish Diaspora already extended to Persia in the east and Spain in the west, where two other languages were added to the Jewish ecology: Judeo-Persian and Judeo-Latin, respectively. One result of the conquest was to confirm Judeo-Arabic in this repertoire; another was to limit this addition, as Jews entered permanent status in Islamic countries as second-class residents, under the terms of the Pact of Umar and its application to *Dhimmi*, which prevented or discouraged non-Muslims from acquiring and using the classical language.

After Egypt had been conquered, the next target of the conquering Arabs was the land held by the Sassanian Empire, where Jews had lived since the Babylonian exile. The conquest of Iran took eight years, from the first invasion in 642 CE to effective control of the main routes, with most areas starting to pay tribute to the Arabs by 650. The invading armies destroyed the defending Persian army in 642, at the battle of Nihavand. Shortly afterwards the city of Hamadan was taken, the town where Esther and Mordechai are reported to have been buried,[33] and where the edict of Darius allowing the rebuilding of the temple was said to have been discovered.[34] Isfahan was next, close to a Jewish village called Yahūdiyya. One by one, other cities surrendered, with only brief resistance. By 650 only the capital city, Istakar, was still holding out; it too was taken, and its inhabitants massacred. The last stand of the Persian king was at Merv, which was occupied, and the king killed. Fighting continued in the border regions, until the Muslim armies were finally blocked in southern Afghanistan. Nor did they fully conquer the vast mountainous areas of the immense land: while the Muslims were tied up with the civil war that established the Abbasids in Baghdad, revolts in eastern Iran by Zoroastrian and other nativists had long-lasting effects.[35]

While many Arabs moved into Iraq, there was no major settlement in Iran, so that, although Arabic became the language of administration and of religion and philosophy, it did not replace Persian as the language of everyday life. The independent Iranian Muslim dynasties of the ninth and tenth centuries used Persian, written in Arabic script and with many Arabic loanwords, as the language of the court. As well as language, many aspects of the high Persian culture and of the pre-Islamic beliefs also survived. Persia was thus the border that the Arabic language failed to cross completely; it influenced but did not replace the local languages.[36]

Jews who had lived in Persia for some centuries before the Muslim conquest adapted and continued to use the Persian language. Iraq and Iran in the eighth to tenth centuries were both prosperous, and Jews lived in many cities, constituting – according to a tenth-century Muslim geographer – the third largest group in Iran after the Zoroastrians and the Christians. The major Jewish centers were in Surah and Pumbeditha (the location of the two Yeshivot) and Baghdad, founded by the Abbasid caliph Al Mansur to be capital of the Islamic Empire.

Under Muslim rule, Jews, like other non-Muslims, suffered the prescribed discrimination against *Dhimmi*, but their communities remained autonomous. During the period there was some messianic activity, and the Karaite movement spread from Iraq to Iran. In the troubled ninth and tenth centuries there was emigration westward. In the early fourteenth century there was a flourishing of Judeo-Persian literature.[37]

The Jews of Persia adopted the local dialects, writing Persian[38] in Hebrew letters and adding words and expressions from Hebrew. Judeo-Persian, called *Farsi* by Jews and *Zidi* or *Jidi* by other Persians, was a community language for the Jews who could speak Muslim Persian with government and non-Jewish neighbors. Judeo-Persian was used for writing biblical translations and commentaries, sermons, and official and legal documents.

There is written evidence of Judeo-Persian as early as the eighth century (there are rock inscriptions in Hebrew letters in Afghanistan) and some letters in the early ninth century, and other documents until the Mongol invasion in the thirteenth century. Judeo-Persian writing was revived in the fourteenth century with poems by Shahim and other writers.[39] There is a sizable corpus of Judeo-Persian texts written between the eighth and twelfth centuries, including Bible translations and commentaries, commercial and personal letters, Halachic and grammatical writings, and poems. Many are Karaite; all are single exemplars. The earliest is a 226-page translation with interspersed commentary on the Book of Ezekiel, written in two different dialects by four authors. It dates from the tenth or eleventh century and was written in northern Iran. There is also an early personal letter from a merchant in the eighth or ninth century, found in Chinese Turkestan. A collection of texts was found in *genizot*.[40]

Though it ultimately became Islamic and adopted Arabic script, Iran as a whole never shifted to Arabic. The Jewish spoken vernaculars of Persian were based on local dialects; there were also some coded vernaculars that other Persian speakers might not understand. The literary Judeo-Persian (*Farsi*), while using Hebrew script, was close to the *Dari* in which classical Persian literature was written in Perso-Arabian script. The earliest examples of New Persian are in Hebrew script: tomb instructions from the eighth to twelfth centuries. There are many other religious and secular works in Judeo-Persian. Belle-lettristic literature appeared in the fourteenth century. A number of major Persian epic poems were transcribed into Hebrew script. The fourteenth-century poet Mahlana Shahin-a Shirani translated biblical works, including Joshua and Ruth, into Persian verse that combined Jewish and Persian elements. Many other writers imitated and developed these epics. There was also religious and secular poetry, including bilingual (Hebrew/Aramaic or Hebrew/Judeo-Persian) and Hebrew poems. There are two major historical texts from the seventeenth and eighteenth centuries, and some philosophical writings. The use of Hebrew script kept the material isolated, though it shows many Persian features.[41]

There were probably Judeo-Persian versions of the Bible as early as the Sassanian period: there are biblical quotations in ninth-century Pahlavi works, showing that Bible translations existed prior to the Arab invasion. Also composed in the ninth century, but known now only in fragments, were Judeo-Persian Karaite commentaries of biblical books, including Ezekiel, Psalms, and Daniel. The earliest surviving Judeo-Persian manuscript, containing a translation and commentary of the Pentateuch, is dated to 1319.

The first Judeo-Persian Pentateuch was printed in 1546 for the Constantinople Polyglot Bible. Other translations were made in the early twentieth century. R. Shim'on Ḥakham published in 1904 a Judeo-Tājīk translation of the Pentateuch together with commentaries. Ḥakham also translated and published

Judeo-Tājīk translations of Joshua, Judges, I and II Samuel, I and II Kings, Isaiah, and the Song of Songs. Other Judeo-Persian translations of individual books of the Hebrew Bible have been published. Judeo-Persian biblical translations and commentaries provide useful evidence of the history of the Persian language.

The medieval Jewish community of Persia was one of the high points of Muslim–Jewish relations, although it was under constant tension and faced regularly, in every generation, the probability of persecution and forced conversion. While maintaining its isolation from full assimilation, the community produced a rich culture and literature that combined Islamic and Persian features with traditional Judaism.

The conquest of Iran was more or less complete by 651 CE, and the next challenge for the Arabs was the unconquered territory across the Oxus, where many different Turkish chiefs ruled. For the next half-century Arab governors led raids across the river. By 601 CE the Umayyad caliph controlled Damascus, but had trouble regaining power over the northeast frontier. Starting in 705 CE Arab forces had entered Bukhara and Samarkand. The Turks (who at the time had not yet moved into Byzantine Turkey) were fine warriors, and strong opponents of the invading Arabs.

There were Jews in Herat in Afghanistan before the Arab conquest. After the conquest Umar II forbade them to build new synagogues, but protected those that existed. There was a Jewish community from 1012 to 1249, as shown by graves inscribed in Judeo-Persian, but the earlier community probably had emigrated, or been killed or converted. In 1840 there were still twenty to forty families and a synagogue, joined by 300 families from Mashhad in Iran, who returned from forced conversion; the city prospered. The original inhabitants spoke a Jewish dialect close to Afghan Dari; the newcomers spoke a different Jewish dialect. In 1856 the Jews were expelled by invading Persians, but they were allowed to return in 1858 after the Paris peace agreement; the population, about 5,000, lived in good relations with the British. Herat was attacked during the Khan wars and there were regular persecutions. The community was the main Jewish center in Afghanistan, providing trained Jewish professionals. There were four synagogues. Jews from Herat made Aliya in various waves: 300 left between 1882 and 1914, more between 1933 and 1939, and illegally; 2,000 came after the State of Israel was established.

From 715 to 739 there were regular invasions of central Asia by the Arabs, and much land was taken. Finally, by 751, Arab overlordship of this part of central Asia was established. At the end of the period there was a battle at Talas at which the Chinese under Tang were defeated by the new Abbasid caliphate, which came to mark the furthest extent of Arab and Chinese conquests. In the early eighth century CE Arab forces conquered Sind, a part of present-day Pakistan, much of it occupied by semi-nomadic tribes. After the conquest both Brahmins and Buddhists were recognized as *Dhimmi*.

The spread of Islam soon came up against the opposition of the Eastern Roman Empire, based in Byzantium. In 655 there was a major sea battle off the Lycian coast between Byzantine and Arab forces, the Arabs being victorious. In 674 a Muslim naval force failed in an attack on Constantinople. Another attempt, in 716–718, including land forces also failed. There were other raids in the Mediterranean. For Jews, Byzantine rule in Syria was a time of persecution, relieved during the Persian invasion, but renewed later. The Arab conquest promised further relief.

As a general rule, for some time after the conquest, the borders of the Muslim provinces remained fluid, but gradually fortresses were built. To start, Arabs were settled in separate new towns or suburbs, thus avoiding contact and subsequent friction with the conquered peoples, but slowing the process of Arabicization. They left mountainous areas to later missionary activity; it was in mountainous areas that Aramaic sometimes survived, Syriac among Christians, and Judeo-Aramaic among Jews.[42] Compulsory conversion was not Islamic policy; Islam was open to all, but conversion was so attractive that, by 1000, much of the conquered populations had become Muslim.

Muslim conquest of the Maghreb

At the same time as the eastern expansion, the Arab conquest continued to spread west across north Africa. Israelites may have first come to Carthage in north Africa with the Phoenicians. In any case, there already was a significant Jewish community in Cyrenaica (Libya) in the Hellenistic period, settled according to Josephus by the Ptolemies as military colonists and bureaucrats. Under Roman rule, Jews lost their protected status, but there was continued immigration from 31 BCE until 117 CE; the Jewish population became Romanized and Greek-speaking. The community grew with the arrival of refugees after the destruction of the Second Temple. There are synagogue inscriptions in Greek attesting to the organization of the Jewish community. The imposition of a heavy tax and restrictions on Jewish farming led to a revolt in 117 CE, but it was put down by Trajan and the area was devastated.[43]

Some Jews had returned by the fourth century CE.[44] A small synagogue built in Naro (south of Tunis) in the fourth to sixth centuries has an inscription in Latin on its mosaic floor.[45] Some rabbis in the Talmud are said to have come from Carthage.[46] There were Jews in Mauretania (Morocco) who arrived after the destruction of the Temple and paid a capitation tax to the Romans. They prospered, especially under the Vandals, the east Germanic tribe that defeated the Romans in 429 CE but continued to use Latin for administration in north Africa.[47] Their strength made Jews a target for Church councils, resulting in a decree by Justinian that was directed against them and others considered heretics.

Until the start of the fifth century north Africa had been part of the Roman Empire, with Roman cities and prosperous agriculture. It was conquered by Germanic tribes in the fifth century CE, and brought under imperial rule by Justinian in 533 CE. The language of the new rulers was Greek, but there were religious tensions between the north African Christians and Constantinople. With the breakdown of trade, the area became poor and marginal. Many towns and villages were abandoned.

The archeological evidence suggests that the area was sparsely populated at the time of the Muslim invasion. There were some remaining Greek-speaking Byzantine soldiers (called *Rum*, Romans, by the Arabs); in Tunisia, there were *Afariqa*, a term used by the Muslims for Christians speaking a dialect of Latin and perhaps Punic; but the main population consisted of Berber, a collection of tribes speaking a related set of six major language varieties (Tamazight). They moved freely across the region, just as the Arabian tribes seem to have moved.

The Muslim invasion began in 642 CE, led by Amr; the treaty called for a tribute and for Berbers to sell their children into slavery to pay it. A new army was sent west in 647 CE, and the Byzantine forces were defeated in southern Tunisia. Much booty was taken, but it was not until 670 CE that a further attempt at conquest was made. A major incursion was led by Uqba, who was defeated by the Berbers. Carthage remained in Byzantine hands. Only in 694 CE did the Umayyad caliph have sufficient strength to take Carthage, finally ending Roman power in Africa. The Berbers continued to resist until their defeat in 698 CE. It took another decade to complete the conquest of Tunisia. Algeria and Morocco remained unconquered, and Muslim control depended on relations with the Berber leaders, who revolted unsuccessfully in 740–741 CE.

There are unsupported reports of conversion of Berbers to Judaism; many Jews certainly settled among the Berbers and acquired their language, producing the Judeo-Berber that many Jews from Morocco, especially from communities in the High Atlas and the Sous and Drâa valleys, ultimately brought to Israel.[48]

The development of local varieties of Arabic

The Islamic conquests of the seventh and eighth centuries brought the majority of world Jewry under Muslim Arab rule. Arabic became the dominant language of the new Islamic Empire, just as Aramaic and Greek had been beforehand. Along with the other conquered peoples, Jews began to adopt the new international language of culture and administration.

Kees Versteegh argues for rapid Arabicization following the Muslim conquest and proposes the development of what he calls New Arabic,[49] renamed by Blau as Middle Arabic, and more recently called Mixed Arabic, and growing into the regional Arab dialects that are the L variety in Arabic diglossia. The Arabic distinction between a high-status (H) Classical variety (*fus'cha*), based on the Qur'an and maintained as the language of religion and the ideal for literacy, and the various local (low-status, L) varieties (Maghreb, Egyptian, Levantine, Iraqi, etc.), used as vernacular spoken languages but never written, was the critical case that led Charles Ferguson to develop the important theoretical notion of diglossia.[50]

Versteegh believes that Arabicization was probably faster even than Islamicization. Before Arabic became the dominant language, the language situation in the territories that were later conquered was something like this. There were pockets of South Arabian in Yemen and the south. Aramaic remained the main language of Iraq, with Pahlavi as an administrative language and Arabic used among the nomads. In Syria, Greek was the language of administration, although isolated Christian communities continued to use Syriac, a version of Aramaic. Pahlavi remained the administrative language of Persia for a while, but after the conquest it was replaced by Arabic, which by the ninth century CE was also the language of high culture. In the Persian provinces, Dari (a colloquial version of Parsi that had been the language of the Sassanian court) became the vernacular by the ninth century CE. In Egypt, Greek had been the language of the elite, and Coptic the vernacular of the masses, but there was constant migration from Arabia, so that by the tenth century CE the Coptic patriarch was complaining that Copts no longer spoke Greek or Coptic and were communicating in Arabic. In north Africa, Arabs occupied the few urban centers, and in the tenth century Arabic spread to other towns, though Berber remained the language of the countryside and the nomads. A million Bedouin were then settled in north Africa, spreading Arabic wherever they settled. After the conquest of Spain, Arabic became the language of administration, religion, and literature, and was widely spoken.

Each of these New Arabics involved major phonological changes and morphological simplification. The traditional Muslim view of the process was corruption, producing *fāsad al-luga*, a state of corruption that had to be corrected by the Arab grammarians intent on preserving the purity of the language in which God had given the Qur'an. Versteegh claims that it was the problems of the conquered peoples in learning Arabic that produced the regional varieties, and that these problems are responsible for "a category of texts with deviations from the classical standard language".[51]

"Judaeo-Arabic" (as he spells it) and Christian Middle Arabic were special varieties, with their own norms. Judeo-Arabic developed early on, and the first Jewish literary texts in Arabic date from the ninth century CE; non-literary texts have been found from the tenth century. These are not the result of learners' errors but a variety for Jewish internal use, for Maimonides could write Classical Arabic when writing to Muslims. The variety is marked by use of

Hebrew script – a clear sign of Jewish isolation – and by a large number of Hebrew loanwords. It draws on both Classical and post-Classical Arabic, and on various dialects of spoken Arabic, includes Hebrew and Aramaic features and pseudocorrections, and constitutes a mixed religiolect.[52] In fact, it was the double barrier (internally and externally imposed social isolation) that generally explains the development of Jewish varieties.

During the first two Islamic centuries the Arabic language underwent a variety of changes, simplifying and borrowing from the languages with which it came into contact, and evolved into various Middle Arabic dialects. Middle Arabic, a name proposed by Joseph Blau for what he calls the "missing link between Classical Arabic and modern dialects",[53] refers to the spoken variety of the Arabic language. The H variety – following the strictest rules of the language used in the Qur'an – was preserved for sacred and literacy use. The L variety was widely spoken but was written mainly by Christians (there are manuscripts from the ninth and tenth centuries) and Jews (though there are Muslim letters written in it), who also were not permitted to study the Qur'an, which was the model of the classical language. These L varieties dropped some of the morphology of the old Arabian dialects and of the classical literary language, putting more weight on the syntax and requiring an enriched lexicon. More recently, some scholars have proposed it be called "Mixed" rather than "Middle" Arabic.[54]

By the tenth century CE a variety of Middle Arabic had become not only the daily vernacular of Jews from Iraq in the east to Spain in the west but also their language for nearly all forms of written expression, ranging from every-day personal and business correspondence to religious queries and answers, legal documents, biblical and textual commentaries, philosophy and theology treatises, and works on Hebrew grammar and lexicography, which were developed on Arabic models. Over half the fragments in the Cairo Genizah are in Judeo-Arabic. It was probably not a serious problem for Jews to switch from the Aramaic they were speaking – which was also the language of the surrounding Gentile communities – to the Arabic that was being adopted so widely. Arabic became the language of Jewish daily life, and was also used for religious writing.[55]

Many thousands of Judeo-Arabic letters, documents, and books were discovered in the Cairo Genizah. According to Jewish law, Jewish sacred writings (which include private letters that include a blessing) may not be discarded or burned, but they have to be hidden (*ganuz*) in a room attached to a synagogue, and are usually buried later in a cemetery. The discovery of such a room attached to the Ben Ezra synagogue in Cairo in the eighteenth century, and its exploration by the British scholar Solomon Schechter in 1897/8, produced a store of more than a quarter of a million manuscript fragments (193,000 of which are now at Cambridge University), resulting in a set of sources for medieval Jewish studies that had an impact not unlike that of the Dead Sea Scrolls at Qumran for biblical studies.

From this evidence, we learn that Jews normally wrote Arabic in Hebrew characters, which they had learned in early childhood for reading Hebrew prayers and sacred texts. It is evident from the material in the Genizah that those Jews who could read Arabic script with some degree of proficiency, and who sometimes wrote in Arabic script for non-Jews, had books by Muslim writers transcribed into Hebrew letters for more convenient reading, or perhaps because they were nervous about owning a Qur'an in Arabic letters.[56]

There were several levels of Middle Arabic. At the highest level was a Classical Arabic with some Middle Arabic elements, used in works of philosophy, biblical translation and exegesis, treatises on grammar and poetry, and belle-lettristic essays. Less formal, with a great deal of colloquialism, would be the personal correspondence of people of various levels of education. Furthermore, Middle Arabic written by Jews included many linguistic elements, especially nouns, borrowed from Hebrew and Aramaic. There were regular quotations from the Bible and other religious texts. It was probably because of their limited proficiency in Classical Arabic, however, that Jews wrote poetry not in Middle Arabic but in Hebrew.[57] Blau points out also that texts showed signs of attempts at classicization, or what might be called hypercorrection.

Jewish sacred texts of the period were written primarily in Hebrew and Aramaic but there were also translations into Jewish varieties such as the Judeo-Aramaic Targumim. In later Judeo-Arabic, this genre is known as *sharḥ* (plural *shurūḥ*). It is found in other Jewish varieties, including Judeo-Italian, Judeo-Aramaic, Yiddish, Ladino, Judeo-Persian, Judeo-Berber, Judeo Malayalam, and others. These *shurūḥ* or Targumim are not so much translations as interpretations or commentaries, reflecting a continued tradition of Jewish teaching by the teacher reading a sentence in the original Hebrew and then explaining it in the vernacular language of instruction. The existence of these Bible translations does not prove a popular loss of Hebrew proficiency but, rather, the development of instruction in the vernacular.

The *shurūḥ* are sometimes said to have been composed primarily for the use of women and children whose Hebrew was not good enough.[58] In fact, Jews continued to read the Bible in Hebrew all over the world, although with an Aramaic Targum. The Judeo-Arabic translations were written mostly in Hebrew characters, and sometimes included Hebrew and Aramaic words and elements; they followed the syntactic structures of the Hebrew or Aramaic original rather than those of the Judeo-Arabic.[59]

A tradition of biblical translation, which had already been used in the Targum, no doubt played a key role in shaping the *sharḥ*. The translations imitated the Hebrew original as literally as possible, so that the *shurūḥ* gained acceptance as holy texts themselves. There were two exceptions. In the tenth century Sa'adya Gaon, appointed head of the Yeshiva at Surah in spite of his birth in Egypt, produced a Judeo-Arabic translation of the Bible that followed the model of post-

Classical Arabic; it became a popular text that was widely used and read throughout the Arabic-speaking Jewish world. Other writers followed his example.[60] Later, in the fifteenth and sixteenth centuries, more literal translations were produced for educational reasons.[61] They were also intended for women.

Jewish communities of medieval north Africa

After the defeats of the Bar Kokhba rebellion and the rebellion in Egypt, the Jewish community in Egypt had virtually disappeared. Once Diocletian had put down rebellions in Egypt at the end of the third century CE a peaceful period followed, during which there was slow growth in established Christianity. Jewish names and Hebrew inscriptions reappeared. But, apart from an account of the pogrom of the patriarch Cyril, who in the early fifth century expelled some or all of the Jews from Alexandria, there is little evidence of Jews in Egypt until the end of the tenth century.[62] By then a community had developed in the new Arab city of Fustat (which was destroyed in the twelfth century and incorporated into Cairo). There were commercial ties with Tunisia, relations with the Yeshivot in Babylonia, and the growth of Jewish communities settled by Jews from Palestine, Babylonia, and Syria, each of which established their own synagogues. There were also Karaite communities. Under the Fatimids in the tenth century CE, Jews shared in the prosperity and tolerance of the rulers, developing major trade relations with India and the Far East. Benjamin of Tudela, visiting in about 1171, estimated a Jewish population between 12,000 and 20,000 – a marked contrast with the tiny communities he reported in Europe. Jewish scholarship also developed, and an academy existed at Fustat by the end of the tenth century.

At the end of the Fatimid dynasty, Salah al Din renewed the discriminatory laws against non-Muslims, but there was little or no active persecution until the Mamluks came to power in the thirteenth century, when Jews and Christians suffered alike. This continued until the conquest by the Ottomans in 1517, with varying levels of tolerance according to the governor of the time. The population was increased by the arrival of Jews expelled from Spain. In the sixteenth century there were three distinct communities: indigenous Arabic-speaking Jews (*musta'arabim*), Spanish immigrants, and *Mograbim* (Jews from the Maghreb).[63]

Further west, the area named by the Romans *Provincia Africa* included present-day Tunisia, western Algeria (also known as Numidia), and eastern Libya. There are reports of early Jewish settlement in Punic Carthage, and evidence of Jewish communities there under Roman rule. There are many Jewish lamps and Latin inscriptions with a menorah in cemeteries around Latin Carthage, which is also known for major Talmudic scholars from the second to fourth centuries CE.

There were large Jewish communities throughout the area, with important synagogues. Under Constantine, persecution started, and there was forced conversion under Justinian, which led to many Jews fleeing to Berber areas.

Under the Fatimids, Jews prospered and founded a number of Yeshivot. The communities included many scholars as well as successful merchants, who traded with the Far East. In 1159 Tunisia was invaded by the Almohads, who forced Christians and Jews to convert. Only after 1228, with Tunisian independence, were they allowed to return to their religion, and conditions for trade improved. During this period Jews played a major role in trade with Spain. Djerba became a major center. Many Jews moved from Spain to north Africa after the persecutions of 1391, and more refugees came after 1492.[64]

A Judaized Berber tribe ruled by a Jewish *kahina* (woman priest) had won a number of victories against the invading Muslim Arabs in the seventh century CE, but the defense collapsed after her death in 693; Jewish inhabitants either converted or moved west and south. The invading Arab armies were followed by Jews from Arabia or other Berber areas, who established communities in the urban centers. They were in touch with Fez and Kairouan, as well as with the Babylonian Yeshivot. There were also Karaites among the Berber tribes.[65]

During the Almohad period the Jewish community of Tlemchen in Algeria was destroyed, but it was restored in the thirteenth century. In the thirteenth and fourteenth centuries many merchants from the Maghreb carried on active trade with Catalonia, Languedoc, and other Aragonese territories. Many Spanish refugees arrived in 1391. Important Jewish centers of learning developed. Some refugees came from Spain in 1492, but Muslim attacks on Tlemchen and Christian raids on Oran damaged the communities; subsequently, communities developed in Oran and Bougie, and *Anusim* and Italian Jews settled in Algiers. From the seventeenth century onwards each developed its own ritual, with disputes in Algiers in the eighteenth century over liturgy. The French conquered Algeria in 1830,[66] introducing European settlement and a new language, French, which most Christians and Jews adopted quite rapidly.

The earliest evidence of Jewish settlement in Morocco is second-century CE Greek and Hebrew inscriptions near Fez and near Rabat. Muslim historians report that Berber tribes were converted to Judaism. Thousands of Jews moved to the region after the Visigothic persecutions of the seventh century CE. Jews and Judaized Berbers lived throughout the region. After the Arabic conquest important centers of learning developed, and the migration to Spain did not weaken the communities. Maimonides (who was born in Cordoba in 1135) and his family settled in Fez after leaving Spain because of the Almohad persecutions. Here he studied at the university and composed a commentary on the Mishnah. In 1168, after a brief time in Palestine, he settled in Fustat in Egypt. Most of Maimonides' works were written in Judeo-Arabic, but the *Mishne Torah* was written in Hebrew. Almohad domination in 1154 ended this period of tolerance in Morocco, and there was persecution and forced conversion to Islam, which gradually worsened after 1165. Many Jews moved to Christian Spain, settling in Aragon, Catalonia, and Majorca. The fourteenth century was more favorable, with Jews essentially controlling the Sahara gold trade. Some Jews, but not learned ones, came to Morocco after 1492, and *conversos* continued to arrive.[67]

Some questions about the relationship of north African Jewry to Ashkenazi and Sephardi Jews have been answered by a recent genetic study, which reported finding distinctive north African population groups.[68] Linguistically, the Jewish settlers adopted Arabic or Berber; some from Spain preserved Judezmo. By the late fifteenth century modern varieties of Judeo-Arabic started to appear, some of which absorbed Spanish borrowings. Literature was produced in Judeo-Arabic, but rabbinical works continued to be written in Hebrew. There were translation of sacred texts, and biblical commentaries written in Judeo-Arabic. Ethical literature (*musar*) and handbooks of Jewish laws, particular those aimed at women, were written by rabbis in Judeo-Arabic. From the fifteenth to the nineteenth centuries there was a shift in Judeo-Arabic, reflecting the increased isolation of Jews from Muslims in Jewish quarters: texts were written for the general Jewish population, and scholars starting to prefer writing in Hebrew.[69]

In the nineteenth century Judeo-Arabic newspapers and periodicals began appearing, especially in Tunisia, where more than seventy appeared between 1878 and the late 1930s. They played an important part in modernization. After World War I Judeo-Arabic periodicals increasingly gave way to French publications, from Morocco to Egypt, on account of the tremendous educational influence of the schools of the Alliance Israélite Universelle and the impact of French colonial rule. In the twentieth century Judeo-Arabic started to develop local centers with clear dialectal differentiation.[70]

Arabic took its place as a major language of the Jews partly because of conversions and migration but even more as a result of the Islamic conquest of regions where Jews lived. Being a Semitic language, Arabic was not very difficult for Jews to learn, so there was generally a fairly rapid development of Judeo-Arabic as a vernacular, replacing the Judeo-Aramaic or Judeo-Greek that had become common. Islam was on the whole more accepting of Judaism and Jews than Christianity was, though it insisted on a second-class status for *Dhimmi* minorities and regularly persecuted Jews, forcing conversion or expulsion. It generally enforced an isolated status, which led to the development of Judeo-Arabic rather than the learning of the Classical Arabic language, for writing as well as speaking. In Chapter 9 we will follow this connection into Spain (which, together with north Africa, formed Andalusia) and find a move to Judeo-Latin, which developed into Judeo-Spanish; after 1492 many expelled Judeo-Spanish speakers returned to north Africa, where they developed another Jewish language, *Haketia*, a Moroccan Romance variety.[71] First, however, we look at the settlement of Jews in Tsarfat, the area that is now northern France.

The languages of the Jews of Tsarfat

Medieval France, which included the Norman French-speaking Jewish community of medieval England, illustrates what Fishman has defined as diglossia, for all the evidence suggests that the Jews spoke a variety of French and wrote Hebrew. There is a dispute about the existence of Judeo-French, some arguing that "there never existed a Judeo-French dialect with specific Jewish traits, but they did speak Old French as mother tongue and within the community as well as in intercommunity relations".[1] Others argue that the Jews there switched regularly between Hebrew and French.[2]

The evidence for the high level of Hebrew knowledge among Jewish scholars is in the continuing significance of biblical and Talmudic commentaries written at the time. When one is studying the Torah nowadays, the first and most important commentary is that written by Rashi; and, when one is studying a page of Talmud, the major commentaries on the left and right of the Talmudic text are those by Rashi and what are called "Tosafot", which are "additional" commentaries that expand on or contradict Rashi and are mainly written by Rashi's children, grandchildren, and pupils in France – although, showing the close relationship of Tsarfat (northern France) and Loter (Germany), also by other Tosafists living in Germany. Without these commentaries from medieval France, the task of studying these fundamental Jewish texts would be significantly more difficult.

The evidence that the Jewish community spoke French rather than Hebrew is the fact that Rashi and the writers of the Tosafot provided glosses in Old French for a large number of the Hebrew words in their commentaries. These glosses, it has been suggested, are, like the Aramaic Targumim, to be seen more as interpretations than as translations, but nonetheless they imply that these scholars were writing for a French-speaking readership. As we shall see, this period of strong bilingualism and high Jewish scholarship took place during 300 years of very mixed acceptance by the Gentile world and was closed by expulsion of the Jews. The adoption of French does show, however, that there must have been a period of comparatively easy relationship with the Christians among whom the Jews lived.

The parts of Gaul

While France is nowadays again a major center of Jewish population, the Jews living there today are not the continuation of a long history of settlement, for, just as English Jewry had to be reconstituted after several centuries of being banned, the expulsion of Jews from France in the thirteenth and fourteenth centuries broke for several hundred years the chain of Jews living there. Nor, as was the case with Spanish Jews, was it preserved afterwards in a distinctive language or culture, but it merged into the Jewish culture of Loter, forming Ashkenaz.[3] The Jewish medieval varieties of both northern and southern France disappeared, preserved only in contemporary written sources[4] and in a few words in the Yiddish[5] that those who moved east spoke next. In spite of the regular persecutions and expulsions, though, the Jewish scholars of the region made major contributions to the building of a rich literature of biblical and Talmudic commentaries.

Gaul, we learned in the days we read Caesar in school, was divided into three parts. It was conquered by Julius Caesar in the Gallic Wars (58–51 BCE). By the fifth century CE, when the Germanic invasion began, it was largely Romanized. Clovis I, at the end of the fifth century, united the Franks into a unified kingdom; a Christian, he was also a Roman official. He founded the Merovingian dynasty, which ruled for the next two centuries, to be replaced by the Carolingians, whose major figure, Charlemagne, was crowned emperor by the Pope in 800 CE.

Under Charlemagne, Jews belonged to the emperor and were allowed to engage in trade. By the end of the century, however, central rule ended and France was divided into a number of local units, each ruled by its own prince and recognizing the king only as a religious authority. It was not until the thirteenth century that France was once more under central control, but this was followed by the Hundred Years War, between the French Capetian kings and the English Plantagenets, and by the devastation of the Black Death and civil wars; in the aftermath there were many attacks on Jewish communities, and ultimately Jews were expelled from France as well as England.

By the time Jews first arrived in Gaul, the territory had been Romanized and its inhabitants were speaking a variety of Latin that had replaced the original Celtic and that had been influenced by the invading Germanic tribes – the Franks, the Alemani, the Burgundians, and the Visigoths in different areas – later developing into the various dialects of Old French. Old French was the variety that developed in the north from Old Frankish; the earliest documents are the Strasbourg Oaths, dated to the middle of the ninth century CE and trilingual, in Medieval Latin, Old French (*langue d'oil*), and Old High German. Already, at the beginning of the century, priests had been instructed to preach in the vernacular, either Romance or Germanic, as people no longer understood Latin. In the south, the major variety was Old Occitan (*langue d'oc*), also called

Old Provençal, with half a dozen dialects, which was first written in the ninth century, and from which Catalan later developed. Essentially, until the linguistic reforms initiated by Cardinal Richelieu in the eighteenth century,[6] the French population spoke many dialects, and presumably Jews picked up the local variety wherever they lived.

There is very little evidence of early Jewish settlement. One of the earliest references concerns Archelaus, the son of Herod, appointed as Ethnarch (head of the province of Palestine) by Augustus Caesar in 4 BCE, though he was bitterly opposed by Antipas (his younger brother) and by many Jews because of his slaughter of Pharisees; in 6 CE he was deposed and banished to Vienne in Gaul.[7] Antipas (reputed to be responsible for the death of John the Baptist and Jesus) was, in turn, exiled by Caligula to Lugdunum (which may have been Lyons or a smaller town on the Spanish border). A legendary source claims that three shiploads of Jews were sent to France after the destruction of the Temple. There are possible Jewish remains in Arles and Bordeaux, and possible written evidence of Jewish presence before the fifth century CE, when there is stronger evidence of Jewish settlement in a number of towns.

Jewish migrants originally settled in the Mediterranean ports, but signs of northward movement started to appear as early as the sixth century CE, with reports of Jewish physicians, tax collectors, and farmers in Merovingian Champagne. In the middle of the century a Church council at Troyes banned Jews from being out of doors or in contact with Christians during Holy Week. Laws were passed against intermarriage, and, in 538, against Jews and Christians eating together. There are reports of Jews being killed, and papal decrees on forced conversion. In 629 King Dagobert ordered Jews to be baptized or expelled, and there were no Jews reported in the Frankish kingdom for the next century.[8]

The Jewish population was re-established by immigration from Visigothic Christian Spain in the seventh century and by proselytism.[9] To understand Christian attitudes to Jews in this period, we need to recognize the origins of Christianity close to and within Judaism, creating an early need to repudiate the Jewish religion and establish a clearly differentiated identity. While there are now many who accept that the division was not early,[10] the period of shared views made the need to emphasize the distinction even more pressing. Jews were seen as a threat because of their ability to argue against Christian beliefs and their claim to have better interpretations of the biblical sources that both accepted because they knew Hebrew. Constantine, when he was converted to Christianity, set restrictions on Jewish life, such as forbidding them to convert slaves. Augustine confirmed the requirement to preserve and protect Jews, both as evidence of the sin that had led to their exile and in the anticipation of their ultimate conversion. This ambivalence – the Jewish right of existence, and the need to place restrictions on them – was the basis of treatment of the Jews by the

Christians.[11] By 1000 CE, when Jewish numbers in Christendom started to rise, they had been used to living as subject peoples, under Babylonian, Greek, Roman, and – later – Islamic rule, maintaining their own autonomous existence but without independence, and finding in their institutions and religion a firm set of personal and communal guidelines.[12]

Southern France

While unified under the Romans and again in the eighteenth century, in between France was mainly broken up into local lordships. From the Jewish perspective, the major distinction was the border between the south, with connections to Sepharad or Spain, and the north, which merged into the Rhineland and Loter-Ashkenaz. In southern France, Jewish settlement dated back to Roman times. Among the handful of small communities, Narbonne in Occitan was especially well known. It was under Muslim rule until 759 CE. A seventh-century epitaph in Latin includes a menorah and the words *Shalom leyisrael* misspelled in Hebrew. When Narbonne became subject to a Carolingian viscountancy, Pepin, its ruler, is reported to have invited Jews from Baghdad to settle there, and there are several legendary reports of Jewish "kings".

The Jewish population of Narbonne, the westernmost of the southern towns, grew to between 1,500 and 2,000 in the twelfth century. There were at least two synagogues and a Jewish hospital. Jews were expelled in 1306, but some returned at the end of the century. The community was distinguished for Jewish scholarship. Narbonne was important for the development of two Jewish language varieties, Chuadit (Judeo-Provençal)[13] and Tsarfatic (Judeo-French).[14]

The Kimhi family lived there; the father was Joseph, an important twelfth-century grammarian and biblical commentator who had left Spain because of Muslim persecution. One son was Moses, who was born in Narbonne and wrote essays on grammar, and a second son was David Kimhi, known as the RaDak and famous for his biblical commentaries, his grammatical works and dictionary, and his work in philosophy and science. Benjamin of Tudela wrote about Narbonne as a city of Jewish learning, with 300 Jews.[15]

Under the Capet dynasty, which ruled France from the late tenth century to the early fourteenth, there were many cases of persecution, and canons forbidding Jewish–Christian relations. Jews were believed to be plotting with the Muslims to destroy the Church of the Holy Sepulchre in Jerusalem, which led to a number of Jews being expelled in 1010. Jews were expelled from Narbonne in 1394.

Further east, Montpellier was another medieval Jewish center, the community having been established by a number of Jewish physicians and strong commercial activity in the twelfth and thirteenth centuries. Ejected at the beginning of the fourteenth century, allowed to return in mid-century, forced to wear a badge, the Jews of Montpellier were finally expelled in 1394. There was a highly respected Yeshiva there in the twelfth century.

Jews settled early on in Béziers, where they were persecuted by the Visigoths, but conditions improved under Carolingian rule. In the thirteenth century many Jews died when the city was captured by Count Simon de Montfort, and conditions afterwards remained bad. This town too had a number of important Jewish scholars.

Jews were reported to have lived in Lunel even before the Roman conquest, and it became a major center of Jewish learning later. Benjamin of Tudela praised the learning of the town and the hospitality of the wealthy Jewish citizens, who supported students studying in the Yeshiva. Conditions were generally good until the fourteenth century.

Although the community of Posquières was not large, it was also recognized for its Jewish learning. The Rabad (Rabbi Abraham ben David), who died in 1198, was a well-known Halachic critic.

There were distinguished Talmudists in St. Gilles, especially known also for a Jewish magistrate appointed by the king in the middle of the twelfth century. There were Jews in Arles quite early on, and conditions were reasonably good under the Carolingians. Benjamin of Tudela reported that there were 200 Jewish families, headed by six rabbis, living in a separate quarter. There were severe restrictions in the second half of the fourteenth century. The first Hebrew concordance of the Bible was written in Arles.

A number of Jews settled in Marseilles, the easternmost of the southern communities in the sixth century. When Benjamin of Tudela visited, there were two synagogues and about 300 Jews there. Conditions varied in the thirteenth century: Jews were citizens but with limited rights, being required to wear badges and not work on Sundays. In the fourteenth century they were permitted to engage in all trades; most were merchants, tailors, or brokers; some were physicians. The Jews were protected into the fifteenth century, though there were massacres towards the end of the century and demands for their expulsion. A royal decree of banishment was finally put into effect at the end of the century. There was a Jewish quarter, called "Insula Jazatarie", with two synagogues and a hospital. A number of famous Jewish scholars lived there; Maimonides addressed a letter on astrology to them.

During the twelfth and thirteenth centuries the Jewish communities of Languedoc (the five communities west of the Rhone) were particularly creative, but Jews were banished in 1306 by the Capetian rulers.[16]

Jews as others: the basis for anti-Semitism

From time to time before the First Crusade, and regularly after it, Jewish history in Christendom is marked by distrust, hatred, persecution, slaughter, and expulsion. The Albigensian Crusade and the killing of those who were later called Cathars is the topic of a recent book by Robert Moore.[17] His main thesis is that the "heretics" who were burned – a method of killing that exempted the Church from the sin of shedding blood – were not in fact heretics or dualists, like many Eastern Orthodox sects, but simply extreme reformers whose existence challenged the political power of the Pope. But they were regularly excoriated not just as dualists but as part of the category of "enemies of the Church" – "Jews, tyrants, false brethren, heretics" accused not only of heresy but of being "Jews or Muslims, of being homosexual, of being lepers, of being witches, and so on. . .".[18]

In the 1140s Peter the Venerable wrote three treatises, one each against the Petrobrusians, the "obstinacy of the Jews", and the Muslims.[19] Chalices and sacred Christian objects left with Jews would be kept in privies and foully treated, he wrote; this became a theme of twelfth-century anti-Semitism.[20] Raymond of Toulouse was humiliated in 1209 for, among other things, employing Jews.[21] Thus, there was strong religious backing for the hatred and persecution of Jews as "others", aliens who did not fit a Christian society.[22] There was no Pact of Umar to define their subordinate conditions, but only with protection from bishops and civil rulers who benefited from their trade and lending practices could they live in Christian territory.

Jewish communities in northern France

Northern France was different from the south, for the Jewish communities were new, not having been under Byzantine or Muslim rule. Jews in Tsarfat and Loter started to develop the culture defined as "Ashkenaz". The region was marked by the growing power of the French monarchy, forming the basis of Western political structure; in particular, it showed an alliance of government with the Church.[23]

There had been earlier Jewish settlement, but there are no physical or other traces, so that the history of the Jewish communities in the north starts in the eleventh and twelfth centuries, though there is still little information from this early part of the period. Jews seem to have moved here with the goal of engaging in trade in a region that was developing rapidly and that was prepared to accept Jewish immigration. Of particular importance was the enterprise of moneylending, which grew rapidly in the twelfth century. While successful economically, it was an activity that led to more hatred of the Jews. There were bursts of anti-Jewish violence associated with the First Crusade and with regular reports of the blood libel, the false accusation that Jews used the blood of Christian children for ritual purposes, such as making unleavened bread at Passover. Jews were often protected by the king and other nobles, but regularly suffered from confiscation of wealth and cancellation of Christian debts to Jews.

In response, the Jewish communities developed methods of defense and cooperation. This was also a period of intense Jewish religious and literary creativity, as demonstrated by Rashi and his followers.

At the end of the twelfth century, with the accession of King Philip Augustus, there were major changes. First, Philip extended the royal territory, bringing more Jews under his control. Second, he set out to restrict Jewish movement and to exploit them financially: in 1210, for instance, Jews in northern France had much of their property expropriated. Third, after complaints from the Church, he instituted a number of restrictions on Jewish moneylending. This was followed by an attack on Jewish learning and the Talmud in particular, and the burning of Jewish books: in 1242 Louis IX ordered the burning of about twenty cartloads (10,000 volumes) of Jewish manuscripts. Under Louis IX there was a ban on Jewish usury. In the thirteenth century forced conversions and expulsions began, and in 1306 Jews were ordered to leave royal France. Louis X allowed Jews to return in 1315, but at the same time set many new restrictions on Jewish usury and difficult conditions on repurchasing synagogues and other property. Some Jews returned, but the communities remained weak, so that the final expulsion order of 1392 had little effect.

Jewish communities in the north

Spreading north from the Mediterranean, Jewish settlement followed the Rhône, the normal means of trade and movement. Avignon had a Jewish quarter by the fourth century CE, and there probably were Jews there as early as the second century. The Jewish quarter, known as the Carrière des Juifs, was rebuilt in the thirteenth century. The community was semi-autonomous, under the supervision of the Church. In the fifteenth century there was an influx of Jewish refugees from the south, and conditions became bad after a series of attacks on the city and plagues. Heavy taxes were levied on the Jews.

There was a Jewish community in Vienne by the tenth century, a Jewish quarter, and – later – a beautiful synagogue. A number of scholars lived there, including one Tosafist. Jews lived in Dijon from quite an early stage, and there were two Jewish quarters. In the fourteenth century there was a small community, and the expulsion order reduced it further. There was no effective return until the French Revolution.

By the sixth century CE there was a Jewish community in Paris, praying in a synagogue built on the Ile de France that was converted into the church of St. Madeleine in 1183.[24] At the beginning of the seventh century CE the sixth Council of Paris decided that Jews who held public office had to convert to Christianity. By the tenth century the Jews of Paris were reported to be wealthy and to own much land.[25]

A blood libel in Blois in 1171 resulted in the imprisonment of thirty-one of the forty Jews said to live there.[26] A ritual murder accusation had been made at Norwich and Gloucester a few years earlier, and was repeated in Paris in 1180 and later elsewhere in France and in Germany. As a result, in 1182 Philip Augustus ordered Jews to be expelled, and confiscated their houses, some of which were given to the drapers and furriers of Paris. Jews were permitted to return in 1198, and a new Jewish quarter created, which in 1294 became a ghetto.

Troyes, where Rashi was rabbi, was a small community in central France, settled in the early eleventh century, where Jews owned vineyards and, from the thirteenth century, were moneylenders. In 1288 there was a blood libel and thirteen Jews were publicly burned. A few Jews continued to live in Troyes after the expulsion of 1322.

The crusades

The First Crusade, preached by Pope Urban II, gathered in France in 1095 on its way to Germany, attacking Jews in Rouen and Lorraine on their way to their attacks on Jewish communities in Cologne and Mainz. There were massacres of Jews in these and other German cities – Speyer and Worms (which also included Jews who had been protected by the local bishop), Trier, Regensburg, and Metz, and in Prague and towns in Bohemia. When the crusaders finally reached Jerusalem, in 1099, they killed Muslims and Jews alike, wiping out the Jewish community there.

The Second Crusade, in 1145–9, was aimed at the Jews of the Rhineland; the Jews of France were comparatively spared. The Third Crusade (1189–92) had its main effects on the Jews of England, where several communities, including that of York, were massacred. In 1236 there were massacres in central France, and in 1320 a "popular" crusade of young "shepherds" (*pastoureaux*), though threatened with excommunication by the Pope, marched through France, wiping out 120 Jewish communities south of the Loire and carrying out massacres in the town of Midi and in northern Spain. A number of ineffective directives were issued by the popes against these excesses.

From the twelfth century on, Christians saw the Jews as alien and enemies. Many Jews wrote about martyrdom in prayers and in *piyyutim* that mourned the massacres. In time, most of the destroyed French Jewish communities were re-established, and in the later twelfth century Jewish scholarship, especially the work of the Tosafists, the medieval rabbis who continued the work of Rashi in expounding and developing the Talmud, flourished, showing a high level of Hebrew and Aramaic knowledge. But the economic role of Jews as traders diminished, and their status as moneylenders become more significant.[27]

Anti-Jewish persecution continued regularly, with periodic expulsions – from Gascony in 1289, from Paris in 1306, from Lorraine, Alsace, and the rest of France in 1394. After this, Jews moved to Germany, Spain, and Italy. From time to time after this some Jews were readmitted for the financial services they provided, but for limited periods only, and persecution and massacres continued. Even in these difficult time, Jewish scholarship – mainly in the form of biblical and Talmudic commentaries and liturgy in the north, and grammatical and scientific studies and translation from Arabic and Latin in the south – continued to flourish.[28]

After the expulsions, it was not until the seventeenth century that many Jews returned to France, but they were soon expelled again; only in the eighteenth century was a community of Portuguese and German Jews tolerated in Paris. The Jewish question was debated at the end of the century during the French Revolution, and some Jews were awarded citizenship. In 1791 a resolution of the National Assembly granted full rights to Jews, and, while there were various modifications later and under Napoleon I, only in 1846 was the More Judaico, a humiliating oath administered to Jews since the Middle Ages, abolished. Jews could assimilate, but French anti-Semitism continued, especially with the Dreyfus affair and again under the Vichy regime.

Judeo-French

It was during the twelfth century that the major Jewish languages of France developed. There had been Jews in the south since Roman times, speaking a Jewish variety of Provençal (Provense or Chuadit), a continuation of Roman-Loez, and a compromise between the language varieties of Spain and northern France.[29] It was in the south that many major Spanish Jewish works – the *Kuzari* and *Moreh Nevukhim* (*The Guide to the Perplexed*), for instance – were translated from Arabic into Hebrew by Samuel ibn Gibbon, who translated the *Moreh Nevukhim* from the Arabic in which Maimonides had written it into Hebrew at the request of scholars of Lunel.

There were dense patterns of Jewish settlement in the south, and also north of the Loire, but little in between. Weinreich suggests that Troyes in the north was spiritually closer to Mainz in Germany, and even to Prague, than it was to the cities of Provense: Tsarfat, Loter, and Knaan (Slavic regions) formed a kind of union. Rashi, living in Troyes, knew no Arabic. Judeo-Provençal, on the other hand, showed no signs of German influence, but was influenced by Judeo-Arabic. Even though Jews were expelled from much of the south in 1394, they remained in Provence proper and the independent Carolingian state until the sixteenth century, and in Comtat Venaissin (which was under papal rule) until 1791; evidence of the Jewish variety persisted. Provense persists also in glosses from the twelfth century and in a fourteenth-century novel. It is closer to

Judezmo than to Judeo-French. The modern variety, attested as late as 1977, is known as Chuadit:[30] Armand Lunel, who died then, learned it from his grandparents and remembered a song in it.[31] This lack of connection between the south and Loter explains, Weinreich argues, the lack of Judezmo influence on Yiddish.

There are few Jewish works in Old French. There is a translation from Hebrew of an astronomical book, *The Beginning of Wisdom*, written by Abraham ibn Ezra and translated by Hagin de Juif. Exceptionally, it was dictated to an amanuensis who was probably a speaker of the Picard dialect.[32] There are many errors and Hebraisms in the text. But glosses (*le'azim*) in Rashi and the Talmud provide valuable information on the nature of Old French.[33] These glosses give in Hebrew letters translations and explanations of difficult Hebrew and Aramaic words: they date from the eleventh century, the largest number being in the writings of Rashi (about 1,300 words) and the Talmud (over 3,500). The first major collection of these words was made in the 1930s;[34] a larger collection, intended for students of Old French, of 10,500 glosses compiled from fifty medieval Jewish manuscripts has been published.[35]

An article on the Jewish languages research website by Marc Kiwitt, a researcher on the *Dictionnaire Étymologique de l'Ancien Français*, summarizes the evidence on the nature of the French used by Jews in the medieval period.[36] He notes first the disagreement between scholars of Jewish languages such as Solomon Birnbaum and Weinreich, who believe that there was a distinctive Jewish variety,[37] and scholars of Old French such as Arsène Darmesteter[38] and Menahem Banitt,[39] who argue that Jews simply spoke the local dialect. The texts are written in Hebrew letters. The earliest written examples in the eleventh century appear in Rashi; there are no further glossed texts after the expulsion in the fourteenth century. There are three types of texts: glosses in biblical commentaries, in glossaries, and – towards the end of the period – in secular texts. The texts show the dialectical features of the regions in which they were written – Champenois, Lotharingian, Burgundian, and Norman – revealing the diffusion of Jewish settlement in medieval France. While there have been some suggestions of possible differences, there is no definitive statement that differentiates Judeo-French from the non-Jewish varieties.[40]

Jews in England before the expulsion

The *loazit* glosses provide evidence that French was the language of the Jewish culture zone of Tsarfat.[41] It was also the language of the Jewish colony in England until their expulsion in 1290. Small numbers of Jews were brought to England from Rouen by William the Conqueror in 1066. The Jews of England followed the same ritual as the Jews of Tsarfat.[42] Small Jewish communities existed in London, Oxford, York, Norwich, and Bristol. The Pipe Roll, an Exchequer document from 1130, mentions Rubi Gotsche as owning property; he may be the Rabbi Joseph Bechor who wrote a commentary on the Torah; there is evidence that his sons kept up connections with Rouen.[43] In 1130 the Jews were fined for a claim that they had killed a sick man, and in 1144 the first blood libel, concerning William of Norwich (who, it seems, had a fit, died, and was buried by his relatives), led to the trial and killing of some Jews.

There was a further influx of Jews to England at the end of the twelfth century. Jews were prominent as financiers and valuable as the source of taxation. Persecution continued, including the 1190 massacre at York. Taxation on Jews increased, and, after England had lost its Norman possessions, trade became more difficult. Under John there was an increased financial burden. During the reign of Henry III there was a temporary improvement, but Jews were soon required to wear a special badge. There were major levies on the Jews; the Church took the lead in persecution, including the burning of copies of the Talmud, and the king treated the Jews as a source of money. The discovery of a dead body (Hugh of Lincoln) led to trials after which 100 Jews were convicted and hanged. Anti-Jewish riots continued, and Jewish property was confiscated. By the return of Edward I from the crusades the Jewish communities had been ruined by the heavy taxation and the non-payment of loans owed them. Finally, in 1290, the Jews were expelled and their property confiscated by the Crown.

The size of the Jewish communities in England is hard to estimate, with London's, numbering some 2,000, making up perhaps a quarter of the total. Most Jews in England came from northern France, spoke French, and had French names such as Benedict, Deulebenie, Deulacresse, Gentilia, as well as Hebrew names such as Isaac. They were serfs of the king, who treated them as a source of funds. Their main occupation was as moneylenders – a profession forbidden to Christians. But there were also physicians and goldsmiths.

All internal legal documents of the community were in Hebrew. All male Jews were literate in Hebrew and most families had tutors. Contracts outside the community, written in Latin, were signed by Jews in Hebrew. Many English Jews were distinguished scholars, the authors of liturgical poems, grammatical works and commentaries, and lexicographical works.[44] Moses ben Isaac HaNessiah of Cambridge, who wrote a grammar called *Sefer ha-Shoham* ("the onyx book"), knew Arabic.[45]

We learn how these tiny persecuted communities kept their identity and language knowledge from the "Code of Jewish education". At the age of five every Jewish boy was to be brought to the "small school [*Yeshiva ketana*] in the provinces" and taught to read a portion of the law in Hebrew, then in the vernacular, then in the Aramaic of the Targum. At ten he began to study the Mishnah, and at thirteen the Tractate *Berakhot* in the Talmud. At sixteen he could go on to the big school (*Yeshiva gedola*) in the capital for seven years. The schools in the provinces were in buildings of two stories; each had 100 pupils, ten teachers, and a "rector", who had to be allowed to go home for the Sabbath. All teachers had ten pupils and went over lessons twice. The boys were expected to examine each other every evening. Teaching was from the book and not by heart. Each member of the community paid two pence yearly as school fees. While the educational system was for boys, even Jewish women were able to draw up deeds in Hebrew.[46]

The tiny but wealthy Jewish community of Angevin England was multi-lingual: it spoke Western Loez, or Norman French, and Middle English and had a good knowledge of Hebrew and Aramaic; some Jews also knew Latin and Arabic. They and the Jews of northern France were expelled in the thirteenth and fourteenth centuries, and permitted to return legally only much later, to England under Cromwell and to France in the eighteenth century. The Jews of Tsarfat, like those of Knaan, disappear from history after the expulsion, though there were three communities in Piedmont reported in the nineteenth century still to be using the French liturgy.[47]

The return to France

The Jews who returned to France from the eighteenth century onwards acquired Modern French, especially once the reforms initiated by Richelieu started to affect the education system in the nineteenth century. There were important effects of the policy of *francophonie*, when the Jews and Christians of the French north African colonies were among the first to switch from Arabic to French; this meant that the quarter of a million Mizrahi Jews who emigrated to Israel from Algeria, Morocco, and Tunisia in the 1960s, forming a majority of the Jewish community, were already French speakers. Their knowledge of French was also the result of the diffusion effects of the Alliance Israélite Universelle, which, starting in 1860, opened schools in Morocco, Tunisia, Turkey, and Palestine to provide French education and culture to Jews in the Middle East.

The linguistic importance of Tsarfat and Provense, the Jewish medieval communities of what is now France, was not in the continuity of the communities (they later migrated to Loter further east and were assimilated into Ashkenaz after the expulsion – unlike the Jews of Sepharad, who moved to north African and Ottoman lands, where they built distinctive communities) but in the contribution that the Jewish variety of Tsarfat made to the development of Yiddish, and the major contributions of Jewish scholars from the region to Jewish culture and knowledge. Although, of course, we do not know very much about the spoken French of the Jews of medieval France, it appears clear that French was the language of the community but that many of them were highly proficient in Hebrew and knew the Hebrew–Aramaic of the Talmud.

Jews in Spain

Jewish settlement in Spain took place at much the same time as settlement in France, and there were contacts between the two communities. The period under Christian rule in Spain was divided in two by an Islamic conquest, however, so the migration of Jews to Spain served to confirm the place of Arabic as a major language of the Jews as well as adding a Romance language, which was the foundation of Ladino, Judezmo, and Haketia.[1] It also provided another example of the growth of Jewish multilingualism resulting from living in societies in which several languages were used, and increased the demand for individual plurilingualism as Jews chose or were continually required to move from one place to another. Each of the three periods of Jewish residence in the Iberian Peninsula ended with the choice of conversion or expulsion, whether by the Visigothic Catholic Hispano-Romans, or the Almohad Berber fanatic Muslims, or the Castilian Catholic monarchy in 1492 (see Map 7). The Jews who converted (*Anusim*)[2] sometimes continued to practice Judaism in secret, and, later, some *Anusim* managed to escape and return to Jewish life in western Europe, north Africa, or the Balkans and Turkey.

There is no evidence to support the legends of Jews in Spain in biblical times, but Jews may have settled there during Roman rule, which started in about 200 CE; a description of Jews attributed to Hecataeus of Abdera, a town on the south coast of Spain from the third century CE, suggests Jewish presence. Latin was the dominant and official language of the Iberian Peninsula by this time, with Vulgar Latin the vernacular, as a result of extensive Roman colonization.

Early Christian Spain

The Romanization of Spain dates from 218 BCE, when Roman soldiers were sent there at the start of the Second Punic War, and the language shift to Latin started with colonization a decade later, in 206 BCE. Over two centuries there was a slow spread of the language, faster in the east and south, where immigration from Latin-speaking areas continued, and slower in other regions; in the

7 Jewish centers in medieval Spain
Source: Stillman (2010b).

Pyrenees, for instance, Basque has persisted up to the present. Urban areas were Latinized more rapidly than rural.

As early as the fourth century CE Ulfilas, a descendant of captured Roman soldiers, ordained by Eusebius and sent as a missionary to the Goths, knew Latin and translated the Bible from Greek into Gothic; according to Arian traditions, he was responsible for the mass conversion of the Goths to Christianity. After the conversion of Spain to Christianity, the Synod of Elvira (now Granada) in the early fourth century was concerned with establishing order in the Church, but it also included a number of canons intended to keep Jews and Christians apart. They forbade marriage between Christians and

Jews or heretics; ostracized a Christian for adultery with a Jew; forbade the blessing of Christian crops by Jews; and forbade Jews and Christians to share a meal.

The process of Romanization was encouraged by groups of captured Roman soldiers who maintained their Roman identity and language and, when freed, intermarried with Goths. In the sixth century some – perhaps most – of the liturgy of the Arian Christians was in Gothic. In the Ostrogothic kingdom of Italy, Romans and Goths were in contact, and learned each other's languages. Amalaswintha, queen of the Ostrogoths from 526 to 534, was said to be more Roman than Goth, and to speak Latin and Greek as well as Gothic.[3] Theodoric, a Goth and follower of Arianis, who had ruled Italy from 493, died in 526, and the Ostrogothic kingdom of Italy was defeated by the Byzantines.

The Visigoths, who entered Spain in the fifth century, were already bilingual in Latin and Gothic, having added Latin in their earlier contacts with the Romans.[4] After the Reconquista – the defeat of the Moorish rulers – when Christian power was re-established, many Spanish historians appealed to myths they found or created describing the Visigothic period to depict an idealized past.[5] There was in fact rapid integration of Visigoth and Hispano-Roman people, however, and the Gothic language started to disappear soon after the conversion to Catholicism. Gothic identity was, it is now believed, reserved for a restricted group of Gothic freemen, a fifth to a half of any multi-ethnic Gothic group. In 376 a large Gothic army had come to the Danube (the limit then of Roman territory) asking for asylum. Two years later they defeated the Eastern Roman emperor Valens at Hadrianople (in European Turkey). In 410 the Gothic king Alaric conquered and sacked Rome.

Visigothic literature in Gothic has been preserved in manuscripts. The major history written in the sixth century CE by Jordanes, a Goth in Constantinople, was in Latin. Visigothic rule – but not language, however – survived in Spain until the Muslim conquest. While there were succession and political problems in the sixth century CE, a new Gothic elitism based on land ownership and including Hispano-Romans developed. Christianity was completely Roman, and in the fifth century included access to Latin biblical texts.[6] By 476 CE King Euric controlled the whole Iberian Peninsula. He knew Gothic; perhaps it survived into the seventh century as a domestic language, but after the conversion to Catholicism it lost its last remaining religious function. Very few Visigothic place names remain, and only a handful of Gothic words are preserved in Spanish.

The Romanized Visigoths who had invaded Spain in 415 established their capital at Toledo, and by 585 they controlled the peninsula. Latin was set as the official language. In 587 the Visigothic king Recarred was converted to Catholicism.[7] At the Third Council of Toledo (589 CE) Arianism was denounced and some anti-Jewish legislation was passed. The fourteenth canon forbade Jews to have Christian wives, concubines, or slaves, required the children of such unions to be baptized, and barred Jews from any positions where they would be able to punish Christians; their slaves were to be freed.

In 613 CE, under King Sisebul, Jews were to be converted; thousands of Jews left Spain for Ceuta and other places in north Africa; others were converted but remained Jewish, secretly forming the first Spanish Crypto-Jews.[8] These latter returned to Judaism under King Swintila (621–631), but the Fourth Council of Toledo, under King Sisenand, required them to continue as Christians. The situation deteriorated under King Chintila (631–639), who forced the Sixth Council of Toledo (638) to establish that only Catholics could live in Spain: Jews had either to convert or to leave. Many did one or the other. The next king stopped enforcing this ban, so that his successor brought the issue to the Eighth Council in 653, setting new rules requiring forced conversion and banning circumcision and keeping the Sabbath (but allowing converts not to eat pork!). Enforcement was weak, so that again, at the Tenth Council, the rules had to be confirmed.

King Wamba (672–680) expelled Jews from Narbonne. His successor, King Erwig (680–687), issued twenty-eight laws condemning the Jews at the Twelfth Council of Toledo, demanding their conversion or expulsion, and setting penalties for any nobles who did not enforce the laws. His successor in turn, Egica, added financial penalties, confiscating Jewish property and forbidding them to do business with Christians. At the Seventeenth Council of Toledo, Egica went even further: all Jews were to be enslaved and their children baptized. Some escaped – mainly back to Muslim north Africa – so that, when the Muslim forces entered the Iberian Peninsula, there were no Jewish communities and only secret Jews left.[9]

Summing up the Jewish experience in pre-Muslim Catholic Visigothic Spain, the continual anti-Jewish canons and royal persecution, compared with the experience of greater freedom (if second-class status) in north Africa, would surely have led the Jews to support the Muslim invasion, but the Seventeenth Council's banishment made sure that only Jews who had moved to north Africa or were on the surface practicing Christians were left to confirm the Christian fears. The sociolinguistic effect was to produce many enslaved former Jews in Spain who were already speakers of the Vulgar Latin that was developing into the Spanish dialects, and others who may have combined this incipient Spanish with a north African variety of Arabic, and even Berber. Again, the Jewish experience produced plurilingual individuals for multilingual communities.

Al-Andalus under Muslim rule

The Muslim invaders, let by a Berber general, invaded Spain in 711 CE. To start, the Jews (*Anusim* released from slavery or returning exiles, for all practicing Jews had been expelled) benefited from the Muslim conquest, being called upon by the conquerors to garrison a number of towns including Cordoba, Granada, Seville, and Toledo, where they were perhaps able to retrieve some of their lost possessions. Initially, during the early days of Muslim rule and the ensuing internal struggles between northern and southern Arabs, on the one hand, and Berbers and Arabs, on the other, Jews seem to have kept very quiet.[10] Under the Umayyad dynasty, established in 755 CE in what was known by Arabs and Jews as al-Andalus, there was relative prosperity and the Jewish population increased. Jews as *Dhimmi* were taxed heavily, but able to work in agriculture, medicine, crafts, and business.[11] Under comparatively tolerant Umayyad rule, the Jews of Spain were able to share in the blossoming Arab culture. Arab historians, Norman Stillman suggests, were more concerned with the struggles with the Christian kingdoms. Jews were an assimilated minority and not a threat like Christians. There was contact between Jews and Christians, with some Christian heresies suggesting Jewish influence.[12]

There was a famous case in 839, when a young Frankish priest named Bodo, brought up in the Carolingian court and taking advantage of the general tolerance at the time of Louis the Pious, set off for Rome, but instead converted to Judaism. He took the name Eleazar, married a Jewess, and moved to Saragossa, where he attempted to convert local Christians to Judaism; he also engaged in a correspondence with a Jewish convert to Christianity, but his letters have been censored.[13]

But Jews remained a tiny minority in al-Andalus, rarely constituting more than half a percent of the total population, though they reached as much as 20 percent or more in a city such as Granada. The Arabs too remained a minority, settling mainly in cities and the south. That is where Muslim and later Jewish culture flourished. The Jews of al-Andalus spoke Arabic in the ninth century CE, but added the Romance varieties of the Christian majority developing from Vulgar Latin, the ancestors of Castilian, Catalan, other Spanish dialects, and Portuguese. Arabs too were bilingual, and some of the poetic forms of the eleventh and twelfth centuries involved mixtures of Classical Arabic and Romance, or Maghreb Arabic; Jewish versions include Hebrew. During this period Jews seem to have been well integrated in their *Dhimmi* status, and not presenting the problems that Christians gave to the ruling Muslims.[14]

Immigrants from north Africa and the Near East added to the Iberian Jewish community, which maintained active communication with the Jewish world. Starting in the ninth century, the Babylonian Gaonim, heads of the two Yeshivot, corresponded with Andalusian rabbis. Teaching of the Talmud began in Spain in the late years of the eighth century CE; a complete prayer book for Andalusian Jews was written by Amram ben Sheshna, Gaon of the Surah Yeshiva; the *Seder Rav Amram* formed the basis for Spanish and Portuguese and German–Polish liturgies. Many *responsa* (answers to

Halachic questions) came to Andalusia from Babylon, especially from the Yeshiva at Surah.[15]

In the tenth century CE, at a time when independent caliphates were developing in Egypt and Baghdad, Amir Abd al-Rahmin III built up the power of the caliphate of Cordova. The Jewish community flourished, as shown by the status of Hasdai ibn Shaprut, Jewish physician to the court, community leader, and adviser to the caliph, for whom he negotiated with the Christian kingdoms in the north and the Holy Roman and Byzantine Empires; he was a distinguished scientist responsible for important translations and discoveries. As leader of the Jewish community, he hosted a regular gathering of artists and intellectuals, and was a patron of a number of poets and scholars. These included Menahem ibn Saruq, a philologist who wrote the first Hebrew–Hebrew dictionary, and Dunash ben Labrat, who strongly criticized the dictionary, which led to a wide public debate on Hebrew grammar. Dunash had studied at Surah and was among the first to write Hebrew poetry with the Arabic meters that later became the standard.

Under the influence of Hasdai ibn Shaprut, the Jewish community of Cordova became independent of Babylonian religious leadership, and he was responsible for the selection of the Italian rabbi Moses ben Hanokh as *Rav Rosh* (Chief Rabbi). The legendary story of his appointment is told by Ibn Daud in the *Sefer Hakabbalah*, written in 1161. Traveling with three others to collect funds for the Yeshiva, he was captured by a Moorish admiral, who fell in love with his wife; with her husband's approval, she drowned herself. Moses was taken to Cordova, where he was redeemed by the community; his learning was recognized, and he was elected rabbi.[16]

After Hasdai's death, in 975 CE, there was a dispute over the position of Chief Rabbi, which remained vacant. Political struggles were also taking place between Berbers and Arabs, and in 1009 Andalusia was split into a number of small kingdoms, in many of which Jews became influential courtiers and bureaucrats.

In Granada, Samuel Ha-Nagid ("the Prince", as he called himself) became vizier in 1037, and was entrusted with an army command, defeating the armies of Seville, Malaga, and the Berbers in 1047. He wrote much poetry in Hebrew and founded a Yeshiva. He wrote a major Halachic work in Aramaic and Hebrew. He was attacked by Muslim scholars on the questionable grounds of having written a criticism of the Qur'an. He was succeeded as *Nagid* by his son Jehoseph, who was skilled in Arabic literature and language and wrote poetry in Hebrew and Arabic. He in turn was bitterly attacked in a poem by a Muslim fanatic.[17] He was assassinated in 1066 by a mob, which then burned down the Jewish quarter and killed its inhabitants. But Jews continued to be influential until the middle of the twelfth century, when the success of the Reconquista led to anti-Jewish attitudes among Muslims.[18]

When the Christian king Alfonso VI captured Toledo in 1085, the Muslims realized that the small independent Arab kingdoms were too weak to resist, and the Almoravids, a dynasty of Berbers ruling Morocco, defeated Alfonso and took over one kingdom after another. They were stricter in observing rules against *Dhimmi*, but Jews continued in the civil service, and Andalusian Jews were prosperous in business and still lived quite comfortably. Jewish religious scholarship and Hebrew poetry continued to flourish.

Some Jews moved north into Christian territory, among them Moses ibn Ezra, a philosopher, linguist, and poet born in Granada in about 1055 and educated at Lucena, a city in Cordova founded by Jews and with a large Yeshiva founded by Isaac Alfasi. He lived in Cordova until the Almoravid destruction of the Jewish community, when he fled north without his family and wrote "in exile" in uncultured Castile. He wrote of being in exile, away from al-Andalus. Among his works was a treatise on poetry and rhetoric in Judeo-Arabic; he wrote poems and liturgy in Hebrew. He could also write in Classical Hebrew.[19]

In the early twelfth century Andalusian Jews sensed the end of a peaceful period and were affected by a wave of messianic feeling. Many were disillusioned, among them Yehuda Halevi, who had been born in Toledo or Tudela in 1075 and lived for a while in Granada and other cities. He was educated in Arabic (in which he wrote prose) and Hebrew (in which he wrote poetry). Halevi was a "foundational figure in Andalusi-Jewish culture".[20] Among his poems was a cycle of "Songs of Zion" expressing strong Zionist feelings. In the Judeo-Arabic philosophic work *The Kuzari* he defended rabbinic Judaism but went on to argue against Andalusian Diaspora life in favor of life in the Land of Israel. He himself traveled to Egypt and on to Palestine in 1141, and died there.

Starting in 1147 a new dynasty, the Almohads – a Berber revivalist movement that did not recognize *Dhimmis* and tolerated no other forms of Islam – spread throughout the Maghreb, and by 1172 it ruled Andalusia too. Jews and Christians were converted or massacred (Christianity was wiped out in north Africa). Many Jews and Christians moved north; others accepted Islam, but converts too were persecuted and forced to dress differently. Some *Anusim* moved to Fez in north Africa and later to Egypt, where they could practice Judaism again; Maimonides was a member of such a family.[21]

Most of Andalusia was taken by the Christian Reconquista: only Granada in the south remained Muslim until 1492. Many Jews remained, but Andalusian Jewish culture moved north to Christian Spain. Andalusian elite Jewish culture was marked by pride in the purity of their language, their lineage, and their religious belief, not unlike the particularism of the Muslim elite. Moses ben Ezra praised the superiority of descent from the people of Jerusalem, who excelled in "the purity of language and the tradition of legal science". Arabs considered their language and literature a treasure; Jews accepted this judgment and believed this gave the Arabs the ability to rule over so many languages. Jewish pride in Hebrew language and literature emulated this, and the writing of poetry in neoclassical Hebrew was a mark of "linguistic nationalism" echoed by the grammarians' efforts at linguistic purity. This elitism was also marked by Andalusian Jewish persecution of Karaites, in contrast to the cooperation between Rabbanites and Karaites in Egypt and elsewhere.[22]

Linguistically, then, al-Andalus, the Muslim rule of Iberia, with all its continued discrimination and ultimate expulsion, was a rich period for the Jews, confirming the place of Judeo-Arabic, beginning the addition of Romance, which was the predecessor of Judezmo, Haketia, and Ladino, and continuing to affirm the position of Hebrew at the apex of Jewish languages.

Reconquista

As the Catholic reconquest of the Iberian Peninsula from the Muslims progressed, the situation of the Jews changed, but not for the better. In Oviedo (the capital of Asturias in northern Spain) the new Christian kingdom resumed the Visigothic policies against Jews and Muslims. In Leon and Castile, however, the small Jewish communities had almost equal status with Christians, as the kingdoms needed trade and industry. At the beginning of the eleventh century CE Jews (perhaps escaping from Berber Spain, or else from France) were encouraged to settle by Alfonso V of Leon (995–1028), who was active in rebuilding the northwestern Spanish kingdom. Jews in these kingdoms belonged to the king, and depended on his protection. By the late eleventh century there were sixty major Jewish families in Barcelona owning much land, for which they paid tithes to the Church.[23] Under the counts, the community was left alone, but in the middle of the thirteenth century royal control increased, though it still left considerable autonomy.[24]

Jewish culture developed. Major Jewish writing was produced by Reuben al-Bargeloni (of Barcelona, a Talmud scholar and poet), Abraham bar Hiyya Ha-Nasi (an astrologer who was familiar with Arabic science but wrote only in Hebrew; he was responsible for coining many scientific terms[25]), and Judah ben Barzilai (who argued with bar Hiyya about the date of a wedding, but completed a codification of Jewish law that was overshadowed by the later codex of Maimonides).[26]

The reconquest of Spain continued: Toledo fell to Alfonso I of Castile in 1085 (Jews continued to live there with royal protection), Tudela to Alfonso I of Aragon in 1115 (Jews were permitted to remain), and Saragossa in 1118, and there and in other towns Jews remained. Legally serfs of the king to whom they paid taxes, their communities, known as *aljama* (a term for self-governing Jewish and Muslim communities), were autonomous but usually under the local authority of the bishop or a royal functionary. At about this time a dispute over the works of Maimonides split the Jewish world, including Spain.

By the middle of the twelfth century only Granada remained in Arab hands, and everywhere the privileges of the Jews were restored, so that their land ownership and commerce increased. The privileges were defined in *Las Sietas Partidas*, a code of law drawn up by Alfonso X in the middle of the thirteenth century; it allowed religious freedom but limited the size and number of synagogues, forbade Jews to have Christian slaves or live in the same houses as Christians, and required the wearing of a Jewish badge. Jews could serve the monarchs as high functionaries, and Jewish courtiers were common. The communities were autonomous and under royal control.

During the thirteenth century a Christian campaign against the Jews was under way, controlling moneylending and forbidding Jews to employ Christian servants. The first blood libel appeared in 1250. A major disputation took place in Barcelona in 1263 between Nachmanides and a Christian priest; Nachmanides had to leave Spain in 1265, and settled in Jerusalem. The Inquisition was authorized to investigate *conversos* and Jews. Tension developed between the *aljama* and the Christian municipality. At the end of the century Jewish courtiers lost their influence in Aragon, but not in Castile. Kabbalistic teaching became popular, and the dispute over the works of Maimonides broke out again.

The position of the Jewish courtiers continued to fluctuate, and the Jewish situation deteriorated, but not until 1391 did a major period of persecution begin, with riots in Seville and attacks in other cities that were unchecked by the monarchy. In many small communities Jews were killed or converted. The position of the *conversos* too worsened. In 1415 Jews were ordered to submit their copies of the Talmud for the censorship of anti-Christian passages. Local persecution and forced conversion continued. An attempt was made by the Jews to reorganize small communities by requiring that a teacher be hired wherever there were fifteen or more Jewish families.

There was persecution also of New Christians. In 1469 Isabella (heiress to Castile) and Ferdinand (heir to Aragon) married, and the two kingdoms, united a decade later, set up the Inquisition to investigate New Christians as Judaizers; many were burned at the stake. Tomás de Torquemada was appointed Inquisitor-General in 1483, and soon thousands had been condemned. Granada fell to the Christians in 1492, and an edict requiring all Jews to convert or leave Spain was passed. Some moved to Portugal (from where they were expelled in 1497), the rest to north Africa or Turkey. The last Jew left Spain on July 31, 1492.[27]

It was during this period that Old Spanish (sometimes called Medieval Spanish) developed from Vulgar Latin, and later was transformed into Castilian. The major work in Old Spanish was the *Song of the Cid*, an epic assumed to have been composed sometime in the twelfth century dealing with a hero who fought in the Reconquista; the earliest manuscript is from the fourteenth century. A number of Spanish dialects developed: Castilian was distinct from Leonese and showed Basque influence; another variety was Galician–Portuguese, developing in the northwest and with some documents; Catalan developed in the eastern end of the Pyrenees mountains and valleys with an extensive literature from the eleventh century, including poems and thirteenth- and fourteenth-century chronicles.

In Christian Spain until the expulsion, Jews had continued as scientists, physicians, and astronomers. Some upper-class Jews shared in education with their Christian counterparts, but most Jews continued Jewish traditional education, with study of the Bible and Talmud. By the eleventh century CE Spanish rabbinical scholarship had developed its own methods. The study of Hebrew grammar was important. Hebrew poetry reached a high level with the work of Judah Halevi, Moses ibn Ezra, and Solomon ibn Gabirol, who wrote both religious liturgical and secular poems. Grammatical treatises on and in Hebrew were influential in Europe as well; biblical commentaries were produced too. Talmudic studies started by Isaac ben Jacob Alfasi and reaching a high level in the Hebrew and Arabic texts of Maimonides were important, as was philosophy. The *kabbalah* became significant, especially through the work of Nachmanides; the *Zohar*, written in Aramaic, was published by Moses de Leon. There were major codices written by Maimonides and others.[28]

Major Jewish communities in Andalusia

Jews may have been in Cordova as early as the eighth century, but the first references are in 840 CE to a debate involving the Jewish proselyte Bodo-Eleazar. Cordova became the capital of the Umayyad caliphate; Hasdai Ibn Shaprut, physician and adviser to the caliph Abd al-Rajman III, brought many Jewish intellectuals to Cordova in the tenth century, and Talmudic studies developed. In the eleventh century, with the Berber conquest, Cordova declined, but it revived in the twelfth century until the invasion of the Almohads. After the Reconquista there were heavy taxes imposed on Jews, and most of the Jewish community were massacred or left in 1391. The community ceased to exist in 1485, and subsequently the Inquisition was active dealing with the *Anusim* there.[29]

While there is no hard evidence, Jewish tradition holds that Toledo had Jewish settlers from the time of the destruction of the First Temple. A Jewish quarter with a wall and a fortress dates from the early ninth century CE. In the eleventh century, under the Berbers, there were about 4,000 Jews, divided into communities according to place of origin, such as Cordova and Barcelona; there were also Khazar and Karaite communities. Jews were engaged in trade and crafts, and also in translation; this continued under the Christians in the twelfth century, with the translation by Jewish scholars of mathematical and astronomical works from Arabic to the vernacular and to Latin. From the eleventh century to the thirteenth, Jews conducted their business, oral and written, in Judeo-Arabic. At the beginning of the fourteenth century they stopped using Arabic for documents. The Black Death killed many in Toledo in 1348. There are estimated to have been 350 families in the fourteenth century; in 1368 some 6,000 Jews were reported to have been killed during the siege. Widespread anti-Jewish riots in 1391 led to the destruction of the synagogues and to massacres and mass conversions. The Jews of Toledo were expelled in 1492; some went to Fez and others to Turkey and Palestine. There were remains of ten synagogues and five batei midrash described in the fifteenth century. Inquisitions and riots against *Anusim* continued for at least two centuries.[30]

There are also traditions of early Jewish settlement in Granada – the Moors called it *Gharnatat al Yahud* (Granada of the Jews) – but the first evidence that there were Jews in the Muslim garrison there dates from 711 CE. When Granada became independent in the eleventh century, Jews were prominent in administration. Jews were for a while a majority in the town, but they were estimated to be a fifth of the 26,000 population in the late eleventh century. There was a revolt in 1066, with many Jews killed, and, under the Almohads, Jews were banned from the city. Jews returned in the thirteenth century, including *Anusim* who returned to Judaism, to be expelled again in 1492.[31]

Barcelona, in Catalonia, is mentioned as having a Jewish community in the middle of the ninth century CE. While one Arab chronicler thought there were as many Jews as Christians in the city, only sixty names were listed in 1079. There was a Jewish quarter from the eleventh century, and Jews were under the authority of the counts. Jews in Barcelona were mainly merchants and craftsmen. At the beginning of the thirteenth century the community was renowned for scholarship and wealth. There was a public disputation between Nachmanides and four Christian priests, of which both Latin and Hebrew summaries remain. In the fourteenth century Jewish trade was restricted, and the community suffered during the Black Death. Many Jews were killed or converted during the 1391 riots. An attempt was made to re-establish the community in 1401, but it was blocked by the Christian residents.[32]

Tudela, in Navarre (northern Spain), was probably settled much later; both Judah Halevi (1075) and Abraham ibn Ezra (1092) were born there. Muslim rule ended in 1115 and it became part of Aragon; Jews were permitted to return; they paid taxes to the new Christian king. Jews in Tudela were slave traders, traded in wool and textiles, and were craftsmen. Benjamin of Tudela began his travels through the Jewish world in about 1160. Navarre came under French rule in 1234; Tudela was a haven for refugees from France in 1306. There was persecution a few years afterwards, damage from invading armies in the rest of the century, and an economic decline in the fourteenth century. After the expulsion in 1492, many Jews moved from there to Provence.[33]

Jews probably settled in Saragossa (in Aragon in northeast Spain) in the Roman and Visigothic periods, but the community grew during Muslim rule. During the eleventh century the Jews made up about 6 percent of the population of the city. The Jewish quarter inside the city walls included several synagogues. After the Reconquista, in 1118, Jews maintained some privileges in return for taxes; individual families continued to receive special rights. The first blood libel in Spain appeared in Saragossa in 1250, and another in 1294, but the child was found. The majority of the community was wiped out in the Black Death in 1348. Afterwards, the community prospered under the leadership of the de la Cavalleria family: Judah Benveniste de la Cavalleria had a royal post (he signed state documents in Hebrew) and a home that was a center of Jewish culture. Most of the family was baptized by the middle of the fifteenth century.[34]

Jewish languages and Judeo-Spanish

The Jews who left Spain took with them the language they had spoken before the expulsion. In north Africa, Turkey, and the Balkans this developed into a variety of Judeo-Spanish, known as "Haketia" (*haketiya*) in Morocco,[35] as "Judezmo" (with various spellings) in the eastern Mediterranean, and as "Ladino" in the re-Hispanicized formal written language of Sephardi Jews. There are other names and varieties, such as "Tetuani" for the dialect of Oran, "Spanyiolit" in informal Modern Hebrew, but in this chapter we will deal with the simple question: did Judezmo exist in Spain before the expulsion? Another way of putting this is: was there a difference between the Romance/Old Spanish spoken by the various religious groups in Christian Spain? But, first, we need to return to the question of what constitutes a Jewish language.

I selected the title of this book for two reasons. First, it seemed an appropriate continuation to my two earlier books, *The Languages of Jerusalem*[36] and *The Languages of Israel*.[37] The second reason was not to beg but, rather, to delay to an appropriate point attempting to answer the question of what a Jewish language is. This seems to be such a point.

It is a question that was delayed until the later part of the twentieth century, for fairly clear reasons. The speakers of the pre-eminent Jewish language, Yiddish, seldom recognized it as a language, calling it *zhargon* to mark its low status. For the German-speaking Jewish scholars of the Haskalah (Enlightenment) and the *Wissenschaft des Judentums* (Jewish Studies movement of the nineteenth century), Yiddish was, as Moses Mendelssohn put it, a "jargon [which] has contributed not a little to the immorality of the common man", to be cured by "the increasing use of the pure German language".[38] The state should not support Yiddish or the "*Vermischung der Sprachen*" (mixing of languages) but should use only "*rein deutsch, oder rein hebräisch*" (pure German or pure Hebrew). Mendelssohn attacked the translation of the Torah into Yiddish by Yekutiel ben Isaac Blitz (published in Amsterdam in 1679) and made his own translation into "decorous and refined Hebrew such as that spoken in our time", as a model to raise the status of Jews.[39] Later Jewish writers, including some who wrote in Yiddish, accepted his views that Yiddish could be spoken (he spoke it himself) but not be written.[40]

It was only in the late nineteenth century, with the efforts of Yiddish writers such as Mendele Mocher Sforim (the pseudonym of Solomon Moiseyevich Abramovich, who published fiction in both Hebrew and Yiddish), that it began to change its status, so that at the 1908 First World Congress for Yiddish, at Czernowitz, the supporters of Yiddish were satisfied to proclaim it as "*a* Jewish language", leaving the definite article for Hebrew.[41] Given the bitterness of the struggle between Hebraists and Yiddishists,[42] it is no wonder that Zionist Israeli scholars too were reluctant to give status to Diaspora Jewish varieties.[43]

Only with the work of YIVO (Institute for Jewish Research) and its publication in 1973 of the Yiddish original of Max Weinreich's *History of the Yiddish Language*[44] did we have a sociolinguist starting to explore the nature of Jewish languages, followed up by two collections published by Joshua Fishman.[45] Weinreich is credited with the often quoted definition of a language as "a dialect with an army and a navy". Weinreich used it first in a speech at the 1945 annual YIVO conference in Yiddish. He later explained its origin:

A teacher at a Bronx high school once appeared among the auditors. He had come to America as a child and the entire time had never heard that Yiddish had a history and could also serve for higher matters. . . Once after a lecture he approached me and asked, "What is the difference between a dialect and language?" I thought that the *maskilic* (Enlightenment, anti-Yiddish) contempt had affected him, and tried to lead him to the right path, but he interrupted me: "I know that, but I will give you a better definition. A language is a dialect with an army and navy." From that very time I made sure to remember that I must convey this wonderful formulation of the social plight of Yiddish to a large audience.[46]

One of the issues affecting Jewish varieties is that their speakers seldom recognize them as a language: note the many names for "Judezmo", or the use of the word "jargon" for Yiddish. A number of years ago, when I was teaching a course on sociolinguistics, I mentioned Judeo-Aramaic and brought a copy of a book on it[47] into the class. One of the students asked to borrow the book; she brought it to class the next week and announced excitedly that this was the language her parents spoke. They told her they never knew it was a language; they just assumed it was the way people in their village in Persia spoke.

In his definition of varieties of language,[48] William Stewart identifies a standard language as having a dictionary and a grammar book, both of which were provided for Yiddish by Max Weinreich's son Uriel.[49] Yiddish could also fit Stewart's definition of a creole, a pidgin that developed native speakers. But none of the Jewish languages we will be considering (except Hebrew, whose status needs further discussion) has ever had an army and a navy, or even a flag; and in fact, with a few exceptions (Yiddish, Ladino, Judeo-Arabic, Judeo-Aramaic), they have generally not been written but spoken varieties, which Stewart would call a vernacular (if considered independent) or a dialect (if not).

Notice that I am here falling into the common lay and professional habit of labeling a variety with a name, treating it therefore as an identifiable object. This ignores the preference of many sociolinguists today, such as Blommaert,[50] who have pointed out the problems with this approach. One is that a language name such as "English" refers to all the varieties (the "World Englishes", as Braj Kachru has labeled them) such as British English, American English, Australian English, South African English,[51] and all the dialects such as Texan, Cockney, and Queensland, to name just a few; it also covers all the regional, social, and gender varieties, and the varieties modified for media or style; and allows for the constant changes going on in a language.

This degree of variation also affects Jewish languages, such as Eastern and Western Yiddish, and the effects of the major isogloss between Litvak and Galizianer Yiddish,[52] and differences between Maghreb and Iraqi Judeo-Arabic, and between north African and Balkan varieties of Judezmo. So language labels cover a wide variety of linguistic differences, even at times including varieties that are not mutually intelligible (I remember when British films were still subtitled for showing in the United States).

The second problem, also very pertinent to the situation of Jewish languages, is that, in the modern increasingly multilingual city, code switching and code mixing are more and more common, and the resulting fusion varieties are flexible and complex to identify. All of this, then, is to prepare us for the difficulty of defining Jewish languages.

Weinreich discusses at some length what marks a Jewish language in his consideration of what constitutes an independent language.[53] Danish and Norwegian, he notes, are very close but considered separate languages; Sicilian and Tuscan are remote, but considered dialects of Italian.[54] He then talks specifically about Jewish varieties; do the "little peculiarities" persuade the scholar that they should be treated as separate and distinct? He argues that it is useful to give Jewish-oriented names to these varieties "to emphasize their independence in the Jewish framework".[55]

He suggests giving names to the Jewish "correlates" of the Romance languages, which are commonly referred to in Hebrew medieval manuscripts as "Loez", a word that in Psalm 114 is translated as "strange language" and that later came to mean any language other than Hebrew. The Jewish correlates of Romance languages can be called Loez languages; specifically, he recognizes four varieties: "Dzhudezmo" (his spelling) for the correlate of Spanish, and also Catalonian and Portuguese; "Chuadit" for Jewish Provençal; "Western Loez" for Jewish French; and "Southern Loez" for Jewish Italian.

The most thorough investigation of the genesis of one of these languages, Weinreich says, is in the work of David Blondheim on the Jewish Romance vernaculars.[56] He studied twenty-five Bible translations, commentaries, and glosses, finding differences from Jerome's Vulgate and the pre-Jerome versions known collectively as *Vetus Latina*, arguing that these were derived from unwritten Jewish versions. He goes further, and proposes that these were in a vernacular that may have been localized and that would be intelligible to non-Jews but have sounded sufficiently different to be identified as Jewish. But the opposite position is taken by the Romance scholar Leo Spitzer (who succeeded Blondheim as professor of Romance philology at Johns Hopkins University in 1936):

Blondheim's assumption of a common Judeo-Romance language, however, has been refuted by Italian Jewish scholars. They are content with explaining the peculiarities of medieval Judeo-Italian, Judeo-Spanish and the rest as parallel outgrowths of the religious conditions which were alike for Jews in all the Latin countries.[57]

A similar position is taken by the Judeo-Spanish scholar Haim Vidal Sephiha,[58] who points out that the few differences between the Old Spanish spoken by Jews in pre-exilic Spain, such as *alhad* for *Domingo* (Sunday), would not be enough to distinguish the variety spoken by Jews, Christians, and Muslims.[59] We have, then, a negative answer to whether Judeo-Spanish existed as a distinguishable variety before exile, and, indeed, he argues that it was only around 1620 that it became a marked Jewish language.

The Hebrew linguist Haim Rabin has tackled the question of what constitutes a Jewish language, noting that the term was new and a scientific artifact. He makes a distinction between Jewish languages and languages spoken by Jews.[60] My favorite example of this would be Eyak, an Alaskan language related to Athapaskan, the last native speaker of which died a few years ago, leaving a Jewish linguist as the last remaining speaker. Rabin has a similar difficulty with the suggestion that it is a variety spoken within a Jewish community and recognizable as distinct, especially by anti-Semites. He finds more promising the notion of a variety that exists in a diglossic relationship with Hebrew (or, rather, Hebrew–Aramaic), which would help explain why these languages are commonly written in Hebrew script and borrow so many words and expressions from the Bible and the Talmud and other Jewish religious texts. There is a similar phenomenon uniting the vernacular versions of Arabic through their status as the lower variety of their diglossia with Qur'anic Arabic. As happened with the Romance vernaculars, these lower varieties may be raised, as Yiddish and Ladino were, by their use in the higher literary domains.

Joshua Fishman also offers a definition, one that is somewhat more inclusive and helps establish the field that Weinreich calls Jewish intralinguistics:[61]

I define as "Jewish" any language[62] that is phonologically, morpho-syntactically, lexico-semantically or orthographically different from that of non-Jewish sociocultural networks and that has some demonstrably unique function in the role-repertoire of a Jewish sociocultural network, which function is not normatively present in the role-repertoire of non-Jews and/or is not normally discharged via varieties identical with those utilized by non-Jews.[63]

There are, Fishman hastens to admit, borderline cases, made more complex by the fact that the parameter favored for identification may be psychological (because Jews or non-Jews believe them to be different)[64], sociological (because of their use for Jewish functions in Jewish networks), or linguistic (because of structural differences), and because of the differences of opinion in each case. Various scholars produce different lists. Fishman notes that the *Encyclopedia Judaica* includes Judeo-Alsatian, Judeo-Arabic, Judeo-Berber, Judeo-Catalan, Judeo-Corfiote, Judeo-French, Judeo-Greek, Judeo-Italian, Judeo-Persian, Judeo-Portuguese, Judeo-Romance, Judeo-Tajik, Judeo-Tat, Judeo-Tatar, Ladino (Judeo-Spanish), and Yiddish (Judeo-German). Another pioneer in the field, Nathan Birnbaum, objects to the use of "Judeo-", which he says would be acceptable only if French were known as "Gallo-Latin" and English as "Anglo-German". He prefers names such as Yevanic, Italkian, Tsarfatic, Arvic, Ma'aravic, Parsic, Bukharic, Tatic, and Gruzinic.[65] Weinreich adds Targumic (Judeo-Aramaic). The Jewish language website adds Jewish Dutch, Jewish English, Jewish Malayalam, Jewish Latin American Spanish, Jewish Polish, Jewish Russian, Judeo-Georgian, Judeo-Slavic/Canaanic, Karaim, and Yiddish Sign Language. Adding the criterion of religion, they can be called "religiolects".[66]

One question that might be raised at this point is whether Hebrew in any of its varieties is usefully considered a Jewish language. One Israeli linguist is clear that it is not, for in Israel it is the language of the country (Jews and non-Jews alike) and, earlier on (and still in the Diaspora), it was the language of religion.[67] But, of course, I am protected from being caught in this, because I am writing about the languages of the Jews, and not Jewish languages alone.

I will return to this question in the last chapter, when I have more evidence. In the meantime, I will continue this exploration of the addition of new varieties to the Jewish sociolinguistic repertoire, arranging my consideration by what Weinreich labels the "culture areas" into which the Jewish people were divided from 900 CE until 1200 CE: "Loter" (Alsace, which became Ashkenaz); "Tsarfat" (northern France); "Provense" (southern France); "Sepharad" (the Iberian Peninsula); "Knaan" (east and west Slavic lands); northern and central Italy; "Yavan" (southern Italy, the Balkans, Asia Minor, and the Greek islands);

"Ishmael" (the Muslim Arabic area, north Africa, Palestine, and the Arabian Peninsula down to Yemen); the "Targumic" area (where Iraq, Turkey, and Iran meet); and "Paras-umaday" (Persia and the Median Empire).[68] But, as we shall see, the communication and active travel connections between these zones make any strict ordering irrelevant.

The languages of the Iberian Peninsula[69]

To sum up, the major languages of the Iberian Peninsula were Gothic (disappearing), Latin (developing into Hispano-Romance, Classical, and Andalusian), Jewish Arabic, Hebrew, and probably Berber. The Visigoths had been Romanized; their thinkers wrote in good Latin, and they spoke what became Hispano-Romance, called *latīnī* or *ajamī* (foreign) by the Muslims. The variety of local Andalusian Arabic spoken by the Muslims and Jews was influenced by Hispano-Romance, and influenced it in turn, suggesting code switching as a norm. The Almoravids, who were Berber, probably kept up that language for a while; their first leader definitely spoke it. The Jews, many of whom knew Hebrew well, and Aramaic, probably spoke much like their neighbors, whether Arabic or Hispano-Romance, but presumably with code switching into Hebrew. They could write Classical Arabic, but most of their writing was in a variety of Judeo-Arabic called Middle Arabic. It was only after their expulsion and departure from the peninsula that the specifically Jewish varieties of Spanish developed.

Jews in Ashkenaz

Leaving aside for the moment the question of whether or not Hebrew is a Jewish language,[1] Yiddish is without question the premier Jewish language, as its name proclaims.[2] While German scholars of the Enlightenment and Zionist Hebrew Israeli scholars denigrated it, modern students of Jewish varieties all see it as the prime example of an autonomous Jewish language. It may have started as a fusion language, but it gained standardization, vitality, and vernacular functionality, achieved a distinguished literary use, and still has surviving secular and religious supporters endeavoring to overcome the murder of most of its modern speakers. True, most secular speakers are old, and the religious are members of a few Hasidic sects. Other secular supporters now form the kind of "metalinguistic community" that is typical of many disappearing indigenous languages without vitality.[3] But, because of its continuity among Hasidim,[4] Yiddish is the best example of a surviving Jewish variety with natural intergenerational transmission.

Its birth, commonly assumed to be in the Rhineland area of the Loter-Ashkenaz Jewish culture area sometime around the end of the first millennium CE, with all the uncertainties of medieval Jewish life and society and with the controversies that have arisen about its Slavic environment and component, must be the center point of a study of the languages of the Jews. This gives added importance to studying the Jews who created it and the non-Jewish environment in which German first became a language of the Jews (see Map 8).

Max Weinreich, its principal historian and scholar, names the communities of Loter,[5] on the banks of the Rhine and the Moselle, as the location where Yiddish was born; specifically, he suggests Cologne, Mainz, Worms, Speyer, Metz, and – further east – Regensburg.[6] Dovid Katz is among those who question the Rhineland origin,[7] however, citing both Matthias Mieses,[8] who favors Bavaria, and Jacob Gerzon,[9] who favors East Central German as the dialect contributing most to the Germanic component of Yiddish; Katz himself then guesses at Regensburg as the "cradle of Yiddish". He goes on to express doubt about the Romance component, derived from Weinreich's assumption that the

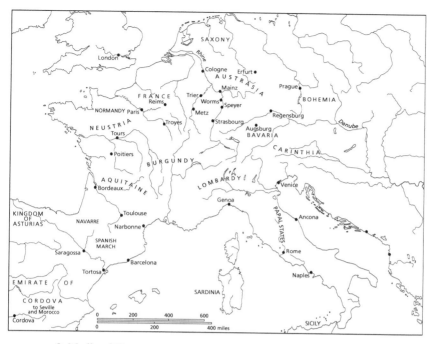

8 Medieval Europe
Source: Chazan (2010b).

first speakers were from France and Italy – a proposition that has only very weak lexical support.[10] There are other scholars who support the idea of a Regensburg origin, with the Bavarian dialect as the base.[11] The third[12] theory as to where Yiddish originated might be labeled the "Judeo-Slavic scenario", of which there are two current versions: one holds that Czech is the origin of Eastern Yiddish,[13] and the second, more radical, holds that Yiddish is a relexified form of Sorbian or Judeo-Sorbian.[14] But the situation in the Rhineland communities does give a useful background to the linguistic speculation.

The Rhineland

There were Jews in Cologne in Roman times – in 321 CE Constantine abolished their exemption from municipal office – and they continued to live there during the Frankish period after 462 CE, with relatively good relations with the Christians. In 881 CE invading Normans destroyed the city, but Jews were part of the rebuilt city, which included a Jewish quarter, a synagogue, and a Yeshiva founded by the legendary rabbi Amram of Mayence.[15] In 1010 a new synagogue and hospital were built, and the community was headed by an *episcopus Judaeorum* (bishop of the Jews),[16] with ten *Dayyanim* (rabbinical judges) forming a council with authority over the Jews. Jews traded in all commodities, and many were becoming wealthy. The Cologne fairs brought traders from all over Europe, and Jews among them from as far away as the Ukraine.

When the First Crusade approached the city in 1096, the Jews tried to hide, but they were eventually discovered, and most were massacred. Re-established by the remnant and with new Jewish inhabitants, the community suffered again during the Second Crusade fifty years later. The rebuilt community had to cope with a ban on trading and exclusion from craft guilds, so that Jews had to move to moneylending, a trade permitted them but forbidden to Christians.[17] In the twelfth century Jews were heavily taxed by the archbishop, whose serfs they now were. In the early thirteenth century they benefited by supporting the city against the archbishop, and refugees from other towns increased the Jewish population. Asher ben Jehiel (known as Rabbeinu Asher or the Rosh) was active in Cologne and later in Worms, but moved to Toledo in 1303. In the early fifteenth century Jews were expelled, and permitted to return only at the end of the eighteenth century.[18]

The earliest evidence of Jews at Metz comes from 888 CE, when a Church council forbade Christians to dine with them. Some bishops and the dukes of Lorraine at the end of the tenth century were said to be favorable to them, and during this time the "sages of Lorraine"[19] were said to reside in Metz. But the persecutions of the First Crusade started there, with twenty-two victims in 1096. There was a Jewish quarter. In 1257 Jews passing through had to pay a tax but were not permitted to reside. All Jews were finally expelled in 1365, and allowed back only in the late sixteenth century.[20]

There are hints but no solid evidence of Jews elsewhere in Germany before the ninth and tenth centuries CE apart from traders. Then, a number of Jewish families from Italy (including the Kalonymus family) moved from Lucca to Mainz, in the Rhineland.[21] The family name may derive from Greek: *kalo* (beautiful) + *numos* (name) – in Hebrew, *shem tov*.[22] There are family branches also in Provins (Provence) and in Venice.[23] There is doubt about when the family was brought to Germany, whether by Charlemagne or another king;[24] various dates are proposed, ranging from 787 to 962, but this establishes the Southern Loez or Yavanic (which includes Italy) origin of many of the earliest settlers in Loter-Ashkenaz. Linguistically, this connection might provide a Judeo-Greek and Judeo-Italian component in Yiddish as well as the assumed Judeo-French or Western Loez elements, and explains the scholarly prominence (and so Hebrew knowledge) of the region.[25] The Kalonymus family produced many scholars and liturgical poets.

When there were doubts about interpretations of Jewish law, communities in Loter sent questions to Italy, to the famous Yeshiva at Kiwan in Tunisia, until the community was destroyed by Bedouin in 1050, or to the Yeshivot in Palestine or Babylonia. Other leading scholars in Germany among the Hasidei Ashkenaz included Rav Yehuda Ha-Hasid of Regensburg (born in 1150 in Speyer and author of *Sefer Hasidim*; his father was Rav Shmuel Ha-Hasid) and Rabbi Eleazar of Worms, his principal disciple, and author of a major Halachic guide.

Jewish communities were mentioned in Mainz, Worms, and Regensburg in the tenth century CE. Jewish settlement was concentrated on the Rhine and in Lorraine; in the eleventh century, Jews were attracted to southern Germany by trade possibilities. The Yeshivot at Mainz and Worms were major centers for German and French Jews. Jewish communities depended on royal and ecclesiastical support, and were governed by a complex set of laws that guaranteed their rights while restricting their status.[26] Most communities were small – several hundred or a few dozen families – but Mainz in the eleventh century is said to have reached a population of 2,000 Jews.

Mainz (Mayence) was the center of the Christianization of the German and Slav peoples; its archbishop was one of the seven Electors of the Holy Roman emperor, and occupied the only Holy See apart from Rome. It was a central site for Jewish life too, as Rabbi Gershom ben Yehudah (960–1030?) was said by Rashi 100 years later to be the teacher of all Ashkenaz; he headed the Yeshiva founded by the Kalonymus family earlier in the century. He provided crucially important leadership after the decline of the Babylonian Yeshivot. He was born in Metz, and his students included Eleazar ben Isaac and Yaakov ben Yakar, the teacher of Rashi. He produced revised texts of the Mishnah and the Talmud. Around 1000 he organized a synod that banned polygamy for the next thousand years, required that women give permission for divorce, modified rules concerning Jews forced to become apostates, and forbade the reading of private mail.

The Jews, who had played a major role in local trade, were expelled from Mainz in 1012 but allowed to return soon afterwards. They were expelled again in 1082, and a number of them moved to Speyer. Those who returned were slaughtered by crusaders in 1096 in spite of a protection order from the emperor, the survivors then being attacked during the Second Crusade (1145–9) but protected by the emperor during the Third (1189–92). They were ordered to wear a Jewish badge in 1259, 1472, and 1474. The community was attacked by mobs, who burned the synagogue, during the blood libels in 1201 and 1283. Many Jews left Germany in 1289 with Rabbi Meir ben Boruch of Rothenberg (who died in prison in Alsace), while most of the remaining members of the community were killed, and 6,000 were burned alive in 1349, when they were charged with causing the Black Death.

Some Jews returned to Mainz after 1356, but the community remained small and was burdened with heavy taxation. There were disputes with the city government about taxes and continued expulsions up to 1483, when the synagogue was converted into a church. Trade and, later, moneylending were the main activities of Jews in Mainz. Jews were allowed to own houses until the Black Death, and a *Judengasse* is mentioned in 1218. Mainz, Speyer, and Worms were the main German Jewish medieval communities at this time. By the early sixteenth century few Jews remained in Mainz, but a new community was established in 1583 with immigration from Frankfort, Speyer, and Hanau. During the seventeenth century the French government limited the number of Jewish families to twenty and, later, ten, all required to live in the ghetto. After the French Revolution the Jews of Mainz became French citizens, but, under renewed German rule in 1816, they lost their civil rights.[27]

There were some Jews in Speyer before the millennium, but the numbers increased significantly in 1084, when the bishop allowed Jews from Mainz to settle there and granted them privileges, including the right to build a wall and to sell meat to Christians (hindquarters that were not kosher), and granted them exemption from some taxes. The emperor Henry IV confirmed these rights and allowed Jews freedom to trade. The community, headed by Rabbi Judah ben Kalonymus, survived the First Crusade and built a new synagogue. It grew during the twelfth century, becoming a center of Jewish learning with such scholars as Eliakim ben Meshullam ha-Levi, Kalonymus ben Isaac, Jacob ben Isaac ha-Lavi, Meir ben Kalonymus (all recognized as writers of Talmudic commentaries), and Judah ben Kalonymus ben Meir, author of a Talmudic lexicon.

There were attacks on the community as a result of a blood libel at the end of the twelfth century, but the emperor intervened and ordered the rebuilding of the synagogue and the destroyed houses. As a member of the three-city league known in Hebrew as *Shum* (Speyer, Worms, and Mainz), Speyer shared in the synods that established Ashkenazi Judaism. Relations with non-Jews were comparatively peaceful; some Christians lived in the Judengasse, and Jews were permitted to own property outside it. There were attacks associated with the blood libel, but the community continued to grow, building a hospital for the indigent and a *matzo* (unleavened bread) bakery. During the persecutions at the time of the Black Death in 1349, however, the community was virtually wiped out, all debts to Jews were cancelled, and Jewish property was confiscated. During the fifteenth century attempts were made to rebuild, but there were regular expulsions and anti-Jewish decrees and confinement to the ghetto; by the sixteenth century, and until the nineteenth, there were only individual Jews living in what had once been a major community.[28]

Jews lived in Worms at the end of the tenth century, built a synagogue in 1034, and owned the Heiliger Sand cemetery (claimed to be the oldest in Europe) by 1076, the date of the earliest tombstone.[29] The Jewish merchants of Worms are mentioned prominently in a charter dated 1074 by the Holy Roman emperor, King Henry IV, who was at the time engaged in a struggle with the Church in Rome over the right of the emperor to appoint bishops. Around 1090, when Henry was probably invading Italy, he issued a charter granting privileges to the Jews of Worms to travel freely, to lend money, to hire Christian servants, to own property, to be judged according to their own law, and to be autonomous, subject only to the king. Among the prominent Jewish scholars at the time were Meir ben Isaac, who composed an Aramaic poem, *Hadamot*, of ninety couplets;[30] Jacob ben Yakar, a co-founder of the Yeshiva of Worms and a teacher of Rashi; Isaac ben Eleazar, a Talmudist and liturgical poet, also a teacher of Rashi; his four sons were also distinguished scholars; Kalonymus ben Shabbetai, who was born in Rome, where he was president of the community, and was called to Worms to be rabbi and head the Yeshiva; and Solomon ben Samson, mentioned as among the scholars of Vitry, where an important *Machzor* (prayer book) was composed, and who may have been the head of the community of Worms to whom the charter was addressed. The scholars of Worms added to the Talmud studies for which Mainz was noted the writing of Bible commentaries and *piyyutim*. The community at Worms suffered during the First Crusade in 1096; 800 Jews were killed, and many others were forced to convert. But Henry IV allowed the converts to return to Judaism, and the community was re-established and granted a customs exemption in 1112 by the emperor Henry V.

Commerce was replaced by moneylending. Arguing that this was not so bad as it seemed, Robert Chazan[31] starts by citing Salo Baron, who was the first to take a more positive view of Jewish life in the Middle Ages.[32] Chazan goes on to point out that, in 1000 CE, the bulk of the Jewish world population lived under Muslim rule, and only tiny groups were starting to move, as traders, into Christian northern Europe. They specialized in commerce and, from the twelfth century, in moneylending, thus meeting society's special needs and being enabled to grow numerically and economically, if at the same time their role produced negative imagery. But there was a strong demand among the barons and royal courtiers for this necessary service, so that there was often protection offered to the Jews. He cites William of Chartres' biography of St. Louis as saying that the barons objected to a proposal to banish Jews who provided moneylending: moneylending was needed, they said, and, if Jews weren't available, Christians would have to do it. Jews, Chazan argues, were able to exploit this demand. But Louis made sure the borrowers did not suffer:

He stablished also, for to have away the burning covetise of the usurers, that other public usurers by letters, ne by none other manner, to pay or yield to them their usury or growing.[33]

Further east, a Jewish community existed in Regensburg (Ratisbon) in Bavaria by 1020, when a Jewish quarter was built. The community was forced to convert to Christianity during the First Crusade, in 1096, but was permitted by the emperor to return to Jewish practices. A charter issued by Emperor Frederick I Barbarossa confirmed "their ancient customs" and allowed them to trade with Slavic countries "in gold, silver, and merchandise of any sort". In the twelfth and thirteenth centuries Christians lived in the Jewish quarter. A synagogue was built in 1217. By the end of the century Regensburg was an important Jewish center. Its scholars included Baruch ben Isaac (who was born at Worms and wrote *Tosafot* [additional commentaries] on the Talmud), Ephraim ben Isaac (who lived as a youth in France, was a Tosafist, and was considered the greatest *payyatan* [writer of *piyyutim*] of Germany), Isaac ben Moses (who was born in Bohemia and wrote his major work in Vienna), and Judah ben Samuel (who was born in Speyer, founded the Hasidei Ashkenaz,[34] and wrote *Sefer Hassidim*). The Yeshivot developed their own style of learning, *pilpul* and *chilukim*.[35]

The community's wealth, largely from moneylending, enabled it to weather the fourteenth-century persecutions, and it became a refuge for other Jews. At the end of the century it suffered when Emperor Wenceslaus annulled all debts owed to Jews. After the Black Death the community was heavily taxed; it survived with imperial protection until 1519, when, on the emperor's death, the remaining Jews were expelled and the synagogue destroyed. The city was declared *non recipiendis Judeis* in 1545, but a small community was re-established in 1669 under the protection of the duke.[36]

Nuremberg is another Bavarian town; Jews may have been there as early as 1146, but the first mention in local records is 1182. A synagogue was dedicated in 1296, and 798 Jews were killed two years later. Jews had returned by 1303; ten years later the city was allowed to admit more, but two years later their houses were destroyed. In 1331 they fled the city because of taxes, but returned soon, the Jewish population reaching 2,000 by 1338. The city council opposed any further Jewish ownership of houses, and in 1344 King Louis said they could no longer buy houses from Christians. In the Black Death massacres of 1349, 560 Jews were burned to death and the rest expelled. Charles IV allowed the city to demolish the Jewish houses and build a church on the site of the synagogue. Two years later they were readmitted, and in 1352 they were required to live in a Judenstrasse (Jewish street); all debts to Jews were cancelled. There were over 500 Jews living there by 1382. In the fourteenth and fifteenth centuries every head of a Jewish family had to pay a fee, provide guarantors, and swear an oath of loyalty. Jewish residents needed permission to travel. Foreign Jews could not live in the city. Newly married couples needed a residence permit after four weeks. Jews and Christians could not use the same bathhouses. Moneylending was restricted: Jews could not sell meat, some other food, wine, or beer to Christians. There was conflict between the king and municipality over the Jews, each competing for the taxes they could charge them.

In the second half of the fifteenth century there was growing tension between the city and the Jews, who were expelled in 1499, their houses and the synagogue confiscated. Some moved to nearby villages. During the sixteenth century a number of Hebrew books were printed in Nuremberg by non-Jews, including a polyglot Bible by John Hutter in twelve languages. Jews were allowed to enter the town for trade at the end of the seventeenth century, but only in the middle of the nineteenth century was the community re-established.[37]

Further east, Prague (Praha, in Czech), in Bohemia, may have had Jewish residents in late Roman times, but they were first mentioned in 970 CE. The community was first documented in 1091, when two Jewish districts developed, one settled perhaps by Jews from further east and the other by Jews from the west. The community was massacred during the First Crusade in 1096 and re-established on the right bank of the river Moldau, and the *Altschul* synagogue built there. As the Jews already spoke Czech, the glosses added to their Halachic works were in Old Czech.[38] From the thirteenth to sixteenth centuries they increasingly spoke German. From the thirteenth century they were considered serfs of the king, required to wear special dress, and restricted to the ghetto and to moneylending.

More Jews arrived from Germany in the thirteenth century, and the Altneuschule synagogue was built in 1270. There were serious pogroms in 1298 and 1338, and most of the community was massacred in 1389. The restored community suffered from the cancellation of debts in 1411. There were problems during the Hussite Wars (1419–36), including mob violence in 1422. Attacks continued through the century, at the end of which permission was given to Christians to lend money; Jews were thus forced to look for other sources of income. Slowly the economic position of the Jews improved, in spite of tension with the city and attempts to expel them; the Jewish population doubled from 600 in 1522 to 1,200 in 1544, and the Jewish quarter expanded. In 1543, however, the king agreed to expel the Jews, allowing them back two years later and expelling them again in 1559. Abraham ben Avigdor, who was the rabbi during this period, wrote a poem, *Anna Elohei Avraham*; he also published a four-volume commentary on the *Arba'a Turim* (a major Halachic work). Jews were allowed to return in 1562. A Hebrew printing press had been set up in Prague by Gersonides, the family of Gershon ben Solomon Cohen, who published prayer books and *Haggadot*; he moved to other cities and printed other works, including *Chumashim* and Rashi commentaries, and in 1543, at Augsburg, a Judeo-German version of Kings and Samuel in rhyme.[39]

The situation of the Jews of Prague continued to improve in the seventeenth century, with the population reaching 6,000. Among its distinguished scholars was Judah Loew ben Bezalel (the *Maharal*), an important Talmudist and philosopher; probably born in Poznan to a family from Worms, he moved back to

Poznan after some years in Prague. Among his students was David Gans, the astronomer, mathematician, and author of *Tsemach David*, the first Jewish history book to deal with world history.

The Counter-Reformation in the middle of the century produced anti-Jewish legislation. The plague in 1680 and a fire reduced the Jewish population; anti-Jewish feeling finally led to a brief expulsion in 1745. At the end of the eighteenth century restrictions on Jews started to be abolished; as part of a Germanization movement, they were compelled to adopt family names, to establish secular education, to do military service, and to stop using Hebrew and Yiddish in business transactions. Jews in Prague were emancipated in 1867.[40]

Jews arrived in Vienna in the twelfth century CE and managed to build a synagogue in time for it to be destroyed during the Third Crusade, in 1196. A second synagogue in the center of the city was built by 1204, and the community was granted autonomy in the middle of the thirteenth century. By the end of the century there was a community of 1,000 Jews, and Vienna had a number of distinguished Jewish scholars. The city was spared the Black Death persecution of 1348, but a fire destroyed the synagogue at the beginning of the fifteenth century and there were serious attacks in 1421, in which year Duke Albrecht ordered that all Jews in Austria be put to death. Some escaped to Bohemia, but after the "Wiener Gesera" (the Vienna Decree), leading to the killing or expulsion of all Jews and the forced conversion of their children, the community no longer existed and Vienna became known as *Ir Hadamim* (city of blood).

Individuals returned to Vienna during the sixteenth century and a ghetto was established in the seventeenth, with rights granted to them to trade. In the middle of the century some refugees from the Cossack massacres in the Ukraine arrived; hatred of the Jews continued, and all were expelled in 1670, the Great Synagogue being converted into a church, the Leopoldskirche. At the end of the century a small number of wealthy Jews were allowed to return, but during the eighteenth century the numbers continued to be restricted until the emancipation and the nineteenth-century arrival of Jews from Hungary, Galicia, and Bukovina. Wealthy Jews became assimilated by the beginning of the nineteenth century; the Reform movement grew, but the new synagogue, the Stadttempel, which was opened in 1826, maintained Hebrew traditional prayers.[41]

It was among these tiny, shifting, persecuted communities, regularly forced to live in close quarters and constantly taxed by city and overlords, that the Ashkenazi community took shape and added local varieties of German to their linguistic repertoire, which in due course developed into Yiddish. But, as elsewhere, they remained multilingual, with knowledge and use of Hebrew and access to other Jewish varieties.

Jewish multilingualism at the millennium

A thousand years after the events he recreates, the Israeli writer A. B. Yehoshua published a novel that included a detailed account of Jewish multilingualism in 999 CE, almost a century before the First Crusade.[42] It tells of the voyage of a Jewish merchant, Ben Attar, accompanied by his two wives and his Muslim partner, Abu Luth, from Tangier in Morocco to Paris and then on to Worms (where Jews lived in a separate section)[43] in Loter.

Yehoshua is deeply interested in the communication problems involved in this crossing of language borders, and provides a clear and plausible description of the linguistic proficiency of each of the characters and how they conversed with the Jews and non-Jews they met. Ben Attar and his wives speak Arabic to each other and to their Muslim companions; he knows Hebrew, but "had never seen fit to endow his wives with any words of the holy tongue".[44] This contrasts with the language skills of the wife of his Jewish partner, Mistress Esther-Minna, herself from Worms, whose father Kalonymos and late husband had taught her to read Hebrew and trained her that a "a meal without words of Torah was likened by the sages to eating the sacrifices of the dead".[45] Her own speech is normally in "the Frankish tongue. . ., with quotations from Bible stories and rabbinic writings".[46] On one occasion she whispers in Hebrew, "as though fearful of uttering the words in the local tongue, lest she arouse the Frankish servant who slept by the doorway".[47] Her new husband, Abulafia, is Ben Attar's nephew and able to converse in Arabic and vernacular Latin; his Hebrew is good enough to convince Rabbi Kalonymos of his Jewish faith.[48] The Muslim partner and the ship's Muslim crew do not understand the Hebrew of the Jewish partners. Ben Attar has taken with him a rabbi from Seville "in order to interpret the unfamiliar Capetian environment by means of the Latin he commanded".[49] Rabbi Elbaz speaks Judeo-Arabic with the partners, composes a poem "all in Hebrew, following the meter and rhyme scheme that had been brought to Andalus from the east by Dunash Ben Labrat",[50] recites "a few verses in Latin that he recalled from the prayers of Christian friends in the little church in Seville" and uses "sign language" with the first two young Franks the boat meets when it starts up the river Seine on the way to Paris.[51] He is accompanied by his young son, who also speaks "soft Andalusian Arabic".[52]

When Ben Attar arrives in Abulafia's house in Paris, his learned brother-in-law from Worms speaks to the north African in "clear, simple, and very slow Hebrew, as though the worry was not only about some difference in accent, dialect, or vocabulary but about a mental gap dividing north from south";[53] indeed, the central point of the book is the contrast between Sephardi and Ashkenazi customs, philosophies, and views of Jewish law, such as the new ban on bigamy of Rabbeinu Gershom. Abulafia attempts to "soften the question in trilingual speech" by addressing his brother-in law in Frankish, his uncle in

Arabic, and continues "in the holy tongue that they could all understand".[54] His skills become central later at a trial, when Ben Attar makes his case in Arabic and Abulafia translates his words into Frankish, which I assume to be the then current version of Romance, or Old French, rather than the Germanic variety known as Franconian; later he summarizes evidence "in archaic Hebrew with the Jerusalem accent", which a local scribe clothes "in the local language for the benefit of his fellow judges".[55] Mistress Esther-Minna presents her own case "volubly in the local Frankish dialect",[56] Abulafia translating from Frankish to Arabic. As the hearing continues, the rabbi chooses Arabic rather than "the ancient holy tongue";[57] again Abulafia interprets, but later the rabbi switches to Hebrew so that his own young son should not understand, calling on the local scribes to translate into Frankish.[58] At a second trial in Worms, the brother-in-law bursts "into a frantic discourse in the harsh local German dialect, leavened with flattened Hebrew words"; Ben Attar makes his complaint in Arabic, which the rabbi translates into Hebrew.[59]

Summing up, Arabic is presented as the main language of the north African Jews; the Andalusian rabbi knows Hebrew well, and Arabic (though his Spanish dialect is different from the north African), and the men (and some women in Europe) have varying levels of proficiency in Hebrew. In each region, Jewish varieties are about to develop: Judeo-Arabic in Muslim lands, Judeo-Spanish in Andalusia, Judeo-French in France, and Yiddish in Loter-Ashkenaz. Communication in this multilingual situation depends on the plurilingualism of individuals able to translate for others.

The birth of Yiddish

This historical sketch and the novelist's convincing reconstruction provide useful background for speculating on the language situation in Ashkenaz in which Yiddish could have developed. First, one notes the high level of proficiency of the many scholars in Hebrew and Aramaic, in both of which they wrote prose and poetry. Second are the close connections with Loez, both with Yavanic or Southern Loez (see the next chapter) and Tsarfatic or Western Loez, where some of them were born and with which they had regular communication. Third, Jews appear generally to have lived in concentrated sections of the town, whether open or closed Judengasse. Sometimes they were allowed Christian servants, but there were regular canons or laws against this. Fourth, the communities were regularly attacked or destroyed, and often expelled for a time, whether short or long. Fifth, their occupation as moneylenders would allow communication with non-Jews who were wealthy or powerful enough to borrow money.

Considering their background as speakers of one of the two varieties of Loez, depending on whether they came from the Yavanic area (Italy) or the Tsarfatic

(France), and their deep knowledge of Hebrew and the Judeo-Aramaic of the Talmud, it makes sense to claim[60] that Jews in Loter were multilingual, adding knowledge of the co-territorial vernacular German, and producing in the course of time a distinct fusion variety that formed the basis of Yiddish.

Each of the languages involved contributed significantly to the new spoken language of the Jews. Hebrew and Aramaic are responsible for most of the Jewish terms. If you listen to a Talmud class today, whatever the main language is (Yiddish, Hebrew, French, English), every sentence is likely to include several Hebrew or Aramaic phrases and words, and it is normal for this professional lexicon to be learned by all students. Of course, this assumes that we are dealing (as clearly was the case in the small communities of Loter-Ashkenaz) with a learned population. From Loez (the Jewish varieties rather than the Romance languages) may have come a small number of lexical items: *bentshn* (to bless), the origin of which must have been *benedicere*; *leynen* (to read aloud from the Torah), from *legere*; and probably *shul* (Jewish place of worship), which is more likely to be from Latin through Loez *schola* rather than from the Germanic Latin borrowing *schuola*.[61] There are even words that can specifically be traced to Western Loez. One example that Weinreich spends some time on is the word *tsholnt* (the combination of meat and vegetables cooked slowly starting on Friday to be eaten on Shabbat), which he traces to the Latin word *calere* (to be warm), which reflects the development of Latin initial /k/ into Old French /č/, which was deaffricated into /š/ in the thirteenth century, giving the modern French *chaud*; thus, he argues it was borrowed by Old Yiddish before the thirteenth century. Weinreich presents other examples to show the Loez base.[62]

There are only a few words that come from Southern Loez or Yavanic: one is the word *trop* (a melody for the cantillation of the Torah), which Weinreich derives from Greek *tropos*,[63] also used among Greek Christians for liturgical chant. The basis for Yiddish was a Middle High German dialect, for Yiddish often agrees with Middle High German rather than with modern German; but which variety? In fact, assuming that Yiddish started to emerge before 1150 (taken as the boundary of Old and Middle High German), Old Middle German was the first contact continued after 1150 with Middle High German. But, as Weinreich points out, the Middle High German that we know is preserved in texts and thus a normalized version of the spoken dialects.

Weinreich analyzes the complexities of trying to map features of Yiddish (at various times) onto known settlement history, with a gradual movement eastward and the reconstruction of Old High German dialects and their later developments. He gives pride of place to the Rhine–Moselle cities; there are others who argue for East Central German and Bavaria; Weinreich acknowledges, and Katz and Robert King favor, Regensburg in Bavaria, to which many Jews from the Rhineland fled in the fourteenth century because of its protection of Jews.

According to the Rhineland and Bavarian theories, the Slavic element first came into Yiddish with Knaanic (Slavic) Jews moving west, though of course its main influence was to be when large numbers of Ashkenazim later moved east.[64] But the early influence was slight, Weinreich believes. From the thirteenth century to the sixteenth there was a "great migration", after which the language was greatly modified, not just adding many lexical items and "thousands, thousands" of words, but also affecting the structure of the language. There was, for instance, the addition of what Weinreich calls "aspectoid" forms of the verb, signalling, for example, duration, repetition, or completion. Many Slavic suffixes, such as -even (in a disparaging sense) or the diminutive -nik, were also added. The Yiddish sentence never places the verb at the end, and there are many influences on phrase structure. Phonological influence is also observable. In terms of sociolinguistic influence, Weinreich observes evidence of non-Jewish servants and workers, and the close relation of Jewish peddlers with non-Jewish villagers. But, Weinreich argues, Yiddish was a fully formed language by the time the Jews moved into Slavic lands.[65] Both the Rhineland and the Danube hypotheses assume a single origin of Yiddish, but a new theory – which I shall present in more detail in a later chapter – argues that Western Yiddish had a Germanic origin but Eastern Yiddish developed separately on the basis of Czech.[66] There is a radical and contrasting hypothesis, discussed in Chapter 12, that is presented by the Israeli scholar Paul Wexler, who claims that in fact Yiddish was not Germanic but originally Slavic, and emerged in Sorbia, a region of Germany and Poland settled by Sorbs, who spoke a Slavic language.[67]

Except for artificial languages such as Esperanto, the beginning of a new variety is always a difficult event to date, for it is likely to be gradual. Yiddish fits this pattern, emerging over a long period in central Europe and taking its recognizable shape in eastern Europe, where it reached its cultural and literary apogee. To follow this, I turn in Chapter 12 to Jewish linguistic history in Slavic lands. First, though, to provide background, we need to look at Southern Loez, which Weinreich calls the Yavanic region of Greece (Yavan in Hebrew) and Italy.

11   The Yavanic area: Greece and Italy

Greece and Italy

In earlier chapters we traced how Alexander's conquests introduced the Greek language into Palestine, where it became a common vernacular of Jews there, and in Greek colonies and Byzantium; we also saw the development of Latin as the language of Jews in the Western Roman Empire, including in due course Andalusia (Spain) and France, constituting what Weinreich labeled Western Loez. In this chapter we explore the development of what Weinreich calls Southern Loez in Greece and Italy, preparing ourselves to look for evidence of the northward movement into Slavic lands, where we will see the traces of Knaanic (Judeo-Slavic) and the spread of Yiddish and the post-expulsion migration of Judeo-Latin (actually, Judeo-Spanish – Ladino, Judezmo) into the Balkans, Greece, and Turkey.

In this chapter, we look at the developments in Greece and Italy that provided the source for some of the Jewish migrations already described. By now the general picture should be clear: Jewish sociolinguistic ecology (which, remember, is the topic, rather than the historical and geographical processes that are its cause) was being modified by migration, as Jews picked up new languages (and sometimes dropped old ones) as a result of voluntary movement (usually the pursuit of trade) or involuntary expulsion (basically, the effects of anti-Semitic outbursts sparked by Christian or Muslim fanatics). The learners of these new languages were involved in assimilation, which could be sped up by forced conversion or encouraged by economic and social acceptance, or blocked by external or internal isolating forces, and which regularly suffered major losses of speakers through massacre or plague. On occasion, the conversion of others to Judaism added a language to the repertoire. In all this, one sees the maintenance of historical Jewish multilingualism, especially in the development of plurilingual proficiency, but including a continued central role for Hebrew – or, rather, Hebrew–Aramaic – as sacred and literate languages. We start with Greece.

Greece

There is evidence of Jewish residence in Greece in the biblical period, with references to Jewish slaves in the second century BCE and Jewish fugitives during the reign of Antiochus IV. Jews spread to many Greek cities during the Hasmonean period: the list provided in I Maccabees 15: 23 and matched in Philo includes Sparta, Rhodes, Crete, and Cyprus.[1]

As was the case at Alexandria, Jews in these places generally shifted to using Greek for all except sacred purposes, but they also read the Septuagint. In the case of Cyprus, there were major problems during Jewish wars in the reign of Trajan. The third-century Greek historian Cassius Dio, presenting an early version of the blood libel that was constantly to excuse Christian mobs attacking Jews, reports massacres and cannibalism by Jews in Cyrene and their expulsion in the time of Trajan.[2]

In spite of anti-Jewish feelings and actions, the Diaspora communities in the Greek colonies continued into the Byzantine period, from 330 CE until 1220. Under Constantine, the communities were recognized but restricted. Heraclius in 632 CE ordered but did not carry out the conversion of all Jews to Christianity. A similar attempted conversion was proclaimed by Leo III in 721 CE, reversed by the Council of Nicaea in 787 CE, and ordered again by Basil I in 874 CE and Romanus I in 932 CE. Christians on their way to Jerusalem for the First Crusade in 1096 attacked and looted Jewish communities, and many Jews escaped death only by fleeing from Salonika to Palestine.

Under the laws established by Constantine, Jews were excluded from the army and the government. There were civil limitations too, but Jews were active as craftsmen and farmers, and also as physicians and traders. Hebrew remained the religious language, but there was little literary activity except in south Italy (which Weinreich includes in the Yavanic region). Karaites appeared after the First Crusade, and Karaite and Rabbanite Jews arrived in Yavan from Muslim lands. In spite of the negative report of the medieval traveller Pethahia of Ratisbon (Regensburg) in the twelfth century, the conditions of the Jews in Byzantine seem to have been more favorable than in the Western Empire. From the beginning of the thirteenth century, however, persecution was common until the Ottoman conquest in 1430.

Greek-speaking Jewish communities continued to exist in many Greek cities, such as Crete, Corinth,[3] Coron, Modon, Patras, and Chios.[4] The Romaniotes, as they were called, in these communities continued to speak Judeo-Greek[5] until modern times, but in the fifteenth century Jews from Spain and Portugal joined them, speaking their own variety of Judeo-Spanish, Judezmo. They were later joined by Jews from Hungary (in the aftermath of the Black Death) and Italian speakers expelled from Corfu in southern Italy. Other Jewish immigrants arrived during the sixteenth and seventeenth centuries, so that the multilingual community also included former *Anusim* and refugees from Polish persecution.

Each of these groups built its own congregation (*kehilah*) to maintain heritage, religious, and perhaps linguistic practices. Patras,[6] for instance, had four synagogues: Kehilah Kedoshah Yevanim (the Greek Holy Congregation), Kehilah Kedoshah Yashan (the Ancient Holy Congregation, of Jews from Sicily), Kehilah Kedoshah Hadash (the New Holy Congregation, of refugees from Naples and small Italian towns), and Kehilah Kedoshah Sephardim (the Sephardic or Spanish Holy Congregation). Several important Hebrew scholars lived there.

Further north, the first synagogue in Arta (Kehilah Kedoshah Tassavim) was built by Romaniote Jews from Corfu during the Byzantine period; later, the Pugliese synagogue was built by Jews from Apulia in Italy; there were also said to be synagogues built by Jews from Calabria and Sicily.[7] The Jews of Arta continued to speak Yavanic (Judeo-Greek) until modern times, when the community was exterminated by the Nazis in 1944.[8] These developments show the effect of successive waves of migration of Jews from different countries, each bringing with them its own traditions and languages, and commonly establishing separate communities and synagogues to maintain them.

In the late Byzantine and Ottoman periods Salonika, in northeastern Greece, was the largest Jewish community. The Greek-speaking Jewish community there had been visited by Paul, and lasted through Roman and Byzantine periods. The Christian rulers of Byzantium enforced anti-Jewish laws, and the community remained small (Benjamin of Tudela reported 500 Jews) and was persecuted until the thirteenth century. Jews from Hungary arrived in 1376. But the community continued to grow. Under Venetian rule in the fourteenth century, many Jewish merchants did well but were heavily taxed. Larger numbers of Jewish immigrants arrived in Salonika after the Ottoman conquest in 1430; in 1470 Bavarian Jews built an Ashkenazi synagogue alongside the existing Romaniote one. In the fifteenth and sixteenth centuries Jews expelled from Spain, Portugal, Italy, Sicily, and France by the Christians and refugees from Muslim zealotry in north Africa arrived and established their own synagogues. *Anusim* (*conversos*) were also accepted into the Jewish community.

By the middle of the sixteenth century there were 20,000 Jews in Salonika. They lived in three main areas: near the port (the merchants), in the *Frank* (foreigner) quarter, and near the Hippodrome (mainly Greeks). There were some thirty independent *kehilot*, each with its own leadership and internal charitable, legal, and educational organizations. There were Yeshivot and distinguished rabbis, and the city was known for Kabbalah scholars and for composers of *piyyutim*. The immigrants maintained trade relations with their cities of origin, a pragmatic reason for continued plurilingualism. In the seventeenth century, in spite of plagues and fires, the Jewish population continued to grow. The false Messiah, Shabbetai Zvi, after he was expelled from his native Izmir, arrived in

1657 and was at first well received; he was later driven from Salonika, but, after his conversion to Islam, some of his followers, the *Doenmeh* (Turkish for apostates), were centered in Salonika. In 1680 the thirty synagogues united under a supreme council elected for life, and rabbinical courts were set up. In Salonika, the port was in Jewish hands and closed on the Sabbath.[9] The main Jewish language in Salonika was Judezmo, although, after Greek rule in 1912, Greek was taught in school and become the Jewish vernacular. French was added by Alliance schools, and Italian too.[10]

There were other Jewish communities in Greece – Thebes,[11] Patras, Chalcis,[12] and Nataukos – all of which were destroyed by the Greeks during their wars with the Turks in the eighteenth century.

Greece, then, was important both as an early Diaspora and for its later willingness to accept Jewish refugees from persecution elsewhere. One linguistic effect was the continuation of Judeo-Greek and its development into Yavanic by the Romaniote Jews; a second was the provision of an environment for the development of Judeo-Spanish (Judezmo and Ladino). At the same time, after a tendency to move away from Hebrew in the Roman period, Hebrew (and Hebrew–Aramaic) remained significant languages for most Jews from the Byzantine period. Another important fact bearing on language development is that some Jews later moved northwards from Greece into Slavic lands.

Italy

Weinreich distinguishes between northern Italy, which he groups with Tsarfat (northern France) and Loter (Germany) in Ashkenaz, and southern Italy, which he combines with Greece to make Yavan.[13] Jews had lived in Italy from the Maccabean period without a general expulsion, but with many local ones, and generally had peaceful relations with non-Jews.[14] Indeed, the Roman Jewish community claims to be the oldest continuously inhabited Jewish Diaspora community. By the time of Augustus there was a large Jewish population in Rome, among whom Christianity spread. Many Jewish slaves were brought to Rome after the destruction of the Temple in 70 CE, celebrated by the Arch of Titus in the Forum.[15]

During the first century CE there were estimated to be 50,000 or more Jews in Italy, many or most of them living in or near Rome, constituting one of the largest foreign groups. Many of them were former slaves who were generally poor and knew little Hebrew; there were a dozen synagogues. Jews slowly spread from the coastal towns to the interior. There was a good deal of proselytism among pagans, providing fertile ground for Christianity to develop later. There was a Yeshiva in Rome in the second century CE.

Much of the evidence of language use comes from collections of inscriptions in Italy; outside Rome, most are in Greek, a smaller number in Latin, but there are also a good number in Hebrew.[16] In Rome also, particularly in the cata-combs,[17] Greek is the most common language for inscriptions, with about half that number in Latin and only a few in Hebrew.[18] It has been suggested that the Latin inscriptions are later than the Greek, arguing that the Jewish community was bilingual, maintaining Greek, which may have been used in worship, but slowly shifting to Latin; perhaps this was also associated with class.[19] Knowledge of Latin was probably required for upward mobility, but the Christians continued to use Greek until the second century. The community was poor.[20]

When the Roman Empire adopted Christianity the Jewish situation changed from tolerance to subjection. From the fourth century CE Jewish rights were reduced, marriage to Christian women was forbidden, and keeping Christian slaves was not permitted. Legal codes established a lower status for Jews, including a ban on building synagogues. As the empire collapsed, there were changes depending on the rulers: there was greater freedom under the Goths, and persecution under the Byzantines. In the ninth and tenth centuries there were periods of forced conversion to Christianity, and Arab raids in the south. In Sicily, conditions became better under the Saracens in the ninth to eleventh centuries.

By the end of the eleventh century there were only a few Jews in Verona and Pavia in northern Italy and Lucca in Tuscany, but a larger community continued to exist in Rome, and there were many Jews in the south and Sicily. Some Jews were artisans, others farmers. By the tenth century tombstones were being inscribed in Hebrew. In a study of public texts in south Italy, especially Solenot, although ninth-century Jewish inscriptions were found to be in Hebrew, by the eleventh and twelfth centuries they are in Greek and Latin.[21] There were Yeshivot in Lucca (where the Kalonymus family lived), in Rome, and in the south in several towns, including Bari in Apulia and Siponto, noted as a center of Jewish learning in the twelfth century.

In the thirteenth century the bulk of Jewish settlement in Italy continued to be in the south,[22] apart from 200 families in Rome and a few dozen families in Pisa and Lucca. The first Jewish settlement in Naples may have been as early as the first century CE; there was an important community there by the fourth century, and a synagogue and school in the eleventh. When Benjamin of Tudela visited Naples, he reported that there were 500 Jews. In the twelfth century there were anti-Jewish riots, and the synagogue was converted into a church. Under the rule of Robert of Anjou in 1330, however, Jews from the Balearic islands were invited to settle in Anjou and Naples; 100 years later, under the rule of Aragon, Jews from many parts settled there.[23]

The attitude of non-Jews to the Jews in Italy varied, with popular antagonism sometimes controlled by nobles and bishops. Pope Calixtus II (1119–24) had issued a bull, *Sicut Judaeis*, calling for protection of the Jews, which other popes confirmed,[24] but decisions at the Third (1179) and Fourth (1215) Lateran Councils set important restrictions on Jewish life.[25] Soon after that the Inquisition started to investigate Jews and *Anusim*, and after 1240 the campaign against the Talmud that had started earlier in France reached Italy.

In the south, Jews continued to be protected, and Benjamin of Tudela reported that there were about 1,500 Jews in Palermo[26] and as many in Apulia. When, at the end of the thirteenth century, southern Italy came under Angevin rule, a blood libel pogrom took place in Trani, one of the largest Jewish communities in Apulia during the twelfth century and the birthplace of the great Talmudist Rabbi Isaiah ben Mali di Trani, leading to a campaign of conversion and massacre until 1294, during which synagogues were converted to churches and communities annihilated.

But Jewish learning (which depended on knowledge of Hebrew) continued. There were Yeshivot in Rome, Bari, and Otranto. Parts of south Italy were under Byzantine rule from the fifth century to the eleventh, with a large number of wealthy Jewish communities in larger cities and ports reported to be under constant pressure to convert to Christianity. The Jews of Oria had a high reputation for Hebrew scholarship; ten rabbis were reported to have been slain during the Muslim conquest of the city in 925 CE. Survivors moved to Bari or Otranto. Bari was in commercial contact with Byzantium, where there was an important rabbinical court. The town had been destroyed by the time Benjamin of Tudela visited.

Otranto had been founded by 5,000 Jewish prisoners settled by Titus after the destruction of Jerusalem. There were 500 Jews there when Benjamin visited. Among the learned Jews were a number of poets. Taranto also dates back to the Roman period; in the fourth and fifth centuries CE funerary inscriptions were in Greek and from the seventh to the ninth in Latin, Hebrew, or bilingual. The Jewish community may still have been Greek-speaking when Benjamin found 300 Jews there, but the bishop and clergy were Latin-speaking. There were highly cultured Jews in Rossano. Jews used the language of their co-territorial Christians: Latin in Apulia, Greek in Calabria. There is good evidence of knowledge of Hebrew.[27]

It was around the twelfth century that Jews in southern and central Italy began to speak dialectal varieties of Judeo-Italian, a practice that spread to the north in the fourteenth to sixteenth centuries. Corfu, the northernmost of the Ionian islands, was a good example of the development of Jewish communities in the Yavanic region after the thirteenth century (earlier, there had been only one Jew there, according to Benjamin of Tudela). The first group of Jews to arrive was from Thebes, brought as prisoners and slaves by King Roger of Sicily; they spoke an Apulian dialect. They were required to serve as galley slaves, to provide lodging for soldiers, to act as public executioners, and to come to court on the Sabbath. At times there were attacks by the local population.

Corfu was the "rallying point of modern Greek and of the Venetian and Apulian dialects as spoken and written by Jews".[28] Corfiote Jews started speaking Greek, but added other varieties as more Jews arrived between the twelfth and fourteenth centuries.

Under Venetian rule, starting in 1386, Jews in Corfu were forbidden to buy land and forced to wear badges, and they were heavily taxed for the wars against the Turks. In 1622 they were forced into a ghetto. The Greek-speaking community was absorbed, in time, by the Apulian, but it preserved some customs, such as celebrating Shushan Purim[29] and reading Greek *piyyutim* on the fast of Tish'a B'Av. The Greek synagogue was the oldest, and it kept up for some time variations in liturgy and a distinctive melody for prayer. In the sixteenth century there was a Greek or Romaniote community that followed what was called *Minhag Korfu* (the Byzantine ritual), and an Italian community, enlarged by Jews from Apulia, exiles from Spain and Portugal, including former *Anusim*, and Ashkenazim who had adopted a Sephardi ritual; by 1563 the Sephardim formed the majority of the 400 or so Jewish population, but most Jews spoke the Apulian dialect with Greek words. The Jews of Corfu were traders, artisans, and moneylenders, and were granted privileges not allowed to the Jews of Venice. Some Greek *piyyutim* were maintained in the Corfu Greek synagogue into the nineteenth century. The "better class" of the community spoke Judeo-Venetian, with some Greek words, but official documents were in Italian, which became the language of instruction in Jewish schools. Jewish exiles from Spain quickly picked up one of the two local vernaculars, and others settled briefly in Albania before continuing to Salonika, which became a center of Judeo-Spanish. Apulians settled in Corfu, and composed love songs in Apulian and Hebrew. Venetian, Apulian, Italian, and Greek were still spoken in Corfu at the end of the nineteenth century. In 1829 a New Testament was printed in Judeo-Spanish.[30] Yavanic speakers had lost their language by the nineteenth century, but kept some words and names.

Venice and the ghetto

Although ghettos were not restricted to Italy,[31] the name was first used there for the area of Venice in which Jews were permitted to live in 1516. It is, of course, common for new immigrants to tend to cluster in a city in the same area; their relatives and others speaking their language are there, as are appropriate shops and institutions. For observant Jews, it is important to live close enough to a synagogue to walk there on the Sabbath, when travel is forbidden. An extra motivation was the danger of attacks by Gentiles. This is the explanation given for the walled *mellah* of Fez in Morocco, established in 1438 and described originally as a beautiful area, protected by a surrounding wall. A second *mellah* was set up in Marrakesh in the second half of the fifteenth century, with two gates locked every night.[32] In Venice, and in Florence after 1570, the ghettos were similarly enclosed, but the cause was a decision not of the Jews but of the local government.

The existence of ghettos raises the issue of the degree to which developments in the Jewish community were internally motivated or the result of external influence.[33] Jonathan Israel argues that European Jewish culture was strongly influenced – indeed, shaped – by its non-Jewish environment.[34] Robert Bonfil and other scholars,[35] on the other hand, argue for greater internal agency. Whatever the original motivation, the forced enclosure in the ghetto of Jews of different status and origin both made the presence of Jews in a Christian state legitimate and gave opportunity to Jewish institutions to develop "secular and religious modes of accommodation, adaptation, and resistance".[36]

The separation established by the ghetto and the *mellah*, whether internally or externally motivated, had important sociolinguistic effects. First, it reduced contact with non-Jews, especially when the ban on Jews having non-Jewish servants was enforced by Christian or Muslim rulers, and when the main contact with non-Jews was by Jewish moneylenders or physicians working outside the ghetto. Second, it reinforced the formation of Jewish varieties of the co-territorial vernacular, first adopted during times when there was easy outside contact or when it had been introduced by higher-status males who had opportunities to trade outside the ghetto. Third, it led to later Jewish migrants adopting the established Jewish variety as they settled into the community. The developments of the Jewish Italian dialects and of Judeo-Arabic and Haketia (the north African variety of Judeo-Spanish) in north Africa was a sociolinguistic mode of "accommodation, adaptation and resistance", picking up enough of the co-territorial vernacular to do business with non-Jewish neighbors, but forming and maintaining a marked variety that supported and signaled Jewish identity.

Venice itself provides a vivid example of the combination of Jews from different regions and languages. In the fourteenth century the Venetian Senate gave permission to some Jews to reside in Venice for a limited time, but in 1397 Jews were expelled and forced to move across the lagoon to Mestre, being permitted to come to the city only for fifteen days at a time. They were forbidden to own property there. Some Jews found ways to stay in the city, and in 1424 a law forbade sexual acts between Jewish men (traders) and Christian women (presumably their servants). In 1496 the Senate required Jews in Venice to wear a yellow hat. A new charter in 1502 required Jews to do business from neighboring Mestre, but allowed them to move to Venice in case of war, which they did in 1508. Jewish second-hand shops were permitted in the Rialto in 1514.

After 1516 all Jews in Venice were required to live in the ghetto, an area surrounded by a wall and patrolled by guards, with the gates closed at night. A new charter authorizing second-hand shops and pawnbroking and requiring a 5,000 ducat annual tax was adopted in 1533, and renewed later at a higher tax rate. The most important group in the new ghetto consisted of the Ashkenazim, called the *Natione Todesca*, many of whom had lived in Italy for many generations, but also including recent immigrants. Jewish physicians among them were allowed to leave the ghetto at night.

In 1541 the Venetian Senate gave permission to the magistrates to admit Levantine Jewish merchants also to lodge in the Old Ghetto; these were former *Anusim* from Portugal and Spain who had been living in Constantinople and Salonika, and who had trading connections with Romania, the Balkans, and the Ottoman Empire. Now there were Ashkenazim in the New and Levantines in the Old Ghetto. In 1555, under papal direction, the *Anusim* in Ancona (a city on the Adriatic with a large Jewish community) were arrested and killed, deported, or converted; the Levantine Jewish merchants declared a boycott, which strengthened the Venetian traders.

In the renewal of the Venetian charter in 1558, Jewish moneylenders were instructed to keep their accounts in Italian rather than Hebrew.[37] The charter was renewed, but conditions worsened in 1566. During the second half of the sixteenth century the Inquisition was active among the *Anusim* in Venice, as elsewhere. Pressure was also brought on the growing number of printing presses in Venice; Hebrew publishing was banned from 1553 to 1563, and censorship was later imposed; thousands of Hebrew books were destroyed in 1568. In the sixteenth century the rabbinate began to censor Hebrew books to make sure they were not offensive to Judaism or the Catholic Church.

The third wave of Jewish immigration to Venice was the arrival of Iberian Jews, known as the *Natione Penentina* (Western Nation), as noted in the charter of 1589. The three communities, each with its own synagogue or Scola, formed the University of the Jews (*Università degli Ebrei)*. Jewish life slowly improved, as new areas for trade developed; there was tension between the communities, however, especially the former *Anusim*, and with the Senate, as each community had to negotiate new charters regularly.

After a first century of problems, the Jews of Venice were established, with their mixture of languages: "Hebrew chants and Mediterranean dialects were superimposed on the colorful tones of Spanish, Turkish, Portuguese, and Greek, along with the argot spoken by some of the Polish and German refugees and with the many Italian dialects: a true Babel of people and tongues."[38] In the New Ghetto were the Scola Grande Todesca (built in 1528), the Scola Canton (a second Ashkenazi synagogue built in 1531), and the Scuola Italiana (built in 1571). In the Old Ghetto there were the two largest synagogues: the Levantine, built in the middle of the sixteenth century; and the Spanish, built a little later. Hebrew may well have been the only common language until all learned the Venetian dialect, of which a Jewish variety developed; the Sephardim spoke

Judezmo, the Ashkenazim Yiddish. A Haggadah was published with Hebrew text and translation into Judeo-Spanish, Judeo-Venetian, and Yiddish.

While the various Italian Jewish communities were in touch with each other, the fact that vernacular varieties of Italian were regional and local until quite recently – an Italian school inspector told me twenty years ago that at that time most schoolchildren did not meet a non-dialectal version of Italian until they came to school – there was no Judeo-Italian, but Jewish varieties of local dialects: Judeo-Roman, Judeo-Venetian, Judeo-Florentine, and about nine or ten other distinct varieties.

Although currently the second largest Jewish community in Italy, that of Milan had a very checkered past: a few inscriptions from the Roman period; the destruction of the synagogue in 388 CE, which the bishop regretted he had not burned down; the synagogue rebuilt and sacked in 507; vague references in the tenth century; revival in the thirteenth century (along with other northern communities); expulsion in 1320, but permission to settle in Lombardy in 1387; expulsion again in 1489, but permission to return to Lombardy (but not Milan for longer than three days shortly afterwards – a situation that lasted until 1597, when Jews were expelled from all of Lombardy). Only in 1714, under Austrian rule, did Jews start to return; a synagogue was built in 1840, and full rights were granted in 1859 under Italian rule.[39]

Jewish publishing

The development of printing in the fifteenth century had major effects on Jewish culture as well as on general culture. Gutenberg's Latin Bibles appeared in 1455; the first Hebrew Psalter was published in 1477, printed probably in Bologna by some German printers, Joseph Neriah, Chaim Mordekai, and Hezekiah Montero de Venturo, using Rashi characters. Hebrew printing developed rapidly in Spain; an edition of Rashi's commentary on the Bible was printed in Guadalajara by Solomon ben Moses Alkabis Halevi, and there was high-quality Jewish printing there until the expulsion in 1492.

The first Jewish printers in Italy, the next major center, were from Germany. A Pentateuch was printed in Pesaro in 1482, and an edition with commentaries in Bologna at about the same time. In 1487 a Jewish press was set up in Naples by the German Joseph ben Jacob Gunzenhausen. Before the summer of 1492 his successor, Joshua Solomon Soncino, published the full Hebrew Bible in Naples. A third Naples printer was Isaac ben Judah ibn Katorzo from Spain, who printed Nachmanides' Pentateuch in 1490.

In the same year Eliezer Toledano published in Lisbon a number of separate books of the Bible with commentary and Targum. In 1493 the Soncino Press (headed by Gershom Soncino) was publishing in Brescia. After the expulsion

Hebrew printing ceased in Spain and Portugal, and it was not renewed until 1510 in Italy.[40]

Jews adopted the technology of printing very early: in the first half of the sixteenth century more than 1,300 Hebrew books were published. Manuscripts of sacred texts, such as *Sifrei Torah* (scrolls) to be read in synagogue and the passages to be enclosed in *mezuzot* and phylacteries, continued to be written by scribes following strict rules, but for other purposes print quickly replaced manuscript. While there was some debate about the status of books, the technology was as acceptable to Jewish religious authorities as it was to Christians and to Muslims in the Ottoman Empire (elsewhere it was banned by Muslims until the eighteenth century, or even the nineteenth).

One effect of the new technology was the collaboration it led to between Jews and Christians, the former responsible more for content and the latter for editing (including censorship) and book production. New classes of readers (people of moderate education and means) and of authors (itinerant preachers and young rabbis) also appeared. Italy was the early center of this activity. Nearly half the Hebrew books published between 1539 and 1639 were printed in Italy, with Venice publishing a third of them. There was state or Church control of printing in Italy, leading to censorship. Italy was in an ideal place to serve as the center for Jewish publication, which lasted until the late seventeenth and eighteenth centuries, when Amsterdam became important.[41] Geneva too was important for publishing Hebrew books, but these were for non-Jews, for there was no Jewish community; the books included Bibles or polyglot Bibles, Latin treatises on Hebrew grammar, and works in French or Latin with Hebrew quotations.[42]

The printing of books in Hebrew confirmed and increased the status and use of the language, for most Jews could afford a prayer book and a Bible, and scholars could be encouraged to publish their commentaries and scientific works. The rich literature in Hebrew guaranteed the prestige of the language and provided a treasury of developing lexicon to handle traditional as well as modern concepts.

Yavan

In this chapter, we have followed the addition and development of languages of the Jews in the Yavanic region and in northern Italy. We saw first the continuation of Jewish use of Greek from the Greek conquest of Palestine and the continuing Roman rule, and its adoption by Jew in Greek colonies and Byzantium. Later, a Jewish variety emerged that lasted through the nineteenth and twentieth centuries, until it was lost through migration and assimilation to co-territorial varieties (including, of course, Modern Hebrew in Israel) and the Nazi destruction of European Jewry and its languages.

In Italy, we saw the adoption of local varieties of Italian, until they were replaced in the middle of the twentieth century by standard Italian; thus Jews acquired Venetian and developed a variety of Judeo-Venetian, reported to be spoken as late as 1979.[43] Other dialects include Judeo-Piedmontese, attested to by Primo Levi,[44] which some of his elderly relatives still spoke; Judeo-Florentine; Judeo-Ferrarese; and Judeo-Mantuan.[45] There is also a distinct variety of Judeo-Roman, which may still be spoken. A number of religious and literary texts appeared in Hebrew letters in Judeo-Italian dialects in the thirteenth century, and continued to be published until the eighteenth century.

Other languages were brought into Italy by Jews expelled from Spain and France, or seeking a better life than was currently available in Muslim or other Christian lands. This led to the development of multilingual Jewish communities, with separate Scola (*shuls*) that outlasted the acquisition of the local vernacular, and accounted for periods when Jews in Italy spoke Judeo-Arabic, Judezmo, and Yiddish. The establishment of Jewish education (there were Yeshivot in many towns with distinguished rabbis) and the development of Jewish printing in Italy encouraged (and attested to) continued proficiency in Hebrew and Aramaic in the Yavanic region.

12   Jews in Slavic lands

Where did they come from?

There are two conflicting views of Jews in Slavic lands. The standard view, supported by most scholars, goes like this. Starting with the First Crusade, in 1096, Jews in Spain, France, and Italy suffered regularly from periodic pogroms and other persecutions, and were from time to time expelled from the towns and countries in which they lived. This pressure for migration continued for several hundred years, and, with no outlet to the west yet available, the obvious direction was to the east, through Loter (which was the foundation of Ashkenaz), into the countries that were now largely occupied by the Slavic peoples – Indo-Europeans who had moved into the region from the sixth century (see Map 9). One of the linguistic effects of this migration was the addition to the Jewish repertoire of varieties of Slavic, identified in Jewish linguistics as *Knaanic*. The term is a pun on the word "Slav" as slave, and the biblical category of Canaanite slaves. Knaanic, as some linguists following Solomon Birnbaum[1] call it, was eventually replaced by Yiddish.

The alternative view is that there was only a comparatively small and temporary eastern migration, followed rapidly by a return to Loter. In this view, the bulk of Jews in eastern Europe either were there already,[2] perhaps local converts (the Sorbian and Ukrainian hypothesis), or came from the Caucasus or Persia (including the Khazarian theory). In either event, we are left with the question of how Knaanic or other Slavic varieties were so completely replaced by Yiddish.[3]

Early migrations to Slavic lands

In any case, there is evidence that Jews had reached eastern European regions before the Slavic invasions. The earliest reference appears to be a first-century CE tradition that Jews assisted King Decebelus of Dacia in fighting the Romans. Dacia, a Thracian kingdom inhabited by a relatively unknown Indo-European people, was bounded in the south by the Danube, which provided a border with ancient Greece (whose inhabitants considered them barbarians) and included

9 Jewish centers in early modern Europe
Source: Shear (2010).

present-day Bulgaria, Serbia, Hungary, Romania, and the Ukraine. In about 100
CE Dacia was conquered by Rome and became a Roman province. Decebelus,
the last Dacian king, was defeated by the Romans and committed suicide, but
before that is said to have invited Jews into his kingdom. Later, Jewish prisoners
were said to have been transferred to the Roman province, and rebellious
legions, which had included Jewish soldiers, were transferred there. A number
of inscriptions give evidence of Jewish presence in the second and third

centuries CE, including a reference to an *archisynagogos Iudeorum* in Intercisa in the Roman province of Pannonia in the early third century.[4]

The region was occupied successively by Huns, Ostrogoths, Lombards, Gepids, Byzantines, Avars, various Slavs (from the sixth century), Magyars (from the eighth century), the Holy Roman Empire, Ottomans, and Serbia. In 960 CE letters mention Jews in "Hungarin" and an Arab geographer mentions Hungarian Jews trading in Prague. So there is evidence of Jews in the east well before the migration from western Europe.

In 1092, in the reign of Saint Ladislaus I, the Synod of Szabolcs passed a ban on Jews marrying Christian wives or having Christian slaves, emulating earlier west European anti-Jewish policies. The next ruler, King Coloman, restricted Jews to cities with bishops where they could be supervised. While sometimes opposed by local rulers in Hungary, crusaders were said to have attacked Jews.

As a result of the pogroms in France, Germany, and Bohemia, Bohemian Jews sought refuge in Hungary, and, to start with, were accepted. In the early thirteenth century some served as government officials, but in 1233 the Pope required Muslims and Jews to wear distinctive badges. After the Mongol invasion that followed, Jews were granted a *privilegium* that remained in force until 1526, with exceptions and persecution under various foreign rulers and a period of expulsion in 1360. There was a brief period of protection under the emperor Maximilian but a major change after the Ottoman conquest in 1526, when Jews were scattered and sent to Constantinople, Sofia (where there were Romaniote, Ashkenazi, Sephardi, and Hungarian synagogues), Plevna in Bulgaria, and Kavala in northern Greece.

The eastward movement

There had been Jews in Loter in Roman times, but Ashkenaz as a Jewish cultural center started to develop only in the ninth century. Originally, Jewish observance in Loter was answerable to the rulings of the Yeshivot of Babylonia and Palestine, but by the time of Rabbi Gershom, with his ban on polygamy in the eleventh century, Ashkenaz had become independent in deciding questions of Jewish law. In the eleventh and twelfth centuries Jews moved east into Slavic lands, and the center of Ashkenaz also moved east. This movement is at the heart of the Rhineland hypothesis about the origin of Yiddish, which, although it has been attacked,[5] remains the majority consensus.

A major figure was Rabbi Jacob Pollack, who in around 1500 left Prague for Poland and founded a Yeshiva in Cracow.[6] Language, Rabbi Pollack argued, reflects life, and the development of Yiddish came about with this major change in Jewish life. There is no clear evidence of the actual beginning of Yiddish, however. Weinreich recognizes four periods: before 1250, from then until 1500, from 1500 to 1750, and modern Yiddish after 1750. There are, of course, many dialects of Yiddish.

Yiddish is a fusion language, with four components: Hebrew, Loez, German, and Slavic; the first three were original and the fourth was added several hundred years later.[7] Up to the middle of the thirteenth century Yiddish existed in German-speaking territory; after that it developed in territory where the language was not German. Jews migrated for non-linguistic reasons, of course, but their languages were affected by these migrations.

Jews had come to Slavic lands earlier from four sources: from the Yavanic communities north of the Black Sea, from Byzantium, from the Caucasus, and from Khazaria; they settled in Kievan Russ. Some may have come from the west before the major movement. These early migrants presumably learned to speak a Slavic variety, the Eastern Knaanic, of which little evidence remains, and which was ultimately replaced by Yiddish.[8] Because of the paucity of hard evidence, there are a number of fairly radical hypotheses about what else might have happened. One is the notion that the Khazars who had converted to Judaism were a major source of the Ashkenazi population, and so the first speakers of Yiddish. We start with this suggestion.

Conversion of the Khazars

The Khazars[9] were a Turkic people who moved into eastern Europe in the seventh century CE and established a kingdom that lasted until the tenth century, at the end of which they were conquered by the Russians. In the middle of the eighth century their royal family and a part of the Khazari population were converted to Judaism. For the next two centuries the Khazar kingdom extended as far west as Kiev and as far east as the Caucasus, forming a buffer between Christians and Muslims. Their language was Khazarian, written in a runic script, but any surviving written works are in Hebrew.

Starting from the middle of the eighth to the middle of the ninth centuries, and still attested in the thirteenth century, Jewish Radhanite traders – said by the Persian geographer Ibn Khordadbeh to speak Persian, Slavic, Spanish, Frankish, Greek, and Arabic – traded in the region; one of their routes was from Regensburg to Kiev, another from Prague to Kiev. Most Radhanite traders were observant Jews, with knowledge of Hebrew; some theories hold that the Khazars adopted Jewish practices from them. Other traders in the region were Rus', Arabic or Chinese.

In the tenth century there was a series of letters in Hebrew between King Joseph of Khazaria and Hasdai ibn Shaprut of Andalusia. Hasdai mentioned the problems he had in establishing contact, and asked about the conversion and the Jewish practices of the Khazars. Joseph replied giving details of the conversion and of the reform under King Obadiah, when rabbinic Judaism was introduced.

In an updated version of a popular but detailed and richly annotated account,[10] Kevin Brook gives useful background not just to the controversial account of the Khazar contribution to Jewish genetics proposed by Arthur Koestler[11] but to the process of Jewish settlement in Slavic lands. The area of Khazaria became, Brook suggests, a region of refuge for Jews, some of whom introduced Judaism to the Khazars. King Bulan converted to Judaism, as did many nobles and possibly many other people, and the Judaized Khazars later adopted rabbinic Judaism and Hebrew names, studied the Torah and Talmud, and replaced their runic script with Hebrew writing.

Brook acknowledges that the genetic contribution of the Khazars to the Ashkenazim is much less than Koestler believes, but still holds that East European Jews descended from a mixture of "Khazars, Slavs, Middle Eastern Jews, German Jews and Czech Jews".[12] The Khazars, like other nomadic Turks, were racially mixed, with both Slavic and European features, but there is no clear evidence of their origin. The independent Khazarian state was founded in the early seventh century CE, a multi-ethnic and multi-religious empire that assimilated many peoples. After the conversion, only Judaized Khazars were eligible to become *kagan* (king, later modified to spiritual leader when the *bek* was the secular leader and army commander). But any detailed study of the Khazars is hampered by the shortage of written records.[13] There are few traces of the Khazarian language, which has been partly reconstructed from runic texts, assumed Khazar words in Hebrew texts, and place names and personal names.[14] It seems that some converted Khazars learned Hebrew, which was known by the Jews of the region (St. Cyril was able to study Hebrew in Cherson in the Crimea in the late ninth century). Many Khazars were traders, taking advantage of their position at the center of major trade routes. The Khazars minted coins, some with errors in the Arabic, suggesting that they were not fluent in Qur'anic Arabic.

There were Jews settled in Pannonia in the third century, who left inscriptions in Latin. Jews also lived in early Bulgaria. Thousands of Jews migrated to the Hellenistic kingdom of Bosporus, settling on the Crimean and Taman Peninsulas. They spoke Greek and used it on their inscriptions. Liberated Jewish slaves were welcomed in some synagogues. In Cherson, a Christian basilica was built in the fifth or sixth century CE on the remains of an earlier synagogue. Archeological finds attest to Jewish settlement in the later sixth century. There are Jewish traditions of these dispersions.

It is not certain that these Jewish communities continued, but, if they did, Crimean Jewry would have come into contact with the invading Khazars. In any case, Khazaria became a refuge for Jews in Byzantium seeking to escape the forced baptisms of Heraclitus at the beginning of the seventh century CE and of Leo III a century later and the persecutions of the ninth and tenth centuries. Some of these Jewish refugees married Khazars; they maintained circumcision but not Sabbath observance. There are also reports of Jews from Mesopotamia and Persia moving to Khazaria.

Before their conversion to Judaism, Khazars followed Tengri shamanism, the animistic polytheistic religion common among Turks, Mongols, Bulgars, and Hungarians. King Bulan was the first Jewish ruler, who, according to some accounts, selected Judaism after a debate between an Arab mullah, a Christian priest, and a rabbi. Yehuda Halevy tells of an angel who warned Bulan of the need to convert, and of the circumcision that marked the event. Confirming his twelfth-century Jewish account, a ninth-century cleric, Christian of Stavelot, attests that Khazars were circumcised and observed the laws of Judaism. Another near-contemporary account is a letter to Hasdai ibn Shaprut (discovered by Solomon Schechter in the Cairo Genizah) that initiated correspondence between Hasdai and King Joseph. Hasdai was a doctor and vizier to the Umayyad caliph and lived in Cordoba, a city in Andalusia, at the end of the tenth century. It took some time for his letter, which was sent via Hungary and Bulgaria asking about the conversion and Khazarian life, to reach Khazaria. A reply written around 955 gave details of Bulan's conversion and told of a later king, Obadiah, who brought in Jewish scholars to teach rabbinic Judaism. The succeeding kings all had Jewish names.

There are indications that Muslims were also proselyting, and in 860 Saints Cyril and Methodius were sent to the Khazars by the Byzantine emperor Michael III as missionaries. Cyril studied Hebrew and engaged in a public disputation, as a result of which a few Khazarian nobles and some common people converted to Christianity. More evidence is provided by a Hebrew letter discovered in the Cairo Genizah written about the beginning of the tenth century by Jews in Kiev trying to raise money for a Jew imprisoned for debt. It has a word added in runic, thought to be Khazarian for "I have read". The names of the signatories suggest that some may have been proselytes; otherwise, they might be Khazar names adopted by Jews. The important question is: did common people convert to Judaism, or only the king and some nobles? And, if so, when? Brook concludes that not just the royalty and nobles but also a significant proportion of the common people adopted rabbinic Judaism. But there is no hard evidence of how many Khazars converted, or how fully they followed Jewish practices, and there are few Turkic words in Yiddish: *kaftan* (coat),[15] *yarmulke* (skullcap),[16] *davenen* (to pray),[17] and a number of other equally questionable borrowings, and none that is certainly from Khazar. As mentioned above, most current genetic studies find only a tiny proportion of Slavic (and perhaps Khazar) markers in east European Jewish DNA – not enough to suggest a large number of converts intermarrying.

Over the centuries the Khazarian Empire was engaged in wars with its neighbors – Muslim, Byzantine, Hungarian – but the most serious struggle was with the Rus', who seized the city of Kiev in 965 and continued to invade their territory. Shortly after this some cities came under Muslim rule, and many Khazars converted to Islam. Much of Khazaria came under Slavic control, and the Khazar Empire ended early in the eleventh century, when the Byzantines and the Rus' attacked Khazaria, effectively ending the independence of the last Jewish nation until 1948. Khazars moved to Hungary, Transylvania, Byzantium, Spain, Azerbaijan, Bulgaria, Lithuania, and elsewhere. Some intermarried with other Jewish communities, others converted to Islam or Christianity.

The genetic evidence

There appears to be little hard evidence of what happened in these cases but enough references to Jewish Khazars to provide a basis for the Koestler and Wexler hypotheses. A number of studies of Jewish DNA have been cited as throwing light on the issue, but these are hindered – and, indeed, rendered highly questionable – by lack of evidence of Khazar DNA, there being no clearly identifiable descendants. We need less biased or more sophisticated studies to clear up this mystery. In the meantime, there is some DNA evidence suggesting a slight Khazar influence, and insufficient evidence of any language influence for us to take the hypothesis seriously; Weinreich considers the theory "fantastic",[18] commenting that "nothing is known about the language of the Khazars",[19] and even Brook finishes up with little enthusiasm for the claim, concluding that "there is a small Turkic Khazarian element among" east European Jews.[20]

Keeping the issue alive, though, a recent unpublished study compares the hypothesis of the Khazarian origin of east European Jewry with the Rhineland hypothesis using genome-wide data from Caucasus populations,[21] and claims that the east European population clusters with the Caucasus rather than the Middle Eastern populations, providing support for the Khazarian hypothesis and for the views of Wexler and Koestler.[22] The issue is clearly still being debated, but the argument has not yet shaken the consensus view, which is also supported by a survey of genetic evidence.

How trustworthy is the genetic evidence of the development of the Jewish people? A controversial Israeli historian, whose book[23] attacks the notion of Jewish peoplehood and the historiography on which it is based, has been cited as attacking geneticists (including those whose views seem to support his arguments) as generally ignorant of history and dangerously seeking evidence to support unfounded theses.[24] In a recent review of two books on Jewish genetics,[25] Richard Lewontin, a pioneer of population genetics, is skeptical of studies that attempt to reconstruct the genetic structure of ancestors. He argues against biological determinism, pointing out the speculative nature of these attempts. Noting the conclusions and motivations of the three books he mentions in his review might help us judge better the confused picture that emerges.

In the first, an Israeli geneticist, in a book still available only in Hebrew,[26] finds genetic support for the links between present-day Jews and the land that has been "the glue of their social bonds". In a popularized account of his and other research, a geneticist, Robert Ostrer,[27] also finds a genetic basis for tracing Jewish history. A recent study in which he has been involved[28] finds shared ancestry between Middle Eastern and Ashkenazi Jews, and is claimed to refute "large-scale genetic contributions of Central and Eastern European and Slavic populations to the formation of Ashkenazi Jewry" such as that claimed by Eran Elhaik.[29]

Elhaik offers an opposing view, claiming that the present-day Ashkenazi population descends from converted Khazars and not from former Middle Eastern "Judeans". Thus, he supports the hypothesis of Koestler (as repeated by the linguist Wexler) of the Khazarian origin of Yiddish.

While still holding to a form of biological determinism in her claim that "who we really are collectively and individually is given by and legible in biological data", Nadia Abu El-Haj,[30] in the third book reviewed, is highly critical of the work of Israeli and "self-identified Jewish scientists" in building up a case for Jewish peoplehood. She does not believe, however, that work on the genome can be conclusive one way or the other in proving or disproving historical facts.

Can genetics answer our questions? Shlomo Sand and Abu-El-Haj suggest that our answers will be predetermined by our beliefs. Lewontin not only sees uncertainty, but wonders why we are asking the questions. The field is developing too rapidly for us to be confident of applying it: studies based on a few genetic elements of selected parts of large populations are unlikely to do more than confirm the prejudices we have. So, again, we are left with *Teiku*: the question remains unanswered.

The murky origins of Yiddish

Scholars who follow Weinreich believe that Yiddish developed from the German of the Rhine Valley. There were certainly Jews, probably speakers of Judeo-Latin, living with the Romans in the Rhineland in the fourth century, but they probably left when the Romans withdrew. There was a community in Cologne[31] mentioned by Constantine. Jews reappear only 500 years later, and the territory that Jews called "Loter" includes Metz,[32] Aachen,[33] Mainz,[34] Worms,[35] and Speyer,[36] with evidence of Jewish settlement dating from 800. There were probably a number of other cities with Jews, such as Trier (Treves), where Jews survived persecution in 1066 and again in 1096, and Bonn, where Jews were martyred during the First Crusade in 1096. There was also an important Jewish community on the Danube, located in Regensburg at least from 981. It was, Weinreich believes, one of the first colonies of Loter settled by Jews from the west, south, and east, and creating their own fusion language with German as the main component.[37] And there were, as we have mentioned already, Jews further east in Knaan, such as in Prague.

The evidence for Jewish life in Loter is scattered, but it is reasonable to assume, as Weinreich does, that the community took shape between 800 and 1000. This was the area ruled by the grandson of Charlemagne, Lothar, between France and Germany. This Jewish borderland separated from Tsarfat about 1000, probably as a result of the influence of settlers from Italy such as the Kalonymus family. The term "Loter" coincided roughly with the kingdom of Lorraine (Lotharingia); its main Jewish settlers came from Tsarfat, but there is evidence of a link to Italy with the coming of Kalonymus from Lucca. It is possible that, while the greater number came from France, there were other distinguished scholars who came from Italy.

Jewish Loter maintained its traditional ties with earlier rabbinical authorities; questions of doubt would be sent to Italy or to the Yeshivot in north Africa, or even to Babylonia; Rabbi Meir ben Baruch of Rothenburg, who had studied in Mainz and in French Yeshivot and founded his own Yeshiva in Germany in the middle of the thirteenth century, is quoted as saying that "we follow the customs of the Babylonians". But, soon, Jewish Loter became autonomous with its own rabbis, who ruled independently of the Yeshivot in Babylonia and Palestine and, like their heads, were cited as Gaonim (a term for head of one of the major Yeshivot). It was in Loter, Weinreich believes, that Yiddish emerged, "because western Loez speakers and southern Loez speakers, with Hebrew as their mediated language, created a small gathering of exiles in an area where the co-territorial non-Jewish population spoke different variants of German".[38]

The linguistic bases of Yiddish

Yiddish was formed from four components (Weinreich uses the word "deter-minants"): *loshn koydesh*, Loez, and German, to which Slavic (Knaanic) was later to be added. Each of these he considers in detail, his account based mainly on lexicon.[39]

Weinreich first considers Hebrew, the original, dominant, and characteristic language of the Jews. He sees a difference between the Merged Hebrew, which formed part of Yiddish, and the whole Hebrew, which is *loshn koydesh* (the Yiddish for what is in Hebrew *leshon hakodesh*, the language of sanctity, the holy tongue). To illustrate, he gives the example of a guest invited by the *bale'bos* (Yiddish for "host") to recite the grace after meals in which he includes a verse thanking the *baal habayis* (Hebrew for "host"). Other obvious pairs are the Merged Hebrew (Yiddish) *Rabbonon-kadish*, in contrast to the Hebrew (or actually Aramaic) *kadish derabonen*.

Hebrew continued as a written language and a language of worship over the years, its pronunciation slowly varying according to the other languages that Jews spoke. Weinreich suggests that two systems of reading Hebrew developed in the Middle Ages, Sephardic and Ashkenazic, with differences in vowels (/o/ versus /a/) and in consonants (/s/ versus /t/); there are also differences in stress. These differences are in part reflections of differences in Palestinian and Babylonian traditions. The Merged Hebrew of Yiddish derives from changes that preceded Yiddish. It provides a good proportion of the lexicon of Yiddish, especially with regard to objects and concepts related to Judaism.[40]

There are only a few examples of the Loez component in Yiddish, such as *bentshn* from Latin *benedicere*, *tsholnt.* (a dish kept warm in an oven and served on the Sabbath), *leynen* (to read), *shul* (synagogue, which we noted earlier from Italian); all these derivations are disputed. There are a few more cases, and a number of names, that he looks at carefully, but it is not hard to see that he bases the cases largely on the assumption that the Jews of Loter came there from Tsarfat, where the glosses in Rashi give us evidence of the Judeo-Romance language they had developed, and from Italy, with the evidence of Jewish scholars who moved to Loter.

It is most difficult to be precise about the German determinants of Yiddish, because contact lasted so long and was limited by the antagonism that followed the First Crusade. It is unlikely that Jews ever spoke pure Old or Middle High German, and they were in contact with various dialects at different times. For this reason, it is not surprising to find other theories about the home of Yiddish. One needs to be reminded that the name itself is new: Weinreich points out that, for many centuries, the Jews referred to their spoken language as *taytsch* ("German"). In Hebrew, the language was regularly referred to as *leshon Ashkenaz* ("the language of Germany"). In the eighteenth century the term *Jüdisch-teutsch* ("Judeo-German")[41] started to appear. In the nineteenth century the term *zhargon* ("jargon") is used. Only at the beginning of the twentieth century does the word "Yiddish" start to appear regularly.

There are arguments about the German base. Eckhard Eggers has presented evidence that Yiddish derived instead from the Bavarian dialect.[42] Katz[43] says this was first proposed by Matthias Mieses,[44] who rejected western Germany as a source for Yiddish, and cites Robert King and Alice Faber as asking "Where is Loter?",[45] echoing Mieses and joining him in proposing Bavarian as the German dialect from which Yiddish developed (Birnbaum had shown features of both Bavarian and East-Central German). Both King and Katz independently favor Regensburg[46] as the place where Yiddish was developed, thus arguing that the colony of Loter in Bohemia was a more likely place of origin. But Brook goes on to cite Alexander Beider, who argues that it is unlikely that Yiddish came from a single dialect but, rather, was the merger of elements from different regions, as Birnbaum and Weinreich have said.[47] So, summing up the views on the birthplace of Yiddish, we are left with locating it as far west as the Rhineland and as far east as Regensburg.

Czech origins

A new hypothesis on the origin of Yiddish has recently emerged.[48] Using mainly lexical evidence, Beider notes the strong presence of Czech elements in Eastern Yiddish but their absence from Western Yiddish. On this basis, he argues that the two varieties developed separately, and that there was not a single proto-Yiddish. The absence of hard evidence, as in much about this period, leaves the question far from closed. As the Jews from Loter moved east into Slavic lands, speakers of Yiddish came into contact with the Jewish variety Knaanic and with local Slavic speakers, adding a new component. There was presumably a period of bilingualism, but one may assume that it was the weight of numbers and the comparative isolation of Jewish migrants that made the difference. The Yiddishization process varied geographically – Brest before Grodno, both in Belarus, for instance. Yiddish replaced Knaanic (Czech and East Slavic) in the Grand Duchy of Lithuania by the seventeenth century, as shown by chosen names.

But the numbers remain a problem, as a number of scholars have pointed out. Jits van Straten[49] makes the case very strongly, reporting that he cannot find in the records any references to large numbers of Jewish migrants from Germany moving east. The problem is how to account for half a million Jews in Poland by the middle of the seventeenth century[50] when, in 1500, there could be at the most 80,000 Jews in western Europe.[51] No reasonable rate of population growth would fit, so there must have been more Jews already in eastern Europe than is normally accepted.

Some Sephardic refugees from Spain arrived in the Slavic region in the fifteenth and sixteenth centuries. Synagogues were built in Przemśl in south-eastern Poland, and Linsk close by, in the sixteenth century. Early on there was, for a short time, a Sephardi community in Zamość, which built its first syna-gogue in 1588. Some Romaniote Jews also settled in the area. There were Jews in Kiev and elsewhere in the Ukraine until 1495, with ties to the Babylonian Yeshivot and to rabbis in Loter and Tsarfat. There had been Jews in western Ukraine in the twelfth century. In the 1240s Mongols destroyed some of these communities.

Jews moved into Poland and Lithuania after the fourteenth century. There were Jews in Poland before the Mongol invasion; the main settlement came in the fifteenth and sixteenth centuries. The Council of the Four Lands was set up in 1519 and lasted until 1764. Jews had settled in Belarus in the early twelfth century, and in Lithuania by the thirteenth century. There were Jews in Grodno in 1128 and Kaunas in Lithuania by 1280. Jews lived in

Vilnius by 1593. There were Jews in western Hungary (including Buda) by the thirteenth century. But the numbers normally cited for these settlements are low, explaining why the Khazar hypothesis, or the Caucasus origin, seems so attractive to some.[52]

The question is not a new one, and was recognized but not solved by Weinreich himself.[53] It is in the meantime open, as scholars seek new data and propose competing hypotheses. One is the Sorbian origin.

The Sorbian heresy

The established view of Jewish languages is, as most scholars following Weinreich agree, that they were the result of Jews speaking an earlier language and learning a new co-territorial vernacular: thus, speakers of Hebrew acquired Aramaic and later Greek, both of which they Judaized; speakers of Judeo-Greek and Judeo-Aramaic acquired Judeo-Arabic or Judeo-French, or perhaps Judeo-Slavic; speakers of Judeo-French and Judeo-Romance acquired Middle High German, and produced Yiddish; speakers of Knaanic developed Yiddish as the area was colonized by Bohemian Germans; speakers of Judeo-Arabic acquired Spanish and produced Judezmo; and so on. The new variety continued to include Hebrew (or Hebrew–Aramaic) terms, and its grammar was modified by interference. But there are demographic and other problems. There is an alternative theory, strongly promoted by Paul Wexler, which is that Jewish languages were created by non-Jews when they were converted, who relexified their previous language as a result of their new situation.[54]

Wexler's hypothesis is that Yiddish was originally a Slavic language that emerged in Sorbia, a region in eastern Germany and southwest Poland between the rivers Oder and Elbe. The Sorbians were a Slavic tribe that conquered Lusatia, a central European region between Germany and Poland. Wexler appears to believe that some of them were converted to Judaism, developing a Judeo-Slavic variety, and that they later relexified their language with Old High German words, forming a basis for the later merger with the Judeo-German, which developed in the Rhineland, and the Judeo-Turkic, in the Kiev–Polessian (Khazar and Karaite) and Polack–Rejazan (Karaite) lands.[55]

The relexification hypothesis that Wexler is touting was developed in the study of pidgins and creoles. The Dutch linguist Pieter Muysken has described a language he discovered in his studies of Ecuadorian Quechua, a variety named *Media Lengua* spoken by young Quechuans who had come to Quito to help build the railway. It is a mixed language, with its grammar based on Quechua but most of its lexicon drawn from Spanish, serving to build an identity between the two.[56] The relexification theory is applied to pidgins and creoles, in its original and most radical form constituting the monogenesis theory of the German Romance philologist Hugo Schuchardt, an expert on the lingua franca of the Mediterranean, who argued that all creoles developed from a single original version.[57] Wexler, who has doubts also of the Jewish origins of Sephardic Jews,[58] is not as certain about the process of relexification in Romanian to which it might easily apply as he is in the case of Yiddish, Modern Hebrew (seen as relexified Yiddish), and Haitian Creole (a Caribbean language relexified with French words).[59]

Few scholars agree with Wexler's claims, and certainly not historical linguists. Erika Timm and Gustav Adolf Beckerman disagree fundamentally, pointing out that Yiddish is grammatically more German than Slavic. They trace many detailed etymologies, including the complex and disputed origin of the word *dovenen* ("pray"). They agree with Weinreich, Birnbaum, and others about the western origin of Yiddish.[60] Katz traces the history of studies of Yiddish, noting that scholars in the Enlightenment tradition considered it a jargon and "bastardized";[61] the first to see it as a product of linguistic creativity, with a stable grammar and lexicon, was Mieses.[62] Katz attacks Wexler's work in what he calls "Jewish interlinguistics" as "sensationalist", consisting of "fanciful etymologies" and producing an "Alice in Wonderland" view of relationships, built by assuming direct connections even when there is evidence of several intermediate occurrences and failing to follow the established practices of comparative linguistics.[63] A study of the political basis of Israeli linguistics labels the theory as "most bizarre" and an extreme example of the "anti-revivalist perspective", which I discuss later when talking about the revitalization of Hebrew.[64]

Are there any data? The earliest mentions of Jews in the area are tenth-century Jewish sources and ninth-century non-Jewish ones. Ibrahim ibn Jaqub, a tenth-century Jewish traveler probably from al-Andalus, visited Rome and described Poland; he also mentioned Prague. He reported that Jews lived on the river Saale in Germany. The Polish scholar Tadeusz Lewicki has collected material on Arabic visits to Slavic lands; he includes a passage from a ninth-century Persian geographer about medieval Jewish traders called Radhanites who were reported to speak Arabic, Persian, Roman, and the Frank, Spanish, and Slavic languages. Wexler questions the linguistic ability of these merchants, who seem to have continued to travel and trade up to the tenth century. But there is no evidence they settled anywhere. Jews are mentioned in Bohemia in the ninth and tenth centuries and there is a reference to a monolingual Slavic-speaking Jew in the tenth century. While there is little likelihood that any Jewish settlements (if they ever existed) survived the Tartar invasions in the thirteenth century and the wars in Thrace and Macedonia, the linguistic evidence does hint at early contacts. There may have been Armenian, Iranian, and Byzantine immigration to Khazaria in the eighth and ninth centuries, and Jewish and Judaized Khazar immigration into the Ukraine in the tenth century.

Wexler acknowledges that Jewish languages developed on a substratum of earlier varieties that stretch back to the spoken Hebrew of Judah. For example, he notes an "unbroken chain" from Hebrew to Judeo-Aramaic (sixth to eighth centuries BCE) to Judeo-Greek (fourth century BCE) to Judeo-Latin (first century CE), becoming varieties of Judeo-Romance, to Yiddish (ninth to tenth centuries). He also recognizes what he calls "Judaicized" languages, which developed when a non-Jewish language changed or a Jewish group moved elsewhere without adopting a new variety (Judaicized Iraqi Arabic is his example). There were also Jewish languages developed to translate Hebrew or Aramaic texts: these he calls "calque" languages. Finally, there are varieties that hardly differ from the non-Jewish variety except for an occasional borrowing, which he call "Jewish". Wexler identifies a number of distinctive Jewish subculture areas, namely Judeo-Greek, Judeo-Romance, Judeo-Germanic, Judeo-Turkic, Judeo-Tat, Judeo-Georgian, and Judeo-Slavic.

Weinreich proposes a different set of Jewish cultural areas for the period from 900 to 1200: Loter, which became Ashkenaz; Tsarfat (northern France); Provense (southern France); Sepharad (the Iberian Peninsula); Knaan (the Slavic area, divided into east and west regions); northern and central Italy; Yavan (including southern Italy and the Balkans); Ishmael (the Arab cultural sphere); Targumic (where Iraq and Persia meet); and *Paras u-maday* (Persia and the Median Empire). These areas do not coincide with non-Jewish regions, but depend on "Jewish geography". The Diaspora spread through the then accessible world. When the world was divided between Muslim and Christians, Jews had a major role in trade between them.[65]

In a later paper, Wexler is willing to accept three separate origins for Yiddish: first, a Judaized German developed in the Rhineland on a Romance basis (this is the common Weinreich view); second, a (Judeo-)Slavic developed separately in Sorbian lands between the ninth and thirteenth centuries, and relexified to High German lexicon in Kiev–Polessian lands by the fifteenth century, and relexified later to Yiddish and High German lexicon; and, third, Judeo-Turkic, in the Kiev–Polessian (Khazar and Karaite) and Polack–Rejazan (Karaite) lands.[66]

In a review of two of Wexler's books, Herbert Paper tackles the hypotheses that Modern Hebrew has been so influenced by Russian as to become a Slavic language and that "Yiddish is a Germanic metamorphosis of (a textually unattested) Judeo-Sorbian, and hence is also a Slavic language in an Germanic outer garb". Both arguments are, he says, flawed: "[B]y the standard tests of linguistic genetic affiliation, Modern Hebrew remains a Semitic language and Yiddish remains a Germanic one." But he agrees that there was "a long-standing and widespread Slavic–Yiddish bilingualism among Jews in their long co-territorial existence with Slavic speech".[67] This leaves the interesting question of how long Knaanic continued as a Jewish language.[68]

Summing up, while it is fair to note that Wexler makes a case for his "heretical views", they do not in the end shake the accepted scholarly view that Yiddish developed in German-speaking areas and was brought by Jews to Slavic lands, where it grew into a major community variety. Nor does he shake the accepted view that converts were only a small part of the Jewish population, and not the major portion that he and Koestler claim.

The dialects of Yiddish

A stereotypically prejudiced joke[69] is regularly told about the young Litvak (a Jew descended from a family from Lite[70]) who revealed to his father the background of the girl he wanted to marry. Shocked, the father complained: "We carefully taught you not to consider marrying a non-Jew (a *shikse*) or someone with dark skin (a *schwartze*), but we assumed you would know not to marry a Galitzianer." It also reminds us of the importance of what has been called perceptual dialectology,[71] which may not coincide with linguistic observation.

The distinction between northern (Litvak) and southern (Galitzianer) dialects of Eastern Yiddish is a critical one, not just in dividing Jewish dialect areas but also in setting up cultural borders, for, while Galitzianers preferred to add sugar to such food items as gefilte fish, Litvaks insisted on salt rather than sugar. An equally serious difference is that Galitzianers (the majority) tend to follow Hasidism while Litvaks are traditionally *mitnagdim* (opponents of the Hasidic movements).

Given its development as a spoken language over a long time and area, and the lateness of written Yiddish and attempts at standardization, it is no wonder that Yiddish produced a complex mix of dialects. The building of a linguistic atlas of Yiddish started in the 1950s and has continued since then.[72] The first major distinction in Yiddish dialects is between the older Western Yiddish, itself divided into three branches, and Eastern Yiddish. The three Western branches were Northwestern (Holland and northern Germany), Midwestern Yiddish (central Germany), and Southwestern Yiddish (Switzerland, Alsace, and southern Germany). This was the language of the first printed works in Yiddish in the 1540s, but it was soon swamped by the development of Eastern Yiddish and faded as its speakers were attracted to standard German as a result of the emancipation. A few elements of Western Yiddish survive.[73]

The major split in Eastern Yiddish, which developed as Jews moved into Slavic lands, was between the north and the south. There was indeed a feature reflecting the biblical shibboleth, as northerners (or Litvaks) were reputed to use /s/ instead of /sh/, whereas in fact they either used a single intermediate sound or switched.[74] There were also major differences in vowels, such as the northern /ey/ as in *teyre* rather than /oy/ *toyre* ("Torah"); /o/ in *zogn* instead of /u/ *zugn* ("say"); or /u/ *hunt* instead of /i/ *hint* ("dog").[75] There were further divisions: the southern branch divided further into a central and southeastern variety.[76]

In the southern region of eastern Europe, in reaction to the genocide of the Cossack massacres in the Ukraine in the middle of the seventeenth century, there was a readiness for the spiritual movement that came to be called Hasidism. An important linguistic effect of the new movement was the publication of Hasidic texts in Yiddish as well as Hebrew, and in particular the work of Reb Nachman Bratslaver, published in 1815 in a Yiddish version with a Hebrew translation. The struggle between the northern opponents of Hasidism (*mitnagdim*), who founded a network of Yeshivas, and the southern populist Hasidim was played out in part in varieties of Yiddish and in a Hasidic tendency to make Yiddish sacred; part of the arguments in the attacks on Hasidism in Vilna in 1771 included a charge of using Yiddish in prayer. But, in the course of time, the intensity of the battle diminished as both were challenged by emancipation and westernization.[77]

In Slavic lands

In the sixteenth century, under Polish rule, many Jewish communities built fortified and armed synagogues. In the middle of the seventeenth century relations with Christians deteriorated, and in 1648 thousands of Jews in Galicia and Ukraine were slaughtered by the Cossacks, led by Bohdan Khmelnytsky. This led both to the Hasidic movement and to the beginning of a western return of the Jews.

Pressure continued. In Russia, a ban on Jews living in Moscow and Russia proper was initiated in the seventeenth century, and confirmed at the end of the eighteenth century by Empress Catherine. Jews were then confined to what was called the Pale of Settlement, restricted to 20 percent of Russia and largely corresponding to the former Polish–Lithuanian Commonwealth. With its mainly Catholic and Jewish populations, the region had been conquered by Orthodox Russia in the late eighteenth century and first half of the nineteenth century, and held until 1917.

The Pale, with its small towns (*shtetl*; plural *shtetlach*), was the center of east European Jewish life. Jews there lived a poverty-stricken life, in uncomfortable contact with non-Jews, and with only 10 pecent permitted to receive public education. It was in this area that the modern Yeshiva system developed, with students leaving home and being provided with meals by local Jews. Jews commonly worked as artisans or were peddlers. The population and poverty both increased as time went on. Much of the picture of the *shtetl* is based on literary sources, such as Sholom Aleichem, but there has started to be more serious scholarship.[78] There were hundreds of these small towns with large and compact Jewish settlements throughout eastern Europe, and over the last thirty years they have been receiving multidisciplinary study.[79]

Differing markedly from earlier patterns of Jewish settlement, Jews in a *shtetl* were often a majority, constituting as much as 80 percent of the town's population. Also different from the earlier Knaanic period, the Jews of the *shtetl* spoke their own variety, Yiddish,[80] rather than the various co-territorial vernaculars, usually but not always Slavic languages. There was considerable variation in Jewish occupations, ranging from a small number of wealthy entrepreneurs and contractors to a majority who were poor tailors, carters, and water carriers.

The Jews were commonly invited to settle on the estates of Polish nobles, who instituted a system of leases and sub-leases. The center of the *shtetl* was a market square, often with a church on one side and Jewish institutions and homes on the other. Jews and non-Jews from the countryside would come to market days. Many *shtetlach* developed in conjunction with the rapid growth of the Jewish population at the beginning of the eighteenth century. It was in this environment that Yiddish flourished, and developed its rich literature and culture.

The rise (and fall) of Yiddish

Weinreich identifies four historical periods for Yiddish: Early Yiddish (from around 1100 until 1250), Old Yiddish (from 1250 until about 1500), Middle Yiddish (1500 to 1700), and New Yiddish (from about 1750).[81]

Early Yiddish he divides into two: in the first, the three determinant varieties, *loshn koydesh* (Hebrew–Aramaic), Loez (Judeo-Romance), and German, entered into a fusion state in Loter and Regensburg; and, in the second half, this variety was spread to the basin of the river Main, the upper Rhine, and the upper Danube; these two areas Weinreich calls Ashkenaz I. There are no written documents from this time of voluntary Jewish isolation, which was a period that brought Jews into the region, driven by the First Crusade in the west and the Mongolian attacks in the east, and fed in part by a Babylonian renaissance.

The second period is that of *Old Yiddish* (which has some documents in Western Yiddish), and covers the spread to Ashkenaz II, which means a move to the middle Danube and adding Bohemia, Moravia, Poland, and Lithuania, and also Palestine. The Jewish population moved east, propelled by the Black Death and expulsion from large cities in Germany and Austria as Slavic states accept migration; Slavic entered the fusion.

Middle Yiddish dates from 1500 to 1700, when southern and western Lithuania were added to Poland. The Thirty Years War, the Cossack massacres, and the Swedish War encouraged Jewish migration back west to Alsace, Holland, and northern Germany, and north to eastern Kurland (part of Latvia).

Jews left the larger cities (because of expulsion or taxation) and moved into smaller towns, as *landjuden* in the west or in *shtetlach* (small towns) in the east, coming under the protection of local lords. Dialects developed in Eastern Yiddish, which was separated from Western.

New Yiddish dates from about 1750, its population growing in Ashkenaz II and Palestine, and crossing the Atlantic. This is when Hasidism developed, Europe was urbanized, and many Jews abandoned religious observance. Yiddish was greatly enriched by taking on secular functions: it became the language of social movements; there was an active press; it became the language of instruction in secular schools; and literature started to be published in Yiddish. The written language, originally in Western Yiddish, was gradually taken over by Eastern Yiddish; it became standardized and a language of secular culture.

Spoken and written Yiddish

Developing as a spoken vernacular alongside the higher-status *loshn koydesh* (Hebrew–Aramaic), Yiddish entered into a diglossic relation with Hebrew, which continued to serve most written functions. Rabbis would teach or give sermons in Yiddish, but publish their work in Hebrew; business and general letters would be written in Hebrew, and records would be written in it. Yeshiva students would write to their fathers in Hebrew, adding a few lines in Yiddish for their mother.[82] But gradually Yiddish started to be written. The breakthrough came in Yiddish supplicatory prayers (*Tkhines*), the first printed version of which appeared in Prague in 1590; many editions followed. Other prayer books included Yiddish text below the Hebrew. A Yiddish prayer book was published in 1543. But Yiddish did not replace Hebrew as the language of prayer, and, while some arguments were presented for prayer in the mother tongue, they were generally unsuccessful. A few Yiddish passages and songs were added to the Haggadah. And a Yiddish prayer to form part of the Havdalah service was printed at the beginning of the eighteenth century. Yiddish is reported to have been used in some divorce documents. Before printing, there may have been some Yiddish literature, but it was largely lost. The earliest remaining copy of the Tsene-rene, a Yiddish-language adaptation of the Pentateuch, Haftorahs, and Five Scrolls (*megilot*) read as part of the liturgy in synagogue, was printed in 1622 and became popular as a book for women. These works were printed not in the square characters used for Hebrew but in a script closer to the written variety called *taytsch* or *vaybertaytsch* ("women's letters").

Most early written Yiddish was in Western Yiddish, but in the nineteenth century Eastern Yiddish elements began to appear, and Yiddish books started to appear even earlier in square letters.[83] A good number of Yiddish religious books were published in Cracow at the end of the seventeenth century. Some secular works started to appear, for which the Tsene-rene was intended as a replacement. Books of stories also started to appear.[84] The motivation is often explained in a preface, saying that the book was for women and for men who hadn't studied sacred texts.

A new literary tradition developed in the east, in both Hebrew and Yiddish: the first Hebrew novel was *Love of Zion*, published in 1853 by Abraham Mapu; a Yiddish newspaper, *Kol Hamevaser*, appeared in Odessa in 1862 as a supplement to a Hebrew newspaper, and in it was published a novel in Yiddish by Sholem-Yankev Abromowitz under the pseudonym Mendele Mocher Sforim (Mendel the Bookseller) in 1864.[85] Popular Yiddish works, attacked by many for their immorality, appeared in the 1880s. Another major writer, Sholem Aleichem (his real name was Sholem Rabinowitz), started publishing at about this time. These two were joined by Y. L. Peretz, the three forming the foundation of modern Yiddish literature.

Around the beginning of the twentieth century Yiddish made its first claim to be a national language (associated with the secular non-territorial movement), but it was weakened by Jews assimilating and adopting co-territorial languages (including revitalized Hebrew in Palestine), and, of course, millions of its remaining speakers were wiped out by the Nazis. I will discuss later what remains: a glorious secular vernacular and literary past, earnestly and devotedly pursued by a metalinguistic community, and a living presence among some contemporary Hasidic groups, for whom it serves as a method of separation from mainstream Israeli or Diaspora Jewish communities. In spite of its murky and highly disputed beginnings, Yiddish grew into one of the major languages of the Jews.

13 Linguistic emancipation and assimilation in Europe

Into the modern world

We have followed the addition of languages to the Jewish sociolinguistic ecology historically and regionally: the adoption of Hebrew in Canaan; the addition of Aramaic and Greek in the ancient world; the spread of Greek and addition of Latin in the Mediterranean Diaspora, and of Judeo-Persian in the eastern; the spread of Arabic to Jews as well as others as a result of the Muslim conquest; the development of Judeo-Romance varieties in Western and Southern Loez; the process from German dialects to Yiddish in Ashkenaz and further east; and the period of Judeo-Slavic (Knaanic) before Yiddish took over in eastern Europe.

This survey took us through the ancient and medieval worlds, with surprisingly little variation in pattern as Jews, usually forced to migrate by conquest or persecution, added new languages to their repertoire, modified them when isolated by internal or external pressure, and, throughout, generally maintained Hebrew as their heritage, sacred, and literary language. In Renaissance Europe, the expulsion of Jews in 1492 from the Iberian Peninsula did not just spread Judezmo as far as Turkey, but also was associated with a flurry of translations by Jews of Classical texts via Arabic to western languages. Essentially, in the next two chapters we trace the next stage of development in what might be called the modern world, remembering that modernization, industrialization, political emancipation, and westernization came to different parts of that world at different times; earliest in Germany, and never in some Islamic nations, whose Jews were emancipated as citizens only after their escape to a western Diaspora or to the new State of Israel.

Generally, until the modern period, Jews continued to suffer discrimination, persecution, forced conversion, slaughter, and expulsion whether they were living under Muslim or Christian rule. Political and social emancipation had a linguistic effect; sociolinguistically, it meant that Jews were more likely to acquire the co-territorial dominant languages of their countries of residence, being allowed access (though sometimes still limited by quotas such as the *numerus clausus* of many universities and professions) to public secular education and to a wider range of occupations and professions.

Emancipation didn't mean the end of anti-Jewish attitudes or activities. The Dreyfus affair in France at the turn of the twentieth century, the Nazi murder of some 6 million Jews, and the Arab expulsion of 2 million Jewish residents came after many of these countries had granted citizenship to their Jews, making it even more shocking to the victims; one thinks of the German Jews whose fathers had served in the German army in World War I and whose university education in German would seem to have guaranteed acceptance for those who had assimilated or even converted to Christianity, and how difficult it must have been for most of them to understand the fate that the German people and its leadership had in store for them. And one has only to note the way that many people in western Europe have so easily and rapidly transferred their historical hatred of Jews to demonization of Israel and support for the Islamic movements that are trying to clear both Jews and Christians from the Middle East.

But, when it worked, emancipation seemed to grant linguistic freedom to Jews as well as others, and to offer anyone who managed to acquire proficiency in the dominant version of the national language equality of opportunity and the chance to pass. Because their skin is not black, many assimilated European Jews were able to be successfully integrated once they had developed educated proficiency in the national language; it surprises the Jewish traveler to be told regularly by locals about having a Jewish grandfather.

A topic debated recently is how far this process would have gone had it not been blocked by the growing anti-Semitism of European nations in the 1930s and the subsequent extermination of a large part of European Jewry in the 1940s. One position on this question is taken by Bernard Wasserstein, who argues that "by 1939, two years before the Nazi decision to commit genocide, European Jewry was close to terminal collapse".[1] He proposes that existing Jewish languages (including Judezmo and even Yiddish) were losing strength as Jews shifted to the co-territorial Turkish, Greek, German, Polish, Czech, Russian, or other dominant national languages. He is disagreeing, therefore, with the Fishmans, who hold, rather, that Yiddish in particular was still flourishing after World War I, only to be destroyed by external actions.[2]

There is little disagreement about the results, as Jews assimilated or escaped to the West or Israel, where they adopted the local dominant languages, or were slaughtered if they remained in areas that came under Nazi rule. The debate concerns, rather, the extent to which this assimilation and language shift were the result of external pressure alone. Again, this is a critical question (such as how late was Hebrew spoken alongside Aramaic and Greek, or where did Yiddish begin?), to which the only honest answer remains *Teiku*: the question remains unresolved. We look in this chapter at emancipation in Europe, starting

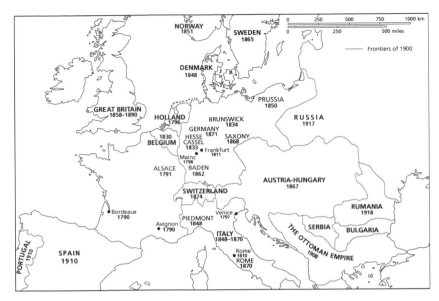

10 Emancipation of European Jews
Source: Rozenblit (2010).

in the west and later as it affected central and eastern Europe (see Map 10). In the next chapter, we will go on to Britain and the New World.

Jews in Renaissance Europe

What do I mean by "the modern world"? Mostly, in the rest of the book I will be talking about the nineteenth and twentieth centuries, but it is worth starting earlier and noting the Jewish position in western Europe during the Renaissance. An interesting harbinger was Solomon Ibn Verga, born in Malaga about 1452, who came to Italy fifty years later, after being expelled from Portugal and Spain, and wrote in Hebrew a book listing sixty-four historical persecutions of Jews (the book was printed in 1554 in Turkey). An independently minded skeptic, he also made use of his new freedom by attacking the Talmud, Maimonides, and Judah Halevy.[3]

The Renaissance was the time at which ghettos were being established in Italy and elsewhere, inside which Jews were developing an active intellectual and social life while struggling with second-class citizenship and suffering frequent pogroms and expulsions.[4] It was, as we saw earlier, a period of increasing multilingualism both outside and inside the Jewish communities.

Many Jews welcomed the Reformation, because it seemed to be a rejection of the worst persecution by the Catholic Church. Not unlike Muhammad, Martin Luther started off seeking support from Jews, but, upset by their refusal to convert to Christianity, turned on them bitterly in a 1543 pamphlet ("On the Jews and their lies"), which Johnson terms "the first work of modern anti-Semitism".[5] Going beyond this, Luther helped expel Jews from German towns in the 1540s. But Luther's opponents were no better for the Jews: the Counter-Reformation in its turn attacked Jews as well as Protestants.

In the seventeenth century, suffering from widespread persecution, many Jews turned to messianic hope and were attracted by the Lurianic kabbalah and then by Hasidism. Large numbers were excited and attracted by a new Messiah, Shabbetai Zvi, who was proclaimed as such in Gaza and accepted by many in the Jewish world. His apostasy when he became a Muslim disappointed his followers, but left a movement that lasted for a century, flaring again in the middle of the eighteenth century with a reincarnation around another false Messiah, Jacob Frank.

But there were more promising developments too. It was in the middle of the seventeenth century, during the rule of Oliver Cromwell, that a conference of English lawyers found that there was no English law banning Jews from coming to England; the 1240 decree that expelled them had been a royal decree only, and not a law. Taking advantage of this, a group of *Anusim* migrated to London, returned to Judaism, and leased their first synagogue. In this way, almost by accident, England became the first country with a modern Jewish community. About the same time, the first small group of Jews sailed from Europe to the Dutch colonial town of New Amsterdam, forming the beginning of the American Jewish community.[6] Thus, the way was paved for the addition of English to the languages of the Jews, and to its development as partner or competitor to Hebrew as a medium of contemporary Jewish culture.

Another significant development in the formation of the modern Jewish world were the writings of Baruch Spinoza, born in Amsterdam in 1632, the son of a Sephardi refugee from Portugal who became a successful Dutch businessman. When the Netherlands declared independence from Spanish sovereignty in 1581, its constitution included a clause guaranteeing freedom of religion, intended to allow Protestantism to replace the former Roman Catholic rule. But it also allowed many *Anusim* still in Spain or Portugal to escape. The members of the new Portuguese community of Amsterdam were former *Anusim*. They spoke Portuguese, and used Spanish as a high language and Hebrew for the liturgy.[7]

Spinoza grew up in this community. His lack of respect for the divine origin of the Bible resulted in his excommunication but he had a major influence in the development of modern Western secular philosophy. He also represents the beginning of the process of a weakening of the hold of traditional religion, and thus a lessening of the sacred status of Hebrew. Spinoza wrote most of his works in Latin, but knew Hebrew[8] and Dutch; he expressed a preference for writing in his native Portuguese in a letter written in Dutch, which he asks his correspondent to correct.[9] The Netherlands, as I shall shortly explain, was important as one of the most tolerant of countries, and so attracted many refugees from Spain and Portugal, who were later joined by Jews from eastern Europe escaping persecution there.

The Enlightenment in western Europe

Germany

It was in Germany that ideas of emancipation were raised when Gotthold Lessing, a young dramatist, published[10] in 1779 a one-act play, *Nathan der Weisse* (*Nathan the Wise*), which for the first time presented a Jew as a rational human being. The central character, Nathan, was modeled on Lessing's Jewish friend, Moses Mendelssohn. Coming from Dessau,[11] Mendelssohn started to publish philosophical writings, and was granted by the emperor the right of residence in Berlin. He argued for the possibility of combining Judaism with modern secular enlightenment. At a time when many Germans were still writing in Latin or French, and some Jews were writing in Hebrew or increasingly, for women, in Yiddish, Mendelssohn chose to follow Lessing and write in German. He also translated the Torah into German, and argued for the study of Hebrew to replace the use of Yiddish.[12]

Gradually there was growing recognition of Jewish rights. Frederick the Great in 1750 passed a Jewish law that granted some rights but restricted residence to one descendant, set high tax rates for Jews, and limited Jews to certain trades and professions. In Austria, the poll tax and the yellow badge were abolished, but Yiddish and Hebrew could not be used for business or public records, and Jews were required to perform military service; there were residence restrictions in Vienna. In 1787 Austrian Jews were required to adopt German family names. In France, the poll tax on Jews was canceled, but their rights to lend money and trade in cattle were curbed.[13]

The Frankfurt parliament, after the 1848 revolution, granted equal rights to members of all religions, and slowly full civil rights were granted to Jews and others in all parts of Germany. From 1871 onwards German Jews were legally equal, but they were still denied appointments as army officers or full professors in the universities. They were active in business, science, literature, and the arts. Large numbers assimilated; combined with birth control, conversion to Christianity and intermarriage, this meant that the community kept up its numbers only as a result of a steady influx of Jews from the east, the "Ostjüden", who were commonly resented by Jews as well as Gentiles. The community was strongly organized and highly respected among world Jewry.[14]

In 1901 the Hilfsverein der deutschen Juden was established, partly as a response to the activities of the Alliance Israélite Universelle, which was an agent in the francophone language diffusion program.[15] At first the Hilfsverein operated in eastern Europe, but after a decade it started to work in the Middle East and was responsible for developing the small but highly significant educational network in Palestine.[16] To start, the Jewish studies program of these schools was in Hebrew and the general and scientific studies in German, but gradually the schools, which catered to half the non-Haredi Jewish population, became a center of Hebrew language revival and were active in the Language War of 1913 over the proposed policy for the planned tertiary institute.

Over 100,000 German Jews served in the army during World War I, after which all restrictions were cancelled by the Weimar Republic, in which Jews played important political roles. But, especially with the Yiddish-speaking Ostjüden, Jewish difference continued to feed the growing anti-Semitism during the economic crisis. At the same time, with the growing number of Hebrew writers escaping from the Soviet Union, Hebrew publishing increased, and many Jewish schools taught the language.

All this ended when the Nazis seized power in 1933 and proclaimed that "no Jew can be a German". Anti-Jewish demonstrations began; Jews, classified as non-Aryan, were removed from the professions; the Nuremberg laws of 1935 cancelled Jewish citizenship. Soon, even assimilated Jews were targeted. The goal of a "Judenrein" Germany was adopted, with encouragement of emigration; 300,000 emigrated between 1933 and 1939. In 1941 the "Final solution" was adopted, and Jews remaining in Germany were sent to extermination camps and murdered, along with Jews from conquered territories. Communities re-established in Germany after the defeat of the Nazi government include large numbers of former displaced persons and refugees from eastern Europe.[17]

France and the French Revolution

Emancipation developed in full force in revolutionary France. Jews had begun to return to France in small numbers in the sixteenth century, mainly *Anusim* – or "Portuguese merchants", as they were named in the letters patent that Henry II granted – settling mainly in Bordeaux and nearby. Only a few returned to Judaism; because they maintained Spanish or Portuguese, they were suspected of being spies for Spain; their goods were confiscated and they were heavily fined; they were confined to a few towns including Avignon, and to restricted quarters. When the towns of Lorraine (Metz, Tours, and Verdun) were ceded to the French in 1648, the Jews living in them were permitted to remain – the first legal Jewish residents since 1394.

Much of Alsace also became French. In 1651 a group of Sephardi Jews from Amsterdam received permission to settle in Charleville in the Ardennes,[18] and, at about the same time, Jews from Ukraine and Poland, escaping the Cossack massacres, arrived in Alsace and Lorraine. Jews from north Africa and Italy also moved into Savoy, which was suffering economically after the Thirty Years War. From the beginning of the eighteenth century Jews began to arrive in Paris from Alsace, Lorraine, Bordeaux, and Avignon, and even Germany and Holland, organizing themselves into a southern and an Ashkenazi group. At the end of the century public discussions began on the possibility of granting civic rights to Jews.[19]

The place of Jews was debated during the French Revolution, and emancipation was formally granted in 1791: under revolutionary rule, and later under Napoleon Bonaparte, many ghettos in France and Italy were opened up. The French Enlightenment did not cancel the anti-Semitism that had been expressed in the work of Voltaire and Diderot, however, instead adding a "secular superstructure" to modern anti-Semitism.[20] But, significantly, following the earlier support for the standardization of Parisian French by Cardinal Richelieu,[21] the Jacobins during the Revolution proclaimed that Parisian French was to be the national language, required of all civil servants and used as the language of instruction in all schools. It took many years for this to be implemented (there weren't enough teachers fluent in standard French), but its effect was to impose the French language on French Jews.

At the time of the French Revolution there were 40,000 Jews living in France, an Ashkenazi and mainly Yiddish-speaking majority ("German nation") in Alsace-Lorraine and France, and a "Spanish, Portuguese, and Avignonese" group in the south. After long discussion the second group became French citizens in January 1790, and the Ashkenazim in September 1791. Individual rights were granted, but at the same time religious-legal group autonomy was abolished. During the Reign of Terror, synagogues had been closed, together with churches. The ghettos were opened, and Jews began to move out.

Napoleon called together a States General of French Judaism in 1806, and a Sanhedrin a year later. As a result, every department of France with more than 2,000 Jews established a consistory, which had authority over Jewish religious life in the department. Economic laws too were passed; all debts to Jews were annulled. Jews were required to adopt surnames, they were not permitted to provide substitutes for military service, and there were regulations on where they could live. In 1829 a central rabbinical seminary was established, and in 1831 the state took responsibility for the payment of communal rabbis.

Many Jews, especially among the leadership, took advantage of the new freedom to convert to Christianity. In 1846 the *more judaico* (Jewish oath, with its accompanying humiliating practices such as standing on a sow's skin and calling down curses if the oath were broken) was abolished.[22] A Jewish school system began to be set up in 1818, and received state support until primary education was made compulsory for all in 1882, and state and Church were separated in 1905. There were minor reforms in Jewish religious practice: more sermons, ministerial garb for officiants, fewer *piyyutim*, shorter services, and religious initiation for girls; this flexibility allowed for the absorption of Jewish migrants from north Africa and averted efforts to establish Reform or Orthodox communities, as happened in Britain and the United States.

In 1860 the Alliance Israélite Universelle was formed and began to play an important role in organizing francophone Jewish education in north Africa and the Middle East. Towards the end of the century political anti-Semitism grew stronger; a proposal was made to expel the Jews from France; then, in 1894, the Dreyfus affair, in which a Jewish officer was falsely accused of spying for Germany, led to a bitter public struggle and finally to a law separating Church and state, which now meant that the organization of French Jewry was voluntary.

The pogroms of 1881 in Russia resulted in the first major influx of Russian, Polish, and Romanian Jewish refugees. More Jews arrived after the 1905 Russian Revolution. Many Jews arrived after 1908 from Ottoman countries. Between the wars there continued to be significant Yiddish-speaking immigration, increasing the proportion of Ashkenazim. Social assimilation continued.[23]

About 90,000 of the 300,000 Jews living in France when it surrendered to Nazi Germany in 1940 were deported, with the collaboration of the Vichy government, and killed. About 180,000 French Jews remained after World War II; some displaced persons settled there, and they were joined by 100,000 Algerian, Egyptian, Moroccan, and Tunisian Jews. After Algeria became independent almost the entire community of 110,000 moved to France; large numbers of Moroccan and Tunisian Jews arrived in 1968, half of whom remained. Many of these north African Jewish immigrants had already become French-speaking during the colonial period. At the same time, the Libyan Jewish community escaped to Rome and North America.

In 1968 ten of the forty Jewish periodicals published in France were in Yiddish. Fewer than 5 percent of Jewish children at that time studied in French schools, but now most do. State schools could teach Hebrew, by virtue of a matching teaching of French in Israeli French schools. But there has been an upswing in private education, and it is estimated that only 25 percent are now in Jewish schools.[24] With the addition of Jews from north Africa, France is now a major Jewish community, making French a major language of the Jews.

The Netherlands

The success of the rebellion of the Netherlands against Spanish (and so Catholic) rule made the Netherlands one of the earliest important sites of emancipation. Jews probably came to the Netherlands first with the Roman armies, but the earliest reliable evidence of Jews living there is from the twelfth century. The Black Death persecutions seem to have wiped out the limited Jewish settlement, however, and only at the end of the sixteenth century did Jews – actually *Anusim* from Spain via Portugal – reappear, founding in about 1600 a secret community in Amsterdam that was chartered a few years later. A second community was set up in 1608 and a rabbi appointed, but only in 1619 were the towns of the Netherlands authorized to define the status of their Jewish residents. In Amsterdam, Jews could settle but not become burghers nor work in many trades; in other towns, there were no such restrictions. Many Portuguese took part in the expedition to Brazil in 1634, but returned when Portugal took over Brazil twenty years later. Some Dutch towns allowed Jews complete freedom, but others (Groningen in 1710, Utrecht in 1713, Gouda and the province of Friesland in 1712) imposed restrictions after a spate of robberies that were blamed on Jews.

With economic expansion in the seventeenth century, the Sephardi Jews in the Netherlands were successful in business, taking an important role in the East India Company; they were also very active in the diamond industry and in printing. The seventeenth century was a "golden age" for Sephardi Jews in Amsterdam; they were leaders in medicine, and as artists. Scholarship developed, focused on some Yeshivot and supported by the printing of religious, scientific, and literary works in Hebrew. There were religious conflicts: Spinoza was only one example, and in 1666 there was enthusiasm for the false Messiah, Shabbetai Zvi. The union of three Sephardic communities into the Esnoga synagogue in 1675 produced one of the most beautiful Jewish buildings in Europe, and marked the wealth and power of the community.

In the early years of the seventeenth century there began the immigration of Ashkenazim, who settled in Amsterdam and throughout the Netherlands, the first wave coming from Germany but after that from Poland and Lithuania. Much poorer than the Sephardim (they generally were peddlers, butchers, and cattle dealers), they soon outnumbered the Sephardim. They spoke Yiddish, with an admixture of Dutch words, and had little contact with the non-Jewish population. For a short time they wrote Yiddish as well, in a number of books on Jewish history.[25] During the French Revolution, when the Netherlands was occupied by the French, complete emancipation was proclaimed. Under King Louis Bonaparte, an 1810 *concordat* established relations between Ashkenazim (about 50,000) and Sephardim (some 5,000). Jews were required to adopt surnames, and a Bible translation into Dutch accompanied efforts to persuade them to use Dutch.

In the nineteenth century economic conditions worsened: half the Jews of Amsterdam were paupers in 1849, and King William I worked to integrate Jews.

In 1821 schools were opened, and in 1857 public education was made compulsory, leaving Jewish education to Sunday and afternoon schools. There was a struggle within the Ashkenazi community, and a radical group founded a new synagogue that called for complete integration. Part of this movement for assimilation was a campaign affecting schools and synagogues and calling for the replacement of Yiddish by Dutch.[26]

Economic conditions improved later in the century, with the growing diamond business in Amsterdam and a successful cotton industry in the east, and urbanization followed. Many upper-class Jews were baptized or intermarried; the community started to favor liberal Judaism or socialism. Mixed marriages increased from 13 percent of the total in 1901 to 41 percent in 1931. Orthodoxy was weakened, and there was a small Zionist movement, but the general movement was towards assimilation. Jews were active in Dutch society. Four weekly Jewish papers were published in Dutch. In the 1930s working-class Jews in Amsterdam spoke their own patois.[27] Of the 140,000 Jews in the Netherlands in 1941, about 27,000 survived the Nazi occupation.[28] There are reports of a variety of Dutch that includes vestiges of Yiddish, producing a kind of Jewish Dutch.[29]

Belgium

There was early Jewish settlement in the region, but it did not survive the Black Death persecutions or the Brussels massacre in 1370, which was followed by expulsion. *Anusim* arrived in the sixteenth century, and, returning to Judaism, established a secret synagogue in Antwerp, where they were becoming active in the diamond and other trades. Under Austrian rule, starting in 1713, Jews paid special taxes. Under French occupation (1794–1814) and Dutch rule (1814–1830) there were fewer restrictions on Jewish residents, and Ashkenazim started to arrive. After Belgian independence in 1830, Judaism was recognized.

Brussels, which is a French-speaking "island" surrounded by Dutch speakers, provided an environment for quite rapid assimilation. In Antwerp, however, a Dutch-speaking city, Jews continued to be religiously observant and to speak Yiddish. After the 1880 pogroms in Russia many east European Jews arrived, and the Antwerp community increased rapidly, reaching 50,000 by 1939 and building synagogues and schools. Some 25,000 Belgian Jews perished in the Holocaust. Currently about 15,000 French-speaking Jews live in Brussels; 18,000 live in Antwerp, many of them religiously observant. There are many synagogues and a large number of Hasidic groups represented in the community. Jews in Antwerp are commonly plurilingual, speaking Dutch, French, and Yiddish, and acquiring Hebrew in the Jewish schools, which cater for 95 percent of the Jewish population.

Thus, western Europe – the Netherlands, Belgium, Britain, France, Germany – and the New World[30] came to offer what seemed a safe refuge for persecuted Jews, and its major languages were added to the Jewish repertoire.

Jews in Nordic lands

The first Jews in Scandinavia arrived in Denmark at the end of the sixteenth century: some Portuguese-speaking Sephardim settled in Elsinore in 1619, but the first community was licensed in Altona, north of Hamburg, in 1640.[31] The community grew gradually, with both Sephardi and Ashkenazi migrants, reaching 700 by the middle of the eighteenth century, when the idea of equality for Jews began to be accepted. Schools for poor boys and girls were started in the early part of the century, and teaching in Danish encouraged the switch from Yiddish. There were disputes inside the community over reform. Full emancipation came by royal decree in 1814. The 1848 constitution gave Jews full rights. But the overall picture is complex.

Even after Finnish autonomy, the Swedish ban on Jews was preserved until the late nineteenth century, though a few lived there earlier.[32] There has never been an organized Jewish community in Iceland, but there were services conducted by British and US forces stationed there during World War II. The extreme nationalism of Icelanders kept down the number of Jews admitted before and after the war. There are only a handful of Jews in Iceland, which continues to be anti-Semitic and anti-Israel.[33]

A few Jews came to Norway in about 1905, augmented by 500 refugees from Germany, Austria, and Czechoslovakia before World War II. Some 60 percent of Norwegian Jews survived the Holocaust by escaping to Sweden; the rest were murdered in Auschwitz. A number of displaced persons were permitted to settle after the war. There are currently about 2,000 Jews in Norway.[34]

Jews who came to Sweden in the eighteenth century were required to convert; only in the late eighteenth century were they allowed to practice their religion and establish congregations. In 1782 a statute established the right of Jews to reside as aliens, marry each other, and conduct their own affairs, but they could not hold public office or give evidence in court. In 1815 Jewish migration was restricted, but in 1838 the statute was abolished and Jews were recognized as "Swedes of the Hebraic faith". Most civil rights were granted in 1870. Synagogues were founded, and refugees arrived from Russia from 1880 to 1930. In 1938 the borders were closed to Jews, but in 1942 and 1943 Norwegian and Danish Jews were sheltered. In 1951 a law on freedom of religion was passed and civil rights were granted.[35]

Originally under Swedish rule, during which period Jews were banned, Finland came under Russian rule, and Jews who had served in the Russian army were permitted to remain. In independent Finland, in 1917 Jews were granted full citizenship. During the Winter War, in 1939, Jews served in the Finnish army fighting the Soviet Union. Later, Finland joined Germany as an ally, but Finnish Jews were not persecuted; some foreign Jewish refugees were handed over to the Nazis in 1942. There is a small Jewish community in Finland, most of whom speak Finnish or Swedish; Yiddish, German, Russian, and Hebrew are also said to be spoken in the community.

While Scandinavian ethnic nationalism and state religion tended to restrict Jewish immigration, Jews who did move there appear to have switched to local national languages, so that we can add Swedish, Danish, Norwegian, and Finnish to the list of languages of the Jews, though it must be noted that the Scandinavian countries are marked by a high level of proficiency in English.

East Europe and the addition of co-territorial vernaculars

Russia

In eastern Europe, Jews continued to be restricted and persecuted, and emancipation was much later than in the west. While the Yiddish-speaking *shtetl* remained the environment of most east European Jews until the 1917 Russian Revolution, many individual Jews managed to move to cities and even Moscow, where they started to acquire Russian or other local languages.

In 1897 (the year of a census) over 5 million Jews lived in Russia, 94 percent of them in the Pale of Settlement, where they were allowed to reside and constituted a tenth of the population. Originally under the rule of Poland–Lithuania, in 1772 these regions had been annexed by Russia. Until then Jews had formed a middle class between the landowners and the peasants, working as innkeepers, tradesmen, and craftsmen. Under Russian rule they were heavily taxed, and the Russian government saw a "Jewish problem" that needed to be solved, by expulsion or assimilation. The push for assimilation came with the "Jewish statute" of 1804, which authorized the admission of Jews to Russian schools and permitted Jews to establish their own schools, in which the language of instruction could be Russian, Polish, or German. At the same time, Jews were prohibited from living in the villages, leasing land there, or selling alcoholic beverages.

Expulsion started in Belorussia in 1822, an alternative to conversion to Christianity. Under Tsar Nicholas I, the military conscription of Jews and their expulsion from Kiev and other towns began. The adoption of Russian as a Jewish language was a slow process, partly dependent on the recruitment of Jews into the army in 1827; 70,000 Jews served for the next twenty-five years. *Cantonists*, as they were called, were Jewish children between the ages of twelve (or even as young as eight) and eighteen; a high quota (thirty per 1,000 males during the Crimean War) was required to be provided by Jewish communities for preparatory training, during which they were forbidden to pray or speak Yiddish and required to attend Christian instruction. They were forced to accept baptism, and at the age of eighteen to start on twenty-five years of military service.[36]

In 1844 some government schools were established for Jews, the purpose of which was to convert them to Orthodox Christianity. Jews were now classified as useful or not useful; the useful included wealthy merchants, craftsmen, and farmworkers. Conscription increased. Under Alexander II, who came to the throne in 1855, peasants were emancipated and some limited rights were granted to some Jews. In 1874 there was a change in the army draft, and Jews had to serve for only four years. Those with secondary school education had better conditions, even though Jews could not become officers. This encouraged Jews to go to Russian schools. Education in Russian permitted many Jews to move into journalism, literature, law, theater, and the arts, where they soon became prominent – a focus for expressions of popular anti-Semitism.

The Russian Jewish population continued to grow, but the emancipation of the serfs meant that a plan to move Jews into agriculture would not work. One result was the beginning of emigration, at first from Lithuania and Belorussia in the direction of southern Russia. New communities appeared in towns such as Odessa and Kremenchug in the 1870s, but emigration towards western Europe and the United States also became common; these Yiddish-speaking *Ostjüden* (eastern Jews), as they were called, were generally despised by established assimilating Jews.

There were important ideological changes too, with the development of the Haskalah (Jewish Enlightenment movement) in the larger cities such as Warsaw, Odessa, and Riga. Some favored complete assimilation, but most sought a way of preserving national and religious identity. The *maskilim* (followers of the Haskalah) were at first opposed to Yiddish, arguing for adopting the language of the country; others proposed Hebrew, and there were Hebrew newspapers as well as Yiddish and Russian ones. Many appreciated Yiddish; an active and rich secular Yiddish literature started to develop, with writers such as Mendele Mocher Sforim, who also wrote in Hebrew. In 1863 a society was founded in Moscow for Haskalah and encouraging use of the Russian language. Jews started to attend Russian–Jewish and Russian schools in increasing numbers.[37]

The situation changed drastically in 1881, when a wave of looting and pogroms followed the assassination of the tsar. Jewish "exploitation" was blamed, and Jews were expelled from the villages. A quota of 10 percent in the Pale and 3 percent outside was set for Jewish admission to secondary schools. The pogroms ended in 1884, but administrative pressure on Jews and anti-Semitic propaganda in the press increased, leading to a surge of emigration.

There had been Jews in Moscow from the seventeenth century; some converted to Christianity in order to be able to remain. Slowly, Jews classified as "useful" – the wealthy, discharged soldiers, pharmacists, dentists, and midwives – were allowed to live in the city; others were restricted to short visits. A cemetery and synagogue were set up in 1871, by which time there were about 8,000 Jews in Moscow. Jewish merchants of the highest class were seen as important to the economy. In 1891, however, Jews were banished by order of the governor-general, and an imperial quota in 1899 limited Jewish membership of the first guild of merchants. Under Nicholas II, this pressure on Jews to convert or emigrate continued, with more violence in 1904/5. A law in 1912 forbade the appointment of Jews, apostates, and their children and grandchildren as officers in the army. In 1913 the blood libel trial of Mendel Beilis drew world attention; he was acquitted.

Emigration surged: 2 million Jews left Russia for the West between 1881 and 1914. In 1891 the government approved an agreement with Baron Maurice de Hirsch for 3 million Jews to move to Argentina in the next twenty-five years; about 200,000 did actually emigrate there. By the end of the nineteenth century there were over 5 million Jews in the Russian Empire – 2 million in the Ukraine, and over 1 million in Lithuania and Russian Poland. There were 200,000 in the interior of Russia and Finland. Most of the Jews in the Pale worked in trade or crafts, with a growing proletariat. Many young Jews joined the radical movements – the Social Democrats and the Socialist Revolutionary Party.

Political parties had their own language policies. In 1897 a Jewish workers' union, the Bund, was formed, which aimed at Jewish autonomy, the recognition of Yiddish as a national and school language, and the development of a Yiddish press and literature. The *Hovevei Zion* (Lovers of Zion) movement was also formed after the pogroms; it called for a return to Palestine, and established newspapers in Hebrew, Russian, and Yiddish. A few of its members moved to Ottoman Palestine and founded agricultural settlements that were active in the revival of Hebrew as a vernacular; we will follow this development in the last chapter. Members of the youth movements formed Jewish self-defense forces during the pogroms of 1903. Disagreements between the Bundist non-territorial movements, which supported Yiddish, and the Hebraist Zionist movements led to a bitter dispute both in Europe and, soon, in Palestine.

In Russia, the language choices became more complex and reflected, it has been suggested, political and economic ideologies. Thus, Jews in Odessa in 1905 might have chosen as their favored language Russian if they were active in socialism and communism, like Leon Trotsky; German if they wished to study in western Europe, like Chaim Weizman; Hebrew if they had become Zionists, like Eliezer Ben-Yehuda or David Ben Gurion, and planned to emigrate to Ottoman Palestine; and Yiddish if they remained orthodox or if they favored secular non-territorial Jewish cultural nationalism.[38] These languages and the political ideologies with which they were associated were often in bitter conflict.[39]

After the revolution, in which many Jews were active, there was under Lenin a brief period of Jewish emancipation and recognition. In line with the Leninist policy of supporting some minority languages, Yiddish was promoted by the Soviet government. Hebrew was discouraged, however: the last Hebrew book was published in Russia in the mid-1920s, and Hebrew was virtually banned after the 1930s.[40] For a while, even under Stalin, Jewish schools and other institutions were allowed to continue, but the Communist Party soon moved to control the Jewish masses, abolishing in 1919 Jewish community organizations, prohibiting religious education, closing Yeshivot, and taxing rabbis (the leader of the Habad movement was expelled in 1927). Hebrew and its teaching were also banned; in 1921 a group of Hebrew writers emigrated, and a few years later the Hebrew theater *Habimah* moved to Palestine; many remaining Hebrew writers were sent to forced labor camps.

One other Jewish language, Judeo-Tat (spoken by about 30,000 "Mountain Jews" in Daghestan), was officially recognized: newspapers were published in it, plays produced in the 1930s, and a literary circle established; but, like other minority languages, in 1929 it was required to be written in the Latin alphabet and in 1938 in Cyrillic.[41]

Arguing that Hebrew was bourgeois and that Yiddish was "the language of the Jewish toiling masses", the Soviet government decided to establish a "Jewish proletarian culture", based on a modified Yiddish. The orthographic system was changed so that Hebrew words were transliterated rather than spelled as they were in Hebrew, and Slavic words replaced Hebrew; this was proclaimed as a Soviet reform. A bitter conflict over spelling developed between the Soviet Yiddishists and those in Poland associated with YIVO. An Institute for Jewish Proletarian Culture in Kiev had over 100 researchers by 1935.[42] A Yiddish press was set up, with newspapers in Moscow, the Ukraine, and Belorussia, and a Yiddish theater network was established. Yiddish institutions came under party control. A major network of Yiddish schools was established in the Ukraine and Belorussia in the 1920s, using Sovietized Yiddish but with little other Jewish content; a third of Jewish children attended them at one stage, but the lack of matching secondary and tertiary programs and the ideological changes led to their unpopularity, so that they disappeared by the late 1930s.

In spite of this brief official support, the speaking of Yiddish in Soviet Russia diminished rapidly. In 1926 70 percent of Jews claimed a Jewish language as mother tongue; by 1939 only 40 percent did. In Moscow 81 percent of Jews declared Russian to be their mother tongue; only in Minsk did the figure go down to 50 percent. Wasserstein cites David Fishman as blaming this loss on "creeping official liquidation", but he himself believes that this was not because Yiddish was specially targeted. In Stalinist language policy, Russian was promoted over all minority languages. Wasserstein says it was a result of pressure from below rather than above, reflecting the economic advantage seen in knowing Russian: for example, Jews in the republics chose Russian over Ukrainian or Belorussian.[43] In 1939, he says, the government gave strong support to events celebrating the eightieth birthday of Shalom Aleichem. Wasserstein concludes that "the decline of Yiddish everywhere was primarily a consequence of decisions taken by Yiddish speakers themselves rather than of policies imposed from above. The downward trend was similar whether in Western Europe, Poland or the Soviet Union."[44]

Most Jewish children attended Russian schools; assimilation and intermarriage were common, and economic changes wiped out many traditional Jewish occupations. Some Jews were moved into agriculture, and, lacking sufficient space in the Ukraine and Crimea,[45] a Jewish settlement area was set up in the Far East on the Chinese border. Birobidzan, an area of 36,000 square kilometres, was to be an autonomous Jewish region with Yiddish as its national language, and was declared to be the cultural center of the working Jewish Soviet population. But the Jewish population of Birobidzan reached only 18,000 (a quarter of the total population) and declined to 14,000 by the 1959 census (and was reported to be 6,000 in 2010; only one of the sixteen schools still teaches in Yiddish[46]).[47]

During World War II, Yiddish culture in Ukraine, Belorussia, and Lithuania came to an abrupt and brutal end, with the annihilation of much of the Jewish population and of Jewish schools and institutions. The majority of the 2 million Jews who survived the war were no longer Yiddish-speaking. For a brief period there had been official support for Yiddish publications and theater, but this ended with the "doctors' plot", in which a group of Moscow doctors, many of whom were Jewish, were charged with conspiring to assassinate Soviet leaders; anti-Semitic publications were accompanied by the dismissal of many officials with Jewish names; pressure eased only after the death of Stalin in 1953, when it was admitted that the charges had been made up. According to the 1959 census, three-quarters of Jews declared Russian as their mother tongue; 18 percent (most in Lithuania, Moravia, and Latvia) declared Yiddish, though this has been interpreted as a claim of identity rather than of proficiency; 35,000 claimed Georgian,[48] 25,000 Judeo-Tat,[49] and 20,000 Tajiki (in Bukhara).[50] In the 1970 census the Jewish population was lower, and only 11 percent claimed Yiddish. In the 1960s many Jews sought to emigrate to Israel, but most were refused; some of the "refuseniks" (many of whom lost their jobs) protested by learning Hebrew. In the late 1980s and 1990s permission was finally granted, and over a half of Soviet Jews left the country, many to Israel.

Summing up, over the century Russian Jewry started off speaking Yiddish, built a rich Yiddish culture, assimilated, and switched almost completely to Russian or to some local languages, and half emigrated in the 1990s, settling in Israel, the United States, or Germany where they learned Hebrew, English, or German.

Yiddish under attack in west and east

During the emancipation there were strong attacks on the use of Yiddish in the West. Many anti-Semitic works attacked "jargon" as a code used to fool Christians and harm Christianity in secret, or as a language used by criminals.[51] Jews too saw Yiddish as a handicap: for instance, David Friedlander, an associate of Moses Mendelssohn, published in 1798 a piece arguing that the improvement of education for Jewish children depended on using correct German and correct Hebrew, and not Yiddish.[52] Publication in both Hebrew and Yiddish virtually ceased, but the Jews of Germany continued to speak Yiddish at home, certainly into the middle of the nineteenth century, or at least to speak German with a Yiddish accent; some elements of Western Yiddish remained in the Netherlands, Alsace, and Switzerland, and even more in Hungary and Slovakia. Only among the extreme orthodox followers of the Khatam Soyfer,[53] in the Bratislava Yeshiva, did studies continue in Yiddish; in Frankfurt, the orthodox establishment favored *loshn koydesh* and spoken and written German.[54]

In both west and east, Yiddish started to "shrivel and die", more rapidly in the modernizing west, and later in the "socially and culturally" backward east.[55] Closer contact with non-Jews encouraged Jewish learning of Polish and Russian, but, surprisingly, this came after 1860; earlier, the followers of the Haskalah were more influenced by German, which they used sometimes in informal correspondence, rather than the Hebrew they preferred for formal writing.[56] Most *maskilim* agreed with the German Jewish condemnation of Yiddish.

When Mendel Lefin Satanover published a translation of the biblical book of Proverbs in "rich, idiomatic, local Galician–Ukrainian" Yiddish printed in square characters, with vocalization like a sacred Hebrew book, in 1813, it was strongly criticized by Hebraists such as Tuvya Feder for using neither pure Hebrew nor pure German; Feder's book was the first Hebrew work explicitly opposing Yiddish.[57] There were defenders, who argued that Yiddish had been used for 400 years and was still developing. Other later supporters included Mordechai Lifshits, who in the 1870s published a Russian–Yiddish and Yiddish–Russian dictionary, and tried (but failed) to start a Yiddish newspaper, believing one should communicate with the Jewish masses in their own language.[58] But the co-territorial vernacular was not yet a problem: in the 1897 census, 97 percent of Russian Jews declared Yiddish to be their mother tongue. The founder of modern Zionism too, Theodor Herzl, had a negative view of the "jargons", as he called them – the ghetto languages – that he believed would be replaced by German in the Jewish state he envisaged.[59]

In eastern Europe, by the beginning of the twentieth century, written Yiddish was well established, with daily newspapers and novels being published; in the west, Yiddish was being replaced in the secular world by the local language, but in Russia and Poland it had become a method of secularization. A struggle developed between what were later called Yiddishists and Hebraists, but the language question was only one of a number of ideological issues. The practical value of Yiddish was appreciated especially by the Jewish socialists (markedly in the work of the Jewish Labor Bund), who joined language with nationalism. They established schools. But even the Zionists, though theoretically committed to Hebrew, saw the usefulness of Yiddish and established a Yiddish daily newspaper in Russia.[60]

The influence of language claims on politics came to the fore in Austria, where the autonomous provinces granted administrative power to ethnic groups according to the numbers claiming vernacular (*Umgangsprache*) use.[61] Galicia was declared Polish because 1 million Jews claimed Polish as their vernacular; some Jewish leaders there and in Bucovina argued that, by claiming Yiddish, they would gain rights to administrative recognition and Yiddish schools. The assimilationists were against this, but the nationalists (including the Zionists) supported it.

In August 1907 the Conference for the Yiddish Language met in Czernowitz, Bucovina, and quickly the debate turned to the relative status of Hebrew and Yiddish. A final resolution called for the recognition of Yiddish as *a* Jewish language, leaving attitudes to Hebrew to the "personal convictions" of participants.[62] The argument continued among secular Jews; traditional orthodoxy opposed both, just as it opposed any nationalist view including Zionism. While the Austro-Hungarian government did not permit anyone to claim Yiddish on the 1910 census (in fact, it claimed that it was illegal, and some were jailed or fined for trying), Yiddish publishing and schools continued to grow in the pre-war period in eastern Europe in the three states – Russia, Austro-Hungary, and Romania.[63]

After World War I the three states had become eight, with the USSR, Estonia, Latvia, Lithuania, Poland, Czechoslovakia, Hungary, and Romania each coming to grips with their own nationalist ideologies and policies towards minorities, including the Jews. In most the Jews sought cultural autonomy, and sometimes language recognition. Each of these newly created nations signed minorities protection treaties under the terms of the Treaty of Versailles. This could have been a blueprint for language diversity, but, in practice, implementation was quite limited, as feelings of local nationalism downgraded linguistic and ethnic minorities.

Poland

The Polish treaty, signed in 1919 and forming a template for others signed in the next few years, provided "total and complete protection of life and freedom of all people regardless of their birth, nationality, language, race or religion" (article 2). Article 7 established that minority languages could be used in private and public discourse, commerce, religion, and the courts. Article 8 allowed racial, linguistic, or religious minorities to establish their own schools at their own expense and use their own languages in them. Article 9 called for state-supported primary schools in regions with large minority populations, to teach minority children in their own language as well as in Polish. Article 11 allowed local Jewish committees to disburse public funds to religious schools. Yiddish was thus recognized as a language of instruction, but received state support only at the primary level. Weakening any chance of implementation, the final article provided that only a member state of the League of Nations could make a complaint about non-compliance. The details of this treaty took six months of complex negotiation, and were a defeat for those who had wanted a general declaration of minority rights.[64]

Poland between the wars was the "real fortress" of Yiddish, Weinreich claims, with several million speakers, a major Yiddish press, a Yiddish-speaking labor movement, and a well-organized Yiddish education system.[65] Vilna, in Poland, became the center for the development of a standard language, supported by YIVO, a center for research and development with regard to the Yiddish language and literature. In spite of continuing Polish anti-Semitism, Jews attended Polish state schools and started speaking the language. Indeed, one scholar even claims that, "had Polish independence lasted another twenty years, modern Yiddish and Hebrew culture and schools would have inevitably declined to be replaced by Jewish cultural creativity in the Polish language".[66]

The 1931 census did not allow for any claim of nationality, and Jewish political parties called on people to make language claims instead; 8 percent claimed Hebrew, though it was seldom spoken anywhere, and the claim of 31 percent declaring Yiddish as their mother tongue, compared to 70 percent ten years earlier, was probably an exaggeration.[67] In fact, Polish Jews had added Polish to their Yiddish before World War I, and lived in a trilingual community, which these two languages shared with Hebrew.[68] The Polish government in 1921 had granted some recognition to Hebrew, but no government schools operated in Yiddish. In 1926 the Jewish libraries loaned the same number of books in Polish and in Yiddish, and even in Vilna only 8 percent of the loans from the Mefitsei Haskalah Library were in Yiddish. This showed up in the language of public signage too: in 1937 only seventeen out of 129 store signs in a Jewish street were in Yiddish. The Yiddish writer S. Ansky wrote most of his early work in Russian; Max Weinreich, a founder of YIVO, grew up speaking German and learned Yiddish in the Bundist youth movement.[69]

Dovid Katz adds an important element to this story, pointing out that the struggle between the Yiddishists and the Hebraists affected only a minority of Jews: the large majority of orthodox Jews formed a silent but Yiddish-speaking group.[70] Their position came to be represented by the non-Zionist Agudath Israel movement, founded in 1912 but later led by Nathan Birnbaum, who had been one of the organizers of the Czernowitz conference and who during World War I returned to traditional orthodoxy. But his position was not extreme enough for the Hungarian Hasidim, who at the Chop conference, in 1920, led by the Minkatsher rebbe (rabbi) and supported by the Satmar rebbe, condemned Agudath Israel as well as secular Zionists, proclaiming Yiddish as the sole spoken Jewish language.

It appears that Yiddish in Poland was secure only among the decreasing group of orthodox Jews, and that, although it was stronger there than in other countries, both internal pressure and the absence of government recognition meant that the number of speakers was decreasing. The Nazi murders wiped out 90 percent of Polish Jewry, however, and most who survived the Holocaust left Poland after the Polish attacks on them from 1944 to 1946. Wasserstein may have been right in asserting that Yiddish was weakening in the 1930s, but it was the Holocaust that destroyed it.

Czechoslovakia

Czechoslovakia, formed as a unified state in 1918 and more recently divided again into the Czech Republic and Slovakia, included Jews from Bohemia and Moravia – once part of the Hapsburg Empire – and Slovakia and Carpatho-Russia, both previously part of Hungary; the Jewish community organizations followed Austrian or Hungarian models.

The Jews were generally assimilationist, adopting the Czech and German cultures and languages in the west and Hungarian in the east.[71] Czech sociolinguists note that Hebrew was the religious language of the Jews, but found no evidence of Yiddish use later than the seventeenth century; many Jews spoke German.[72] Wasserstein says it was "still current" in the 1930s, however, in the small towns of eastern Slovakia and among traditional Jews in sub-Carpathian Ruthenia.[73] In Bohemia, Silesia, and Moravia, Jewish children attended general schools; there were Jewish elementary schools in Prague and Ostrava and a secondary school in Brno; in Slovakian Jewish schools, instruction was in Hungarian and later in Slovak; and there were Yeshivot and traditional *hedarim* in Carpatho-Russia. Jewish authors, many outstanding, wrote in Czech, German, or Hungarian. Emancipation thus produced conditions conducive to religious, cultural, and linguistic assimilation. Most Czech Jews were exterminated during the Holocaust.

Latvia

Jewish culture in Latvia started well after World War I; with a Jewish population in 1925 of about 100,000, there was a Jewish department within the Ministry of Education responsible for Yiddish and Hebrew schools; in 1933 there were ninety-eight Jewish elementary schools, eighteen secondary schools, and four vocational schools. There were three Jewish political parties in the parliament and five newspapers in Yiddish or Hebrew.[74] In 1934, however, after a coup d'état,[75] minority language education was restricted and all schools were required to teach in Latvian; all political parties were abolished. The influence of religion[76] and Zionism increased, with the beginning of emigration.

After the Soviet occupation of Latvia many Jewish leaders were arrested, and 400,000 Jews were deported to Siberia and central Asia. Most of the remainder were either killed by the Nazis or escaped to the Soviet Union; a few survived, and after the war they were joined by 10,000 former Latvian Jews who had survived in the Soviet Union and another 30,000 Soviet Jews from elsewhere. In 1959 half the Jews in Latvia claimed Yiddish as their mother tongue. When Latvia became independent, in 1991, the Jewish population was about 23,000; following the mass emigration of the next decade about 9,000 remain, served by one Jewish day school and a synagogue.

Lithuania

After World War I the Lithuanian Federation was divided into three separate states: Lithuania, the Belarusian Soviet Republic, and Poland. The Belarusian Republic followed Soviet policy: traditional Judaism, Hebrew language and culture, and the Zionist movement were all suppressed.

In independent Lithuania, with a population of about 150,000 Jews, who formed the largest national minority, most Jews claimed Jewish nationality and spoke Yiddish; some professionals were proficient in Russian, and in time most learned some Lithuanian.[77] There was pressure to emigrate during the interwar period.

The first Cabinet, formed in 1918, included three Jews, one of them the minister for Jewish affairs. In 1919 the Lithuanian government guaranteed that Jews would receive the "right of national-cultural autonomy". A Jewish National Council worked with the Ministry of Jewish Affairs and was responsible for Jewish institutions. When Lithuania joined the League of Nations, in 1922, it agreed to recognize minority rights. These were written into the constitution. In 1924, however, the position of minister of Jewish affairs was abolished, the National Council was banned, and the communities lost their nationalist Jewish content.

Jewish education continued, however. Jewish teachers and schools were supported by public funds. There were three Jewish systems: *Tarbut*, which was Zionist and used Hebrew as its language of instruction; a socialist system, which used Yiddish; and *Yavneh*, the traditional religious sector, which used Hebrew and Yiddish. There were also other religious Jewish schools. In the 1920s the number of Jews in Lithuanian medium schools started to increase; a Jewish school with Lithuanian as the language of instruction was started in 1933 in Kovno (Kaunas). In 1936 there were over 100 Hebrew and Yiddish elementary schools. There were also more than a dozen Jewish secondary schools, which had to be maintained by the parents; some used Hebrew as the language of instruction and two used Yiddish.[78] Some Jewish authors started to use Lithuanian. Evidence has been collected of a Jewish variety of Lithuanian.[79] A Jewish Lithuanian language magazine, which appeared from 1935 until 1940, argued for Lithuanian rather than Russian, and stayed neutral on the Hebrew versus Yiddish debate.[80]

In 1939 Lithuania came under Soviet rule, and Vilna, with its 100,000 Jews, was added. A number of Jews were deported and all social groups and organizations were banned. In 1941 the Germans occupied Lithuania in a one-week campaign, and the extermination of Lithuanian Jewry began immediately.

Estonia

Estonia was another Baltic nation created after World War I with a minorities policy influenced but not governed by the Treaty of Versailles. Jews had appeared in Estonia quite late, migrating from Courland (western Latvia) and Lithuania in the nineteenth century and settling mainly in Tallinn and Tartu; their dialect of Yiddish was distinct. The small urbanized Jewish community was multilingual in Yiddish, German, and Russian, secondary education in the tsarist period being in the two prestige languages. In independent Estonia, after 1918, Jews were granted cultural autonomy in a document issued in Hebrew and Yiddish, and this was in effect from 1926 until Russian domination in 1940.

Although the community was small (about 4,300 in 1934), it was very active. After 1918 knowledge of the national language, Estonian, became critical, but education in Jewish languages was also possible, resulting in competition between Yiddishists (founding the first two schools in 1926 and 1931, with Hebrew as a subject) and Hebraists; a school with Hebrew as the language of instruction was opened in 1928. There was also pressure for Estonian, and some for Russian, but the main controversy was Yiddish versus Hebrew, at times leading even to violence. Jewish cultural autonomy was banned after the Soviet occupation in 1940 and many Jews were deported.

Some 3,000 Jews fled before the German invasion, and the remaining 1,000 were killed by the Nazis. The Estonian Jews who returned after the war were forced to choose between Estonian and Russian, and the many Soviet Jews who came subsequently were Russian-speaking. As a result, after independence, in 1991, there were not enough Yiddish speakers to justify it as a school language; the Jewish gymnasium uses Russian as its language of instruction.[81]

Hungary

Under Ottoman rule, in Buda and other portions of Hungary in the sixteenth century, Jews returned from the Balkans and Asia Minor, and Buda became an important Jewish community. In the Habsburg-dominated areas, persecutions and expulsions continued until the seventeenth century, except in some small neighborhoods in Burgenland. In the eighteenh century, when the Ottomans had withdrawn, the small Jewish population was increased by migration from Moravia and Poland; most were peddlers living in villagers, and the Jewish community had to pay a heavy "tolerance tax". At the end of the century Jews were allowed to settle in royal cities, and by 1787 there were 81,000 Jews there. During the 1830s and 1840s there were suggestions that they be granted civic rights, but restrictions stayed in force until 1859, when Jews were allowed to reside anywhere and work in the professions. A law of Jewish emancipation was passed in 1867, and migration from Galicia led to a major increase in Jewish population, passing half a million by 1869. Jews became active in finance, the liberal professions (including journalism, law, and medicine), and agriculture. Judaism was officially recognized by the state in 1890. A political anti-Semitic movement started to appear in the 1870, and was active especially among national minorities, such as the Slovaks.

Hungarian Jewry had three major divisions: in Oberland, Jews originally from Austria or Moravia spoke German or Western Yiddish; in Unterland, Jews from Galicia spoke Eastern Yiddish; and most of the Jews of central Hungary spoke Hungarian. There were religious divisions too: there was a strong orthodox movement, centered on Pressburg, while Haskalah started in the 1830s and a strong Reform movement (called Neologists) had developed by the middle of the century. In 1868 the government summoned a General Jewish Congress, which split between orthodox and Reform (Neolog), with a third section of status quo communities. Torah study and Yeshivot were strong in western and central Hungary. Hasidic communities developed in the northeast in such towns as Satmar, Munkacs, Belz, and Vizhnitz, each the founding city of a major sect. By the end of the century assimilation, apostasy, and mixed marriages were common in Hungary. A small Zionist movement developed, opposed by assimilationist and orthodox Jews (from whom the anti-Zionist *Neturei Karta* movement developed).

Jews served in the Austro-Hungarian army during World War I (10,000 were killed in action), and were active in the communist movement that was briefly in power afterwards. They suffered during the "white terror" that followed, and from the anti-Semitic policy of the government, which set a 5 percent *numerus clausus* on Jews in higher education.

In 1928 there was an easing of anti-Jewish regulation, and the Jewish community elected two representatives (one orthodox and one Neologist) to the upper house of parliament. But this was a brief respite: anti-Jewish legislation in 1938 restricted the number of Jews in liberal professions and commercial and industrial occupations to 20 percent; a 1939 law applied this also to apostates and their children and reduced the number of Jews in economic activities to 5 percent. In 1941 the Third Jewish Law prohibited intermarriage; the killing of Jews started the same year with the expulsion to Nazi-occupied Galicia of 100,000 Jews and their murder there. Germany pressured the Hungarian government to increase anti-Jewish activity, and occupied Hungary in 1944 with an aim of achieving the "final solution of the Jewish problem". Deportation and mass murder followed, with the result that only about 260,000 Jews of the 865,000 considered Jewish in 1941 survived. Under communist rule, in 1949 Zionist and Jewish education was banned.[82]

Overall, Jews in Hungary were set apart socially and physically "for religious reasons".[83] Large number of Jews migrated to Hungary in the early nineteenth century, and were Yiddish-speaking or used German if they had modern education. After the emancipation in 1867, modernization and assimilation was common. Even orthodox Jews developed a working knowledge of Hungarian; Neolog Jews, living in the cities, were almost completely Hungarian-speaking. Jews were recognized as a religious minority, but not a national minority. By the 1930s Yiddish was limited to the ultra-orthodox.[84] Two-thirds of Hungarian Jewry (more than half a million Jews) were victims of the Holocaust, although the killings did not happen until the German army was retreating, in 1944.

Currently, there are between 80,000 and 150,000 people in Hungary today with at least one Jewish parent – a decline from 1945. Most are highly educated and live in the capital, Budapest. There was heavy emigration after the war and again in 1956/7. Jewish life was reinvigorated after the fall of communism. There are at present forty-two Neolog synagogue districts, twelve in Budapest; there are also three Habad synagogues, one Reform, and a modern orthodox synagogue. The four Jewish schools established since 1991 have about 1,000 pupils in all. Some youth movements were re-established, and there are several periodicals published in Hungarian. Students are reported not to learn Hebrew to any extent; whereas in the past Jewish education produced multilinguals, it now produces graduates with the same language skills as the general population. There is, it is reported, a major gap between the complex structure of Jewish institutions and the largely assimilated unaffiliated Jewish population.[85]

So let's make a language: Esperanto

Concerned about the continuing gap between Jews and Gentiles and the choice between the dominant language and ethnic identity, one proposal at the end of the nineteenth century was to develop a new universal language. The most well known and successful proponent of this radical compromise was Ludwik Lazar Zamenhof.

Zamenhof grew up in Bialystok, the son of an emancipated Jew fluent in Russian, French, German, and Polish who worked for the government as a censor of publications in Yiddish and Hebrew, or, in another account, as a teacher of German. His first language was Russian, but he grew up speaking Polish and knew Yiddish; he later developed fluency in French, Latin, German, Greek, English, and Hebrew. After completing gymnasium training he began medical studies in Moscow but returned in 1881, just before the pogroms. He completed training as a doctor in Warsaw and started to practice medicine.

As early as high school he began to work on his idea of an international language, but only in 1887 was he able to publish a pamphlet giving details of the language. While in Moscow he formed a group that made plans to found a Jewish colony somewhere; in 1882 he published an article proposing to establish such a colony, but not in Palestine, because of problems he anticipated with Muslims, Christians, and the Turkish government. When this suggestion was strongly attacked, his next article accepted the Zionist idea of settling in Palestine. He became active in Hibbat Israel and in organizing the Zionist groups. He proposed modernizing Yiddish, and wrote a grammar of Yiddish, the Russian text and Yiddish translation of which was finally published in 1982.[86] He left the Zionist movement in 1887, arguing that it would not solve the Jewish problem. In that same year Zamenhof published the first full description of Esperanto. In 1914 he is reported to have refused to join a Jewish group of Esperantists, on the grounds that nationalism was a danger to strong and weak groups alike.[87] He died in 1917.

The number of speakers of the language grew, at first in eastern Europe and later internationally, and estimates of the current number of speakers is anywhere between 10,000 and 2 million; there are said to be 1,000 native speakers.[88]

Summing up: the effect of emancipation in Europe

Emancipation turned out to be a negative force for Jewish identity and continuity, for its most common results were a loss of Yiddish, assimilation, apostasy, and intermarriage. Only in Belgium (with a solid Haredi community in Antwerp), France (bolstered by refugees from Arab north Africa),[89] Britain, the United States, and Latin America were the numbers sufficiently high to allow an active minority to build a strong Jewish community outside Israel. Otherwise, a loss of affiliation was common; many Europeans claim a Jewish grandparent!

The movement east into Slavic lands produced a major Jewish culture expressed in a developing Yiddish-speaking and (later) Yiddish-writing life, which supported also a strong Ashkenazi Hebrew literacy. In spite of regular pogroms and expulsions, the east European Jewish communities flourished and grew, taking advantage of any opportunity for economic or social advancement. Restricted to villages in many countries, blocked from general or higher education, banned from many occupations, heavily taxed, Jews nonetheless experienced a rich social and intellectual life until the twentieth century.

In the interwar period, the overwhelming tendency was for east European Jews, no longer restricted to ghettos and *shtetlach*, to abandon religion and language, and assimilate as speedily as they could. The Holocaust, using the Nuremberg laws, which murdered those with one Jewish grandparent alongside those with four, made sure that intermarriage and apostasy were no more an escape than giving up Yiddish and orthodoxy. The anti-Jewish laws of the east and central European nations and the anti-Semitism of those nations after emancipation guaranteed that only emigration would be an escape. It is perhaps not unreasonable, then, to ask what might have happened without the Holocaust; the evidence of the interwar period supports a conjecture that Jewish religious and cultural life and Yiddish might well have continued to fade even in the eastern European centers of Jewish population. But the return to Zion and the revernacularization and revitalization of Hebrew guaranteed vital linguistic and cultural continuity.

A personal history

A recent book dealing with the challenge of postmodernism to those who write Jewish history[1] recognizes the problem of historians' personal history in shaping their views of what they are describing and analyzing. By now, I am sure you have become aware of my prejudices as I have recounted the sociolinguistic history of the Jews: my background as a Zionist modern orthodox Israeli brought up as a speaker of English and now living by choice in a Hebrew-dominated society. In this chapter, which deals with the addition of English and Spanish to the sociolinguistic ecology of the Jews, I start with a personal autobiographical account of the languages of my own background, which will give me a chance to depict the changes that have occurred to many Jews in the last two centuries or so.[2]

My mother's oldest known ancestor was Jane Benjamin, identified in the 1841 British census as a forty-six-year-old hawker living with her daughter in the East End of London. Born in about 1795 in Holland, she probably married in London in 1816. My assumption is that she was a Yiddish-speaking Ashkenazi who picked up enough English to be able to work as a peddler.[3] Her daughter, Esther, was born in London, presumably growing up bilingual in Yiddish and English. In 1860 Esther became the wife of Julius Green, a Polish-born tailor who had arrived in England some time before 1848, when he was married by the Chief Rabbi to Mary Solomons, London-born, who died ten years later after bearing two children.

Julius and his second wife (Esther) had another ten children of their own, my grandfather, Mark, being the eighth. Most of the children were listed in censuses as tailors once they reached the age of ten. Mark and his younger brother attended the Jews' Free School,[4] founded in 1817 in Spitalfields, in the East End of London, to cater for Jewish immigrant children. Its famous headmaster, Moses Angel, who held the post from 1842 to 1898, worked to stamp out Yiddish and teach English language and culture while maintaining Jewish religious observance. Mark thus grew up as a fluent, educated speaker of English (I recall him as an active writer of letters to newspapers and the government to promote his ideas and inventions). When Mark's father died, in 1894, he decided to emigrate, choosing Australia and New Zealand rather than America. He took with him a married sister and a younger brother, and started a haberdashery in Wellington, New Zealand. But both brother and sister died, so, in 1905, he took a trip to the United States. There he visited his business partner's family and quickly married Anna Zelda Barasch, Albany-born daughter of parents who had emigrated from Grodno, probably shortly after the pogroms of 1882. Thus, both my mother's parents were English speakers, and she grew up in England and New Zealand with no knowledge of the Yiddish her grandparents certainly spoke.

On my father's side, I know of my great-grandfather, Nesem Shpolsky,[5] who served in the Russian army (by then Jewish military service was only five years) and, after release, moved to Kremenchug, a city in the Ukraine being settled by Jews from Lithuania, where his son Jacob was born in 1866. Jacob too left eastern Europe after the pogroms, moving in 1890 or so with his wife and members of her family to Glasgow, recruited probably to work for the Imperial Tobacco Company. My father was born there, and, after the troubles of the tobacco industry in competition with the American cigarette makers in 1906, emigrated with his family on an assisted passage to New Zealand, where he entered public school. He knew some Yiddish, but I don't remember hearing him speak it.

Essentially, then, my family was typical of the east European Jews who left for English-speaking countries – Britain, the United States, the British Empire – about the end of the nineteenth century. My wife's family, which made a similar move from Hungary to the United States at about the same time, did leave some relatives in Europe, a few of whom survived the Holocaust and emigrated to the United States only after World War II.

These families typify the major emigration of mainly Yiddish-speaking Ashkenazi Jews from east Europe to the English-speaking world, where they found societies that permitted them to integrate or assimilate, and that encouraged them to add English and drop Yiddish from their sociolinguistic proficiency. A somewhat similar pattern affected those Jews who moved to Latin America, where their Jewish language was replaced by Spanish or Portuguese.

Westernization: Britain and the British Commonwealth

Jews who had been expelled in the thirteenth century started to return to Britain at the time of Cromwell, the earliest being Portuguese-speaking *Anusim*, joined soon by Sephardi Jews from Holland and only later by Yiddish speakers from eastern Europe. In 1655, concerned with the persecutions of 1648 in eastern Europe that were starting to drive Ashkenazi Jews westward, a Jewish scholar from Amsterdam, Manasseh ben Israel, came to republican England to present a petition asking for Jews to be admitted. Oliver Cromwell sent the petition to the

Council, which set up a committee of lawyers. The committee announced that there was no legal bar to Jews coming to England, the 1290 expulsion having been a "royal prerogative" referring only to Jews then living there. But, as they could not agree on conditions for readmission, no formal status was established.

In 1656 a group of twenty *Anusim* living in London claimed that they were refugees from the Spanish Inquisition, and petitioned the Council to be allowed to practice Judaism in private. This was granted, and they brought a Torah scroll from Amsterdam and rented a building for a synagogue.[6] After the Restoration, in 1664 the Privy Council ruled that Jews had the same civil rights as Roman Catholics and Nonconformists, who did not take Church of England oaths. Further privileges were granted, and in 1774 a judgment protected Jews from group libels. Thus, "almost by accident, England became the first place in which it was possible for a Jewish community to emerge".[7]

At the same time, the first Jewish refugees from Brazil came to New Amsterdam, where they were allowed to stay but not to build a synagogue: this became possible only under English rule in 1664, when New Amsterdam became New York. By the early eighteenth century Jews had equal rights, and no need (as in Europe) to establish religious courts and communities to negotiate with the governments. Jews in America had synagogues just as Christians had churches, but no Jewish community was legally mandated.[8] In the United States, there were no civic disabilities forcing Jews to convert to Christianity in order to overcome them; in Britain, this was not the case until the middle of the nineteenth century.

Jewish migrants were the founders of the financial market that grew up in London when William of Orange became William III in 1688. They were committed to trade and developed efficient intelligence systems. Many, such as Isaac D'Israeli, converted to Christianity, as did the millionaire Samson Gideon – his son became a Member of Parliament – and so did Manasseh Lopez, David Ricardo, and Ralph Bernal. Benjamin Disraeli, brought up as a Christian but recognizably of Jewish origin, became an MP, leader of the opposition and, later, prime minister. By this time his fluency in spoken English was demonstrated by great parliamentary skills, and he also became a successful novelist. Only the Rothschilds managed to avoid baptism and be financially successful, when Nathan Rothschild was sent to England to establish the English branch of the international family banking business.[9]

In 1826 all restrictions on Jewish immigration were lifted; in 1833 Jews were allowed to become lawyers, and in 1846 their right to buy freehold land was included in a law. In 1858 the first practicing Jew was elected to parliament.

Bevis Marks synagogue had been built in 1701; Ashkenazi Jews (poorer and of lower class than the Sephardim) established their first congregation in 1690; and two more synagogues were added in the early eighteenth century. Many Ashkenazi Jews were peddlers like my great-grandmother. Some of them started congregations in the country towns and ports where they traded.

In the nineteenth century Ashkenazi congregations in Britain recognized a single Chief Rabbi, thus forming in the middle of the century a central organization. Most immigrants settled in London. Mass immigration after 1881 brought in poor Yiddish-speaking Jews, who tended to live in compact ghettos in east London, Manchester, Leeds, Liverpool, and Glasgow. Earlier, responsibility for education had fallen on the parents, who hired Hebrew tutors or started *heders*, but some of the teachers complained that London-born boys didn't know enough Yiddish.[10] With continued immigration, however, the immigrants started to publish Yiddish and even Hebrew newspapers, established small synagogues, and set up a Jewish trade union.[11] One such paper was the *Arbeter Fraynd*, a radical anarchist paper that first appeared in 1885 but was banned during World War I.

By the 1820s English Jews had started to dress like non-Jews, and even to shave. Yiddish was being challenged by English: wealthier Jews in business needed to learn English, and only the lower classes continued to speak Yiddish. Yiddish almanacs were published for peddlers, but included English words. Yiddish was stigmatized, however: middle-class parents wanted their children to speak English. By 1816 the three major synagogues kept their records in English rather than Hebrew and Yiddish, and in 1826 the leaders of the Great Synagogue required all announcements and notices to be in Hebrew and English, though this was reversed when it became obvious that the majority of the congregation understood neither.[12]

There were three Yiddish daily newspapers in the 1890s.[13] The established Jewish community encouraged Anglicization, working through the Jews' Free School and youth movements. The schools worked hard, "to transform their students into little Englishmen and Englishwomen".[14] For a few years in the middle of the nineteenth century an institute for adults offered classes in Hebrew and general culture. Many Jews moved out of the neighborhoods and joined the middle class, leaving behind minorities of Orthodox, Yiddishists, socialists, and anarchists.

Anti-foreigner feeling developed at the end of the century; a Royal Commission on Aliens in 1903 reported that overcrowding was the only serious problem, and the 1905 Aliens Act allowed for the admission of refugees, and so did not reduce the problem.[15] The evidence suggests a community continually being replenished with Yiddish speakers: a Board of Trade Report in 1894 complained that the concentration of newly arrived foreigners speaking in Yiddish prevented migrants learning English and assimilating. Old Bailey proceedings from the 1890s to 1913 contain fifty-eight mentions of Yiddish.[16] Yiddish posters were used in 1916 to try to persuade the 25,000 Russian-born Jewish aliens, exempt from conscription as citizens of an ally, to volunteer for the army.[17]

Glasgow is a good example of a provincial Jewish community. Originally, in the eighteenth century, there were only a few Jewish traders and medical students[18] in Glasgow. The city grew rapidly in the nineteenth century, the population reaching 700,000 by 1870. There was a tiny Jewish community by 1831, growing to 200 by 1850. The community grew slowly, already serving as a transmigration point for Jews from east Europe aiming to reach the New World. In the 1890s two major employment possibilities developed: an influx of London tailors led to the opening of many sweatshops, and a branch of the Imperial Tobacco Company was recruiting cigarette makers in Europe; others followed, and, as mentioned, that brought my grandfather to Glasgow. Most of the Jewish migrants in Glasgow came from Russia and Poland, and many settled in the Gorbals area of Glasgow.[19] Many hoped to continue to the United States, and some succeeded.

A Talmud Torah school was established in Glasgow in the 1890s, which taught at first in Yiddish. When a new synagogue was consecrated, in 1892, the Rev. Simeon Singer (minister of a London synagogue and editor of the *Authorized Daily Prayer Book*) gave the opening address, in which he called on the Russian Jews to switch to English: "I can conceive no good whatever in keeping up in Scotland for an hour longer than you can help the use of Yiddish. For a few weeks or months it may be of service; after that it is no longer necessary... The wisest thing is to exchange your language for (your neighbours')."[20]

The transition of the community from vernacular Yiddish to English is shown by the newspapers. A Yiddish *Jewish Times* occasionally was issued around the turn of the century. The daily *Glasgow Jewish Evening Times*, started by Zvi Golombek, a Zionist, soon became the *Glasgow Weekly Jewish News*, which did not last long; it was followed by the *Jewish Voice*, also in Yiddish, which lasted only a few years. The Yiddish of these newspapers was said to be full of English borrowings.[21] In 1928 Golombek started a weekly English-language Jewish paper, the *Echo*; he was succeeded as editor by his son Ezra in 1950, who continued to produce the paper until 1992.

Yiddish survived the demise of the newspapers in Britain. In 2011 the *Jewish Chronicle* reported the last meeting in London of a Yiddish literary society, the Friends of Yiddish, founded in 1936 and meeting since then in Whitechapel. The first Yiddish theater had opened in London in 1886, and others followed. The last, the Grand Palais, closed in 1970. But Yiddish remained alive, not among its secular enthusiasts but within the Hasidic world, where it continued to serve as a support for the special clothing, strict rules of *kashrut*, and concentrated living patterns that kept the ultra-orthodox separate not just from non-Jews and non-observant Jews but also from modern orthodox Jews.

Yiddish, as fate should have it, is 100 percent safe for centuries to come among the Southern Hasidim – those that hail from Poland, Ukraine, and particularly Hungary. The average number of children in each family is between six and seven. Most marriages are arranged in the later teenage years, often between brides and grooms of different towns or countries. Nearly all live in compact communities in easy walking distance to synagogues, schools and other institutions.[22]

Katz lists the Hasidic dynasties in the United States and Israel. In the United Kingdom, he notes, "Satmar, the most populous Hasidic dynasty in the world, has a substantial Yiddish-speaking community in London which is also the home to Belzer and others".

An English journalist, Jack Shamash,[23] estimated in an article in *The Times* (6 March 2004) that there were over 30,000 Yiddish speakers in Britain, including "several thousand" children. According to the 2001 UK census, there were 149,000 Jews living in London, out of a total of 266,000 Jews in the United Kingdom. The census data do not provide any tabulation for languages, so the widely used 30,000 figure is based on Shamash, it seems. Among British Satmar, males use mainly Yiddish and consider English a "necessary evil" required by the Education Act; women use English among themselves but are under pressure to use Yiddish.[24]

Britain served both as a way station for Jews who moved on to the colonies or the New World, like my grandfathers, and the location for a new Jewish community, the majority of whom shifted to English and showed signs of assimilation, but also with a significant minority of Hasidim forming part of the self-isolating, Yiddish-speaking ultra-orthodox cluster; there were also a small number (11,892 in the 2001 census) of Israeli-born Jews speaking Hebrew, Arabic, and English.

Language loyalties in the United States

From 1881 to 1911 a series of pogroms in Russia led to massive emigration on the part of Jews: over 60,000 every year. More than 2 million went to the United States, changing the demography: in 1826 there were 6,000 Jews in the US, and 150,000 by the start of the American Civil War, but the numbers rapidly increased after 1880, reaching 1 million by 1900.

But there had been an earlier settlement, starting with the arrival of Jews and *Anusim* in New Amsterdam under Dutch rule and continuing to grow under the freedom of the "virtual absence of religious-determined law".[25] Jews could establish their own synagogues, of whatever form they chose – Sephardi or Ashkenazi (German, Polish, English, or Dutch) – just as Christians were setting up their own churches. In eighteenth-century America, Jews (like those in England) could start businesses without fears of confiscation by Christian or Islamic governments.

The Jews felt free (though there were some minor Jewish disabilities in North Carolina until 1868, when the requirement to take an oath of being a Protestant was lifted).[26] But the US Jewish communities grew very slowly. Many Jews were peddlers, who later opened small businesses in New York, Ohio, and Illinois. Divided regionally and politically, 7,000 Jews served in the Northern Army and 3,000 in the Southern during the American Civil War. There was a brief blink in 1863, when General Ulysses S. Grant issued an order expelling Jewish traders from Tennessee, but the order was cancelled a month later on the instruction of President Lincoln.[27]

For a while after 1840 German Jews, secular and highly educated in German, were the dominant element in the community (succeeding in this Sephardi Spanish and Portuguese Jews)[28] with their ideas of emancipation, and Reform Judaism, with its policy of moving the vernacular into the synagogue service, spread rapidly. The 1881 pogroms changed this balance, resulting in the rapid arrival of masses of poor Yiddish-speaking east European Ashkenazi Jews. The fashionable German Jewish synagogues in New York moved uptown, and refugees were jammed into the Lower East Side, living in "dumbbell tenements", required by the Tenement House Act of 1879 to have access to the air, which was provided by building them around air shafts; a 1901 New Law required a courtyard between buildings. Most Jews were employed making ready-made clothing, working a seventy-hour week. By 1910 there were a million foreign-born Yiddish speakers in the United States; the figure went up to 1,222,658, but was down to half a million by 1960.[29] By 1913 there were 16,552 clothing factories in New York. The average Jewish immigrant stayed in the Lower East Side for fifteen years, moving next to Harlem, then to the Bronx, then to parts of Brooklyn. Some established major businesses; most of their children went to college, and many became doctors and lawyers.

Freie Arbeiter Stimme was a Yiddish anarchist newspaper founded in 1890, and it continued publication until 1977. *Der Tog die Varhayt* was published in New York from 1919; it changed its name to *Der Morgen Tschurnal* in 1938 and continued to appear until 1971. In 1910 there were seven Yiddish daily newspapers in the United States, out of 129 mother-tongue dailies; the number rose to eleven by 1920 but dropped to five by 1960. Circulation reached half a million in 1920, and dropped to 120,000 by 1960. There were eight weekly Yiddish papers in 1910, which doubled by 1920 then fell to two by 1960. By 1920 there were seven mixed Yiddish/English weeklies, which increased in 1930 to thirteen and dropped to four by 1960. During the same period, the number of English-language periodicals intended for Jews grew from thirty in 1910 to 122 in 1960.[30]

By 1920, with 1,640,000 Jews, many of them Yiddish speakers, New York was the largest Jewish city in the world.[31] Another significant language group among Jewish immigrants were the Sephardim; by 1924 there were estimated to be 30,000, mainly in New York, and in the 1930s the Judeo-Spanish press, printed in Hebrew letters and founded by Jews from Salonika, claimed 50,000 readers of Ladino. There were nineteen Ladino periodicals, all but two in New York, between 1910 and 1948. The earliest was *La Amerika*, which was published from 1910 to 1925 and tended to be traditionally religious. There were socialist Ladino papers too, such as *El Progreso* and *El Emigrante* (published in New Jersey). The last issue of *La Vara* was published in 1948; in 1928 it had had 16,500 subscribers. The Ladino newspapers were generally in financial difficulty, and commonly ignored by Ashkenazim. They reported the tensions between the communities, whose language and food and customs were so different.[32] The common belief among US Sephardim is that the language has already vanished, and hopes for continuation are unrealistic.[33]

There was no German Jewish daily in the United States, perhaps because the German Jewish immigrants learned English quickly, or else because there was a non-Jewish German language daily in New York. There were weeklies, however: *Aufbau*, published since 1934, and *Jewish Way*, a rival that appeared from 1940 to 1965.[34] There was also *The Israelite*, founded in Cincinnati by Rabbi Isaac Meyer Wise, a leader of the Reform movement, in 1854; it published *Die Deborah*, a weekly German-language supplement largely for women.

By the end of the century three major groupings of synagogues had developed; the largest was the Conservative movement, which rejected the radical changes of the Reform movement, such as English services; the second was the Orthodox, with a range of traditions and a growing number of institutions certifying kosher food; the third was the Reform movement, moving towards English in the services.

After World War I the comparatively easy integration of Jews in the United States was suddenly challenged by anti-foreigner feeling; one result was the 1929 Immigration Quota, fueled by the fear of Bolshevik Russian Jews. By this time, though, Jews were strongly entrenched in many parts of the economy – finance, real estate, retail, entertainment – and especially in those professions in which, in spite of some Ivy League quotas reminiscent of the *numerus clausus* of Russia, the openness of higher education was particularly attractive.

But all this came with a Jewish willingness to assimilate, dropping religious observance (one common myth is of the Jews who accepted new names at Ellis Island and dropped their *tefillin* into the sea; another marker was the abundance of non-kosher Chinese restaurants in Jewish neighborhoods) and shifting from Yiddish to English as the language of home as well as community. The community grew during the 1930s and 1940s, with continual integration, increased intermarriage, and a loss of immigrant languages. A recent survey shows the changes in US Jews' knowledge of Yiddish (higher with the elderly and low with the young, showing an absence of natural intergenerational transmission) and Hebrew (the opposite, showing the effect of school learning and visits to Israel).[35]

A new wave of Russian Jewish immigration (a quarter of a million or more[36]) came with the collapse of the USSR and the opening of the gates to emigration in the 1990s. Most had been secular since the banning of religion in the Soviet Union, and brought with them a high attraction to the Russian language and Western culture. Many of these former Soviet Jews settled in concentrated areas in New York (especially Brighton Beach, where the community is strong but aging), Boston, Miami (Sunny Isles beach), and San Francisco (Richmond district), where Russian can be heard in the markets; adults keep using Russian at home and with friends. There are several Russian Jewish newspapers published in New York and elsewhere. After-school programs in Russian are provided for children, who attend public English-medium schools. The children who came to the United States under the age of ten are essentially English-speaking, mixing languages with their parents or speaking only limited Russian with their grandparents. All this adds up to the usual immigrant language shift.[37]

Another group that arrived after the break-up of the Soviet empire came from Bukhara, speakers of a Jewish variety of Persian know as Bukhori. About 10,000 remain in Uzbekistan; there are 50,000 in Israel, and a large number in the United States, in New York (especially Queens, where there may be about 35,000: 108th Street is known as "Bukharan Broadway"[38]), Arizona, Atlanta, Denver, South Florida, Los Angeles, and San Diego.

Another significant Jewish immigrant community in the United States is from Iran; there are between 60,000 and 80,000 Persian Jews, mainly in Los Angeles and Great Neck, New York; they are reported now to speak English and a little Farsi. There are some who say that the wealthy Jewish Persian community form a Farsi-speaking enclave, however, with their own stores and restaurants. The first Iranian Jews arrived in Los Angeles in the 1950s, mainly professionals, students, and traders in carpets and antiques, and began to assimilate. They were joined by new waves in the 1970s (concerned over anti-Semitic outbreaks during the Asian Games in 1968, when an Israeli team played an Iranian), however, and before and after the 1979 Iranian Revolution; most of these were quite wealthy, but middle- and lower-class immigrants started to arrive in the 1980s. There were initial problems in integration into the Jewish community, focused in part on the Sinai Temple, which many joined, but it was finally resolved, and later an Iranian Jew became president of the Temple. For the older immigrants, learning English was a problem, and so they established their own synagogues and institutions. The next generation (forty to sixty-five) became bilingual and worked to integrate while maintaining identity; the role of the women in setting up charitable organizations was important. The younger group (fifteen to forty) took full advantage of educational possibilities to become professionals. Some went into politics as well. The oldest generation maintains the Persian language, which is used also for social and communal activities; the middle generation is bilingual; and the third generation is mainly English-speaking, with little fluency in the heritage language. Some of these are reported to study in university Iranian programs, however.[39]

An estimated 41,000 New York Jewish households include an Israeli Jew, making a total of 121,000 living in such households, with about 30,000 having been born in Israel.[40] Many of them speak Hebrew. There are many Israelis in Los Angeles too, where there is a Hebrew-language radio station.

There are also about 12,000 Syrian Jewish households in New York, with a total of 38,000; half live in Brooklyn. They emigrated mainly from Aleppo starting in the 1900s, with another wave of immigration in the early 1990s. The community is relatively young, and women tend not to work. The community is orthodox in observance. A *New York Times* article reports the tight rules against marriage outside the community.[41] They appear to be assimilated in clothing and language, however, though the younger generation may still use some Syrian Jewish words in their English.

For most of the Jewish immigrants to the United States, the pattern has been as set out in Fishman's classic study of US language loyalty:[42] the immigrant generation remains heritage language speakers, who learn enough English to manage; their children are bilingual; and the third generation are English speakers with limited if any knowledge of the heritage language. The process can be speeded up, with younger children acquiring English once their older siblings start school, or slowed down, if there is a concentration of settlement leading to isolation or if there is an internal effort at isolation. In the 1920s this latter feature was associated with the development of secular Yiddish afternoon schools,[43] or in the self-selected isolation of the ultra-orthodox Hasidim. Otherwise, it depended (as does the maintenance of Spanish in the United States) on continuing waves of immigration. So English is well established as the main language of the Jews of the emancipated English-speaking country, but alongside a continued place for Hebrew as the sacred language and the language of the modern Jewish state.

Hebrew is taught in religious schools of all the streams, with the orthodox concentrating on sacred text and prayer book skills. It is taught also in the day schools, carrying on a tradition that dates back to the revival movement of the early twentieth century.[44] Camp Ramah, a Conservative summer camp network, has emphasized use of the language, and offers Hebrew lessons.

Yiddish has, of course, influenced American English: words such as "blintz" and "chutzpah" turn up in the speech and writing of non-Jews. But the existence of a Jewish variety of English is more controversial. One variety that has been described is the English of Haredi Jews, sometimes called Frumspeak or Yeshivish.[45] It is marked by frequent borrowing from Yiddish or Ashkenazi-pronounced Hebrew, and a few syntactic Yiddishisms. Perhaps this is not a separate variety, however, but instead "English with a repertoire of distinctive linguistic features stemming from Yiddish, Hebrew, Aramaic, and other sources."[46] The current significance of English as a language of the Jews is attested to by the extensive publication of religious and secular books in it, and the number of English-language periodicals published for Jewish readers.

Other English-speaking countries

Britain and the United States were early goals of Jewish migration to escape the continuing persecutions of Christian and European institutions and populations, and were renewed goals alongside the new State of Israel when 880,000 Jews left or were expelled from Islamic countries. They were also transit points for those who went on to other English-speaking countries, especially those that were part of the British Empire as it was until the 1920s and the British Commonwealth after that. The sociolinguistic pattern is similar: a move from heritage languages such as Yiddish to English through a period of bilingualism. But the size of migration and its date and the differing local conditions led to interesting variations, which cast useful light on the effects of migration on sociolinguistic patterns.

Canada

Canada is a good example of Jewish linguistic experience, for it has critical similarities to and differences from the neighboring United States. When Canada was under French rule, until 1760, only Roman Catholics were permitted to settle, so the first Jews arrived with the British army towards the end of the century. Jews who arrived subsequently as traders or merchants were not allowed to be elected to the legislature until 1831. There was a small community (about 200) that built a synagogue in Montreal in the 1770s. A synagogue was built in Quebec City in 1892.

Jews escaping the Russian pogroms arrived after 1880; by 1901 there were over 6,000 in Montreal, and by 1930 155,000 in Canada. Most Jewish migrants were poor, but they slowly established social institutions; by 1911 there were Jewish communities in all the major Canadian cities. A survey of Jewish households in Montreal in 1938 found 9 percent using French, 6 percent speaking only Yiddish, and the remainder using mainly English but the other two languages as well. The Folk Shule (Jewish People's School), founded in 1914 by the Labour Zionist movement, taught Hebrew and Yiddish, and merged with the Peretz School in 1971 and opened a high school in 1972. Adults read French and New York Yiddish newspapers, but children mainly English.[47] A Yiddish paper, *Keneder Adler* (or *Odler*, the *Canadian Eagle*), was published in Montreal from 1907 until 1988.[48]

In spite of outbursts of French anti-Semitism,[49] the Montreal Jewish community continued to grow. In 2006, however, although the number of Jews in Montreal had dropped to half the number in Toronto, Montreal still had more Yiddish speakers than Toronto, and Yiddish literature, drama, and education continued.[50]

At its height, Yiddish was spoken by some 149,000 Jews in Canada, in 1931, but the number had dropped to 17,300 in the 2006 census, surpassed in that year by speakers of Hebrew! Between 1905 and 1920 Yiddish was the dominant language of the Jewish community of Montreal, with a daily newspaper and an educational system. In 1931 99 percent of the Jews of Montreal claimed Yiddish as their first language. Leading the activity was the Poelei Zion movement, and also the Arbeter-Ring (Workmen's Circle). During this period the Jewish community constituted a "third solitude" between the French and the English; while they had an agreement for their children to attend the schools of the Protestant system, they had no rights of representation on the school board. But this of course meant that Jewish children were developing proficiency in English, the status but minority language of the city.

Yiddish remained the vernacular of the community, enriched by a strong library and active Yiddish publishing. The socialist-nationalist background of the immigrants to Montreal encouraged the development of a strong Yiddish school movement, the Peretz schools, which used Yiddish and Hebrew. Yiddish during these years was the natural vernacular of the Jewish community. The status of Yiddish continued to grow between the two world wars,[51] supporting a Yiddish literary elite, with important magazines and books being published. The Yiddish schools in Quebec (as in Mexico) offered a full-time program, as opposed to the afternoon schools of the New York movement. But, in spite of this, there was a gradual change as the second generation became Anglophone and as many elements in the community favored Canadianization. The community was too small to support a major permanent theater. And any literature tended to consist of short magazine pieces rather than major works.[52]

Although there was renewed Yiddish-speaking immigration after World War II, by this time the community was essentially English-speaking. The new immigrants were divided between secular and ultra-orthodox, the latter containing Yiddish-speaking Hasidim, who lived in enclaves closed to the rest of the community and who did not value the secular literature that had been a mark of earlier Yiddish culture. There remains a small secular Yiddish movement, forming a "postvernacular culture",[53] or a "metalinguistic community",[54] in which the language is honored, studied – learned, even – but not spoken. While the teaching of Yiddish is declining in the secular Jewish schools of Montreal, it is being increasingly taught in the Hasidic girls' schools.[55]

There were unsuccessful attempts in Canada to establish farming communities in the west. Generally, though, the western movement of Jews was made up of peddlers following the growing railway. The most important early development was in Winnipeg, in Manitoba, which grew rapidly between 1900 (when there were about 1,100 Jews) and 1920 (when there were nearly 15,000). It was considered the "Chicago of the north", serving as the commercial center of the prairies. A Yiddish Peretz school was started in 1914, and it had over 500 students by 1931, making it the largest Yiddish school in North America. A Yiddish newspaper, *Dos Yiddishe Vort*, was founded in 1911, and an English weekly, *Jewish Western Bulletin*, was started in Vancouver. Half the early population of Winnipeg consisted of foreigners, and the Jewish community had to stress its identity through the strength of Jewish educational facilities.[56] The Peretz school closed in 1994, but the endowment trust it left behind funded the opening of Yiddish classes in the Jewish day school, a fellowship for a Yiddish teacher, and some classes at the university.[57]

Most Canadian Jews now speak English, but there has developed a sizable French-speaking Sephardi community in Montreal, many of whom came from north Africa from the 1960s onwards.[58] In the 1960s Jews whose children were educated by special agreement in the Protestant school system of Montreal played a large part in persuading the school board to develop bilingual English/ French schools, even before it was required by the Quebec government. Some Jewish schools in Montreal were offering trilingual (English, Hebrew, and French) or quadrilingual (those three plus Yiddish) programs, showing the Canadian tendency for cultural and linguistic diversity rather than the "melting pot" US philosophy. As result of the rise of the Quebec nationalist parties and the passing of the language laws, however, which permitted children to go to English-language schools only if their parents had gone to them, many English-speaking Jews moved to Toronto,[59] which soon replaced Montreal as the largest Jewish community. About 40 percent of Jewish children in Toronto (60 percent in Montreal) attend Jewish elementary schools; at the high school level, the figures are 12 percent and 30 percent, respectively. Canadian Jews pursue higher education more than the general population (46 percent, compared to 16 percent), and many go on to the professions of law and medicine.

While the numbers were smaller, then, the greater recognition of linguistic diversity and a political response to the need to counter francophone separatism help account for the continuation in Canada of secular Yiddish schooling and institutions, as well as explaining the presence of francophone Jews in Quebec, where, for a number of years, Yiddish was the language of a "third solitude".

South Africa

There were Jews in South Africa during the period of Dutch rule, but they were not permitted to practice their religion before 1804. Effectively, Jewish settlement did not begin until the 1820s, when under British rule religious freedom was re-established. The first synagogue was established in Cape Town in 1841, and Jews played important roles in agricultural and mining industries.

During the Boer republics in the second half of the nineteenth century Catholics and Jews were not permitted to be teachers or students in the schools. Many Yiddish-speaking Jews arrived from Lithuania during the gold rush. Jews fought on both sides in the Boer War; the Jewish population reached some 40,000 by 1914, with Jews spreading to Johannesburg (occasionally known as "Jewburg") and to the country towns as traders. Depending on where they lived, Jews acquired English or Afrikaans.

While Jews received equal rights after the Boer War, anti-Jewish feeling led to the Quota Act in 1930, which curtailed the entry of migrants from eastern Europe, and the Aliens Act of 1937, which blocked German Jews. The Afrikaners were largely anti-Semitic, but when the Nationalist Party came to power in 1948 it did not take an anti-Jewish position; after 1953 there were ties between South Africa and Israel. Jews generally were liberal and supported the opposition parties and anti-apartheid groups. Many Jews left South Africa, a good number going to Israel, and others to Australia. The first Jewish day school was established in South Africa in 1948, and many more have followed. There are also a number of orthodox schools, as the remaining community is largely orthodox. The schools use English as their language of instruction and teach Hebrew as both a sacred and a vernacular language.

Most of the members of the founding migrant community were Yiddish-speaking Lithuanian Jews, who picked up English and Afrikaans from their Gentile environment, and maintained Hebrew as their sacred language and as a modern language for those with a Zionist ideology. English became the main vernacular of the community, with Afrikaans being learned in bilingual schools or acquired for business and work relationships. The pattern, then, is a normal immigrant one, with the loss of the heritage language and the addition of co-territorial vernaculars, but the maintenance of some Hebrew. For a while, though, Yiddish was a strong presence.

Some members of a South African tribe, the Lemba, speakers of Bantu languages, have traditions that they are descended from Jews, and there is genetic evidence of a link to Yemenite Jews.[60] They have traditions including Sabbath observance and circumcision, but their status as Jews has not been recognized by South African Jews or by the rabbinic authorities. As described in Chapter 4, there are other African tribes claiming Jewish descent.

Australia and New Zealand

The first Jews to arrive in Australia, in the eighteenth century, were convicts transported from England. When they were later freed, many became successful merchants, as did another wave of free immigration from Britain in the 1820s.[61]

By 1841, a year after small communities of English Jews had settled in New Zealand in Wellington and Auckland, there were around 1,000 Jews in Australia, mainly in Melbourne and some in Sydney. These numbers were increased by German Jews during the gold rush (which brought Jews to New Zealand as well), so that by 1861 there were nearly 6,000 Jews in Australia. Melbourne grew, with synagogues founded by German Jews.

In the latter part of the century there was another wave of immigration from the Russian Empire, and, to serve them, a new synagogue was opened in 1898, with a Yiddish-speaking rabbi. Synagogues were also opened in Sydney, and, in the 1910s, in country areas such as Newcastle and Broken Hill. The newcomers from eastern Europe could support a Yiddish theater and a Yiddish cultural center, Kadimah, and – later – a Bundist movement.[62] There were also attempts, partially successful, to establish agricultural settlements in Victoria.

Melbourne, it appears, was more pluralistic than Sydney, and Yiddish was stronger there. Small Jewish communities also developed in Brisbane and in Fremantle (a port of entry), and, later, in the towns of the gold rush. In Brisbane, the east European Jews were uncomfortable with the Anglo-Judaism of the established synagogue, and set up their own synagogue, in which one could hear Russian and Yiddish.[63]

A third wave of Jewish immigration after World War II led to major increases in the Jewish community. The demand was met by the establishment of a number of day schools, including one with strong Hebrew orientation and another with Yiddish as its main emphasis.[64] But, as the immigrants settled, the Jewish communities of both Australia and New Zealand remained essentially English-speaking, with a central role for Hebrew as a sacred language[65] and some occasional recognition of Yiddish heritage.

Spanish: a second New World language

The migration of Jews to North America had the principal effect of confirming English as a major Jewish language. Migration to Latin America has had similar results for Spanish and Portuguese.

Argentina

There are currently about half a million Jews in Latin America. The largest number is in Argentina, peaking at over 300,000 in the 1960s, but now down to about 200,000 as a result of emigration to the United States and Israel and intermarriage. In the middle of the nineteenth century the first community was formed by Sephardi Jews from the Ottoman Empire, followed in the 1880s by Ashkenazi Jews from eastern Europe. This immigration was encouraged by the constitution of 1853, which established freedom of worship, by immigration laws that did not discriminate against non-Catholics, and by the establishment of state education in 1884, setting Argentina up as a possible refuge for Jews escaping the anti-Semitic events in eastern Europe. The community was bolstered by a large number of Russian Jews, brought out by the Jewish Colonization Association in order to establish agricultural settlements. Most of them soon moved to the cities; by 1919 the Jewish population of Buenos Aires was 125,000. This continued until 1930, when a right-wing government imposed restrictions on all immigration. It resumed, albeit more slowly, after the war, with a further burst in the 1950s.[66]

Initially the Jewish community of Argentina was Yiddish-speaking, but, with the pressure of the general environment and, in particular, the use of Spanish as the language of instruction in state education, which was open to Jews, the normal immigrant transfer to the co-territorial vernacular took place. Jewish schools continued to teach Yiddish until the establishment of the State of Israel, at which time they started to put considerable emphasis on the teaching of Hebrew. Studies of the linguistic proficiency and attitudes of Argentinian Jews who emigrated to Israel show that they grew up with Spanish and Yiddish as mother tongues, and added the Hebrew they now use first in school and then after they arrived in Israel.[67]

The economic collapse of Argentina in 2001 hit the Jewish community hard, leaving many in poverty. The Jewish educational system, which provided for 65 percent of the population, suffered 30 percent attrition. These schools and others in Latin America now benefit from Israeli support.

Brazil

The situation in Brazil was somewhat different. A number of *Anusim* escaping the Inquisition arrived early, but did not continue as an organized community: the Brazilian census of 1872 recorded no Jews. Some 3,000 Jews moved to Brazil from north Africa at the end of the nineteenth century to work in the rubber industry, but they came without women and married (and converted) local women. Two small farming colonies were established at the beginning of the twentieth century.

During World War I there was an increase in immigration to Brazil, including Europeans and Asians. It became a goal for east European Jews too when they were unable to receive visas for the United States, Canada, or Argentina. By the 1930s there were around 30,000 Jews in Brazil. Although they succeeded economically, their success and the cultural differences made the Jews (and Japanese immigrants) the focus of anti-foreigner feeling. After a period of restricted immigration the numbers of Jews arriving picked up again in the 1950s; by 2000 the Jewish population of Brazil was estimated as just under 100,000.[68]

The largely Yiddish-speaking east European Jewish Brazilian community was served by a Yiddish press at first. In the 1920s there were disputes between proponents of Yiddish and Hebrew. This was reflected in the existence of more than a score of small, poorly funded schools choosing either Hebrew or Yiddish alongside Portuguese. Yiddish remained an important language among Brazilian Jews until the 1940s, serving not just as a vernacular for those of east European origin but also as a symbol of Zionism and Jewish identity, in contrast to the speakers of German and Italian.[69]

Mexico

Although officially New Christians were not permitted in the New World during the Spanish period, a number of *Anusim* did come to Mexico and were targeted by the Inquisition. A few German Jews arrived in Mexico in the nineteenth century, but the first large wave of immigration was from east Europe after the pogroms of 1880. In 1901 Arabic-speaking Jews conducted services in a private home. About 1912 there was a second wave of Jewish immigration, Sephardim escaping the collapse of the Ottoman Empire. Speaking Judezmo, they integrated quite rapidly, moving to Spanish. The third wave came from east Europe after World War I, many of whom planned to go to the United States but were blocked by the new US immigration quotas.

Most Mexican Jews live in Mexico City, where there are over thirty synagogues. Jewish children generally go to the dozen or so Jewish schools, which teach Hebrew or Yiddish. Zionist youth organizations are very active. There are communities in other towns. A number of Judaizing sects have been reported, and there have been reports of *Anusim* in New Mexico, in the United States.

Other countries

There are said to be 20,000 Jews in Chile, though 5,000 of them may be Jews for Jesus. Most live in Santiago, and others in Valparaiso, where Turkish and Russian Jewish immigrants set up a community in 1916. The community in Santiago grew up in the 1930s. There are orthodox and Reform synagogues. There is a Jewish day school in Santiago.

While there were Jews in Uruguay during Spanish rule, it was not until the late nineteenth century that there were many immigrants, and the first synagogue was established only in 1917. Schools were started shortly afterwards, and there are currently Zionist and non-Zionist Ashkenazi and Sephardi schools. More than half the community has emigrated in recent years, mainly to Israel.

There are small communities in other Latin American countries.

Summing up: emancipated Britain and the New World

Escaping from continental Europe to Britain, its colonies, and the Americas, Jews found themselves living in societies that recognized them as citizens and did not confine them to ghettos. There was of course a tendency, as with most new migrants, to live close to others like them, as observant Jews in particular need to live close enough to a synagogue to be able to walk there on the Sabbath. This concentration permits the provision of other services, such as kosher food; it also slows down the loss of heritage languages and the shift to the local co-territorial variety. This is even greater in the self-imposed isolation of ultra-orthodox Jews and Hasidim, who have maintained islands of Yiddish in English-, French-, and Spanish-speaking neighborhoods. The tendency to lin-guistic and religious assimilation is checked only by continued migration, religious or ethnic identity, or, in modern times, by the role of Hebrew-speaking Israel as a Jewish unifying symbol. On the whole, though, emancipation weakened the hold of other languages, including Jewish languages such as Yiddish and Judezmo, and encouraged the establishment of English and Spanish as languages of the Jews.

15   Islam and the Orient

Jews in post-medieval Islam

With brief exceptions during periods of foreign rule, Islamic countries remain under legal systems that do not recognize the equal rights of non-Muslims and so have not yet become emancipated. Any Jews still living in these countries (like Christians and other non-Muslims) remain *Dhimmi*, second-class citizens, with rights limited by religious law as defined in versions of the Pact of Umar. For Jews in north Africa, then, apart from the years of French or Italian rule, civic emancipation was achieved only by emigration, and so the linguistic situation was unchanged until then. In the Near East, too, except under British or French rule, the same situation applied (see Map 11). As these countries became independent, they restored restrictions on Jewish residents and expelled most of them in the middle of the twentieth century.

In the Far East, in contrast, Jews came as traders, occasionally converting their servants but not establishing major communities. In this chapter, we will see the strengthening of Judeo-Arabic and Judeo-Persian, and the addition of some European and Asian languages to the sociolinguistic repertoire of the Jews.

North Africa: Algeria and Tunis

One question to ask is why so many north African Jews turn up nowadays in France and Israel as francophones rather than as heritage speakers of Judeo-Arabic. In the seventeenth century France began to build a colonial empire in North America, the Caribbean, and India, in each of which competition with Britain limited its successes. In the nineteenth century colonization was extended to Asia (especially Cambodia and Vietnam) and Africa. French colonization everywhere brought with it the imposition of *francophonie*, a requirement that government and education be conducted entirely in the French language. Christians and Jews were the first to be influenced.

France invaded Algeria in 1830 and conquered it in seventeen years, using as an excuse a dispute over debts involving two Jewish families.[1] A protectorate

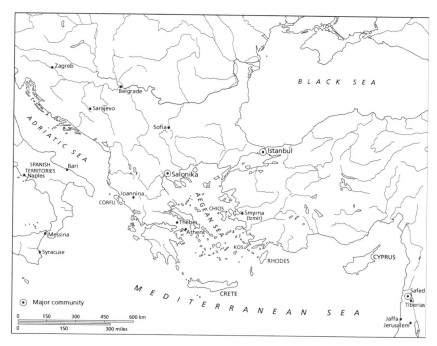

11 Jewish centers in Ottoman areas
Source: Shear (2010).

over Tunisia was established by the Bardo Treaty in 1881. In the next years other colonies were established in sub-Saharan Africa, and in 1912, after competition with Germany that led to the Agadir Crisis of 1911, when the British helped France maintain control of Morocco against German attempts at conquest, Morocco too became a French protectorate.

France encouraged settlement of white Christians in its new colonies. While the emancipated Jews of France considered the Algerian Jews "an uncivilized horde", they accepted responsibility for them, helping them organize a consistorial system[2] and proposing to send Russian Jews there as settlers – a plan blocked by the French army.[3]

French language policy followed a regular principle: any territory under French rule should become French-speaking.[4] Just as the Jacobins had promoted the use of Parisian French throughout France, a similar policy was imposed on the subject peoples in French colonies.[5] The goal was assimilation. In 1886 the French politician Jules Ferry declared that the "higher races" have a right over the lower races and a duty to civilize the "inferior races". Full citizenship rights – *assimilation* – were offered to those who managed to pass through the elitist educational system.

Just as it took a long time to make sure that standard French was spoken in all the schools in France, it took a while to develop French schools in Algeria for the local population. A school for Jewish children was opened in Algiers in 1832, and changed to a school for Jews and Muslims, but both sets of students left when the Roman Catholic bias of the teachers became obvious.[6] In 1836 a school for Muslim boys offered four hours of French studies and four of Qur'anic learning a day. A school for Jewish girls was opened in Algiers in 1837, followed three years later by a municipal school for Jewish boys. Most of these pupils too dropped out and returned to communally directed religious schools. French schools for Muslims and Jews established in other places in the next few years had equally little success.[7]

Public schools opened for the growing numbers of Christian settlers (French, Maltese, German, Spanish, and Italian) were more successful, but only 7 percent of the 9,000 students were Muslim or Jewish. An attempt in the 1850s to establish French-run *médersas* (madrassas, Islamic primary schools) was no more effective.

In 1845 it was decided to establish Jewish consistories in Algeria and provide funding for Jewish schools that would combine religious instruction with French language teaching; they were to be under the control of the Grand Rabbin, who was responsible for avoiding fanaticism. These Jewish schools, but not the Muslim ones, came under the purview of the French educational authorities (the Muslim schools remained under the control of the Ministry of War). Some supporters of reform criticized the fanaticism and unhealthy conditions of the Muslim and Jewish religious schools, and were concerned about how to compete with their greater appeal to the local population. Civil administrators closed many of these community schools, but, slowly, compromises were reached. Working with the Jewish leadership in the consistories, Jewish schools were improved, and a French instructor was added, to teach several hours a day.

Thanks to the efforts of a French Jewish lawyer and politician, Adolphe Crémieux (born Isaac Moïse),[8] Jews in Algeria were granted French citizenship in 1870 along with the European residents (the *pieds noirs*); the decree did not apply to Muslim Arabs and Berbers. Most Jewish children attended school, but only a small proportion of Muslims did.

Jews were not welcomed by the settlers, however, and anti-Semitism grew; there was pressure calling for the abrogation of the decree, which was finally granted by the Vichy government in 1940; the decree was restored reluctantly in 1943. Jewish separation from the Muslim community – stimulated by the 1934 ant-Jewish riots in Constantine in northeast Algeria and the continued anti-Jewish sentiment – helped explain the emigration of most of the Jewish population after Algerian independence.[9]

In a report on life in a large town in Algeria in the middle of the twentieth century, it was noted that Jewish families that used French were considered "progressive" and upper class, while those that used Arabic were "backward" and at the bottom of the social ladder. But there remained traces of Arabic in the French, especially as a mark of intimacy. Jews in the rural areas, who lived in closer contact with Muslims, spoke Arabic, and lived much as they did.[10]

Very little is known about the social development and adoption of languages in north Africa,[11] but there is some evidence in the way in which the Jews of Tunis, different from Muslim communities and even from Jews elsewhere in Tunisia, came to adopt French rather than Judeo-Arabic as their vernacular. Tunis was the largest Jewish community in Tunisia, making up about 10 percent of the population by 1931 (38 percent of the town's inhabitants were European, 53 percent Muslim). Tunis is still marked by the extent of French use; a century ago it was a highly multilingual city with schools teaching in many languages besides Arabic, and a city where plurilingualism was valued.[12] There were around 100,000 Jews in Tunisia before 1948, but almost all except for 1,500 or so left.

After independence in 1962, Jews in Algeria lost their citizenship and rights; 160,000 moved to France (along with 1 million *pieds noirs*) and 25,000 emigrated to Israel. Almost all the rest left in 1994 under threats from a terrorist organization.

Morocco[13]

Under Islamic rule, Jewish life in Morocco varied from peaceful subordination under the Almoravides in the eleventh century to active persecution under the Almihads in the twelfth; in the early fourteenth century conditions were reasonable again, but an economic decline followed. In 1438 the Jews of Fez were forced to move into a *mellah*, a closed Jewish quarter. The sultan welcomed Jewish refugees from Spain in 1492 and Portugal in 1496, but living conditions were unpleasant – there was robbery, disease, and famine – and many left. The earlier Jewish residents were not welcoming to the new arrivals, and the newcomers formed their own communities, where they could maintain their own traditions. Most spoke Haketia – a mixture of Spanish, Hebrew, and Arabic – while a few families continued to speak Castilian. Many *Anusim* arrived in the sixteenth century and returned to Judaism. Jewish religious practice was strong, and so was Hebrew scholarship.

In the nineteenth century European pressure on Morocco increased, and many Jews came under the protection of European consuls.[14] As a result, Jews were seen as agents of European influence, and there was increasing persecution, alleviated only when foreign powers intervened. Jews started moving into Jewish quarters in urban centers, resulting in overcrowding and disease.

In 1912 the Treaty of Fez divided Morocco into French and Spanish protectorates; 100 Jews were killed in the pogroms that followed in Fez, which became French. Jews remained under the protection of the sultan. Upper-class Jews sent their children to French schools, and the Alliance Israélite Universelle established schools whose aim was Westernization. A Jewish middle class grew up, blocked from assimilation by the anti-Semitism of the French settlers. Because Jews were scattered through the country, many lived in small communities with no Jewish education, leading to a high proportion of illiteracy.

In 1948 there were a quarter of a million Jews in Morocco; by 1960, after large-scale emigration, there were only 160,000, and by the end of 1967 there were 40,000; now there are 4,000.[15] Zionist propaganda in the 1930s had been unsuccessful, but after World War II the bitter experiences under the anti-Semitic Vichy government and news of the rebirth of Israel combined to encourage Zionist attitudes among the Jews of the Maghreb. In Morocco, Arab nationalist movements excluded Jews, who were associated with the French. Zionist emigration to Israel started from Morocco in 1947, organized in secret, tolerated by the French, and condemned by pro-Palestinian nationalists. There were riots in Morocco after the establishment of the Jewish state in 1948, which further encouraged Jews to leave. While there were many Moroccan nationalists who opposed Jewish emigration, Jews felt constrained to leave not because they did not support independence but because their conditions continued to deteriorate.[16] Moroccan Jews in Israel formed the largest ethnic community until the Russian immigration of the 1990s, and have generally become Hebrew speakers while maintaining Judeo-Arabic and French.

Egypt

Jews were among the many foreigners who emigrated to Egypt during the later nineteenth century and up to the 1920s. Beforehand there had been about 6,000 Jews in Egypt, increasing to 25,000 in 1897 and probably over 75,000 by the 1930s. There were major concentrations of Jews in Cairo and Alexandria. Sephardim arrived from the Ottoman Empire and north Africa, Orientals from Yemen at the turn of the century, and Ashkenazim from Russia, Poland, and Romania. Most migrants were poor and young, and the leaders of the local community tried in vain to redirect them to Palestine.

Up until the middle of the nineteenth century the Egyptian Jewish community, earlier divided into separate Egyptian, Karaite, Sephardi, and north African communities, had been more or less united, but it remained diverse in religious rites and national origins. Those who had been residents for the longest, with no real evidence of connections to earlier Hellenistic Jewish settlement, were poor and engaged (if employed) in crafts and small trade. They were assimilated culturally and spoke Egyptian Arabic, but lived in a separate *hara* (quarter) with little contact with Muslims and Copts. Some new oriental migrants were poor like them; others were merchants, who quickly joined the cosmopolitan Jewish middle class. This was a Sephardi middle class, descendants of Jews who left Spain, who were more prosperous and plurilingual, speaking Judezmo and also French, Italian, Greek, and an Arabic dialect. Another distinct group was the Italian Jews, some from Livorno but also from other parts of the Mediterranean, who spoke Italian and included craftsmen and laborers, but also many of the leading professionals, merchants, and bankers. While recognizably different, all these groups united to form the Communauté Israélite du Caire, headed by the Sephardi chief rabbi of Egypt.

The Ashkenazim, some arriving as early as the Cossack massacres of 1648 but the main group coming after the 1880 pogroms, and reinforced temporarily in 1915 by 11,000 Jews expelled from Ottoman Palestine, constituted a distinct community; after the expellees returned when the British conquered Palestine, their numbers fell to about 5,000, most coming from Russian and Romania, with 90 percent speaking Yiddish and 10 percent Russian. Two Yiddish newspapers were published for a short time at the beginning of the century, and a theater group performed plays in Yiddish. To start, most worked rolling cigarettes and later moved into various crafts; the second generation became professionals, including doctors. Ashkenazim had a reputation for being engaged in the underworld and prostitution; true or not, they did not easily assimilate with the Sephardim. A small Karaite community (about 4,000 people), mostly poor, lived in Cairo, although some of its members became prosperous. They were organized separately.[17]

Initially, the Jews of modern Egypt were divided sociolinguistically by country of origin: the indigenous spoke Egyptian Arabic; those from Arabic-speaking countries continued to speak the local variety they had brought with them until they learned modern Standard Arabic or Egyptian Arabic; the Sephardim spoke Judezmo and other languages depending on where they came from; and the Ashkenazim spoke Yiddish or Russian. For a while, newspapers were published in Yiddish, Ladino, and Arabic. Later, some of these languages were preserved for home use, but the upper and middle classes (especially the women) generally adopted an international language: Italian in the nineteenth century or French in the twentieth. Most also knew some English for business use. Arabic remained the language of the poorer lower classes, and only in the 1930s was there a Jewish group arguing for a greater use of Arabic. Schools established by the Alliance Israélite Universelle used French as the language of instruction and taught a little Hebrew. Religious and Zionist schools also taught some Hebrew. Except for the poorest, most Jews were plurilingual, which contributed to economic success but weakened community cohesion.[18]

About 20,000 Jews left Egypt after 1948, but a large number remained until the 1956 Arab–Israeli War. The migrants went to France, Latin America, and Israel, establishing Diasporas in each.[19] After 1956 pressure on Jews (sequestration of property, loss of citizenship, expulsion) led to increased emigration; some 36,000 more had emigrated by 1960, leaving under 10,000. By the 1967 Six Day War there were about 2,500 Jews left in Egypt, and by 1970 only a few hundred were still there.[20]

Libya

While there was Jewish settlement in Libya in the Roman period, the modern history starts essentially with the Ottoman conquest in 1551, when the Jewish community began to grow numerically and economically. By the end of the Ottoman period there were well-organized communities with rabbis in many parts of the country. Towards the end of the period, when Ottoman protection was denied, there was much local persecution of the Jews.

Italy conquered Libya in 1911, after which there began the period of intensive colonization, which was strongly resisted. At first Libyan Jews benefited from Italian policy, which aimed to assimilate them until the Italian racial laws started to apply in the late 1930s. The Jewish community of Libya had numbered about 18,000 in 1904. Under Italian rule, about half the Jewish population started to speak Italian.

Anti-Jewish incidents occurred in the 1920s and 1930s. In 1972 Jewish students were required to attend secondary but not elementary school on the Sabbath. This was resolved for a few years, but new problems with government policy developed. The racial laws of 1938 included the expulsion of Jews from Libya and barred them from holding public office. Private Jewish schools were established, as Jewish teachers were not permitted to teach in public schools. In 1939 there were some 30,000 Jews in Libya. In the 1940s foreign Jews were interned in Tunis, Jews with British citizenship were sent to concentration camps such as Bergen-Belsen, and many Libyan Jews were sent to labor camps. The British occupied Libya in 1940 and began a program to deal with the health problems of the Jews in camps. Most Jews were repatriated, but economic conditions remained bad. The Palestine Jewish brigade encouraged emigration to Palestine.[21]

By 1967 there were about 7,000 Jews still there. Anti-Jewish riots took place, and 6,000 Jews were rescued and removed to Rome by air and sea in one month. Some continued to the United States or Israel. Some 5,000 remained in Rome, bolstering the local community and receiving Italian citizenship in 1980.

Summing up, Jews in north Africa in the modern period continued to live in *Dhimmi* status, mostly speaking varieties of Arabic and Berber, but bringing other languages to the area. By the middle of the twentieth century most Jews had left or were about to leave, moving to Israel, France, and the Americas, and bringing to an end two millennia of north African Jewish history.

The Islamic Orient

Jewish communities grew up in a dozen Asian countries, some as a result of traders and others as places of refuge from persecution. Each naturally led to an increase in the languages spoken by Jews. The communities in Iran and Iraq have already been mentioned in connection with the Islamic conquest, but the story is here brought up to date.

Persia (Iran)

After a respite during the Mongol rule in the thirteenth century, Ghazan Khan (who was converted to Islam) and his successors re-established *Dhimmi* statutes. Jews were pressured to convert, but, unlike other Islamic countries, converts in Persia were still stigmatized for several generations. Shi'a rule, starting in the sixteenth century, produced new problems, as Shi'a Muslims avoided contact with Jews. Things were better for a while at the end of the century, but once again, by the middle of the seventeenth century, Jews were required to wear distinctive clothing and avoid contact. In the nineteenth century conditions were reported to be very bad, as Jews were considered unclean. There was constant persecution and debasement. Many Jews emigrated in the late nineteenth and early twentieth centuries. Under the modernizing influence of the Pahlavi, there was a brief improvement; it was even permitted to teach Hebrew in Jewish schools, until they were closed in the 1920s.

Between 1948 and 1953 a third of Persia's Jews, most of them poor, emigrated to Israel. Since the establishment of the Islamic Republic in 1979, many more Jews have emigrated, and the formerly Jewish schools now have Muslim heads and teach in Persian; they do still teach some Hebrew, however. There are about 20,000 Jews still in Iran, served by a good number of synagogues. Judaism is a recognized minority religion, with one representative in the parliament. Jews are conscripted into the Iranian army. Most Jews live in Tehran, but there are communities in some other large cities. Most Jews speak standard Persian, but there have been several Jewish varieties, such as Dzhidi (Judeo-Persian) with an extensive earlier religious literature, Judeo-Golpaygani (once spoken in western Iran), Judeo-Shirazi (spoken by Jews in Shiraz), and Judeo-Hamedani (from Hamedan, said to still have speakers). Another variety of Judeo-Persian is Judeo-Bukharan, also known as Judeo-Tajik, with speakers reported in Uzbekistan, Israel, and the United States.

The Caucasus

The major Jewish variety in the Caucasus is Judeo-Tat, also known as Juhuri, with 24,000 or more speakers still in Azerbaijan and Dagestan; it is classified as an endangered language, with an estimated 70,000 speakers in Israel, living in Sderot, Haderah, and Or Akiva.

Judeo-Tat[22] has four major dialects, that of Derbent being recognized as central since 1928; a newspaper was published there from 1928 to 1941. Originally, Hebrew was the written language of the Jews in the region, but the first books written in Judeo-Tat appeared in the 1870s. Originally written in Hebrew letters, following Soviet policy, Judeo-Tat was written in the Latin alphabet starting in 1929 and in Cyrillic starting in 1938. In that year Russian replaced Judeo-Tat in schools in Dagestan, and Azerbaijani replaced it in Azerbaijan. Jews at the time were regularly bilingual. Some publication in Judeo-Tat resumed after World War II. There was an active theater in Judeo-Tat in the 1930s until the professional theater closed in 1946. Since migration to Israel, a number of writers have continued to publish in Israel.

A sociolinguistic study conducted by SIL International researchers[23] investigated Jewish and non-Jewish speakers of varieties of Tat; the Jews identify themselves as Mountain Jews and name their variety accordingly. It estimated the number of speakers of Mountain Jewish at 30,000, with most members of the community using the language regularly as the home and community language. They also speak Azerbaijani and Russian, which are used in their schools, and, although there are signs of a shift to Russian, the variety is still strong.

Turkey

The quality of Jewish life in Ottoman Turkey depended on the sultan of the time. When Mehmed II conquered Constantinople from the Byzantines, he ordered that Muslims, Christians, and Jews from all over Turkey should resettle it, so that Romaniote Jews became a tenth of the city population and extremely influential. Ashkenazim started to arrive in the fourteenth century, but the major influx was of Sephardim expelled from Spain in the fifteenth century. Invited by the sultan, they settled in Constantinople and Salonika in large numbers and spread throughout the Ottoman Empire, including Palestine. They had autonomy under the *millet* system, which recognized each religious group; the Jews were represented by the Ḥakham Bashi (Chief Rabbi), had to pay taxes like other *Dhimmi*, and suffered various restrictions. In the seventeenth century they were successful in trade and commerce, and became prosperous. In the nineteenth century competition from Greeks led to an economic decline.

Most Jews lived in the European areas of Turkey, and so came under Christian rule when Greece, Bulgaria, and Serbia cast off Ottoman dominion. Judezmo was the dominant language in the Jewish community, but there were speakers of Judeo-Greek. In the nineteenth century the establishment of schools by the Alliance Israélite Universelle meant that many educated Turkish Jews switched to French. Under the republic and Turkish independence, starting in 1923, the strong national language policy introduced by Kemal Ataturk encouraged those Jews who remained in Turkey to learn and use Turkish. Nowadays, Turkish is the main language used in the Jewish schools,[24] but Hebrew is taught as a second language. Only among the older generation are there still speakers of French (once an elite language) and Judezmo, although, up to World War II, most reported Judezmo as their native language. Jews living in Turkey find a tension in identity, marked especially by cosmopolitanism.[25] The Jewish population in 2010 was reported to have dropped to 17,000, and with current pressures many are considering emigration.

Syria

Aleppo had Jews from early periods, and the community was further increased by migration from Spain and Portugal after 1492 and from Livorno in the eighteenth century. As active traders, the Livornese merchants soon had partners in many countries. Under Ottoman rule, in 1893, there were about 10,000 Jews in Aleppo and 7,000 in Damascus. Most spoke Arabic. Their status was as *Dhimmi*, but mitigated by European protection. It was competition between Christians and Jews that lay behind the 1840 Damascus affair, when Jews were accused of killing a Catholic priest to use his blood. There were also pogroms in 1880. Jews worked in crafts and commerce. Jewish schools were traditional until the 1860s, when the Alliance established modern schools for boys and girls. Arab nationalism in the twentieth century led to increased emigration, and few Jews remain.[26] Starting before World War I, Jews moved to the Americas to avoid the draft. At the same time, there was regular religiously motivated immigration into Palestine. Pogroms in 1947 encouraged further emigration, and recently several thousand Jews have been smuggled out of Syria, such that only a handful remain. There are Diasporas of Aleppo Jews in the United States, Israel, Mexico, Brazil, Argentine, Chile, and Panama.

Jews in Asia

In the Far East, the common pattern is that Jewish communities were established by traders, who might have brought their families with them or who quite commonly married local women, converted them to Judaism, and later introduced rules against intermarriage. This pattern is also reported in north Africa and the Middle East, where Judaicized slaves were converted.[27]

China

A Jewish community is believed to have existed in Kaifeng since at least the Northern Song dynasty (about 1000), probably made up of Jewish traders from

Persia or India and their descendants. There was reported to be a synagogue in 1163. Matteo Ricci, the Jesuit priest who brought the Chinese examination system back to Europe, met a Jew from Kaifeng who had come to Beijing in 1605 to take the Imperial Examination, who told him of the community, the synagogue and its books. Ricci sent a Chinese lay brother, who produced evidence that the books were the Torah. The rabbi turned down Ricci's invitation to convert to Christianity, but, after his death, some Jews did and others were said to have become Muslims. The Kaifeng synagogue, drawings of which were made by the Jesuits in the seventeenth century, was destroyed in 1860; it combined Chinese architecture with the needs of a synagogue.[28] The first European Jew to visit the town in 1867 reported that the Jews kept up the cemetery and that their liturgy was taken from the Bible. Most had intermarried, but many kept up the ban on pork. A small number have emigrated to Israel. A Torah scroll in Hebrew is in the British Library, as is a prayer book written in Chinese characters.[29]

The first Jewish settlement in Shanghai consisted of Mizrahi traders, led by a member of the Sassoon family (see below), who opened a branch in 1860. To start, the community consisted of clerks from these traders, but after World War I a number of Ashkenazi Jews arrived. At the end of the 1930s and into the 1940s some 18,000 Jews arrived in Shanghai from Germany, Poland, and Austria, many of them enabled to escape thanks to the efforts of the Japanese consul in Kaunas, Lithuania (Chiune Sugihara), the Chinese consul-general in Vienna (Ho Feng Shan), and the Polish ambassador in Tokyo (Tadeusz Romer) in obtaining the necessary papers. The Japanese occupiers in 1943 required them all to move to a three-quarter square mile area of Shanghai labeled a "Designated area for stateless refugees"; for a while they were supported in difficult conditions by local Baghdadi Jews and welfare organizations. After Shanghai was liberated, in 1945, many Jews worked as translators for the Americans, but after the establishment of the State of Israel and the fall of Chiang Kai-shek, in 1949, almost all of them left.

Russian Jews fleeing the pogroms, and later after the revolution, settled in Harbin, where there was an active community until the Japanese occupation began in 1932. Some then moved to Shanghai. Harbin was a small village on the Russo-Chinese border, settled first in 1898 with the building of the railway. By 1903 there were 500 Jews living there, and a "steering committee" was set up to establish a synagogue, hire a rabbi, and organize religious services. During the Russo-Japanese War of 1905, many Russian Jewish soldiers served in the area, some of whom chose to settle in Manchuria after they were demobilized. They were joined by Jews seeking to escape the pogroms of the early years of the century and others expelled from the western border areas during World War I, and by others fleeing the Russian Revolution. Others arrived during the period of the New Economic Policy. By 1929 the railway town of Manzhouli had a strong Jewish community of 1,500 with a synagogue, school, and library, but these Jews left for Harbin, Shanghai, and elsewhere when Japan occupied Manchuria in 1932.

In Harbin in the 1920s there was a Yiddish newspaper, two Zionist papers published in Russian, and a cultural club that presented lectures mostly in Russian but also in Yiddish. There were two large synagogues. The first Jewish school had been established in 1907, and a high school was added in 1917, though it was closed in 1924 for financial reasons. A Talmud Torah teaching in Hebrew and Russian was established in 1920 and continued until 1950; the pupils went on to high school at the Harbin Public Commercial School, where the language of instruction was Russian, and English, German, and Chinese were taught as foreign languages; Jewish students had instruction in Jewish history and literature. Jewish youth movements existed: Hashomer Hatzair (a socialist Zionist youth group), formed in 1927, was replaced in 1929 by Betar (a revisionist youth group), which lasted until 1945. By 1931 there were about 13,000 Russian Jews, but many left after the Japanese occupation and associated anti-Jewish incidents; only 5,000 remained in 1935. The community survived the war, but difficulties began during the brief Soviet occupation that followed and under the subsequent Chinese Communist rule, when foreigners were encouraged to leave; 1,000 or so left from 1948 to 1951, and all had left by the 1960s.[30]

Apart from the Kaifeng community, many of whom assimilated, the Jews in China commonly maintained their identity and the languages they had brought with them.

Hong Kong

Jews began to move to Hong Kong in the middle of the nineteenth century; the Ohel Leah synagogue (in memory of Sir Jacob Sassoon's mother) was built in 1881 to replace one leased in 1870. In the beginning the community was mainly Sephardi, but Ashkenazim formed a majority of the quite small congregation by 1968. There are now four synagogues, and there has been rapid growth with foreigners coming to Hong Kong for business.

India

There are three main groups of Jews in India, the ones with the longest tradition being the Bene Israel living in and around Mumbai (Bombay). Their oral history claims that their ancestors left Judah as a result of the persecutions of Antiochus in the second century BCE; seven families survived being shipwrecked, and, although they soon forgot Hebrew and had no written texts, they remembered the Sabbath and some holidays and the *Shema*.[31] They settled first in villages in the Konkan, where they switched to speaking Marathi, became oil pressers, and maintained circumcision. They were rediscovered by Cochin Jews in the eighteenth century, and developed their own religious leadership. In the nineteenth century Christian missionaries established schools for them and encouraged them to add English to their language repertoire. The school, founded in the nineteenth century, taught Hebrew and English as well as Marathi. Encouraged by the British government, they moved to Mumbai in the nineteenth century and served in the Indian army and later as white-collar workers. In the early twentieth century many emigrated to other parts of British India and to Burma and Aden. After India and Pakistan became independent in 1948, many emigrated to Israel.[32]

The second group is the Cochin Jews, with records dating to the eleventh century, and recording three waves of settlement. The earliest were the Black Jews, the second immigrants from Spain and Portugal in the sixteenth century, and the third a group of *Meshuarim*, low-caste descendants of Jews and their slave-concubines. The three groups did not worship together.[33] The Cochin Jews lived in Kerala in the south of India and spoke Judeo-Malayalam, a Jewish variety of the local language; it is mutually intelligible with other varieties of Malayalam (a Dravidian language) and is written in the same script, but contains many Hebrew borrowings.[34] Cochin Jews are said to have been traditionally observant; most emigrated to Israel after the state was established. Some of the Jews from Spain were *Anusim*. Among them was Leonor Caldeira, who arrived in 1533 with her husband, Afono Nunes; she was one of those who had undergone mass conversion in 1497 in Lisbon;[35] she lived quietly in Cochin practicing Judaism until 1557, when she, a widow, and nineteen other New Christians were charged by the Inquisition with Judaizing and sent to Portugal, where she was burned to death in 1561.[36]

The third group was called Baghdadi or Iraqi: Arabic-speaking Jews who followed earlier European Jewish traders to settle first in Surat and then later, in 1730, in Mumbai. They formed originally the Arabian Jewish Merchant Community, and came from Baghdad, Aleppo, Basra, Aden, Syria, and other Arabic-speaking places. By the 1830s there were about twenty-five families in Mumbai, where they owned a synagogue. In 1833 David Sassoon and his family set up businesses throughout Asia. To start, all the firm's business was conducted in Judeo-Arabic. Sassoon built a synagogue with an attached hostel and Talmud Torah. His family business continued to grow after his death, and his descendants carried on his philanthropy. The Baghdadi Jews kept up their traditions, learned Hindustani for business but not Marathi or Bengali, and switched in due course to English.[37] Arabic-speaking traders established the Jewish community in Kolkata (Calcutta).

There are other groups in India. The Bene Ephraim are a small community of low-caste Telugu speakers in Andhra Pradesh who have claimed to be descended from the tribe of Ephraim and are reported to have studied Judaism and learned some Hebrew: they are not recognized as Jews. The Bene Menashe are a Tibeto-Burman tribe of about 9,000 in northeastern India who speak Thado and Mizo. They claim to be descendants of the Israelite tribe of Menashe, which is why Rabbi Eliyahu Avihayil, who visited them in the 1970s, named them Bene Menashe. Some have emigrated to Israel, but their status remains controversial.[38]

Japan

The first Jewish settlers arrived in Yokohama in 1861 and built a synagogue. The community moved to Kobe after the 1923 earthquake. Another settlement was formed in Nagasaki in the 1880s, but declined during the Russo-Japanese war. The Kobe community continued to grow, boosted by Russian Jews from Harbin, Iraqi and Syrian Jews, and German Jews. Many Jews escaping Europe, including the Mir Yeshiva, passed through Japan, but were sent to the Shanghai ghetto. After World War II a few Jews in Japan assimilated and married Japanese. There are small communities in Kobe and Tokyo.

Singapore

Jews from Baghdad via India arrived in Singapore in the early nineteenth century and built a synagogue in the middle of the century. There were about 800 Jews in 1931 and 1,500 by 1939. A wealthy Jew, Sir Manasseh Meyer, built a Sephardi synagogue in 1878 and the Chesed El synagogue for Ashkenazi services in 1905 (now only one is used at a time). There are about 300 local and 700 expatriate Jews living in Singapore.

Burma (Myanmar)

Jews mainly from India began to trade and live in Burma in the nineteenth century, but most left during the Japanese occupation. The community's last rabbi left in 1969, and fewer than fifty Jews remain. The Bene Menashe (see India) speak a Tibeto-Burman language; some Chin claim to be Jewish.

Sri Lanka

Jews have been reported in Sri Lanka since the ninth century, and Benjamin of Tudela said there were 3,000 in the twelfth century. These early Jews either assimilated or were forced to convert by the Portuguese Inquisition in the sixteenth century. There were a few Jews in Ceylon under British rule, and a small contemporary community is supported by Habad, the children's aid society.

The Orient: a summary

Jews came to Asia as traders or refugees and established quite small communities, some of which lasted into modern times, but many of which subsequently moved on to Israel or the United States. The oldest communities are the Bene Israel and the Cochin in India; one extinct ancient community in China is the Kaifeng. Many communities were founded by Baghdadi traders, and showed slow assimilation, probably continuing to speak Judeo-Arabic until they switched later to English. Religious, social, and physical differences – easy recognizability, perhaps – helped keep the community closed and supported language loyalty. With the synagogue acting as the main center of Jewish life and the Hebrew school alongside, the role of Hebrew as a sacred language and mark of identity remained, making migration to Israel seem less of a challenge.

16   The return to Zion and Hebrew

Background to the emergence of spoken Hebrew

This book started with two questions that I am regularly asked, the first (in Israel) about whether Hebrew is endangered, which I tried to answer in Chapter 1. The second is the question that is put to me whenever I meet activists who are trying to maintain or revive their heritage languages: how, they ask, was Hebrew revived? What was the magic? No magic, I tell them, and no miracle, unless it was that a group of secular nationalists chose to use as their daily language a variety that had been preserved for sacred purposes by a religious establishment that mainly opposed both their nationalism and their language policy.[1]

Reading the chapters of this book, you have already learned the basis of my answer, which is that, during the two millennia when Jews were in exile and when they learned and spoke many other languages, Hebrew was almost always a significant part of their linguistic repertoire, as a sacred language for religious purposes and as a language of literacy. It was therefore not a matter of reviving[2] a dead language, reconstructing it from ancient manuscripts (as with Cornish) or from isolated elderly speakers (as with Eyak). What was involved, rather, was the expansion of the domains in which the language was currently being used and an increase in the number of uses and users.[3]

There were two critical processes: revernacularization (adopting a formal written and sacred language for normal daily use)[4] and revitalization (adding vitality – that is, speaking the language to babies and so guaranteeing natural intergenerational transmission).[5] Associated with these ecological changes were processes affecting the form of the language (modernization, increase in lexicon, simplification of morphology, changes in syntax, development of phonological complexity) and its status (adding the official, the informal, and the intimate to a sacred and literary variety).

We do have some knowledge of the Hebrew proficiency of Jewish men in eastern Europe at the end of the nineteenth century, when the change occurred. Studies of working-class Jews in Russia and Poland found that quite small percentages were unable to read Hebrew or Yiddish. Being able to read Hebrew

249

did not mean being able to understand it, as many would have had a quite poor *heder* instruction. Only a small elite of Jews went on to study Talmud, so that most Jewish men would be limited to the prayer book and the Bible. Even this knowledge was often restricted. It seems reasonable to assume that good knowledge of Hebrew was a mark of the elite rather than the "ignorant" masses.[6]

But there was variety in the informal written Hebrew in use in the nineteenth century. The best example is the *Kitzur Shulchan Arukh*, a shortened version of the classic sixteenth-century code of Jewish law written by Rabbi Shlomo Ganzfried and published in Hungary in 1864: by 1908 there were said to be about half a million copies in print. The *Kitzur* was written in an informal style very close to the colloquial, and might very well have formed the basis for the spoken language that developed as Hebrew was becoming a vernacular.[7] What is particularly fascinating is that its lexicon included a great number of terms that the scholars who claim to have developed Modern Hebrew said they had to invent; it included about fifty words for fruits, vegetables, and trees, for example, although there is a story of a Hebrew teacher out for a walk with his class wondering about the names of trees.[8] There are also many words for furniture, for medical and anatomical terms, for kitchen implements and utensils, for clothes, and for food. Many of the words in the *Kitzur* are Yiddish, suggesting the close connections between Yiddish and the spoken Hebrew developed by the first speakers at the turn of the century.[9]

In fact, if we accept the normal mixture of varieties, with easy borrowing of lexical and grammatical items,[10] that occurs in the kind of multilingual speech community that we have found to mark Jewish societies for most of their history, then we will find it more natural to understand the easy movement between Yiddish, Hebrew, and their other languages that must have been true of the early Zionist settlers. The beginning of Hebrew vernacular use was not so much an abrupt change as a shift in progress, although one must also imagine language teachers, purists, and activists trying to manage the speech of others by insisting on greater standardization.

This shift towards spoken Hebrew started even before Herzl proclaimed modern Zionist political nationalism, when some east European Jews were starting to suspect that the only solution to the Jewish problem was the establishment of a territorially independent nation. Throughout the long history of persecution and forced emigration that followed the destruction of the Jewish state by the Roman Empire in the first century, the return to Zion was a constant theme of Jewish prayers. Occasionally, it was realized by individuals who set off in the hope of finding a place to live in the Holy Land.[11] In the nineteenth century a goodly number of poor eastern European Jews had moved to Ottoman Palestine, where they joined a number of Sephardi Jews who had been there for 100 years or more. The Sephardim, many of them speakers of Judeo-Arabic and

Judezmo, and some with good control of classical Arabic as well as of Hebrew, were comfortably settled in what was a poverty-stricken backwater of the Ottoman Empire. The mainly Yiddish-speaking Ashkenazi migrants were reluctant to learn Arabic and generally unwilling to work, preferring to depend on charity from overseas Jewish communities to maintain their poor existence.

In the 1880s a new type of immigrant arrived: some of the Jews escaping the pogroms in Russia decided to go to Palestine rather than to the United States. The first important group were the Bilu,[12] fourteen university students from Kharkov who went to Palestine, spent a while on a training farm, then joined a Hovevei Zion (Lovers of Zion) group in setting up a farming cooperative in Rishon le Zion, which later, with the support of Baron Edmond de Rothschild, became the beginning of the local wine industry. Hovevei Zion had been founded in 1884 in Germany, and led by Rabbi Samuel Mohilever and Leon Pinsker. A second group, led by the linguist Ludwig Lazarus Zamenhof, who was at the time writing a grammar of Yiddish and later created Esperanto, was formed in Warsaw about the same time.[13] A third, based in Russia, was registered as a charitable organization with the name "Society for the Support of Jewish Farmers and Artisans in Syria and Eretz Israel".

Hovevei Zion was responsible for the founding of Jewish farming settlements in a number of places, including Petah Tikva (the first in 1878, known as Mother of the Moshavot), Rosh Pinna (1882), Zikhron Ya'akov (1882), Yesud Hama'ala (1882), Rishon le Zion (1882), Gedera (1884), and Hadera (1891). It was in these pre-Zionist farming communities, several of them supported in 1883 by Baron de Rothschild, that the major changes in the use of Hebrew took place. They preceded political Zionism, which essentially began when the first Zionist Congress took place in Basel in 1897, convened by Herzl. In his books, articles, and speeches, this Austrian Jewish journalist, who had been shocked by the recurrence of anti-Semitism in emancipated France during the Dreyfus trial, called for the re-establishment of a Jewish state in the ancient Holy Land. He dreamed that the language of such a state would be German, the main language of educated western Europe. But many others considered that the revived Jewish state should use a Jewish language; some supported Yiddish, and others believed it had to be Hebrew. The question was debated not just in Europe but also in the new farming communities of Palestine.

The Yiddish–Hebrew struggle

The orthodox community in eastern Europe and in Ottoman Palestine continued to use Yiddish as its vernacular and Hebrew as its sacred language, so that it was normal for a rabbi to give his sermons in synagogue in Yiddish and then publish them later in a Hebrew book. It was among secular Jews, however, that the Yiddish nationalist movement developed at this stage, with newspapers,

magazines, books, and plays. There were several competing positive views of
the Yiddish language at the end of the nineteenth century. The ultra-orthodox
view was a traditional utilitarian one: Yiddish was an appropriate language to
use only in publications intended for women and the uneducated. The secular
Yiddish nationalists held that it should be used for the political and social
education of the masses. Going further, there were those who argued that it
had a role to play in expressing Jewish nationalism. Finally, there were those
who believed that it was a totally natural symbolic expression of that
nationalism.

All four views were expressed at the Czernowitz international congress on
Yiddish in 1908.[14] The conference was convened by Nathan Birnbaum, who had
by now broken with the Zionism of Herzl that he had once supported (he later
went on to found the ultra-orthodox non-Zionist Agudath Israel, whose aim was
to strengthen orthodox institutions). The conference was intended by its organizers to deal with practical problems such as spelling and grammar and the status
of Yiddish writers and actors. In fact, it focused mainly on the issue of the status of
Yiddish among Jews. About sixty people attended from various parts of east
Europe, including a number of writers[15] and linguists. It lasted a week, opened by
Birnbaum reading a speech in Yiddish (which he didn't speak) translated from the
German (which he spoke well). The conference was marked by constant arguments about status, but, finally, forty people took part in the vote to accept a
resolution proposing that Yiddish was "*a* Jewish national language" and not "*the*
national Jewish language" – a status preserved for Hebrew.[16]

Hebrew did not have a first congress, but there was an assembly of Hebrew
teachers in Palestine in 1903, followed by two conferences of European Hebrew
organizations in 1907 and 1909, that filled this role.[17] But we are getting ahead
of the story; first, we need to look at the sociolinguistic ecology of Palestine at
the end of the nineteenth century.

The environment of the revival

So far, the general picture that I have painted has been of Jews arriving as
immigrants in a new country and struggling to maintain identity while picking
up the local language. What, then, was the linguistic situation of Ottoman
Palestine in the latter half of the nineteenth century? The language of government was Turkish, but most government officials spoke Arabic. Turkish was the
language in which reports were sent to Constantinople, and the language of the
army and government officials. The main language of the Arab population was a
version of Palestinian Arabic: a village variety outside the main cities, a city
version inside Jerusalem and other large towns, and a third variety spoken by
Bedouin. This pattern was repeated in other countries under Ottoman rule, but
each country had its own set of spoken dialects. Spoken Arabic was the lingua

franca of all in Palestine except the Ashkenazi immigrants. A Yiddish book published in Warsaw in 1841 included a short list of essential Arabic words – numbers, place names, foods, a few phrases – to help them adjust.

Arabic was the language of Muslims, Christians, and Jews. The Sephardi Jews, who generally spoke Judezmo, knew Arabic; there were also native-born Jews (Moriscos, descendants of *Anusim*) who spoke only Arabic. Newly arrived Ashkenazi Jews did not know Arabic, however, but the ultra-orthodox community objected to a proposal to teach it to them. Sir Moses Montefiore tried to improve their educational level, and the Chief Rabbi of the Ashkenazi community approved of a scheme to teach Arabic to Jewish boys using a religious Jewish teacher. But a small faction (mainly Hungarian Hasidim) resisted strongly and managed to persuade a senior rabbi to issue a decree banning the teaching of foreign languages in Jerusalem.[18]

Jerusalem in the nineteenth century was multilingual. The British consul reported the language situation: "Hebrew and Greek, Turkish and Arabic, Syriac, Abyssinian, Hindustani, Russian, German, French, Italian, Spanish and English (and other languages) are daily spoken in Jerusalem."[19] An English archeologist wrote about the difficulties of communication: "The hotel-keeper talks Greek; his cook, Amharic; one waiter, Polish-Hebrew; another, Italian; another, Arabic; the barber speaks French; the washerwoman, Spanish; the carpenter, German; the dragoman [interpreter], English; and the Pacha, Turkish: Sepoys from India mutter English oaths."[20] Each religious community had its head and language: Armenians, Copts, Greeks, Jews, Latin Orthodox, Muslims, Protestants, Russians, and Syrians.[21]

With all this mixture of languages, spoken Arabic was the lingua franca. Sephardi Jews[22] knew it comfortably and were self-supporting, but Ashkenazim[23] were reluctant to learn it. Many of the Jews who came from eastern Europe towards the end of the nineteenth century were fundamentalists, unwilling to adjust to the new situation and dependent on charity sent from home communities or collected locally.[24] As Ashkenazi immigration continued, by the latter part of the century Judezmo, once the dominant Jewish language, was the mother tongue of only a third of the Jews in Jerusalem.[25] By the end of the century Yiddish was becoming the dominant Jewish language, used by Ashkenazim and learned by many Sephardim, and even Arabs, to do business.[26] But established Ashkenazi families would know some Judezmo, to speak to servants and to relatives, as the communities intermarried, and some Arabic was picked up in the streets.[27]

Hebrew was known outside as well as inside Palestine. Fourteen-year-old boys in a Hebrew school in Italy were reported to be able to speak and write Hebrew. A rabbi who went to England in 1828 to collect money was invited to speak in the Portuguese synagogue in Hebrew.[28]

In Palestine it was even more important. The British vice-consul in Jerusalem wrote to the foreign secretary in 1839 asking for the hiring of a Hebrew dragoman, pointing out that the Jews generally wrote contracts in Spanish and Hebrew. Disputing this claim, the British consul-general in Cairo argued that Jews used Arabic and did not know Hebrew. In reply, the vice-consul listed a number of documents he had just received in Hebrew: one was a will and the second a statement of property. Jews, he claimed, conducted affairs among themselves in Hebrew.[29] Although his request was approved, interpretation continued to be a problem: in 1849 the British consul, who had learned some Hebrew himself, found it necessary to employ several Hebrew translators for different varieties. He reported that "in Jerusalem [Hebrew] is the living tongue of everyday utility – necessarily so, for in what else could Jewish strangers from opposite ends of the earth converse to each other? In the Consular office, Hebrew was often heard spoken – on one occasion by a Jew from Kabul who had to enter into explanations with one from California: of course in Hebrew."[30]

Similarly, the Ashkenazi and Sephardi elders of Tiberias were observed to speak to each other in Hebrew during the visit of Montefiore, but they spoke to the British consul and other non-Jewish visitors in Arabic or German.[31] The British ambassador in Constantinople passed on a complaint in 1871 to the British consul in Jerusalem about the fact that a local Christian missionary had posted placards in Hebrew containing "statements of a controversial character seeking to prove to the Jews from the Old Testament that they are in error". The foreign secretary approved the complaint.[32] The differences between Sephardi and Ashkenazi Hebrew handwriting and pronunciation also led to difficulties: the official dragoman (a Sephardi) could not read a Hebrew letter in Ashkenazi script.[33] The north African Jews in 1850 asked for a synagogue of their own because their form of prayer and pronunciation of Hebrew were different from those of the Sephardim.[34] A similar argument was presented on behalf of the Ashkenazi Jews when they asked permission to rebuild the Hurva synagogue.[35]

In nineteenth-century Ottoman Palestine, then, we have seen that Jewish immigration had two distinct sociolinguistic results: Sephardi and Mizrahi Jews easily modified their Arabic knowledge or added knowledge of local spoken Arabic in order to fit in with the non-Jewish population, while only a few Ashkenazi Jews picked up spoken Arabic, but the ultra-orthodox resisted any attempt to learn the local language and continued as speakers of Yiddish or whatever other European language they might have brought with them. In the next section, however, we look at the Zionists, those who combined the return to Zion with the return to Hebrew.

The revitalization of Hebrew: ideology

The movement for the revival of Hebrew in eastern Europe and in Palestine in the latter part of the nineteenth century was influenced by European nationalist movements, which saw the language of a people on its own territory as inextricably bound with its nationhood. But there were major differences: for the Jews, it was necessary to add the third component, a national territory, to the mix. The non-territorial version of Jewish nationalism in Europe had chosen Yiddish as its symbolic language. The small number of Zionist immigrants who came to Ottoman Palestine proceeded to claim Palestine as their national home. They were, in other words, territorialists, and fought off other proposals such as the movement to establish farming communities in South America, the United States, and Australia, and a faction within the Zionist organization that proposed a new Jewish homeland in Africa, such as Kenya or Uganda.[36]

The second major difference from European nationalist movements was the linguistic task: most of the European language movements already had a spoken vernacular, so their challenge was to add a formal written variety. Hebrew, on the other hand, had a high-status sacred and literary variety; the problem was how to develop an informal spoken vernacular.

The revitalization of Hebrew took place in the farming settlements set up by Yiddish-speaking Zionist immigrants from eastern Europe.[37] There were four stages.[38] First, it was necessary to persuade the children of the villages that they should switch from their home language, Yiddish, to Hebrew. Second, they needed to be presented with a model of Hebrew language use in the school. Third, they had to speak the language not just in the classroom but also outside the classroom and at home. Fourth, when they grew up and married, they needed to continue to speak the language and pass it to their own children.

Each of these stages was important and difficult. The ideological struggle between Yiddish and Hebrew had begun already in Europe, but was not resolved at the Czernowitz conference, which, by establishing Yiddish as *a* national Jewish language, left room open for Hebrew to claim the role of *the* Jewish national language. A critical victory for Hebrew had been a decision of the Labor Party in Palestine in 1907 to issue its journal in Hebrew only. This was a year before the Czernowitz meeting.

The ideological struggle continued and was marked by strong rhetoric, and worse. In 1914 Chaim Zhitlowsky visited Palestine and gave lectures in Yiddish in three major cities: his appearance in Jaffa was interrupted by a demonstration of high school pupils. In 1918 the organization of the Yishuv (the Jewish community in Palestine) adopted a resolution requiring knowledge of Hebrew for election to its institutions. In 1927 an attempt to establish a chair of Yiddish at the Hebrew University was defeated. As late as the 1940s there was even violence, with a Yiddish printing press being blown up.[39]

The residents of the new Jewish farming settlements had the kind of ideological fervor for the revival of Hebrew that was found in the writing of Eliezer Ben-Yehuda, who had arrived in Palestine in 1881.[40] An enthusiastic forerunner of Zionism, he had started writing articles supporting the revival of Hebrew and the need to return to Zion as early as 1879. Initially, he did not see this as the revival of the spoken language but in terms of the usefulness of the literary language: he appears to have assumed that Jews would speak their own vernaculars, but use Hebrew as a unifying literary language. It was only a little later, in 1880, that he started to criticize the schools in Palestine that were teaching in French (those run by the Alliance Israélite Universelle) or German (those set up by the German-based Hilfsverein der deutschen Juden), calling for schools that would "teach our offspring in Hebrew, and let us lead a Hebrew life".[41]

Ben-Yehuda followed his own principles. Once he had moved to Palestine, he spoke only Hebrew in his home with his own children, and would not allow non-Hebrew-speaking relatives into the house.[42] But he lived in Jerusalem, where, with a few exceptions, his arguments fell on deaf ears. The majority of religious Jews in Jerusalem continued to restrict Hebrew to sacred functions, and even excommunicated Ben-Yehuda for his heretical arguments. It was in the Zionist settlements that revitalization occurred.

It was the settlers in these small villages who, having given up the city life to which they were accustomed in eastern Europe and become farmers, took on the ideology of the language activists. To start, the schools of the agricultural settlements, under the patronage of Baron de Rothschild, taught general sub-jects in French and used Yiddish for Jewish subjects. David Idelovitch (Yudelovich) was born in Romania and joined the Bilu pioneers in Jerusalem in 1882. After a year in France, in 1886, he became a teacher and later head-master in the Rishon le Zion school, where, in spite of opposition from the officials appointed by the Rothschilds,[43] he started to teach all subjects in Hebrew. To meet the inadequacy of starting to use a new language of instruction in the first year, he added the first Hebrew kindergarten in 1898.[44] He wrote children's books in Hebrew, and organized the first Hebrew teachers' meetings.

The ideological commitment of these settlers was critical to the revival of spoken Hebrew. I have been fortunate enough to observe similar devotion among Māori language activists in New Zealand, when I attended a conference held by the Te Ataarangi movement. The movement had been founded in 1980 by young university students who were learning the Māori language for the first time. Thirty years later they were still gathering each year for a week-long conference, bringing their own children, during which time only Māori would be spoken.[45] Seeing their devotion to the cause and the ideological commitment showed me what the feeling must have been in those early farming communities where Hebrew was revived. A letter written in 1889 tells of a group that came to Jerusalem during the festival of Sukkot, who surprised people by speaking Hebrew in public. "Many of the travelers would still be walking to and fro outside, with the Holy Tongue on their lips. . . This made a strong impression in Jerusalem. All of the travelers walked about together at all times, speaking Hebrew in the streets. . .but the folk of Jerusalem could not believe their eyes: 'Godless people talking the Holy Tongue!'"[46]

Even stronger ideological commitment to radical changes, including the adoption of Hebrew, was shown by the Zionist socialists of the Second Aliya, who established the kibbutzim. Equally committed to working on the land, they went further than the earlier settlers by rejecting private property and forming communal settlements where everything was held in common. There was little or no private space: the children lived in a communal children's house, and there was often a third person in the room of a married couple. Committed absolutely to Hebrew, they changed their names to Hebrew[47] and followed a rule that only Hebrew was spoken in public. A married couple in private might speak their original language, but, as soon as the third roommate or a child entered, the language would switch to Hebrew.[48]

The revival of Hebrew: models and teachers

The second stage of the shift was providing a model. The teachers were well versed in Hebrew, but unused to teaching in it. To start, they followed the normal practice of teaching Hebrew through Yiddish, but, during Ben-Yehuda's brief (and not very happy) spell as a teacher in Jerusalem, he introduced the Berlitz or direct method approach of teaching Hebrew through Hebrew, a model that David Idelovitch also followed in his school. By 1888 general subjects were being taught in Hebrew, and by 1891 teaching was in Hebrew in the other villages as well.

In 1892 nineteen Hebrew teachers met and decided that the direct method should be used, and that Hebrew should be the language of instruction.[49] In 1894 a pre-school program for four- and five-year-old children was instituted in Rishon le Zion, though there were no trained teachers available until 1898, when a candidate was sent to Jerusalem to be trained at the Evelina de Rothschild school, which taught in English. Hebrew kindergartens were opened in Jerusalem in 1903, and in 1904 in Safed, Jaffa, Haifa, Tiberias, Rehovot, Zikhron Yaakov, and Nes Tziona. Just as the Māori pre-school programs (the so-called "language nests", at which grandparents who still spoke the language were brought in to teach the young children) were considered the breakthrough in Māori language regeneration,[50] so these kindergartens were the cutting edge of Hebrew revival: "The child became the teacher of his parents, his brothers, his sisters. . ."[51]

The Hebrew Teachers' Association met in 1895, when it agreed that Hebrew (with Sephardi pronunciation) should be used for instruction (but Ashkenazi pronunciation was to be allowed in the first year and for prayer). It met next in 1903 at the close of a meeting of the Jewish Yishuv called in Zikhron Yaakov by Menahem Ussishkin, the Russian Zionist leader. At this meeting, with fifty-nine teachers present, the principle of teaching Hebrew through Hebrew and the use of Sephardi pronunciation were confirmed,[52] and there was agreement to use Ashkenazi script.

The problem remained of accounting for the teacher's knowledge of Hebrew and ability to start speaking it. It is here that the example of the Hebrew used in the *Kitzur* becomes important. We can imagine the kind of mixed code that was the result of Yiddish speakers attempting to add the Hebrew lexicon they knew to the Yiddish grammar they used. As is normal in the case of languages revived in a school situation,[53] the variety that emerges can be quite different from the variety spoken by native speakers. In the cases of Welsh and Breton, native speakers complained about the language of the children; similarly, many older Māoris were unhappy at the language spoken by children who acquired Māori in school. Ironically, Hebrew was fortunate that there were no older native speakers to criticize the variety being used. It can be argued reasonably that the Modern Hebrew that developed in the early twentieth century was not so much a case of reversing language shift[54] but, rather, the creation of a new variety, combining features of Hebrew, Yiddish, and the other languages spoken by Jews.[55]

The revival of Hebrew: outside the classroom

On my visits to New Zealand to observe the regeneration of Māori, I regularly asked to be told of examples of children speaking the language outside the classroom. For the first few years after 1980 no one could produce hard evidence, but, as time went on, there seem to be more and more cases of this starting to happen. Similarly, in 1891, graduates of Hebrew schools were reported to stop speaking the language when they left school. By 1902, however, young men and women in Zikhron Yaakov were reported to be speaking Hebrew; in 1910 Hebrew was said to be spoken in the streets and homes of Rishon le Zion. As late as 1907, though, a newspaper article expressed surprise that a public speech was given in Zikhron Yaakov in Hebrew, which was understood to be the normal language of children but not of adults.[56]

By the outbreak of World War I there were presumably a good number of young people who had learned Hebrew in school and used it in their daily life: in the farming colonies, in the communal settlements, and in some towns Hebrew now had proficient speakers whose children were the first native speakers since the second century CE. Between 1880 and 1903 more than 20,000 Jews arrived in Ottoman Palestine; many of their children were exposed to Hebrew, and their children in turn were "the first people, after a lapse of 1700 years, who know no language but Hebrew".[57]

The building of the new Zionist city of Tel Aviv was accompanied by a proclamation of the importance of Hebrew. Tel Aviv was to be built close to the largely Arab port city of Jaffa. The prospectus for the new city issued in 1906 made the goal clear:

We must urgently acquire a considerable chunk of land, on which we shall build our houses. Its place must be near Jaffa, and it will form the first Hebrew city, its inhabitants will be Hebrews a hundred percent; Hebrew will be spoken in the city, purity and cleanliness will be kept, and we shall not go in the ways of the *goyim* [non-Jews].[58]

Gymnasia Herzliya was the first Hebrew high school; founded in Jaffa in 1905 in two rooms, it moved to Tel Aviv in 1909. In the 1920s the Gedud lemeginei hasafa (Legion for the Defense of the Hebrew Language) was formed here, and began its public campaigns to spread Hebrew.[59]

It was the high school students who played an active part in the 1913 "Language War". The German-based Hilfsverein der Deutschen Juden, which was already supporting secondary schools, proposed to set up a tertiary techno-logical institute. There was debate over the language of instruction, and, while it was agreed to use Hebrew for general subjects, German, the language of science, was suggested for mathematics and scientific subjects. There was strong objec-tion from the Hebrew-language activists in Palestine, and street demonstrations, and the executive board finally gave in to the pressure. Science classes too, it was agreed, were to use Hebrew as soon as possible. Because of the outbreak of World War I, the Technion did not in fact open until 1924, applying a Hebrew-only language policy, like the Hebrew University of Jerusalem.[60]

But, in 1903, 35 percent of Jewish pupils in Palestine were already in the Hebrew immersion programs in the new settlements and Tel Aviv. Another 10 percent were in traditional ultra-orthodox Yiddish-medium schools. The remaining 55 percent of Jewish pupils were enrolled in foreign language schools – studying in French in Alliance schools, in German in the Lemel School in Jerusalem and in the Hilfsverein schools, and in English in the Evelina de Rothschild school. The changes in the next decade were critical: by the 1916 census 40 percent of the Jews living in Palestine claimed Hebrew as their first or only language.[61]

One of the reasons for the success of Hebrew was the high status of the language. Another was the absence of a serious competitor. Yiddish represented the Diaspora and had ideological support only from the tiny minority of ultra-orthodox individuals and a handful of secular enthusiasts. Arabic was not a reasonable choice: Classical Arabic was banned to non-Muslims, and the spoken language had no written use or status. Support for French waned when Baron de Rothschild removed financial support for education in the settlements. English was not in the picture before 1919, and, as we shall shortly see, German was removed by political action.

Hebrew becomes official

A significant step in the establishment of Hebrew as an official language benefited from Zionist political activity in Britain. The fullest account of the

Language War appeared in a special supplement to the *Jewish Chronicle* weekly newspaper published in 1918, just as General Allenby and the British troops he led were marching into Jerusalem in pursuit of the retreating Ottoman army. This nineteen-page pamphlet[62] combines an account of the conflict over language policy for the tertiary technological institute mentioned earlier with the report of an incident in which the German consul, accompanied by a Turkish policeman, was reported to have entered a Jewish school and forced the teachers to switch from Hebrew to German. At the same time, a Welsh Member of Parliament (a colonel whose young son had been killed while serving in Allenby's army in Egypt) asked the minister of war about the situation in Jerusalem, and whether or not the British occupying forces had already interned the German language teachers found there. The minister replied that he had been told that Jews in Jerusalem spoke Hebrew,[63] and that the army had been instructed to recognize Hebrew as one of the official languages alongside English and Arabic. This recognition of Hebrew was confirmed when the League of Nations awarded the mandate for Palestine to the United Kingdom and it was formally included in the king's Order-in-Council of 1920.[64]

Behind these crucial events, a key figure was, I suspect, Chaim Weizmann. Weizmann, together with Ussishkin, had persuaded the 1913 Zionist congress to support the establishment of the Hebrew University, and both of them had opposed the plans to use German in the proposed technological institute. During the war Weizmann, who had become a British subject, was director of the British Admiralty laboratories, and it was his contacts with British politicians that led to the issuing of the Balfour Declaration, which promised support for the establishment of a Jewish national home in Palestine. It seems reasonable to assume that the Zionist movement and Weizmann were pushing for recognition of Hebrew as an official language, so that political non-governmental activity was mobilized behind the revitalization of Hebrew.

Hebrew language activism

The work of the Hebrew Language Council, the successor of the committees set up by Ben-Yehuda to help modernize Hebrew, was interrupted during the war. Many members were deported to Damascus or Egypt by the Turks, and others left for the United States and Germany. They returned in 1920, and the Council started meeting twice a week in spite of the freezing cold weather, spending their time developing Hebrew terminology for business, carpentry, and kitchen utensils.[65] That same year the presidents of the council (Ben-Yehuda and David Yellin) wrote to the Zionist leadership asking for additional funds to support increased activities: the number of members was to be increased to twenty-three. In 1922 the committee, renamed the Hebrew Language College, wrote to the British High Commissioner explaining the importance of standardizing

Hebrew and requesting that the college be consulted on the translation of all non-secret official documents.[66] The work of the college over the next two decades focused essentially on terminology development, a task that was passed to the Academy of the Hebrew Language, which succeeded it after the establishment of the state in 1948.

Another grassroots organization of activists supporting the revitalization of Hebrew was the Gedud lemeginei hasafa (Legion for the Protection of the Language), led by Ussishkin and established in 1923 at Gymnasia Herzliya. It conducted campaigns against the two principal enemies of Hebrew. Ussishkin, speaking at a conference of the legion, attacked those Jews who used English to claim elite status. He was even more bitter in his complaints against those who used the Diaspora language, Yiddish, and the legion was successful in blocking a proposal to establish a chair of Yiddish at the Hebrew University.

For the first fifty years Hebrew language revival activities were the work of non-governmental grassroots activists, volunteer scholars, and Zionist political leaders, and depended on free acceptance by the minority Jewish community in British-controlled Palestine and by their educational and other institutions. The majority of Palestinian Jews accepted their views, the major exception being the small anti-Zionist ultra-orthodox community, for which Hebrew was too sacred to be used for daily life. The British mandate government, following a general policy of avoiding expenditure in the colonies except for policing and defense, left it to the Arab and Jewish communities to run their own school systems. The Jewish schools thus became the principal instrument of spreading Hebrew to Jewish immigrants and residents.

Hebrew as lingua franca for Jewish immigrants

During World War I immigration to Palestine had come to a virtual halt, but it started again after 1918, when Palestine was occupied by Allied forces. The League of Nations awarded a mandate to control Palestine to the British government in 1922. The British divided the territory into two, proclaiming the eastern sector to be a separate kingdom of Transjordan, where they made Abdullah king rather than returning him to Saudi Arabia. The territory west of the river Jordan was set up as Palestine, with English, Arabic, and Hebrew as official languages.

During the British mandate the population doubled, from about 670,000 in 1919 to 1,970,000 in 1947. The Jewish community of Palestine grew from around 56,000 in 1919 to about 650,000 in 1948.[67] Most of this increase was a result of immigration from eastern and central Europe, initially for political and economic reasons but, after 1933, because of Nazi persecution. The nature of the immigration presumably had an effect on the willingness to adopt Hebrew. For the ideological, this would have been obvious, but most migrants then, and again after the establishment of the state, were escaping from persecution or poverty or other problems, and so were susceptible to the pressure from an establishment encouraging the acquisition of Hebrew, and a situation in which their children were bringing home the language from school. Of course, in 1939 the British government set limits on Jewish immigration, which continued in effect even as the outcome of the Holocaust became public after 1945. There was also some Jewish immigration from Yemen and Asian countries.

Although they greatly outnumbered the early Jewish residents of Palestine, these immigrants came into a Jewish community that had established Hebrew as the language of school and of the community. If they wanted to speak to members of the established community and to immigrants from lands other than their own, they needed a lingua franca, and Hebrew filled this role admirably. In most cases, the children quickly adapted and persuaded their parents to use Hebrew, at least in public. Thus, for the Jews returning to Zion, the process of assimilation meant returning to a traditional heritage language and not to a non-Jewish territorial one. There were the normal exceptions one expects with immigrants: use of the immigrant language in the home, and in neighborhoods where there was an appropriate concentration; and many older people who did not learn.

With the establishment of the State of Israel in 1948, the British-imposed immigration restriction was lifted and the population rapidly increased, with the arrival of survivors of the Holocaust from Europe and a complete emptying of the Jewish population in the Arab countries that now found themselves at war with Israel. Israel was faced with a multilingual population, exemplified in the difficulty of the army sergeant who needed to translate his orders into ten languages before his platoon could move.

The Israeli army tackled this problem head-on by introducing language classes and setting up a program to provide basic primary education for all recruits. The schools continued the policy of teaching Hebrew through Hebrew, and only later started special Hebrew classes for new immigrants. To cater for multilingualism, the government radio stations broadcast news in each of the immigrant languages. Depending on its standard of literacy, each community started its own newspapers, and the government provided a newspaper in easy Hebrew. Finally, the government began special intensive five-month-long programs (called *ulpanim*) that were intended to teach Hebrew and Zionism to immigrants with an advanced education. With the major Russian and Ethiopian surges in immigration in the 1990s, Hebrew *ulpanim* were provided for all.

Hebrew as the hegemonic language of Israel

By now, then, not only has Hebrew been revitalized, revernacularized, and standardized, but it has become the dominant hegemonic language of Israel. As described in Chapter 1, it serves all functions in all domains of Israeli life. It is the language in which you address a stranger, although tourists are likely to reply in English. It is the language likely to be known by minorities, including the Haredi Hasidic men who prefer to speak Yiddish and the Arabic speakers from towns and villages within Israel. It is the language of the physics seminar and the football field, although other languages will be heard where there are concentrations of new immigrants.

There are some who would argue that it is no longer a Jewish language, for it is the language of Israelis of whatever religion. In spite of this hegemony, though, Israel remains multilingual, with space for many of the languages that Jews have picked up over the centuries. Television programs and movies recognize this rich repertoire. Commercial and government offices find ways to cater for speakers of other varieties. Tourists are guided in their own languages, and university programs allow for the presence of foreign students.

With some exceptions, Hebrew has now established itself as the language of the Jews of Israel and of anyone else living there. It has changed in significant ways, developing a pronunciation that is neither Sephardi or Ashkenazi or Mizrahi but that avoids the more difficult sounds of each. Its grammar too has changed, as it has moved from morphological to syntactic constructions, and now shows many Indo-European rather than Semitic features. Its vocabulary, while formally enriched by the products of the Hebrew Academy in all domains, easily accepts borrowed words from all the languages of the Jews, as well as from international academic, scientific, technological, and economic vocabularies.

The languages brought in by Jewish migrants are in most cases locally endangered, as the second and third generations move to Hebrew. There are exceptions: English, as the global lingua franca, is a desirable second language for most; French, Spanish, and Russian are spoken by sizable enough communities, with continued reinforcement from new immigrants; Yiddish and Amharic are used by closed groups to maintain identity; Palestinian Arabic is the first language of a sizable minority. But many of the heritage languages are rapidly disappearing: Judezmo has government support (like secular Yiddish), but its active supporters no longer use it much. Other Jewish varieties have only elderly speakers.[68] Israel remains multilingual, but the number of living varieties is rapidly dropping, and only a few other languages are being passed on to children.

In the continuing Diaspora

Outside Israel, many of the major languages that the Jews have acquired continue to be used. English is clearly firmly established, not just as a language for life outside the Jewish community but also as a language that can be used for writing scholarly and popular Jewish religious texts. The large Jewish communities of the United States, Britain, Australia, Canada, and South Africa now conduct much of their Jewish as well as non-Jewish life in English. They face various problems in terms of maintaining Jewish identity and life, one common feature of which is the difficulty of teaching Hebrew, whether for sacred use or for maintaining association with Israel. In spite of this, Hebrew continues to hold its central status in Jewish communities outside Israel, and there has been no success with earlier attempts to replace it as a sacred language.

The linguistic diversity of these Diaspora communities is maintained in part by continued migration, whether of Hebrew speakers from Israel or speakers of other languages from other Diasporas. Thus, the US communities include recent additions of large numbers of speakers of Russian, Hebrew, and Persian. Russian, Spanish, and French remain strong within regional Jewish communities, as do Russian in the former Soviet Union, Spanish in Central and Latin America, and French in francophone countries. Yiddish is well entrenched in Haredi Hasidic sects, especially in the United States, Belgium, and Britain.

Is Hebrew a Jewish language?

I suggested in an earlier chapter that I would return to the issue of Jewish languages later and ask whether Hebrew is a Jewish language or not. There are good reasons to say it is not,[69] for the common definition of a Jewish language is of a variety (a religiolect) that exists in a diglossic situation with Hebrew. I suppose you could get around this by saying that Modern Israeli Hebrew, the vernacular and dominant hegemonic language variety of Israel, exists for many Jews in a diglossic relation with the sacred Hebrew and Hebrew–Aramaic of the Bible and of Jewish religious writings. For non-Jews living in Israel (Muslims and Christians, for instance), it is not a Jewish language. Another point of definition is that a Jewish variety was commonly based on and shows signs of an earlier variety, as Yiddish was claimed to show signs of earlier Judeo-Romance. This, of course, would fit claims that Modern Hebrew is based in many ways on the Yiddish that its first speakers used; some therefore give it a different name.[70] Others suggest that Modern Hebrew is Yiddish relexified, just as Yiddish was a relexified variety of Sorbian or Judeo-Slavic.[71]

Another way of pursuing the question is by thinking about names. Most of the Jewish languages, if they have a name of their own other than the pseudo-scientific "Judeo-X", are called in the language "Jewish"; this, interestingly enough, was the biblical name of Hebrew, suggesting that it was seen as a Jewish variety. "Judeo-X" makes a somewhat different claim, for it suggests that these Jewish varieties are Jewish dialects (some use the more precise term "religiolect") of "X". Clearly, that won't work for Modern Hebrew.

Another track to pursue is the idea of a sacred or religious variety;[72] this ignores the fact that Jewish varieties, while used for sacred purposes, such as teaching and sermons, and even prayers, are commonly viewed as the vernacular variety in diglossia with sacred Hebrew.

Another defining feature is called for, therefore, and I am starting to suspect that Jewish languages are distinguished by the situation of their speakers as a minority, usually a persecuted one in forced isolation from or subordination to the speakers of the majority Gentile variety. Reading the history of the languages of the Jews, one finds three patterns: Jewish independence; subordination and persecution following, or leading to, expulsion; and an acceptance of Jews as equal citizens after an emancipation period. In the first place, we have the original Hebrew hegemony of the early biblical period and post-statehood sovereignty; in the second case, we have the development of specifically Jewish varieties or dialects of the co-territorial non-Jewish languages; and, in the third, we have assimilation and a loss of linguistic differentiation. Hebrew served in all three periods: in the first, as the vernacular and dominant language for literacy; in the second, restricted to being a sacred language or a literary variety; and, in the third, it depended on a strong educational system for maintenance. Throughout, I have argued that it is *the* language of the Jews, but not a Jewish language. Of course, one problem is that we have no clear evidence of the nature of Jewish languages until they have developed; Judezmo did not emerge as a distinguishable variety until after the expulsion in 1492, and Yiddish became identifiable only after the movement to Slavic areas.

To be accurate, we need to clarify the conditions for the creation of Jewish languages by adding an internal motivation for isolation. There are cases of language maintenance as a method of preserving identity, such as the maintenance of Yiddish and Amish in the United States and Yiddish in Israel as internally imposed isolation. And we have similar evidence of the development of a potential Jewish variety in the growth of Yeshivish among English-speaking newly orthodox Jews.[73]

One of the strongest cases for a similar development by a persecuted minority group of a distinct ethnic variety is provided in the case of African American Vernacular English; in a recent paper, William Labov points out that there is little chance of this variety becoming endangered as long as its speakers continue to suffer the social and economic discrimination that lands its young men in jail.[74] For much of its history, the Jewish people have faced similar external pressure; it is appropriate that we refer to African-American living areas in the United States as ghettos.

As has become customary in this book, we don't finish up with a simple answer to the important questions; I offer this hypothesis not so much as an answer but as a heuristic device to analyze further the phenomena that we have been considering. Noting the way in which Modern Israeli Hebrew has worked as a hegemonic monolingual variety to discourage the continuation of other languages, including Jewish languages brought to Israel by refugees and migrants and including indigenous Arabic, it seems reasonable to claim that it certainly is not a Jewish language in the traditional sense, but one that recognizes its function as a marker of identity. True, it is the dominant hegemonic and official language, but it maintains a role as a marker of a small nation surrounded by speakers of Arabic, threatened by their rulers, rejected by many nations, and in need of constant defense against the pressures of global languages such as English.

If we accept this notion, we see a relation between our two original questions. It is true that Hebrew was easily "revived", because it never died. But, given its situation in the Middle East, surrounded by Arabic-speaking Muslim states, and as a small language among the large global languages competing to dominate the world's language map, it still seems a minor variety even in the nation where it is no longer a minority,[75] its speakers sharing the kind of sense of endangerment that has faced Jews throughout history. We can then easily understand the concern of Hebrew activists for its survival. True, it is no more threatened than other small languages, but two millennia of minority status do not lead to confidence in the future.[76]

History or sociolinguistics?

Whatever its origins and however it has changed over three millennia, a variety labeled "Hebrew" has maintained a central role in the ever-changing language ecology of the Jewish people. Since the Babylonian exile, Hebrew has shared its place with numerous other varieties adopted through conquest or forced or voluntary migration. The first of these was Aramaic, an imperial language in much of the Middle East, but developed as a vernacular in Babylon, where it became a language of the Talmud, and in Judea, where it was adopted in contact with returned exiles and competed with the Greek introduced by Hellenistic and Roman rule. The next major addition was Arabic, with *Dhimmi* status discouraging use by Jews of the Qur'anic Classical variety and leading to the development of spoken Judeo-Arabic and written Middle Arabic. In Christian Europe, isolation and anti-Jewish policies led to the development of Jewish varieties of language such as Judeo-French, Judezmo, Knaanic, and Yiddish. Emancipation brought about the weakening of these languages, replacing them by the local standard languages such as French, Russian, German, and English. But most of these Jewish varieties continued in a diglossic relationship with Hebrew, which resumed its role as a hegemonic variety after the return to Zion and the establishment of the State of Israel. Certainly, it is a different language from that spoken in biblical times, but all languages change, and, after three millennia, there are sure to be major differences. But the core remains. In the meantime, Jews have been changed by their acquisition and use of many other languages, and continue to be individually plurilingual and multilingual as a people. As a continually threatened people, though, it is understandable that some people still ask if Hebrew too is endangered.

Without a doubt, I have learned a great deal about the history of the Jewish people in writing this book. Of course, there remain a great number of unresolved questions – too many cases when my conclusion was *Teiku* – the issue remains uncertain – until we find more conclusive evidence. Some of the most glaring are the origin of Hebrew (did Abraham speak it?), the replacement of Hebrew by Aramaic and later Greek (when between the sixth century BCE and the second CE?), the status of languages introduced by conversion (in Arabia, Africa, and Asia), the disputed origins of Yiddish, the criteria for recognizing a Jewish language, and the potential endangerment of Modern Israel Hebrew. Or it may well be that these are unresolvable questions: competing solutions have been proposed, but it may well be that there will never be evidence to answer them conclusively. But the general picture is quite clear: Jewish history has shown short periods of relative peace and calm and shorter periods of prosperity, broken by regular persecution and expulsion, and each has modified the sociolinguistic ecology.

But what have I learned about sociolinguistics? Has this survey added to my understanding of the nature of language change and maintenance? The answer is twofold: it has confirmed the critical importance of the social environment of a community in its changes in language patterns. Essentially, the changes we have been tracing depended on changes in social situation and external environment. The main driving force leading to the addition of new varieties and the dropping of old ones has been pragmatic – economic or political. As they migrated – voluntarily in search of better social or economic conditions, or involuntarily as they were expelled because of their religion or otherness – Jews generally moved to a new variety of "co-territorial language" provided only that they were not isolated or prevented from reasonable social mobility. As Joshua Fishman has pointed out in his classic early study of language loyalty in the United States,[77] only those groups denied (such as Native Americans or Mexicans) or denying themselves (such as the Amish or Hasidim) upward social mobility and the social and linguistic assimilation that accompanied it did not lose their heritage languages. Thus, it was generally the history that drove the sociolinguistics, leading to a constant reshaping of Jewish sociolinguistic ecology.

But there was a counterforce in the Jewish case: an ideological motivation arising from religious belief and, in modern times, from a secular ethnic pursuit of identity that was expressed in the liturgical and literary status of Hebrew, supported for 2,000 years by religious education and transformed in the modern world into the re-establishment of Hebrew as a living national language as a key component of political Zionism. Without this, Jews might well have switched to Aramaic, as they almost did in Babylon, or to Greek, as they did in Alexandria, or to Judeo-Arabic, as they nearly did in the Islamic world, or to Yiddish or Judezmo or English in the modern world.

There are other groups with this counterforce – religion or ethnic identity – whose language maintenance depends on beliefs that resist pragmatic economic and social pressure, so that this seemingly exceptional case has a lesson for others who wish to preserve or even restore heritage languages. So, while the main lesson for me was the force of non-linguistic events and situations, the study confirmed that ideological beliefs still can play a significant role in language policy, as it did in maintaining Hebrew at the apex of the languages of the Jewish people.

Appendix Estimated current status of Jewish languages[1]

Name	EGIDS[2]	Country	Speakers	Year[3]	Source(s)[4]
Chuadit, Judeo-Provençal	10	Provence	4,850,000	1998	
Hebrew[5]	1	Israel	5,000 (10,000)	1986	Van Cleve
Israeli Sign Language	5	Israel		(2008)	(Meir and Sandler, 2008)
Italkian, Judeo-Italian (various dialects)	8a	Italy	200		Salminen, 1999
Judeo-Alsatian	9	Israel, Alsace	Few	2013	Starck, personal communication
Judeo-Arabic, Iraqi[6]	7	Israel	100,000	1994	
Judeo-Arabic, Iraqi	8b	Iraq	120	1992	Mustafi
			(?)	(2011)	(Yentob, BBC *Today*, November 28, 2011)
Judeo-Arabic, Iraqi	7	India, Iraq, UK	50,000		
Judeo-Arabic, Libyan (Tripolitanian)	7	Israel	30,000	1994	Mustafi
Judeo-Arabic, Libyan (Tripolitanian)	7	Italy	5,000		
Judeo-Arabic, Moroccan	7	Israel	250,000	1997	Mustafi
Judeo-Arabic, Moroccan	7	Morocco	8,930	2000	
Judeo-Arabic, Tunisian	7	Israel	45,000	1995	Mustafi
Judeo-Arabic, Tunisian	7	Tunisia	1,000 + [7]	2013	News reports
Judeo-Arabic, Tunisian	7	France	? [8]		
Judeo-Arabic, Yemenite	6a	Israel	50,000	1995	Kara
Judeo-Arabic, Yemenite	6a	Yemen	1000	1995	Mustafi
Judeo-Arabic, Yemenite	7	Israel	4,230	2001	
Judeo-Aramaic, Lishán Didán, Azerbaijani	7	Azerbaijan, Georgia	200		
Judeo-Aramaic, Lishán Didán, Azerbaijani	8b	Israel	20	2004	Mustafi
Judeo-Aramaic, Lishán Didán, Barzani	7	Israel	7,500	1999	Mustafi[11]
Judeo-Aramaic, Lishana Deni[9]	7	Israel	10,000	1999	Mustafi[11]
Judeo-Aramaic, Lishanid Noshan, Hulaulà, Kurdit[10]	7	Israel	2,000	1992	Podolsky[12] (Chetrit, 1985)
Judeo-Berber	7	Israel	200	2007	Salminen, 2007
Judeo-Crimean Tatar, Krimchak	8b	Ukraine	59,800	2000	
Judeo-Georgian	6a	Israel			

Language	EGIDS	Location	Population	Year	Source
Judeo-Georgian	6a	Georgia	20,000	1995	Wikipedia
Judeo-Malayalam		Israel	8,000 pop. (few dozen speakers)		(Wikipedia)
Judeo-Persian		USA			
Judeo-Tajik, Bukharan		USA			
Judeo-Tajik, Bukharan, Bukhori	6	Uzbekistan	10,000	1995	Mustafi
Judeo-Tajik, Bukharan, Bukhori	7	Israel	50,000	1995	
Judeo-Tat, Juhuri	4	Israel	70,000	1998	
Judeo-Tat, Juhuri	6a	Azerbaijan	24,000	1989	Census
Judeo-Tat, Juhuri		Russian Federation	2,000	2010	Census
Karaim	8b	Israel	0		
Karaim	8b	Lithuania	50		
Karaim	8b	Ukraine	6		
Ladino, Haketia	7	(Moroccan Jews)			
Ladino, Judezmo	4	Israel	100,000	1985	Wikipedia
	(7)[13]		(72,000)	(2013)	(Schwarzwald, personal communication)
Ladino, Judezmo	7	Greece, Puerto Rico, USA	2000	2007	Salminen, 2007
Ladino, Judezmo	7	Turkey	10,000 (7,000)	(2013)	(Wikipedia)
Ladino, Judezmo		USA	3,500	2013	Wikipedia
Ladino, Judezmo		France	2,500	2013	Wikipedia
Ladino, Judezmo		Greece, Brazil, UK	1,000 each	2013	Wikipedia
Marathi (Bene Israel)	7	Israel	12,000	2013	Wikipedia
Marathi (Bene Israel)		India			
Russian		Israel	750,000	1999	Mustafi
Tsarfatic, Judeo-French	10	France	35	1971	Wexler
Yevanic, Judeo-Greek	9	Greece			
Yiddish	4	All	1,505,000	1986	
Yiddish	4	Israel	215,000	1991	
Yiddish	4	Ukraine	634,000		
Yiddish	4	Romania	1,100	2002	Recognized[14]

(*cont.*)

Name	EGIDS[2]	Country	Speakers	Year[3]	Source(s)[4]
Yiddish	4	Sweden	4,000	2000	Recognized
Yiddish	4	Latvia	50,000 (0 ?)	1979 (2013)	
Yiddish	4	USA	148,000	2009	Census
Yiddish		UK	30,000	2002	Shamas, personal communication
Yiddish Sign Language	6a	Israel	?		

Notes

NOTES ON PREFACE

1 Spolsky (1983).
2 Spolsky and Cooper (1991).
3 Spolsky and Shohamy (1999).
4 Fishman *et al.* (1964).

NOTES ON CHAPTER 1

1 Fishman (1991b) presents a graded intergenerational disruption scale to classify language endangerment. Krauss (1998) describes the fate of the 200 or so native North American languages, only thirty-four of which still had young native speakers.
2 *Haaretz* (29 February 2012). Similar developments are reported in Europe; in Denmark and elsewhere, universities are increasingly teaching graduate courses in English, and there are such programs in some Israeli institutions. Even more shockingly for the defenders of Hebrew, in January 2013 the senate of the Hebrew University changed its regulations to allow students to write doctoral dissertations in either Hebrew or English; previously they had required special permission to write in English, a provision sought recently by half the candidates. And in the same month, the Technion (the site of the 1913 victory of Hebrew) announced a new program for first-year students that will offer them content courses in Russian while they are learning Hebrew intensively.
3 All the *Englishes*, as Kachru (1986) would put it.
4 There are probably more speakers of English in India than in all the so-called English-speaking countries together.
5 Myhill (2004: 13) suggests that Jews define membership of their group by personal ancestry and religious affiliation; language and land are also relevant but not central variables, he claims, though I would argue that they have become central to Zionism and Israelis. Later, I will discuss the issue of black Jews, whose existence challenges any definition.
6 Spolsky (2004).
7 Spolsky (2009a).
8 Spolsky (2012).
9 Haugen (1971, 1972a, 1972b).
10 And what about the West Bank?
11 Gumperz (1968).
12 Fishman and Herasimchuk (1969).

13 Labov (1966).
14 Hymes (1974: 74).
15 Hymes (1974: 470). Xu (2004) is a Chinese sociolinguist who agrees that one should start with the speech community rather than the variety.
16 For instance, for an observant Jew, *musaf* is the additional prayer service on Sabbaths and holidays; for a non-observant Israeli, it is the weekly newspaper supplement.
17 There are many Thai agricultural workers brought in for short terms, some of whom stay on as restaurant workers. The caregivers are commonly from the Philippines, brought in originally to look after crippled soldiers and now especially employed for the elderly.
18 *Hasidism* started in the seventeenth century in eastern Europe. They are Haredi, but each sect (known by the town of their first leader) has different customs and policies.
19 Central Bureau of Statistics (2013).
20 The questionnaires were administered in a one-hour personal interview in Hebrew, Arabic, and Russian to about 7,500 people aged twenty and over representing about 4.5 million people in that age bracket (excluding residents of old-age homes, hospitals for the chronically ill, prisons, Israelis abroad for more than a year, diplomats, new immigrants who had arrived less than six months before the interview, and Bedouin living outside boundaries of localities). Those sampled were defined as five population groups: Arabs in East Jerusalem; Arabs elsewhere; immigrants who had arrived in 1990 or later; immigrants who had arrived earlier; and Israeli-born Jews. There were seven age groups, and men and women.
21 It is not explained what happened to speakers of other languages, such as Georgian.
22 There has been controversy concerning the proportion of immigrants from the former Soviet Union who are not Jewish.
23 Chiswick (1993); Chiswick and Miller (1992).
24 Fishman, Cooper, and Ma (1971) describe a community in which English and Spanish had distinct roles.
25 The 2011 Social Survey asks about family, friends, and employment, but not education and religion.
26 Hary (2009: 38) points out that it is not in effect a dichotomous choice between two varieties but, rather, a continuum along which speakers move: he suggests the term *continuglossia*. The notion follows the work of creolists on what is called the post-creole continuum, in which there is a spectrum of varieties ranging from the super-strate official language at the upper boundary to the basolect at the lower (Bickerton, 1975). This model, he convincingly argues, is true of Judeo-Arabic.
27 Schwartz, Kozminsky, and Leiken (2009).
28 Kopeliovich (2009, 2011).
29 Kraemer *et al.* (1995).
30 Levin, Shohamy, and Spolsky (2003).
31 Stavans, Olshtain, and Goldzweig (2009).
32 Baumel (2002).
33 Ben-Rafael (1994).
34 Schwartz and Katzir (2012: 1592).
35 Seckbach and Cooper (1977).
36 Rosenbaum *et al.* (1977).
37 Herman (1961).

38 Suleiman (2011) notes its use in conversations between Israelis and Arabs from the West Bank.
39 Ben-Rafael (1994).
40 Hary (2009: 49).
41 Amara (2010).
42 Amara (2002).
43 Nadel and Fishman (1977).
44 Spolsky and Cooper (1991).
45 Trumper-Hecht (2009).
46 Walter (2003, 2008).
47 More details of this struggle are given in the last chapter.
48 Ammon (2001). A recent study (Bolton and Kuteeva, 2012) reports that using English is a "pragmatic reality" in the sciences in a Swedish university they have studied, but is a "parallel language" with Swedish in the humanities and social sciences. There are Danish and Italian universities that teach graduate courses in English, and Dutch universities that use English at the undergraduate level.
49 Kheimets and Epstein (2005); Ram (2006); Spolsky and Shohamy (2001b).
50 Kreindler *et al.* (1995).
51 There are indications of changes in this, as Israeli courts have held that Haredim should no longer have automatic exemption from army service; this was a disputed issue in the coalition negotiations that followed the 2013 Israeli general election.
52 The second language offered is commonly Arabic; Russian is increasingly the third choice; English is still quite rare.
53 Spolsky and Cooper (1991).
54 Cooper and Carpenter (1976).
55 Deutsch (2001) describes the role of English in the education and professional life of Israeli lawyers.
56 Fishman (1991b).
57 Bakshi (2011) makes the case that Arabic is not really an official language, but he assumes that "official" means much more than it does in practice.
58 Allony Fainberg (1977, 1983) studied the acceptance of Academy terms for automobile parts, showing that army drivers and technical school students were more likely to know them than driving instructors and mechanics; Hofman (1974) looked at the use of Academy terms by psychologists. Another study was that by Nahir (1974).

NOTES ON CHAPTER 2

1 Spolsky (2011) gives details of Fishman, Ferguson, and the other founders of the field.
2 Fishman, Cooper, and Ma (1971) have an account of this major study of a bilingual community.
3 See Blom and Gumperz (1972); Joshua Fishman, personal communication, August 1980.
4 Kuzar (2001) somewhat irreverently suggests that some senior Israeli linguists believe that claiming Modern Hebrew has reached a final form ready to be studied is equivalent to assuming Zionism has completed its task.

5 Harris (1996) has collected a number of classic essays on this topic. Johansson (2005) provides an up-to-date and cautious account of current evidence on the issue. McNeill (2012) proposes a theory of the origin of language that includes both gesture (Sign languages) and speech.

6 Tallerman and Gibson (2011).

7 For example, Lass (1997).

8 Becanus (1569).

9 Lewis (1999: 57). Kvergić argued that the Turkish word for "sun" was based on the exclamation of an individual seeing the sun.

10 Lass (1997: 162).

11 In spite of these difficulties, linguists generally assume the existence of language families.

12 Gianto (1999).

13 Cohen (1979).

14 Stone (2011).

15 Wellhausen (1878).

16 The political scientist Michael Walzer (2012: xiv) describes the difficulty of those of us who are not Bible scholars: "The scholarly literature about these questions is vast, and the disagreements among distinguished and immensely learned scholars are breathtaking."

17 Douglas (1999).

18 Loftus (1996).

19 For example, Finkelstein (2007b).

20 Finkelstein and Silberman (2002: 23).

21 Hezser (2010a).

22 Stone (2011).

23 Finkelstein and Silberman (2002: 90).

24 Broshi (2001: chap. 5).

25 Gzella (2011a: vii).

26 Sáenz-Badillos (1996).

27 Dothan and Dothan (1992).

28 For details on Phoenician, see Gzella (2011b).

29 Greenberg (1950).

30 For a summary of the features of Ugaritic, see Guanto (2011); Sivan (2001).

31 Schniedewind and Hunt (2007).

32 Rabin (1958).

33 Chomsky (1957: 34).

34 Finkelstein (2007b).

35 Hess (1993).

36 Gzella (2011c: 77) says that ostraca give evidence of a northern variety (Samarian) before 722 BCE and a southern variety (Judah), out of which Classical Hebrew emerged.

37 Only recently have linguists started to break free of the implication of distinct and named languages, and looked at the existence of code switching, mixed varieties, and what is called "receptive multilingualism" or "intercomprehensibility", of the kind that enables speakers of Scandinavian, Romance, and Slavic language varieties to

converse with each other. This may well have been the case with the Canaanite dialects.

38 Fellman (1985: 28) says it can be "safely assumed" that from 1000 BCE to 722 BCE there was a standard Hebrew, written and spoken in the capital and the court and comprehensible to speakers of the other dialects.

39 The myths of the Ten Lost Tribes have been used to support arguments for the Anglo-Israel (British Israelite) movement, for the Jewish origin of tribes found in Asia, Africa, and the Americas, and for the Black Jewish claims discussed below.

40 Finkelstein (2007a: 16).

41 Porten (1968).

42 Botta (2009).

43 Rosenberg (2004).

44 Finkelstein and Silberman (2002).

45 Finkelstein and Silberman (2002).

46 Finkelstein and Silberman (2002: 306–7).

47 Van Seters (1999).

48 Finkelstein and Silberman (2002: 298).

49 Ahn (2010) compares the Babylonian exile to other cases including modern ones, but does not deal with language shift.

50 Hary (2009: 6fn and 7fn) objects to the term "non-Jew" and the use of Weinreich's term "co-territorial" language; for the former he suggests being more precise, but here one would need to say something such as "members of other religious, ethnic, and national groups". In fact, the term "Jew" is even more difficult, as I have used it loosely to include early (e.g. residents of Judah and Judea) and late (secular or religious, identified or self-identifying) Jewish people. He prefers "majority" to "co-territorial", but surely what Weinreich wanted to do was to include any other language, whether majority or minority, spoken outside the Jewish community even if it was also used within it.

51 Council of Europe (2001).

52 Dozier (1966).

53 Kulick (1992).

54 Weinreich (1956, 1980, 2008).

55 Garbell (1965).

56 Or receptive multilingualism.

57 Weinreich (1980).

58 Cooper (1982: 31).

59 Paper (1982).

60 Weinreich (1953).

61 Kulick (1992).

62 Spolsky and Cooper (1991).

63 Spolsky and Amara (1986).

NOTES ON CHAPTER 3

1 They are also mainly Israelis and Zionists.

2 For example, He Kupenga Hao i te Reo Māori (2000); Lamy (1977); Statistics New Zealand (1997).

3 A census might ask "What languages are spoken in this family?" or "What is the mother tongue of the residents in this household?". Each would have a different answer, biasing the results considerably.

4 For instance, Judeo-Spanish is also known as Ladino, Dudezhmo, Judezmo, and Spanyolit. Using one name may leave out those people who use another. The problem is especially serious with small minority languages.

5 Some of these are discussed by de Vries (1990); Thompson (1974).

6 Duncan (1931).

7 Petrie and Spiegelberg (1896).

8 Young (1977).

9 For a discussion of the languages of Jesus, see Gerhardsson (1961).

10 Wellhausen (1878).

11 This notion that the Bible represented selected late ideologies is developed by Stone (2011).

12 Person (2010).

13 Young, Rezetko, and Ehrenvard (2008).

14 Young, Rezetko, and Ehrenvard (2008).

15 Lord (1981).

16 Delitzsch (1914b).

17 Delitzsch (1914a).

18 Charpin (2011).

19 Byrne (2007).

20 Rollston (2006).

21 Josephus (1737 [78]).

22 See the work of the psychologist Kahneman (2011). This position is also taken by Abu El-Haj (2012) in questioning genetic studies by Israeli and Jewish geneticists.

23 Finkelstein and Silberman (2002: 301).

24 Fraade (1992: 32).

25 Southwood (2011) provides an excellent analysis of Nehemiah's warning, based on a useful analysis of the relation between identity and language in this and similar cases.

26 Was there national identity then? Certainly not in the modern sense.

27 Southwood (2011).

28 The institution of the reading, whether of the Pentateuch or the Book of Deuteronomy, followed a Persian recognition of local laws that did not conflict with imperial law (Watts, 2001).

29 Jewish Publication Society (1982).

30 Showing the strength of custom, the practice has continued until the present among Yemenite Jews.

31 Kugel and Greer (1986: 28).

32 Kottsieper (2007).

33 This of course ignores the possibility that speakers of Aramaic and Hebrew shared the mutual intelligibility of, say, speakers of Norwegian and Swedish.

34 Rabin (1958).

35 Yadin and Naveh (1989: 9).

36 Kottsieper (2007).

37 The maid's exceptionality is supported by the fact that, elsewhere in the Talmud (Tractate *Moed Katan* 17a), she is reported to have seen a man striking his grown son,

which she interpreted as setting a stumbling block before the blind by inciting him to retaliate, which would have been punishable by death (Exodus 21: 15). As a result, she excommunicated him – a ban that the rabbis respected for three years. But, if she knew archaic Hebrew, who would she use it with if it were no longer spoken?

38 Halliday (1976) defines an "anti-language" as a special form of language generated by an "anti-society". His three examples are criminal jargons of Elizabethan England, Calcutta, and Polish prisons. He concludes that literature can also be a high anti-language.

39 Schniedewind (1999).

NOTES ON CHAPTER 4

1 *Ashkenaz* refers to the Jewish culture that developed in medieval central Europe and spread to include east Europe. It is to be contrasted with *Sepharad*, the culture that developed in Spain and spread after the expulsion to north Africa and the eastern Mediterranean. I will use the Hebrew adjectives *Ashkenazi* and *Sephardi*. *Loshn koydesh* is the Yiddish term: the Hebrew is *leshon hakodesh*.

2 Gruen (2002).

3 Lewy (1938) questions the historical accuracy of this account, suggesting that the "Jewish magician" is cited to provide support for the philosophical views that Clearchus presented as representative of Indian wise men.

4 Josephus (97: 1.22).

5 Gruen (2002: 3).

6 Gruen (2002: 6).

7 Gruen (2010: 724).

8 Van der Horst (2010: 690).

9 There were two Jewish responses to the Septuagint. One was to proclaim the "miracle" of the seventy elders agreeing on a single version. The other was to set a fast day (no longer observed) to mark the translation, which allowed access to a single interpretation of readers without a teacher.

10 Dines (2004: 27) points out that there is little certainty about date or authors. *The Letter of Aristeus*, which claims a pagan author but appears to have been written in the second century BCE by a Jew, has the story of the seventy-two authors.

11 Dines (2004: 112) discusses the various views on the nature of the Greek used in the translation.

12 Rajak (2011) suggests that the Greek of the translation maintained Jewish identity by its Hebraisms.

13 Rabin (1968) argues that Jews there were in fact bilingual, if stronger in Greek.

14 Weitzman (1989) points out that even if Philo did not know Hebrew (and he appeared to have access to some who did) he had a high regard for the language.

15 Lieberman (1942); van der Horst (2010: 690–1).

16 Richey (2012).

17 Van der Horst (2010: 691).

18 Josephus (97: 1.9).

19 Babylonian Talmud, Tractate *Menahot* 64b, Tractate *Sotah* 49b, Tractate *Baba Kama* 82b.

20 Sperber (2012: 116). Sperber's book is a masterful summary of the vast literature on Greek in the Talmud.
21 Babylonian Talmud, Tractate *Sotah* 49b.
22 Sperber (2012: 115).
23 Sperber (2012: 183; emphasis in original).
24 Spolsky (2004).
25 Babylonian Talmud, Tractate *Sotah* 49b.
26 The earlier rabbis responsible for the Mishnah (the core rabbinical development of Bible interpretation) were called *Tannaim*; the next generation were called *Amoraim*.
27 This gender bias in education, still true among many observant Jews, has had important sociolinguistic consequences, especially when reinforced by a Hasidic tendency to keep males at Yeshivah and allow women to go out to work. Thus, among Satmar Hasidim in the United States, men are said to prefer Yiddish and women to speak Hasidic English (Fader, 2009).
28 Fraade (2011: 34).
29 Cited by Fraade (2011: 36).
30 Fraade (2011: 39).
31 There are some who argue for a later date of composition (Ben Zvi, 1991).
32 Fraade (2011: 59).
33 Sokoloff and Yahalom (1985).
34 Sokoloff has edited a dictionary of Babylonian Talmudic Aramaic (2002b) and a dictionary of Jewish Palestinian Aramaic (2002a); he has also published a lexicon of Syriac.
35 Cook (2010: 360).
36 Cook (2010: 360).
37 Lumpkin (2009).
38 "Diglossia" is a term used by Charles Ferguson when two distinct varieties of the same language (e.g. Classical and Vernacular Arabic, German and Swiss German) fill different roles, one more formal (H or high) and one less (L or low), in the same speech community, and extended by Joshua Fishman to cases in which the varieties are different languages (e.g. English and Spanish in the Jersey City barrio, Hebrew and Yiddish in the Pale of Settlement).
39 Cook (2010: 362).
40 Lim (2010).
41 Schwartz (1995).
42 "He imposed it as a decree upon Joseph when he went forth from the language of Egypt; I heard a language I knew not."
43 "For you are sent not to a people of unintelligible speech and difficult language but to the House of Israel."
44 "Deliver my soul, O Lord, from lying lips and from a deceitful tongue." Hebrew *safot* (lips) and *leshon* (tongue) both also mean "languages". Not Psalm 119: 1, as Schwartz (1995) has it.
45 Segal (1927). Born in Lithuania, Segal studied and taught at Oxford, was rabbi of some English congregations, and became professor of Hebrew at the Hebrew University in 1926.

46 A "calque" is a loan translation; a calque language would be one in which the grammar of one language had been relexified with words from another. Relexification is discussed again in Chapter 12 in a theory that Yiddish was a relexified form of Sorbian.

47 Schwartz (1995).

48 Kutscher (1974). Kutscher was professor of Hebrew at the Hebrew University.

49 Such as Spolsky (1985).

50 Schwartz (1995: 17).

51 Bar-Asher (2010). Professor of Hebrew Language at the Hebrew University, he is also president of the Hebrew Language Academy.

52 Smelik (2010: 124). A Dutch Bible scholar teaching at University College London.

53 Perez Fernandez (1997). He taught at the University of Granada.

54 The Tannaim were earlier rabbis, the Amoraim the next generation.

55 Perez Fernandez (1997: 2).

56 Mishnah *Eduyot* 1.3.

57 Xu (2004), a sociolinguist who studies the relationship between Chinese varieties, has stressed this approach to the study of speech communities.

58 Jackendoff (2010a, 2010b, 2012).

59 Teeter (2010).

60 Teeter (2010: 1204).

61 Talmon (1975); Ulrich (1992).

62 Tigchelaar (2010: 169).

63 Talmon (1975: 336).

64 Talmon (1975: 381).

65 Friedman (1997).

66 Kugel (2008).

67 An exception is the journalist Neil Altman, active also as a Jew for Jesus, who wrote some newspaper articles arguing, unconvincingly, that the scrolls are of medieval origin.

68 Golb (1996).

69 Vanderkam (2010). Taylor (2012) reasserts the importance of the Essenes and their connections to Qumran.

70 Frey (2010). One is reminded of the Shakers, who also banned procreation.

71 Levine (2000) provides a useful guide.

72 Eck (2003).

73 Sperber (2012: 196).

74 Halevi (Kirtchuk) (2005): 492.

75 *Midrashim* constitute a form of rabbinic literature that interprets biblical texts, either in the form of *aggadot* (stories) or to establish *Halacha* (Jewish law and practice). Stern (1986, 1996) explores the relevance of Midrash to modern literary theory.

76 Bar-Asher (1999).

77 See, for instance, the dictionaries edited by Sokoloff (2002a, 2002b).

78 Hoyland (2003).

79 Smelik (2010).

80 Smelik (2010: 133).

NOTES ON CHAPTER 5

1 A term that assumes different status and functions for each variety, or if not separate varieties, points on a continuum.
2 Levine (2000).
3 Or even beyond, if you accept the evidence of Evans and Ratliff (2012) of a long transition during which Judaism, Christianity, and Islam shared a culture.
4 A recent study by Botticini and Eckstein (2012) argues convincingly that the introduction of compulsory education for Jewish boys had major effects on the demography and economics of post-destruction Jewry; those families that did not participate were likely to assimilate or convert to Christianity or Islam (explaining the major reduction in Jewish population), but those who did acquired literacy and other skills that prepared then for professional and commercial success.
5 Well described by Fraade (1992).
6 Covered by Levine (2000).
7 Dio (1927 [230]).
8 The Kitos War was the revolt from 115 to 117 CE, named after the Roman general, Lucius Quietus, who crushed it. It also affected some Diaspora communities.
9 Boyarin (2004).
10 Coneybeare (1910).
11 Montefiore (2011).
12 Davis (1983: 280).
13 Fraade (1992).
14 Fraade (1992) argues against the view that the Targum was needed to deal with the loss of Hebrew, as the Septuagint was believed to be needed in Alexandria by Jews who spoke Greek and did not know Hebrew.
15 Fraade (1992: 256).
16 The *hazzan* was also responsible for training young boys in synagogue ritual.
17 Fraade (1992: 265).
18 Fraade (1992: 273).
19 Fraade (1992: 274).
20 Fraade (1992: 284).
21 Breuer (2006).
22 The Tannaim were the early rabbis.
23 The exceptions were in remote and mountainous areas, where both Jews and Christians continued to use it until modern times. Garbell (1965) records a Jewish dialect of Aramaic that survived in Azerbaijan; one of my students reported that her parents recognized it as the variety spoken in their village. Maronite Christians in Israel were recently reported to be teaching Aramaic to their children and seeking official recognition of the language.
24 Goodblatt (2010).
25 Broshi (2001).
26 Safrai (1994: 446).
27 Goodblatt (2010).
28 Dauphin (1998).
29 Goodblatt (2010).
30 Boyarin (2004).
31 Zangenberg and van de Zande (2010).

32 Killebrew (2010).
33 Hezser (2010b).
34 Hezser (2010c). Raphael (2013) considers Josephus one of the first examples of a Jew trying to pass in the Gentile world.
35 Bakhos (2010).
36 Jaffee (2001).
37 Reif (2010).
38 Reif (2010).
39 Horbury and Noy (1992).
40 Levine (2000: 113).
41 Hezser (2010c).
42 Levine (2000: 195).
43 Levine (2000: 196).
44 Shinan (1987).
45 Fine (2011: 444).
46 Noy (1997, 2005b). Other inscriptions in western Europe are described by Noy (2005a). Noy has listed these inscriptions.
47 Blommaert (2010).
48 Dursteler (2012) describes the rich multilingualism of the Mediterranean in the early modern period, citing a 1608 statement that in the Piazza San Marco you can "heare all the languages of Christendome, besides some that are spoken by the barbarous Ethnickes". Thirty years later, he reports, a French traveler noted thirteen languages being spoken at a dinner he attended. About the same time, in the tiny ghetto of Venice, each of the four crowded synagogues had a different language, and a Haggadah was printed in four languages – Hebrew, Judeo-Spanish, Yiddish, and Judeo-Venetian.
49 Delsing (2007).
50 Although linguists write grammars that describe distinct languages, as I mentioned before, Jackendoff (2010a, 2012) has shown how the parallel architecture model can be modified to account for code switching and variety mixing.
51 That is, before the First Crusade signaled the beginning of regular pogroms, expulsions, and persecution.
52 As the young men in Papua New Guinea showed off the Tok Pisin they had learned working in the plantations when they returned to their remote villages.
53 Like the Arab merchants we heard speaking Hebrew to each other as they sat outside their stalls in the *shuk* of the Old City of Jerusalem.
54 In Yap, Kulick reports that the villagers had not noticed that children under twelve spoke only Tok Pisin. Kopeliovich notes that immigrants from the former Soviet Union complained that their children were mixing Hebrew and Russian in a way that they did themselves.
55 Hary (2009) suggests the term "religiolect" for these varieties.
56 Rather, varieties, for Jewish Palestinian Aramaic was different from Jewish Babylonian Aramaic.
57 Other names are *Yevanic* and *Romaniote*.
58 Bowman (2010).
59 Lieberman (1942).
60 Bowman (2010).

61 Bowman (2010: 61).
62 Fine (2011).
63 Levine (2000).
64 The different approaches of these two Yeshivot are preserved in the Talmud in the large number of disputes between Rav and Samuel.
65 Levine (2000: 536–8).
66 A major fast day commemorating the destruction of the Temple.
67 Levine (2000: 474).
68 Bregman (1982).
69 Levine (2000: 552).
70 Novella 146, issued in 553, was once assumed to support Greek-speaking versus Hebrew-speaking Jews in the choice of language of prayer, but is now more widely believed to aim at the conversion of both groups to Christianity. Another theory, however, is that, as long as Jews could read the Hebrew original, they were assumed to have an advantage in disputes with Christians who had access only to the Greek translation. Rutgers (2002).
71 The most recent and complete is that by Sokoloff (2002b).
72 Sokoloff and Yahalom (1985).
73 De Lange (2005: 410).
74 De Lange (2005).
75 De Lange (1996).
76 De Lange (1996).

NOTES ON CHAPTER 6

1 Cush, which occurs in the Bible about fifty times, is translated in the Septuagint as Ethiopia, but may refer to Nubia or include Arabia and Yemen. Although there is no archeological evidence, there is support in biblical references to small Jewish settlements, according to Kaplan (1992).
2 Ellul (1985). Jacques Ellul, a French philosopher and sociologist, was described as a Christian anarchist. He shared Bat Ye'or's attitude to what she called *dhimmitude*. Bat Ye'or is the pseudonym of Egyptian-born Gisèle Littman, who is considered Islamophobic by many scholars.
3 Ye'or (1985).
4 Bloom (2010).
5 Lassner (1993) traces Jewish and medieval Islamic versions of the visit of the Queen of Sheba.
6 Goitein (1974: 4).
7 Newby (2010).
8 Gil (2004: 7).
9 Newby (2010: 359).
10 Stillman (1979: 15–16).
11 The sources are unclear as to where Paul went, whether to Nabatea or to Arabia Felix, and whether he preached to Jews or Gentiles (Barnett, 2008: 80–1).
12 Newby (2010).
13 Jewish Encyclopedia of 1906.
14 Nebes and Stein (2008: 145).

15 Wellhausen (1878).
16 Any expression of doubt is vigorously opposed by current Islamic leaders.
17 Kalisch, a teenaged convert to Islam, was appointed to his position as professor of Islamic theology in 2004. He has remained in it even after his heretical statements and subsequent renunciation of Islam in 2008.
18 Kalisch (2008a, 2008b).
19 Crone (1980: 15) makes this clear.
20 Stillman (1979: 115–18). There are scholars who argue that this "ordinance" is a later composition to justify the treatment of the Jews.
21 Gil (2004: 10).
22 Newby (1971).
23 Abu Ja'far Muhammad ibn Jarir al-Tabari, the ninth-century historian and Qur'anic commentator, believed it was Persia (Gil 2004: 5).
24 The harsh treatment of the Banū Quraysa, who were annihilated, is discussed by Kister (1986).
25 Stillman (1979: 16).
26 Stillman (1979: 19).
27 Friedman (2012).
28 Ye'or (1985: 49).
29 Blau (1965, 2002). Den Heijer (2012) points out that the study of what is now also called Mixed Arabic includes uses of the variety by other minorities besides Jews.
30 Gil (2004: 22).
31 Newby (2010: 360).
32 Adler (1907: 47).
33 Adler (1907: 48).
34 Doughty (1921: 127).
35 Adler (1907: 63).
36 Newby (2010: 359).
37 Johnson (1987: 166).
38 Lecker (1995).
39 Ben Zvi (1963: 16).
40 Goitein (1974: 47).
41 Bowersock (2011).
42 Robin (2003).
43 We find the same uncertainty in the account of the conversion of the Khazars.
44 Tobi (1999: 42–4).
45 A translation is printed by Stillman (1979: 233–46).
46 Tobi (1999: 47). This contrasts with the Ethiopian communities, whose Bible was in Ge'ez; they spoke Amharic or Tigrinya depending on where they came from, and maintained only limited observances until brought into contact with Halachic Judaism in the nineteenth and twentieth centuries.
47 Tobi (1999: 7).
48 Tobi (1999: 49).
49 Meir-Glitzenstein (2011) describes the development of a popular mythic account of this event.
50 Morag (1972).

51 Lewis (2009). *Ethnologue* is the standard listing of languages of the world; while originally focused on Christian Bible translation, its annual editions are now recognized by most linguists as authoritative.

52 Kaplan (1992).

53 Polotsky (1964) studied the words of Aramaic origin in the Ethiopian Bible, which was translated from the Greek of the Septuagint. He believes they are of Jewish rather than Christian origin, suggesting the influence of Judaism on Aksum culture.

54 "Beta Israel" is the term they use for themselves. The name "Falasha" (of doubtful etymology) was first used in the fifteenth century, and the term "Kayla" in the seventeenth century.

55 Kaplan (1992) agrees in many of his views with Quirin (1992).

56 Quirin (1992) presents this analysis after detailed study. He notes that Christian Ethiopians considered themselves Israelites (*esra'elawi*, as descended from Sheba and Solomon), and called the Beta Israel who rejected Jesus *ayhud* (Jews).

57 Beckingham and Huntingford (1954: 54–5).

58 There is said to be some DNA evidence of early Jewish ancestry. Israeli rabbis have ruled that Beta Israel, including the so-called "Falashmura", who underwent forced conversion to Christianity, are fully Jewish.

59 Parfitt (2013), a scholar who has worked with Beta Israel and Lemba and other similar modern groups, provides a recent thorough study especially of historical myths and beliefs about black Jews.

60 Parfitt (2013: 149–69) summarizes the history of white and black group claims. Bruder (2012), inspired in 2001 by a TV program in which Parfitt described the Lemba, carried out fieldwork and wrote a doctoral dissertation under his direction; her monograph describes the various black groups in Africa who have worked to build a Jewish identity.

61 This supports the Hamitic hypothesis, a racist view of the inferiority of the black Africans.

62 Influenced by the reports of Igbos claiming to be Jewish given by Bruder (2012: 143–4), Miles (2012) returned to Nigeria, where he been doing fieldwork, and describes the practices and beliefs of those he calls "Jubos".

63 Parfitt (2013: 37–43) reports on these Nigerian cases, including a later claim that the Igbo language had similarities to Hebrew and that the name "Igbo" is derived from Hebrew.

64 Parfitt (2013: 43–49) deals with black Jews in Ghana.

65 Parfitt (2013: 65; emphasis in original).

66 Parfitt (2013: 66–101) describes developments in the United States. There are about 2,500 Black Hebrew Israelites living in Dimona and two settlements in the Negev; they maintain US citizenship and now have permanent residence status in Israel. One has received Israeli citizenship.

67 Parfitt (2013: 170).

NOTES ON CHAPTER 7

1 Patai (1977). Many are once again moving into Europe.

2 Kennedy (2007). But perhaps he overestimates the speed of Islamicization and Arabicization; there were three centuries of transitional mixed Islamic, Byzantine,

and Jewish culture (Evans and Ratliff, 2012). Recent historical studies, such as those by Bowersock (2013) and Crone (2012), support the view that Islamic conquest, Islamicization, and Arabicization were more complex and gradual than Kennedy implies.

3 Evans and Ratliff (2012).
4 *Shuhad* is plural; the singular is *shahid*. They were promised the famous seventy-two virgins, or *houris*. One source argues that this is a mistranslation, and the meaning is not "virgins" but "white raisins". But, in any case, some Muslims value martyrdom highly, as witness the continuing high number of suicide bombers.
5 They called themselves Romans (*romaioi* in Greek).
6 Donner (1992) describes the history and form of this sixth-century CE map of the Holy Land, with its detailed representation of Jerusalem during the reign of Justinian.
7 A translated text, based on one approved by Tabari, is in Wikipedia.
8 Evans and Ratliff (2012).
9 Erder (2010b) reports that the Cairo Genizah had documents referring to the existence of the Palestinian Yeshiva in Tiberias from the eighth to the twelfth centuries.
10 Fine (2012).
11 Erder (2003).
12 Erder (2010a).
13 See next section.
14 Outhwaite (2010).
15 Evans and Ratliff (2012).
16 Brown (2012: 12).
17 Fine (2012: 115).
18 Lasker (2010).
19 Most dialects of Karaim are reported to be virtually extinct: a few speakers remain in Lithuania and the Crimea but none in Israel.
20 I return to the account by Kennedy (2007).
21 Kennedy (2007).
22 Koester (2000).
23 Wexler (2006) notes that there are indications but little evidence of Judeo-Coptic.
24 Butler (1913).
25 Versteegh (1997).
26 Bareket (1999: 102).
27 Bareket (2010).
28 Recruited as warrior slaves among the Turkic tribes, the status of the Mamluks grew to be higher than Muslims, and they came to power in the Levant, Iraq, India, and especially Egypt.
29 Barda (2010).
30 Wickham (2009).
31 Bachrach (1973).
32 Collins (1989: 11).
33 The mausoleum is said to have been built in the seventeenth century.
34 Book of Ezra, chapter 6. The Book of Esther stresses the multilingualism of the Persian Empire.
35 Crone (2012).

36 Turkey was also a language border, but this was produced by the later migration of Turkish speakers into the region.
37 Moreen (2010b).
38 Gindin (2010a, 2012). The National Library of Israel announced in January 2013 the acquisition of a number of new items from an eleventh-century geniza, some in Arabic and some in Hebrew script in the Judeo-Persian dialect, which was prevalent at the time, and also in Hebrew and Arabic.
39 Gindin (2010a).
40 Gindin (2010b).
41 Moreen (2010a).
42 Garbell (1965) describes one variety of Judeo-Aramaic.
43 There is an account of early Jewish settlement and of the revolt and its suppression by Applebaum (1979).
44 Kerkeslager (2010).
45 Levine (2000: 280–2).
46 Babylonian Talmud (*Bava Kamma* 114b) cites "Rav Chana of Carthage and others say it was Rav Acha of Carthage".
47 Wickham (2009: 75).
48 Chetrit (1985: 262–3).
49 Versteegh (1997).
50 Ferguson (1959). Other examples Ferguson cited were the Haitian distinction between French (H) and Creole (L), the Swiss pair Hochdeutsch (H) and Schweizertutsch (L), and the Greek pair *Karethevusa* (H) and *Demotiki* (L). In his view, the term should be limited to cases in which two distinct varieties of the same language serve in contrasting roles, but Fishman extended the concept to cases in which two different languages served the H and L functions, such as English and Spanish in the Jersey City barrio.
51 Versteegh (1997: 121).
52 Hary (2012).
53 Blau (1965, 2002: 9)
54 Lentin and Grand'Henry (2008); Zack and Schippers (2012).
55 Blau (1965).
56 Blau (1965: 36).
57 Blau (1965: 23).
58 Bar-Asher (1988: 29–30).
59 Hary (1995).
60 Blau and Hopkins (1984); Hary (2009: chap. 2).
61 Bar-Asher (1988: 29–30).
62 Ashtor (1972a).
63 Ashtor (1972a).
64 Corcos (1972b).
65 Chetrit (1985: 262) says that Judeo-Berber was spoken in Morocco even before the Arab conquest in the seventh century, and there were monolingual Judeo-Berber speaking communities such as Tifnut at the foot of the High Atlas region until the twentieth century; most of the Judeo-Berber speakers who emigrated to Israel were bilingual in Judeo-Arabic.
66 Corcos (1972a).

67 Auerbach (1972).
68 Campbell *et al.* (2012). But, as I explain later, one needs to be cautious about genetic arguments that tend to support the opinions of the researchers. See Chapter 12.
69 Hary (2009: 36). Yemen was an exception.
70 Hary (2009: 37) lists Maghrebi, Egyptian, Syrian, Iraqi, and Yemenite dialects.
71 Chetrit (1985: 267–8). There are scholars, such as Bentahila (2010) and Bunis (2008a), who argue that Haketia should be recognized as a variety distinct from Ladino/Judezmo.

NOTES ON CHAPTER 8

1 Banitt (1972) assumes that Jews spoke the local dialect – Norman, or Champagne, or Dijon.
2 Fudeman (2010).
3 Although there are many Ashkenazi families that trace their descent from Rashi's daughters.
4 Such as the words cited by Rashi as *La'az*.
5 Such as *bentshn*, "to say prayers", which is assumed to be from the Latin *benedicere* through Old French. That there are so few words, of course, is a problem. Why did those Jews who left France and moved to the Rhineland shift from Old French to a German variety so speedily, leaving so little trace?
6 Cooper (1989) shows the political basis of Richelieu's establishment of the Académie française.
7 Josephus (65: Book II, chap. 7).
8 Taitz (1994).
9 Blumenkranz (1972a: 9).
10 Boyarin (2004) argues (see Chapter 5) that Pharisees and Christians were very close until what he calls "heresiologists" in each group made the break.
11 Chazan (2006: 35–8). Nirenberg (2013) proposes the term "anti-Judaism" to refer to the European hatred of Jews as "others" whether or not they were present in society; this accounts not just for traditional anti-Semitism, climaxing in the Holocaust, but continued European right- and left-wing anti-Israeli policies.
12 Chazan (2006: 40).
13 Aslanov (2001).
14 Blumenkranz (1972c). Chuadit may have developed from a Jewish variety of Latin; it seems to have been first written by the Jewish scholars at Narbonne. The last speaker of Chuadit died in 1977. Jochnowitz (1985: 244) reports the version of the Passover song *Had Gadya* he heard him sing.
15 Adler (1907: 2).
16 Chazan (2006: 79).
17 Moore (2012).
18 Moore (2012: 6, 7). Nirenberg (2013) expands on this with his proposal of the existence of what he labels "anti-Judaism".
19 Moore (2012: 147).
20 Moore (2012: 149).
21 Moore (2012: 246).
22 Nirenberg (2013)

23 Chazan (2006: 130).
24 Blumenkranz (1972b); Holmes (1962).
25 Blumenkranz (1972b).
26 Dundes (1991: 307).
27 Schwarzfuchs (1972a).
28 Blumenkranz (1972a).
29 Weinreich (1980: 145).
30 The name, derived presumably from *yehudit*, as speakers probably called it, was used by a non-Jewish nineteenth-century writer (Weinreich, 1980: 159).
31 Jochnowitz (1985).
32 Levy (1941).
33 Brisman (2000).
34 Darmesteter and Blondheim (1929–1937).
35 Levy (1964). Word lists continue to appear, such as that edited by Greenberg (1980).
36 See www.jewish-languages.org/judeo-french.html.
37 Birnbaum (1972) calls it Tsarfatic and Weinreich (1980) calls it Western Loez.
38 Darmesteter and Blondheim (1929–1937) published the first important list of glosses.
39 Banitt (1972).
40 Kiwitt (2011).
41 Weinreich (1980: 108).
42 Jacobs (1893).
43 Roth (1941).
44 Roth (1941).
45 What is probably his tombstone was found in Elizabethan times in Ludgate (Jacobs 1893).
46 Jacobs (1893).
47 Weinreich (1980: 109).

NOTES ON CHAPTER 9

1 One scholar of the variety has been heard to remark that this is a language with more names than speakers! I use the term "Judezmo", preferred by linguists such as Harris (1982) and Bunis (1975), for the spoken variety. "Ladino" refers to the standard written variety. "Haketia" is the north African version. Malinowski (1985: 215) also favors the term "Judezmo", which native speakers take to mean "Judaism", as it emphasizes the association between religious observance and language. She also notes that most native speakers refer to their language as *djudo*, "Jewish", or *espanyol*. The complex problems in the naming of Jewish language varieties are discussed by Bunis (2008b), who proposes a taxonomy. An example of confusion is provided by the 2010 US census, which reported only 136 speakers of Ladino; there is good evidence that many Ladino speakers claimed Spanish as their home language.
2 Again, this group has a number of names. I generally use the Hebrew term *Anusim* (forced to convert), and avoid the pejorative *Marranos*. Other terms are *New Christians* and *conversos*.
3 Bradley (1883: 192).
4 Penny (1991).

5 Hillgarth (2009).
6 Heather (1996).
7 Schwarzfuchs (1972c).
8 Another term for *Anusim*. Benveniste (2006) describes the doubts about the effectiveness of conversion and the suspicion of converts in Visigothic Spain.
9 Schwarzfuchs (1972c).
10 Stillman (2010a).
11 Ashtor (1972b).
12 Erder (2010b).
13 Cabaniss (1953).
14 Erder (2010b).
15 Ashtor (1972b); Erder (2010b).
16 Kayserling (1906).
17 Abu Ishaq of Elvira, translated by Bernard Lewis and reprinted by Stillman (1979: 214–16).
18 Erder (2010b).
19 Scheindlin (2006).
20 Brann (2006: 265).
21 Erder (2010b).
22 Erder (2010b).
23 Schwarzfuchs (1972c).
24 Klein (2006).
25 Arribas (2010).
26 Ginsburg (1906).
27 Schwarzfuchs (1972c).
28 Schwarzfuchs (1972c).
29 Beinart (1972a).
30 Beinart (1972d).
31 Beinart (1972b).
32 Avneri and Beinart (1972).
33 Beinart (1972e).
34 Beinart (1972c).
35 Chetrit (1985).
36 Spolsky and Cooper (1991).
37 Spolsky and Shohamy (1999).
38 Cited and translated from his collected works (13: 80) by Grossman (2000: 78).
39 Grossman (2000: 79).
40 Grossman (2000: 82).
41 Fishman (1980, 1991a, 1993b: 327; emphasis in original).
42 Fishman (1991a); Fishman and Fishman (1978).
43 Kuzar (2001) gives a fascinating account suggesting the connection between the linguistics and the political ideology of Israeli scholars.
44 Weinreich (1980, 2008).
45 Fishman (1981b, 1985a).
46 Quoted in Google, which gives the text in Yiddish. There have been other suggested sources. Joshua Fishman wondered if he was the member of the audience, but he was thinking of a 1967 conference. William Bright said some scholars attributed it to the

French linguist Antoine Meillet, but no one has found a source. Jean Laponce, a Quebec linguist, attributed it to Hubert Lyautey at a meeting of the Académie française, but has no evidence.

47 Garbell (1965).
48 Stewart (1968).
49 Weinreich (1949, 1968).
50 Blommaert (2001, 2005).
51 Kachru (1986).
52 Herzog *et al.* (1992–2000). The linguistic isogloss coincides with a food preference, with Litvaks using salt and Galicianers using sugar in making *gefilte* fish.
53 Weinreich (1980).
54 Weinreich (1980: 99).
55 Weinreich (1980: 100).
56 Blondheim (1925).
57 Spitzer (1942), quoted by Weinreich (2008: 104).
58 Sephiha (1985). Just as I was looking up the biography of this Belgian-born son of Turkish Jewish parents and learning that as a youngster he had survived a period in Auschwitz and work camps in Silesia (he later went on to become a professor at the Sorbonne), the sirens sounded here in Jerusalem to mark the annual Holocaust Memorial Day.
59 I cannot resist quoting the footnote he adds (1985: 180): "One should always resist the lure of analogies and approach human language in a very direct way, otherwise matters become confused and one ends up putting a = between Auschwitz and a prisoner-of-war camp."
60 Rabin (1981).
61 Also Gold (1981).
62 A footnote considers the implication of using "language", which he considers to be wider in application than "variety".
63 Fishman (1985b: 4).
64 Fishman also uses the term "ethnolect" for identification related to self-perception.
65 Birnbaum (1972: 68).
66 Hary (2009) prefers this term.
67 Ornan (1985: 22) argues that in Israel it is "the common language used outside – the language of the country; 'the language of the Gentiles'", and so cannot be a "Jewish language", which he considers one that Jews speak only among themselves and that is different from the language used outside.
68 Weinreich (1980: 45–7).
69 López-Moorillas (2006) provides a very useful summary of the development of the languages of the Iberian Peninsula.

NOTES ON CHAPTER 10

1 See Chapter 16 for my answers.
2 True, most Jewish varieties are named, as Hebrew itself was in its early days, "Jewish" in their own language.
3 Avineri (2012). They love the language, and attend lectures and performances, and go to classes where it is taught, but do not intend to use it as a daily language.

4 Katz (2004) stresses the importance of this group of speakers, for whom it remains a "living language".

5 Lotharingia was the eastern division of the medieval Carolingian kingdom, the two western divisions of which were Western and Middle Francia. It included the Rhineland.

6 Weinreich (1980; 2008: chap. 6) sets out in detail the importance of Loter as the foundation of Ashkenaz.

7 Katz (1985).

8 Mieses (1924).

9 Gerzon (1902).

10 Weinreich (2008: 395) states: "At first glance only a few lexical items are involved, not all of which are evenly distributed." He lists a dozen words starting with *bentshn* and adds "probably a few more". In the footnotes (2008: A421) he denies suggestions that there are nearly 100 "Romanisms" by explaining that many are later borrowings from French. But he still holds that "[t]he Yiddish language would have been entirely different had its original pattern not been determined by arrivals with Loez in their mouth" (2008: 396).

11 King (2012); King and Faber (1984). Weinreich (2008: 333) allows that the same process of creation may have taken place in Regensburg as in Loter, but notes that the Italian contact that he considers essential was late, and that the Jews in Regensburg came from Loter already speaking a Germanic variety.

12 Jacobs (2005: 13–15) provides a useful summary of the three scenarios, and suggests that the second two have moved the field to an origin east of Loter.

13 Beider (2012) presents the Czech hypothesis. Weinreich (2008: 542) agrees that Czech is the oldest layer of the Slavic determinant.

14 I give more details of this controversial proposal by Wexler later.

15 The legend concerns the miracles associated with his corpse, carried in an unattended boat from Cologne to Mainz, and given there a Christian burial; a church was later built over the grave.

16 Although there seems to have been one such "bishop" or *Nasi* (president) in German communities, there were as many as four at a time in England (Jacobs, 1892).

17 Christian and Jewish laws forbade lending on interest, but both were permitted to lend to non-co-religionists. Christian nobles and bishops found Jewish moneylenders very useful, for they could easily cancel the debts and expel the Jews when the burden became too heavy.

18 Broydé (1906); Carlebach (1972).

19 They included Rav Simon ha-Gadol, Rav Machir, Leontin, Rav Eliezer (the author of the *Sefer Yere'im*), and especially Rabbenu Gershom Me'or ha-Gadol.

20 Cahen (1972); Ury (1906).

21 Bell (2001: 126).

22 Weinreich (1980: 342) suggests this.

23 Calimani (1988: 40) mentions Calo Calominos as a Jewish physician in the Venetian ghetto at the beginning of the sixteenth century. The family is prominent in Germany and Italy as founders of the Hasidei Ashkenaz.

24 Zfatman (2010) deals with folk myths about the origins of the community, which she says exaggerate the importance of the invitation.

25 Weinreich (1980: 345).

26 Kisch (1949).
27 Weinryb (1972).
28 Cahen (1972).
29 The cemetery was full by 1911, after which only a few reserved spaces were left. It was not destroyed by the Nazis. Rabbi Meir of Rothenberg is buried there.
30 A number of gospel hymns are based on this poem, part of which may refer to a miraculous victory over a Catholic priest in a disputation, which saved the community of Worms from threatened genocide.
31 Chazan (2010a).
32 Baron (1928).
33 See www.catholic-saints.net/saints/st-louis-ix.php.
34 A German Jewish pietist movement, known for strict observance and asceticism.
35 These are methods of intense Talmudic study, criticized by some as casuistry.
36 Wasserman (1972).
37 Editorial staff (1972).
38 Weinreich (1956).
39 Jacobs (1906).
40 Herman and Yahil (1972).
41 Bato (1972).
42 Yehoshua (1999).
43 Weinreich (2008: A141).
44 Yehoshua (1999: 98).
45 Yehoshua (1999: 98).
46 Yehoshua (1999: 54).
47 Yehoshua (1999: 70).
48 Yehoshua (1999: 74).
49 Yehoshua (1999: 80).
50 Yehoshua (1999: 26).
51 Yehoshua (1999: 46).
52 Yehoshua (1999: 82).
53 Yehoshua (1999: 88).
54 Yehoshua (1999: 89).
55 Yehoshua (1999: 126).
56 Yehoshua (1999: 127).
57 Yehoshua (1999: 131).
58 Yehoshua (1999: 135).
59 Yehoshua (1999: 198).
60 As Weinreich (1980: 350) does.
61 Weinreich (2008: 400–2).
62 Katz (1985: 87) is skeptical, however, and argues that "not even a microscope would help find the alleged 'French connection' in Old Yiddish".
63 Weinreich (1980: 418).
64 Weinreich (1980: 525). But this claim is disputed by Straten (2011), who finds no evidence of a mass migration to the east after the crusades or the Black Death, and concludes therefore that east European Jewry must have been of local origin, presumably through the conversion of Ukrainians and Belarusians. Straten also rejects the Khazar hypothesis. King (2012) also has problems with the numbers

involved: he argues that there were too few Jews in Loter to produce the numbers later reported in the east.
65 Weinreich (1980: 539).
66 Beider (2012).
67 Wexler (1987, 2002).

NOTES ON CHAPTER 11

1 Philo (1854 [40]: 281).
2 Dio (1927 [230]: 68, 32).
3 There was a Jewish synagogue in Corinth at which Paul preached for a year and a half. Jews there were poor. They left during the Visigothic period, and those who returned were persecuted by the Byzantine emperors. Benjamin of Tudela found 300 Jews working as silk weavers. The community had disappeared by the fifteenth century, but some individuals returned.
4 A few Jews lived in Chios, an island in the Aegean, according to Josephus. Benjamin of Tudela reported 400 Jews. They had one synagogue in his day, and by 1549 there were several. Jacob ben Asher, author of the *Turim*, was shipwrecked on the island with his students. In the fourteenth and fifteenth centuries Jews mainly engaged in trade. After 1492 Spanish exiles became a majority.
5 Also know as Yavanic. There are no longer native speakers, after heavy Sephardic migration introduced Judezmo, and emigration to the United States and Israel reduced the size of the community (Coverly, 2003).
6 A major city in western Greece, in medieval times Patras was variously under Byzantine rule and held at times by Venice and the Knights of Rhodes.
7 Jews were expelled from Sicily in 1492, and some went to Calabria and Arta.
8 Tsiliyianni (2004).
9 Benmayor (1972).
10 Sephiha (1992: 79–81).
11 Benjamin of Tudela reports a large community engaged in silk dyeing; there are said to have been important scholars. The community was destroyed in the eighteenth century in the Greek–Turkish wars.
12 Chalcis, on the Greek island of Euboea, mentioned by Josephus and said to have 200 Jews by Benjamin of Tudela 1,000 years later, was an important trading city in the Middle Ages, but lost its importance under the Turks. The Jews there continued to speak Romaniot.
13 Weinreich (1980: 46).
14 Milano (1972a). Hary (2009: 6 fn) draws attention to the use of the term "non-Jew" as a "euphemism" (perhaps a translation?) for the Yiddish *goyim* (and *shiksas*), recommending more precision, but here we would need to say something along the lines of "members of other religious and ethnic groups".
15 Some idea of the possible number is given by the fact that Vespasian captured 30,400 slaves in 66 CE after the battles in Galilee (Bloom, 2010: 167).
16 Noy (2005a).
17 In the six Jewish catacombs, there are 110 Greek and forty later Latin inscriptions.
18 Noy (2005b).
19 Cappelletti (2006: 182).

20 Jeffers (1998: 129–30).
21 Safran (2011).
22 Calimani (1988: 4) reviews the evidence and concludes that "all seeming evidence of a stable settlement in Venice during the twelfth and thirteenth century has thus been refuted".
23 Toaff (1972).
24 The words, meaning "and thus to the Jews", were first used by Pope Gregory IX in a letter to the Bishop of Naples referring to the Jews' "lawful liberty".
25 Pope Clement V issued a *Sicut Judaeis* bull in 1348 arguing that as many Jews as Christians were dying during the Black Death, and they would have been foolish to poison themselves (Cohn, 2007).
26 The community grew under Muslim rule, but in the thirteenth century conditions became unfavorable.
27 Von Falkenhausen (1994).
28 Belleli (1906: 310).
29 Jewish law requires the festival of Purim to be celebrated on the 14th of the month of Adar, except in cities that were walled in the time of Joshua, when it is observed on the 15th, as it was in the Persian capital, Shushan.
30 Marcus (1972).
31 The classic study of ghettos, by Wirth (1998 [1928]: 192), deals with European ghettos and then goes on to the patterns of residence in the United States, where now the term refers most commonly to African-American residential areas.
32 Gottreich (2007) points out that the *Mellah* was a Moroccan development, where Jews who often spoke other varieties, such as Spanish and French, chose to live in closed areas for protection.
33 Aziz (2012).
34 Israel (1985).
35 Bonfil (1994); Ruderman (2010).
36 Aziz (2012: 83). Hobsbaum (2005) also stresses that Jewish communities were isolated and inward-looking until quite recently.
37 One is reminded of a ban on the use of Japanese in Hawaiian bookkeeping, overthrown by a US Supreme Court decision.
38 Calimani (1988: 4).
39 Milano (1972b).
40 Schenker (2008).
41 Hacker and Shear (2011).
42 Schwarzfuchs (2011) mentions also one book completely in Hebrew, a translation of a Calvinist catechism for Jews.
43 Fortis (2006).
44 In "Argon", a chapter in his book *The Periodic Table*, Levi refers to Judeo-Piedmontese as "Lassòn Acodesh", which Jochnowitz (1981) considers may well have been a joke, for the term usually refers to Hebrew, as it does in Yiddish. Levi assumes that the Jews of Piedmont came from Spain after the expulsion via Provence; Jochnowitz suspects they were in fact speakers of Judeo-Provençal who were expelled in 1501 and who had their own pronunciation of Hebrew.
45 Jochnowitz (1981).

NOTES ON CHAPTER 12

1 Birnbaum (1972).
2 Weinreich (2008: 85) suggests four "reservoirs" from which Jews came to the eastern Slavic region: remnants of the Yavanic colonies north of the Black Sea; Byzantium; Caucasia (maybe originally from Persia); and Khazaria. The fact that the oldest Jewish center was Kiev suggests that Jews arrived here before the migration from Loter.
3 Wexler (1987: 230) believes that the Jewish Slavic varieties were replaced by Yiddish starting in the fourteenth century, and in the southern Slavic area by Judezmo starting in the sixteenth century; the process was slow, with the last evidence of monolingual Slavic-speaking Jews in the early nineteenth century in the Ukraine. The latest reference reports (Levinsohn, 1828: 35): "[O]ur elders have told us that several generations ago, the Jews in these parts spoke only the Russian language" (cited by Weinreich, 2008: A76).
4 Scheiber (1955).
5 By Wexler and Straten, for example.
6 Weinreich (1980: 4, 724) takes this as the transition to the Middle Yiddish period, which lasted until 1700.
7 Beider (2012) and Wexler (1987, 1991) disagree, arguing for a Slavic origin.
8 Weinreich (1980).
9 There is some question about the first vowel: Judah Halevi used the term *Kuzari* or *Cozari*; his book, written in 1140 in Arabic, was called *Kitab al Khazari*, or, in the many Hebrew translations, *Sefer Hakozri*. It consists of five essays in which a Jew instructs a pagan king on the Jewish religion.
10 Brook (2006).
11 Koestler (1976).
12 Recently, Elhaik (2013) claims to have found evidence supporting the Khazarian origin of Ashkenazim, but the whole issue of genetic evidence remains uncertain.
13 Golden, Ben-Shammai, and Ròna-Tas (2007).
14 Erdal (2007).
15 The word may, instead, be Persian.
16 Probably Turkic origin via Polish or Ukrainian.
17 The origin of this word is disputed and there are more than a dozen guesses.
18 Weinreich (1980: 89).
19 Weinreich (1980: 160).
20 Straten (2011) also rejects the Khazarian hypothesis.
21 Absent any descendants, Elhaik used modern Caucasus Armenian and Georgian populations to represent Khazarian.
22 Elhaik (2013). This debate has political relevance, as it shows various views of the Palestinian source of Ashkenazi inheritance; if Ashkenazim are not of Palestinian origin, presumably they have a weaker claim to Israel.
23 Sand (2009).
24 Aderet (2012) reviews Elhaik's argument. Sand, he reports, was the only Israeli historian or geneticist willing to give an opinion on the paper.
25 Lewontin (2012). A third book is mentioned.
26 Falk (2006).
27 Ostrer (2012).

28 Campbell *et al.* (2012).
29 Elhaik (2013).
30 Abu El-Haj (2012), US-born daughter of a Protestant European mother and a Palestinian, is also the author of a controversial but prize-winning book claiming that Israeli archeology is intended to support political claims.
31 A synagogue was built in Cologne, probably for Latin-speaking Jews under Roman rule, in 1012.
32 There is a complaint to a Church council about Jews living in Metz in 888.
33 Jewish merchants were mentioned there in 820.
34 In about 900 a Church council ruled that anyone who killed a Jew or pagan should be considered a murderer.
35 In 960 the Worms community sent two questions to Jerusalem about Halachic matters. In 1034 a synagogue was built.
36 In 1024 the archbishop granted a privilege to the Jews.
37 We will see that other scholars assume Regensburg to be the birthplace of Yiddish.
38 Weinreich (1980: 347). As mentioned in Chapter 10, however, Straten (2011: 128) reports that he cannot find evidence of an eastward migration of large numbers from Germany. He accepts the origin of Yiddish in Bohemia, Moravia, and southern Germany, and believes that Yiddish was taught to east European Jews by rabbis and teachers as part of religious education.
39 Weinreich (1980: 350).
40 See, for instance, the full listing given by Niborski and Neuberg (2012).
41 Some keep this term for the Yiddish- and Hebrew-influenced German spoken by some German Jews in the presence of non-Jewish servants, and the claim of some German non-Jewish villagers to have learned to speak the variety.
42 Eggers (1998).
43 Katz (1993).
44 Mieses (1924).
45 King and Faber (1984).
46 The older name of Regensburg was Ratisbon.
47 Beider (2010).
48 Beider (2012).
49 Straten (2011). But Dovid Katz (personal communication, 2012) says that many of his points were refuted at the "Knaanic language: structure and historical background" conference, held at Charles University, Prague, from October 25 to 26, 2012.
50 This figure is cited by King from Dubnow (1967).
51 King (2012) points out that this number must have been reduced by the Black Death, the pogroms that led to the migration, and the migration itself. No reasonable rate of population growth would fit.
52 King (2012).
53 Woodworth (2010), in a review of Straten (2011), shows that in notes not included by Weinreich (1980) but recently published in Weinreich (2008) he raises this problem; she shows how he notes that "[d]emographers owe us an explanation" (2008: A136) and finds attractive the notion that many more Jews were living in Slavic lands than the Rhineland hypothesis assumes. Woodworth finds Wexler's hypothesis appealing.
54 Wexler (1987, 2002, 2006).

55 He goes along with Koestler's idea that Ashkenazi Jews are descended from Khazars and have no origin in Palestine.
56 Muysken (1981).
57 The theory was more recently popularized by Taylor (1961) and Thompson (1961), and severely criticized by Bickerton (1977), who thought it required us to accept too many improbabilities. Lefebvre (1986) applied the theory to her study of Haitian Creole, citing Muysken (1981) for defining relexification as the process by which the lexicon of one language is replaced by the lexicon of another.
58 Wexler (1996). Perhaps this claim that modern Jews do not have a Palestinian origin, reflecting Palestinian denial of the existence of the Temple in Jerusalem, is a left-wing Jewish response to Zionist questioning of the existence of a Palestinian people.
59 Wexler (1997).
60 Timm and Beckerman (2006).
61 Katz (1991).
62 Mieses (1915) delivered the opening speech at the Czernowitz conference, a view next presented by Birnbaum (1979) and Weinreich (1980).
63 He also draws attention to the review in *Language* (December 1988) of a book he had edited with the proceedings of a symposium in 1985 that severely criticized all contributions except that by Wexler; the review was signed by "Pavlo Slobodjansk'y". Subsequently the journal published two statements: one that they had since learned that he was a recent immigrant who had been assisted by Wexler; and a second that he did not exist, and so the paper was withdrawn.
64 Kuzar (2001: 123).
65 Weinreich (1980: 47).
66 Wexler (2002: 69).
67 Paper (1995).
68 Beider (2012) argues that the Bohemian colonization of Czech lands in the thirteenth and fourteenth centuries would have led to a shift to what became Eastern Yiddish.
69 Katz (2004: 152) notes that this dichotomy became the subject of much humor.
70 The Jewish region of *Lite* includes Lithuania, parts of Latvia, Estonia, Belorussia, and northern Poland and Ukraine. Jewish Galiciana included western Ukraine and Poland as well as the province of the Austro-Hungarian Empire called Galicia.
71 Preston (1999) draws attention to the importance of what are considered significant dialect differences by speakers of a variety.
72 Until his death in 1964, Uriel Weinreich led the project at YIVO, and since then it has been directed by Marvin Herzog; see Herzog *et al.* (1992–2000)
73 Katz (2004: 140) cites the Dutch *mokem* (city, or Amsterdam, from Hebrew *makom*, place) and German *tfile* (prayer book, rather than prayer). A new study discusses the wide extent of studies of Western Yiddish by German Christian scholars from the sixteenth century to the middle of the eighteenth: Elyada (2012).
74 An analogy is the folk assumption that Japanese speakers of English replace /r/ by /l/ when, in fact, they tend to use an intermediate form of both.
75 Katz (2004: 145–6).
76 N. G. Jacobs (2005) gives a useful summary of the much more complex picture presented in the Atlas.
77 Katz (2004, chap. 6).
78 Katz (2007); Roskies and Roskies (1975).

79 Kassow (2007).
80 Or, obviously for a spoken variety, different dialects of Yiddish (Herzog *et al.*, 1992–2000).
81 Weinreich (1980: 733). One might want to add Postmodern or New Hasidic Yiddish: see Katz (2004).
82 Weinreich (2008: 256). Women would begin their letters in Hebrew but write them in Yiddish.
83 Jacobs (2005: 298).
84 Katz (2004: 96–8).
85 Katz (2004: 204). Mendele wrote an autobiography in Hebrew in 1889.

NOTES ON CHAPTER 13

1 Wasserstein (2012: xvii).
2 Fishman (2005); Fishman (1991c, 1981a). "[O]ne can speak of a new modern Yiddish culture that began to arise in the 1860s and continued its upward trajectory for the next half century, until the outbreak of the First World War, and, in many respects (but not all), during the interwar period as well" (Fishman, 2005: 3).
3 Johnson (1987: 234).
4 Ghettos such as the one in Venice, imposed from outside, were not the only reason that Jews were isolated, however; regularly, Jews appear to have chosen to live close together in their own neighborhoods, whether for more convenient religious observance or for protection.
5 Johnson (1987: 342).
6 Johnson (1987: 286).
7 Nadler (2001: 19).
8 He published a "hyperrationalistic" Hebrew grammar in Latin in 1677, *Compendium grammatices linguae Hebraeae*. One of the aims of the book was to teach spoken Hebrew, which was a goal of contemporary Jewish education in Amsterdam, according to Klijnsmit (1986: 4).
9 Nadler (2001: 47).
10 Banned by the Church, it was first produced in Berlin in 1783.
11 Jews had settled in Dessau in north Germany in 1721, were banished during the Thirty Years War, and readmitted in 1672. The community grew, and established a *bet midrash* in the eighteenth century and a Jewish high school in 1804. A printing press, authorized in 1694, published a prayer book in Hebrew with an appendix for women in Judeo-German.
12 Johnson (1987).
13 Johnson (1987: 306).
14 Weltsch (1972).
15 Ammon (1992) and Kleineidam (1992) describe German and French language diffusion activities.
16 Kushner (1986: 295).
17 Weltsch (1972).
18 Szajkowski (1970: 46).
19 Blumenkranz (1972a).
20 Johnson (1987: 309).

21 Cooper (1989: 10).
22 Originated in sixteenth-century Germany, it lasted there until 1869 and was still used in Romania in 1902.
23 Schwarzfuchs (1972b).
24 Bouganim and Roseman (2011).
25 Wallet (2012) describes Jewish historiography in the second half of the eighteenth century written in Yiddish.
26 Wallet (2006) reports that this had succeeded by the late nineteenth century.
27 Wasserstein (2012: 239).
28 Meroz (1972).
29 Jacobs (2005: 303); Hary (2009: 8).
30 See Chapter 15.
31 Tossavainen (2009a).
32 Lundgren (2009).
33 Vilhjálmsson (2004).
34 Levine (2009).
35 Tossavainen (2009b).
36 Slutsky (1972b).
37 Slutsky (1972b). Domnitch (2003) has collected detailed accounts of Jews as Cantonists and how they were punished for speaking Yiddish.
38 Tobias (1969).
39 Fishman (1976, 1991a); Fishman and Fishman (1974).
40 Wasserstein (2012: 228).
41 Wasserstein (2012: 229).
42 Wasserstein (2012: 231).
43 Wasserstein (2012: 232), citing Fishman (2005).
44 Wasserstein (2012: 233). The same shift from Yiddish occurred in the United States and in Israel, although Shohamy (2007) blames the loss of Yiddish in Israel on Zionist policy. Verschik (2007) notes the emergence of a Jewish Russian, an in-group variety with various degrees of borrowing from Yiddish.
45 The Jewish agricultural settlements in the Ukraine and Crimea were wiped out by the Nazi invasion.
46 Daniels (2010).
47 Slutsky (1972b).
48 Judeo-Georgian is a Jewish variety of Georgian; they are mutually intelligible, but the Jewish variety used for trading includes Hebrew and Aramaic loanwords. There are about 20,000 Georgian Jews still in Georgia and about 80,000 in Israel; there are also some in the United States and elsewhere. The community originated in the time of the Babylonian captivity, but was bolstered by forced immigration under tsarist and Soviet rule.
49 The Jews of the Tat region, half of whom now live in Israel and a quarter in Brooklyn, claim to have been living in the region since the Assyrian period. Their language is a variety of Persian.
50 The Jews of Bukhara speak a Jewish dialect of Tajik. They too claim descent from the Ten Lost Tribes.
51 Katz (2004: 176–7).
52 Weinreich (1980: 281).

53 Born in Frankfurt-am-Main in 1762, he became a rabbi and set up a Yeshiva in Bratislava in Slovakia in 1806, and strongly opposed any innovations in Judaism, including the Reform movement. He objected to rabbis who gave sermons in German (Weinreich, 2008: A279).
54 Weinreich (2008: 283).
55 Weinreich (2008: 284).
56 Weinreich (2008: 285).
57 Katz (2004: 189).
58 Weinreich (2008: 287).
59 Katz (2004: 236).
60 Weinreich (2008: 292).
61 Weinreich (2008: 292–3).
62 Weinreich (2008: 295); see also Fishman (1993a).
63 Fishman (2005).
64 Fink (1998).
65 Weinreich (2008: 302).
66 Mendelsohn (1987: 68).
67 Wasserstein (2012: 224).
68 Wasserstein (2012: 226).
69 Wasserstein (2012: 226–7).
70 Katz (2004: 291–3).
71 Yahil (1972).
72 Nekvapil and Neustupný (1998).
73 Wasserstein (2012: 225).
74 Druviete (1998: 166).
75 Kārlis Augusts Vilhelms Ulmanis was prime minister in 1934; he dissolved the parliament, outlawed political parties, and closed their newspapers. With a motto "Latvia for the Latvians", he increased Latvian literacy and reduced minority economic power.
76 The ultra-orthodox Agudath Israel was given charge of training and certifying teachers for Jewish schools.
77 There is no clear evidence of how many knew Russian. Knowledge of Lithuanian before 1920 was probably limited. Lack of knowledge of Lithuanian was noted as an educational problem, and Jewish schools started teaching Lithuanian in 1920 (Verschik, 2010a).
78 Gar (1972).
79 Verschik (2010a).
80 Verschik (2010b).
81 Verschik (1999).
82 Katzburg (1972).
83 Fenyvesi (1998: 138–9).
84 Wasserstein (2012: 225).
85 Kovács and Forrás-Biró (2011).
86 Zamenhof (1982).
87 Schor (2009).
88 Janton (1993) summarizes the history and status of Esperanto and makes clear how difficult it is to estimate the number of people who know and use the language.

89 As noted in Chapter 11, the Jewish community of Rome was similarly reinforced by refugees from Libya.

NOTES ON CHAPTER 14

1 Rosman (2007).
2 An account of this family history appears as Spolsky (1995).
3 Her first name keeps changing in successive decennial UK census lists. Clearly, she wasn't the one talking to the census taker.
4 The school is now known as JFS.
5 Probably from Shpola, a town not far away.
6 Johnson (1987: 277).
7 Johnson (1987: 278).
8 Johnson (1987: 280).
9 Johnson (1987: 313).
10 Endleman (2002: 65).
11 A meeting of the United Capmakers Union in 1890 was addressed in English and Yiddish.
12 Endelman (1999: 124).
13 Endleman (2002: 149).
14 Endleman (2002: 174).
15 Lipman (1972).
16 Among the poor Ashkenazi Jews in London, there was much crime in the nineteenth century: in the first half of the century 1,000 Jews were among those transported to Australia (Johnson, 1987: 376) out of the total of 145,000 convicts who were sent to penal settlements there; after release, many of them formed the base of the Australian Jewish community (Levi and Bergman, 1974).
17 Endleman (2002: 185).
18 Not requiring an oath, as Oxford and Cambridge universities still did, Edinburgh and Glasgow universities attracted Jews.
19 Collins (1990).
20 Collins (1990: 80).
21 Collins (1990: 205).
22 Katz (2004: 385).
23 He doesn't remember where he found the figure (personal communication, September 10, 2012).
24 Abraham (1999).
25 Johnson (1987: 280).
26 Johnson (1987: 304).
27 Johnson (1987: 368).
28 Kahal kadosh Beth Shalom was the second oldest synagogue in the United States, built in Charleston, South Carolina, in 1749; built originally by Spanish and Portuguese Jews, by 1821 its German Jewish members called for the abridgement of Hebrew prayers and the use of English for worship and sermons. It became the first Reform synagogue.
29 The figures are from Fishman and Hofman (1966).
30 These figures are taken from Fishman, Hayden, and Warshauer (1966).

31 Johnson (1987: 372–3).
32 Ben-Ur (1998); see also Harris (1994).
33 Malinowski (1985: 222).
34 Lowenstein (1989).
35 Benor and Cohen (2009).
36 The 2011 report of the Jewish Community Study of New York, published by the Jewish Federations of North America, estimates 104,000 Russian-speaking Jewish households and 216,000 Jews living in them.
37 Remmenick (2012).
38 Orleck (2001).
39 Pirnazar (2005); also personal communication.
40 These are 2011 figures from the report of the Jewish Community Study of New York.
41 Chafets (2007).
42 Fishman *et al.* (1964).
43 Parker (1978). The 2010 US census confirmed this loss of Yiddish, which was reported to have 162,511 speakers over the age of five (half the 1980 figure) and now outstripped by speakers of Hebrew (216,615 speakers, a language not included in the 1980 report). Even among the Satmar Hasidim, the group assumed to have the highest loyalty to Yiddish, Fader (2009) reports that the women mainly speak Hasidic English; the boys learn their Hasidic Yiddish when they start school, at the age of six or so.
44 Mintz (1993a, 1993b).
45 Weiser (1995). Benor (2012) has studied the use of the variety in the US orthodox community and its acquisition by the newly observant.
46 Benor (2010: 141) reports that the "use of linguistic features correlates with several factors: age, generation from immigration, languages spoken by ancestors, religious observance, traditional learnedness, social networks, and denominational affiliation (especially whether they are Orthodox)". But this produces several distinct varieties rather than a single Jewish language.
47 Tulchinsky (2008: 213).
48 Anctil (2001).
49 Medres (2003).
50 Margolis (2010).
51 This contrasts with the picture that Wasserstein has painted of Yiddish diminishing in eastern Europe. Just as YIVO moved from Warsaw to New York, so Yiddish radical nationalism in North America moved to Montreal.
52 Margolis (2010).
53 Shandler (2006).
54 Avineri (2012).
55 Margolis (2010).
56 Tulchinsky (1993: 163–5).
57 Cherniak (2012).
58 Tulchinsky (2008: 449).
59 Tulchinsky (2008: 448).
60 Parfitt and Egorova (2006).
61 Levi and Bergman (1974).
62 Rutland (2005: 32).

63 Rutland (2005: 33).
64 Rutland (2005: 99).
65 And some accommodation for a small number of Hebrew-speaking Israelis. The communities in both countries have been reinforced by English-speaking South African Jews.
66 Lesser and Rein (2008).
67 Spector (1998).
68 Lesser and Rein (2008).
69 Lesser (1995).

NOTES ON CHAPTER 15

 1 Szajkowski (1970: 1033).
 2 The title "consistory" was given to the bodies established in France and its colonies to govern Jewish communities. The first consistories were set up by Napoleon in 1808; every department with 2,000 Jews could establish a consistory, led by a grand rabbi, a second rabbi, three laymen, and twenty-five notables.
 3 Szajkowski (1970: 1034).
 4 Ammon (1992) points out a contrasting German policy, which held that any German-speaking area should come under German rule; this was the argument used by Hitler when he invaded Austria and the Sudetenland in Czechoslovakia.
 5 This contrasts with British colonial policy, which, after the failure of establishing English as the only educational language, followed a general policy that started elementary education in the local language, introducing English later, certainly by secondary school. Evans (2002) describes the failure of Macaulay's policy in India.
 6 Schreier (2010: 118).
 7 Schreier (2010: 119).
 8 Renauld (2002) provides a biography of this French politician, who was active as a freemason and founder of the Alliance Israélite Universelle.
 9 Abitbol (2003).
10 Bahloul (1996: 88).
11 A study by Bentahila (1983) deals with the attitudes of Moroccan Jews to French and Arabic.
12 Walters (2011).
13 Bensoussan (2012) traces the history of Moroccan Jews up to the present day.
14 Under what were called "capitulations", which were agreements between the Ottoman government and European powers, consuls had rights to protect their nationals; they often expanded this to others, as the British consul in Ottoman Palestine protected Russian Jews.
15 Baïda (2011).
16 Baïda (2011).
17 Krämer (1989).
18 Krämer (1989: 26–9).
19 Beinin (1998).
20 Laskier (1995).
21 Roumani (2008).

22 Shapiro (2010). Bram (2008a, 2008b) describes the current linguistic and social situation of the Mountain Jews (whose language he refers to as Juhuri) after emigration to Israel.

23 Clifton *et al.* (2005) include a detailed study comparing Tat and Mountain Jewish in Azerbaijan.

24 A bilingual Hebrew–Turkish Torah (Genesis) was published in 2002, and other volumes have appeared; a similar prayer book has recently been published.

25 Brink-Danan (2012) describes the current situation of Turkish Jewry.

26 Zenner (2000).

27 Wacholder (1956: 106) concludes that it is reasonable to guess that between the "seventh and twelfth centuries Middle Eastern and North African Jewry doubled as a result of the proselytizing of slaves".

28 Steinhardt (1999).

29 Xin (2003).

30 Bresler (1999).

31 Johnson (1987: 563).

32 Weil (2001).

33 Johnson (1987): 561.

34 Zacharia (2012). Only the first generation is reported to continue to speak the language, which seems to have disappeared in Israel by the third generation.

35 In 1497. Some 20,000 Jews brought to Lisbon with the promise of being able to emigrate were forcibly baptized.

36 Wojciehowski (2011: 212–15) describes the forced double identity of New Christians.

37 Roland (1998: 16–19).

38 In November 2012 the Israeli government agreed to start bringing more of this group to Israel, where they will undergo formal conversion. Some 200 Bene Menashe arrived in 2006. They arrive as temporary residents studying Hebrew and Judaism; after conversion, they will be permitted to apply for immigrant status (Prince-Gibson, 2012). The 2,000th member of the community arrived in January 2013.

NOTES ON CHAPTER 16

1 Eliezer Ben-Yehuda was excommunicated for his arguments for speaking Hebrew (Gold, 1989).

2 If not "revival", then what? Perhaps "regeneration", a word used for the Māori campaign by Hohepa (2000), or "resurrection", a term used for Hebrew by I. Stavans (2008) in a highly personal account of the process.

3 Earlier discussion of this topic appears in Spolsky and Cooper (1991) and Spolsky and Shohamy (1999).

4 The term was first used by Fishman (1996).

5 Vitality was defined in this way by Stewart (1968).

6 Stampfer (1993).

7 This suggestion was made by Glinert (1987).

8 When I observed some Māori immersion classes in the first years of bilingual education, I was fascinated to hear discussions between the teacher, the visiting inspector, and the pupils about appropriate words for new objects (Spolsky, 1989).

The Hebrew writer Ahad Ha'am, visiting Palestine in 1912, spoke of the "word-coining factories"; not just scholars such as Ben Yehuda, but in each school "[e]very teacher is coining with gay abandon" (cited by Morag, 1993: 216).

9 Glinert (1987).
10 The grammatical model suggested is the parallel architecture of Jackendoff (2010a), with items marked for such sociolinguistic features as formality and variety, rather than a grammar that depends on division into labeled languages.
11 That so few went is perhaps a sign of Jewish preference for life in the Diaspora.
12 An acronym for the sentence *Beit Yaakov Lekhu v'Neilkha*, "House of Jacob let us go up".
13 Esperanto was described in Chapter 14.
14 Fishman (1993a, 1993b).
15 Some wrote books in Hebrew as well as Yiddish.
16 Fishman (1980); the emphasis was in the resolution. Fishman notes that the failure of the congress to do more was criticized at first, but, as time went by, a more romantic view emerged. In the light of the destruction of the secular Yiddish world, however, he later (Fishman, 1993b: 330) takes a more realistic view, noting that "history has proved to be much more punishing than an ineffective conference alone could ever be".
17 Glinert (1993).
18 Hyamson (1939: 405). Some argued that the ban was still in effect, and therefore objected to the teaching of English in the state religious school in the Old City of Jerusalem in the 1980s when we lived there.
19 Finn (1878: 2, 103).
20 Warren (1876: 83–4).
21 Luncz (1882–1919).
22 About 6,600 in 1880 speaking Judeo-Espagnol, and about 1,300 from north Africa speaking Judeo-Arabic, according to Luncz.
23 Most of them had arrived in the last twenty-five years. There were some merchants and tradesmen, many living below the poverty level, and a lowest class of laborers and beggars.
24 One wonders how a poor community supported even poorer beggars. Special coins were made out of tin, ten being equal to the smallest regular coin. Luncz (1882) estimated that it would take a beggar a full day to collect enough of these coins to buy a loaf of bread.
25 Ben-Arieh (1984: 356–7).
26 The British consul was proud of his knowledge of Yiddish, which he had started to learn while he was in China in the hope of converting Jews to Christianity (Finn, 1878: 127).
27 Kosover (1966: 114).
28 Loewe (1890: 50, 54).
29 Hyamson (1939: 16).
30 Finn (1878: 127–8).
31 Finn (1878: 360).
32 Hyamson (1939: 400–2).
33 Hyamson (1939: 127–8).

34 Hyamson (1939: 163).
35 Finn (1878: 225–6). Built originally at the beginning of the eighteenth century, the Hurva synagogue was torn down by the Muslims in 1721 for non-payment of debt. It was rebuilt in 1864, and blown up by the Jordanian Arab Legion in 1948. A replica of the old building was reopened in 2011.
36 Herzl received approval from the British government to investigate the possibility of Jewish settlement in east Africa. The sixth Zionist Congress in Basel in 1903 voted to send an investigative commission to east Africa; the seventh congress voted down the proposal.
37 The first wave of Zionist settlers is referred to as the First *Aliya* (*aliya*, "coming" or "going up", means "migration to Israel").
38 This follows and expands Nahir (1988).
39 Fishman and Fishman (1974) describe the refusal of the minister of education to grant time for Yiddish news and radio programs in the 1970s. Shohamy (2007) gives details of pressures from some central government agencies on local bodies to use Hebrew rather than Yiddish in the early years of the state.
40 Fellman (1973).
41 Mandel (1993: 199).
42 Two relevant stories are told about him. One concerns the "dumb" aunt; she was allowed in the house only on condition that she did not speak in front of the children. In the second, his wife came into the study to tell him that a telegram had just been delivered; he spent two days coming up with a Hebrew word for "telegram" before he opened it.
43 Slutsky (1972a).
44 Similarly, noting the problem of Navajo children who met English for the first time, the Bureau of Indian Affairs schools added an extra year prior to the first grade year (Spolsky, 1974).
45 Spolsky (2009b).
46 Cited by Morag (1993: 211–12).
47 David Grün became David Ben Gurion, Yitzchak Ben-Zvi was the son of Zvi Shimshelevitch, Moshe Shertok became Moshe Sharett.
48 A student of mine reported that she was brought up in a children's house on a kibbutz; whenever she entered her parents' room, they would switch from English to Hebrew. Another told me of attending the funeral of her mother-in-law; all the ceremony and eulogies were in Hebrew, but, at the end, old friends came up individually and addressed the deceased (as they presumably did while she was alive) in Yiddish. When he was challenged for speaking Yiddish in the street, the Hebrew national poet Hayyim Nahman Bialik explained that he was talking to his wife.
49 Fellman (1973).
50 Spolsky (1989). A similar model was adopted in Hawaii in language revival programs.
51 Chaim Zuta, cited by Fellman (1973).
52 What happened was somewhat different. The first generation of Jews from Arabic-speaking countries continued to maintain phonetic distinctions that were Sephardi, but gradually all adopted a pronunciation that smoothed out these features, which remain only in a marked class variety and in artificial radio pronunciations.

53 Jones (1998a, 1998b); Spolsky (2002).
54 Spolsky and Shohamy (2001a).
55 Zuckermann (2006).
56 Nahir (1988).
57 Rabin (1958: 73).
58 Cited by Harshav (1993: 143).
59 It was members of this group who were said to have challenged Bialik.
60 The recent decisions of these two institutions to allow PhD students to choose between Hebrew and English for writing their dissertations not surprisingly shocked the Hebrew Language Academy. Until now, this could be done only with special permission of the PhD committee, though permssions appears to have been given in half the cases.
61 This figure is given by Bachi (1956), who reports that the proportion was 75 percent in the young. I am doubtful of these figures: I suspect that, like the later claims of Yiddish knowledge in the Soviet Union, this was a method of claiming identity rather than reporting language proficiency.
62 Cohen (1918).
63 As reported by Bachi (1956).
64 This order was amended by dropping English in 1948, the basis for the assumption that Hebrew and Arabic are now official languages of Israel.
65 Saulson (1979: 57).
66 Saulson (1979: 62–5).
67 Bachi (1974: 40).
68 There are said to be younger people who are reviving Judeo-Arabic songs and possibly even speaking it (Benjamin Hary, personal communication, January 2013).
69 One of the first to deny this was Ornan (1985).
70 Zuckermann (2006) would rather call it "Israeli". And most accept that there is a difference between the Hebrews of the different ages, and call the latest version Modern Hebrew.
71 Wexler (1991, 2002).
72 Fishman (2002) is perhaps hinting at this when he argues for the holiness of Yiddish since millions of its speakers were slaughtered in the Holocaust. Hary (2009) proposes calling Jewish languages (and similar Christian and Muslim varieties) "religiolects".
73 Benor (2012).
74 Labov (2008) suggests we should worry more about endangered people than endangered languages. This account of Jewish history supports his view.
75 Paulston has argued that "minority" refers to lack of power rather than small numbers.
76 There have been reports of the development of Israeli versions of immigrant languages, including English (Olshtain and Blum-Kulka, 1989), French (Ben-Rafael and Ben-Rafael, 2012), Spanish (Berk-Seligson, 1986), and German (Fishman and Kressel, 1974).
77 Fishman (1966) concludes with this analysis, after his erstwhile colleague Kloss (1966) showed the failure of single factors such as numbers and literacy to explain language maintenance.

NOTES ON APPENDIX

1 Most of the information in this table is taken from Lewis, Simons, and Fennig (2013), the current version of *Ethnologue*.

2 The Expanded Graded Intergenerational Disruption Scale is a development of Fishman's GIDS (Fishman, 1991b). 1 is a "national" language. 4 ("educational") is used for 10 percent of the languages in *Ethnologue*, which have educational (or other) uses beyond the home. 5 is "developing", with a start on standardization, graphization, and modernization. 6a is "stable" oral use. 6b is the first endangered level, described as "threatened". 7, "shifting", is a situation in which the childbearing population can still use the language. 8a, 8b, and 9 are "dying" languages, when fluent users are above childbearing age. 10 is "extinct"; this score is assigned by the editors of *Ethnologue* in consultation with a large number of experts.

3 Year of estimate.

4 Unless otherwise indicated, the source is Lewis, Simons, and Fennig (2013).

5 Also known as Israeli, Ivrit.

6 Also known as Arabi, Iraqi Judeo-Arabic, Jewish Iraqi-Baghdadi Arabic, Yahudic.

7 Mainly French-speaking?

8 Probably French-speaking.

9 Also known as Kurdit, Lishan Hozaye, Lishan Hudaye.

10 Also known as Aramit, Galiglu, Hula Hula, Jabali, Lishana Axni, Lishana Noshan.

11 Hezy Mustafi (personal communication) writes: "These were rough estimations based on demographic details in some sources. Most notable for Jewish Neo-Aramaic varieties is A. Ben Yaakov, Qehilot Yehude Kurdistan. The figures are lower today, but I cannot tell to what extent." The book was published in 1981.

12 The editors of *Ethnologue* report: "This reference is to Dr. Baruch Podolsky, who was at Tel Aviv University. Apparently, Dr. Podolsky gave former Ethnologue Editor, Barbara F. Grimes, the following information: 2,000 elderly speakers of Judeo-Berber (1992). We only found a handwritten note to this effect in the paper files."

13 Ora Schwarzwald reports that "the youngest native speakers are over fifty years old", but the language is taught at four universities in Israel and seven elsewhere, and there are activists, some periodical publications, and clubs.

14 Recognized as regional or minority languages under the European Charter for Regional and Minority Languages. Yiddish is recognized in Poland, the Netherlands, Bosnia and Herzegovina, Romania, Sweden, Ukraine, and Moldova.

References

Abitbol, Michel (2003). *Le Passé d'une Discorde: Juifs et Arabes depuis le VIème siècle.* Paris: Perrin.

Abraham, Joan E. (1999). Perceptions of English learning in a Hasidic Jewish sect. *International Journal of the Sociology of Language*, 138, 53–80.

Abu El-Haj, Nadia (2012). *The Genealogical Science: The Search for Jewish Origins and the Politics of Epistemology.* University of Chicago Press.

Aderet, Ofer (2012). Stirring the genetic "soup". *Haaretz*, December 28.

Adler, Marcus Nathan (ed.) (1907). *The Itinerary of Benjamin of Tudela: Critical Text, Translation and Commentary.* Oxford University Press.

Ahn, John J. (2010). *Exile as Forced Migrations: A Sociological, Literary, and Theological Approach on the Displacement and Resettlement of the Southern Kingdom of Judah.* Berlin: Walter de Gruyter.

Allony Fainberg, Yaffa (1977). The influence of English on formal terminology in Hebrew. In Joshua A. Fishman, Robert L. Cooper, and Andrew W. Conrad (eds.), *The Spread of English*, 137–67. Rowley, MA: Newbury House Publishers.

(1983). Linguistic and sociodemographic factors influencing the acceptance of Hebrew neologisms. *International Journal of the Sociology of Language*, 41, 9–40.

Amara, Muhammad Hasan (2002). The place of Arabic in Israel. *International Journal of the Sociology of Language*, 158, 53–68.

(2010). *Arabic Language in Israel: Contexts and Challenges* [in Arabic]. Nazareth: Dirasat – Arab Center for Law and Policy.

Ammon, Ulrich (1992). The Federal Republic of Germany's policy of spreading German. *International Journal of the Sociology of Language*, 95, 33–50.

(ed.) (2001). *The Dominance of English as a Language of Science: Effects on Other Languages and Language Communities.* Berlin: Mouton de Gruyter.

Anctil, Pierre (ed.) (2001). *Through the Eyes of The Eagle: The Early Montreal Yiddish Press 1907–1916* (trans. David Rome). Montreal: Véhicule Press.

Applebaum, Shimon (1979). *Jews and Greeks in Ancient Cyrene.* Leiden: Brill.

Arribas, Josefina Rodríguez (2010). Abraham bar Hiyya. In Norman A. Stillman (ed.), *Encyclopedia of Jews in the Islamic World*, vol. I, 21–3. Leiden: Brill.

Ashtor, Eliyahu (1972a). Egypt. In Cecil Roth and Geoffrey Wigoder (eds.), *Encyclopedia Judaica*, vol. VI, 491–9. Jerusalem: Keter.

(1972b). Spain: Muslim Spain. In Cecil Roth and Geoffrey Wigoder (eds.), *Encyclopedia Judaica*, vol. XV, 222–6. Jerusalem: Keter.

Aslanov, Cyril (2001). *Le provençal des Juifs et l'hebreu en Provence: Le dictionnaire Sarsot ha-Kesef de Joseph Caspi.* Paris: Peeters.

Auerbach, Rachel (1972). Morocco. In Cecil Roth and Geoffrey Wigoder (eds.), *Encyclopedia Judaica*, vol. XII, 326–42. Jerusalem: Keter.

Avineri, Netta (2012). Heritage language socialization practices in secular Yiddish educational contexts: the creation of a metalinguistic community. Unpublished PhD dissertation. University of California, Los Angeles.

Avneri, Zvi, and Beinart, Haim (1972). Barcelona. In Cecil Roth and Geoffrey Wigoder (eds.), *Encyclopedia Judaica*, vol. IV, 208–13. Jerusalem: Keter.

Aziz, Jeff (2012). Review of *Early Modern Jewry* by David B. Ruderman. *Critical Quarterly*, 54, 82–6.

Bachi, Roberto (1956). A statistical analysis of the revival of Hebrew in Israel. *Scripta Hierosolymitana*, 3, 179–247.

(1974). *The Population of Israel*. Jerusalem: Hebrew University.

Bachrach, Bernard S. (1973). A reassessment of Visigothic Jewish policy, 589–711. *American Historical Review*, 78, 11–34.

Bahloul, Joelle (1996). *The Architecture of Memory: A Jewish–Muslim Household in Colonial Algeria 1937–62*. Cambridge University Press.

Baïda, Jamââ (2011). The emigration of Moroccan Jews, 1948–1956. In Emily Benichou Gottreich and Daniel J. Schroeter (eds.), *Jewish Culture and Society in North Africa*, 321–33. Bloomington: Indiana University Press.

Bakhos, Carol (2010). Orality and writing. In Catherine Hezser (ed.), *The Oxford Handbook of Jewish Daily Life in Roman Palestine*, 482–99. Oxford University Press.

Bakshi, Aviad (2011). Is Arabic an official language in Israel? [in Hebrew]. Jerusalem: Institute for Zionist Strategies.

Banitt, Menahem (1972). Judeo French. In Cecil Roth and Geoffrey Wigoder (eds.), *Encyclopaedia Judaica*, vol. X, 423–5. Jerusalem: Keter.

Bar-Asher, Elitzur Avraham (2010). Hebrew. In John J. Collins and Daniel C. Harlow (eds.), *The Eerdmans Dictionary of Early Judaism*, 713–15. Grand Rapids, MI: William B. Eerdmans Publishing.

Bar-Asher, Moshe (1988). The Sharh of the Maghreb: Judeo-Arabic exegesis of the Bible and other Jewish literature – its nature and formation. In Moshe Bar-Asher (ed.), *Studies in Jewish Languages: Bible Translations and Spoken Dialects*, 3–34 [in Hebrew]. Jerusalem: Misgav Yerushalayim.

(1999). Mishnaic Hebrew: an introductory study. *Hebrew Studies*, 40, 115–50.

Barda, Racheline (2010). Egypt. In Norman A. Stillman (ed.), *Encyclopedia of Jews in the Islamic World*, vol. III, 132–41. Leiden: Brill.

Bareket, Elinoar (1999). *Fustat on the Nile: The Jewish Elite in Medieval Egypt*. Leiden: Brill.

(2010). Egypt. In Norman A. Stillman (ed.), *Encyclopedia of Jews in the Islamic World*, vol. II, 126–32. Leiden: Brill.

Barnett, Paul (2008). *Paul: Missionary of Jesus*. Grand Rapids, MI: William B. Eerdmans Publishing.

Baron, Salo (1928). Ghetto and emancipation: shall we revise the traditional view? *The Menorah Journal*, 14, 515–26.

Bato, Yomtob Ludwig (1972). Vienna. In Cecil Roth and Geoffrey Wigoder (eds.), *Encyclopedia Judaica*, vol. XVI, 122–7. Jerusalem: Keter.

Baumel, Simeon D. (2002). Language policies of ethnic minorities as influenced by social, economic, religious and political concentrates: an examination of Israeli Haredim. PhD dissertation, Bar-Ilan University, Ramat-Gan, Israel.

Becanus, Johannes Goropius (1569). *Origines Antwerpianae*. Antwerp: Ex officina Christophori Plantin.

Beckingham, Charles F., and Huntingford, George W. B. (eds., trans.) (1954). *Some Records of Ethiopia, 1593–1646: Being Extracts from the History of High Ethiopia or Abassia, together with Bahrey's History of the Galla*. London: Hakluyt Society.

Beider, Alexander (2010). Yiddish proto-vowels and German dialects. *Journal of Germanic Linguistics*, 22, 23–92.

(2012). Czech lands as the cradle of Eastern Yiddish. Paper presented at the "Knaanic language: structure and historical background" conference, Charles University, Prague.

Beinart, Haim (1972a). Cordova. In Cecil Roth and Geoffrey Wigoder (eds.), *Encyclopedia Judaica*, vol. V, 963–6. Jerusalem: Keter.

(1972b). Granada. In Cecil Roth and Geoffrey Wigoder (eds.), *Encyclopedia Judaica*, vol. VII, 852–3. Jerusalem: Keter.

(1972c). Saragossa. In Cecil Roth and Geoffrey Wigoder (eds.), *Encyclopedia Judaica*, vol. XIV, 858–66. Jerusalem: Keter.

(1972d). Toledo. In Cecil Roth and Geoffrey Wigoder (eds.), *Encyclopedia Judaica*, vol. XV, 1198–206. Jerusalem: Keter.

(1972e). Tudela. In Cecil Roth and Geoffrey Wigoder (eds.), *Encyclopedia Judaica*, vol. XV, 1423–6. Jerusalem: Keter.

Beinin, Joel (1998). *The Dispersion of Egyptian Jewry: Culture, Politics, and the Formation of a Modern Diaspora*. Berkeley: University of California Press.

Bell, Dean Phillip (2001). *Sacred Communities: Jewish and Christian Identities in Fifteenth-Century Germany*. Leiden: Brill.

Belleli, Lazarus (1906). Judaeo-Greek and Judaeo-Italian. In *The Jewish Encyclopedia*, vol. VII, 310–13. New York: Funk & Wagnall.

Ben Zvi, Ehud (1991). *A Historical-Critical Study of the Book of Zephaniah*. Berlin: Walter de Gruyter.

Ben Zvi, Yitschak (1963). *The Exiled and the Redeemed*. Philadelphia: Jewish Publication Society.

Ben-Arieh, Yehoshua (1984). *Jerusalem in the 19th Century: The Old City*. New York: St. Martin's Press.

Ben-Rafael, Eliezer (1994). A sociological paradigm of bilingualism: English, French, Yiddish and Arabic in Israel. *Israel Social Science Research*, 9, 181–206.

Ben-Rafael, Eliezer, and Ben-Rafael, Miriam (2012). Francophonie in the plural: the case of Israel. *Israel Studies in Language and Society*, 4, 39–72.

(2013). *Sociologie et sociolinguistique des francophonies israéliennes*. Frankfurt: Peter Lang.

Ben-Ur, Aviva (1998). The Judeo-Spanish (Ladino) press in the United States, 1910–1948. In Werner Sollors (ed.), *Multilingual America: Transnationalism, Ethnicity, and the Languages of American Literature*, 64–80. New York University Press.

Benmayor, Jacov (1972). Salonika. In Cecil Roth and Geoffrey Wigoder (eds.), *Encyclopedia Judaica*, vol. XIV, 699–704. Jerusalem: Keter.

Benor, Sarah Bunin (2010). Mensch, bentsh, and balagan: variation in the American Jewish linguistic repertoire. *Language and Communication*, 31, 141–54.

(2012). *Becoming Frum: How Newcomers Learn the Language and Culture of Orthodox Judaism*. New Brunswick, NJ: Rutgers University Press.

Benor, Sarah Bunin, and Cohen, Steven M. (2009). Survey of American Jewish language and identity. Cincinnati: Hebrew Union College–Jewish Institute of Religion.

Bensoussan, David (2012). *Il était une fois le Maroc: Témoignages du passé Judéo-Marocain* (2nd edn). Bloomington, IN: iUniverse.

Bentahila, Abdelâlii (1983). *Language Attitudes among Arabic–French Bilinguals in Morocco*. Clevedon: Multilingual Matters.

(2010). Haketia. In Norman A. Stillman (ed.), *Encyclopedia of Jews in the Islamic World*, vol. III, 73–6. Leiden: Brill.

Benveniste, Henriette-Rika (2006). On the language of conversion: Visigothic Spain revisited. *Historein*, 6, 72–87.

Berk-Seligson, Susan (1986). Linguistic constraints on intra-sequential code-switching: study of Spanish/Hebrew bilingualism. *Language in Society*, 15, 313–48.

Bickerton, Derek (1975). *Dynamics of a Creole System*. Cambridge University Press.

(1977). Pidginization and creolization: language acquisition and language universals. In Albert Valdman (ed.), *Pidgin and Creole Linguistics*, 49–69. Bloomington: Indiana University Press.

Birnbaum, Solomon A. (1972). Jewish languages. In Cecil Roth and Geoffrey Wigoder (eds.), *Encyclopedia Judaica*, vol. X, 66–9. Jerusalem: Keter.

(1979). *Yiddish: A Survey and a Grammar*. University of Toronto Press.

Blau, Joshua (1965). *The Emergence and Linguistic Background of Judeo-Arabic: A Study of the Origins of Middle Arabic*. Oxford University Press.

(2002). *A Handbook of Early Middle Arabic*. Jerusalem: Institute for the Study of Asia and Africa.

Blau, Joshua, and Hopkins, Simon (1984). On early Judeo-Arabic orthography. *Zeitschrift für arabisches linguistik*, 12, 9–27.

Blom, Jan-Petter, and Gumperz, John J. (1972). Social meaning in linguistic structures: code switching in northern Norway. In John J. Gumperz and Dell Hymes (eds.), *Directions in Sociolinguistics: The Ethnography of Communication*, 407–34. New York: Holt, Rinehart and Winston.

Blommaert, Jan (2001).The Asmara Declaration as a sociolinguistic problem: reflections on scholarship and linguistic rights. *Journal of Sociolinguistics*, 5, 131–42.

(2005). *Discourse: A Critical Introduction*. Cambridge University Press.

(2010). *The Sociolinguistics of Globalization*. Cambridge University Press.

Blondheim, David Simon (1925). *Les parlers judéo-romans et la Vetus latina: Etude sur les rapports entre les traductions bibliques en langue romane des Juifs au moyen âge et les anciennes versions*. Paris: E. Champion.

Bloom, James J. (2010). *The Jewish Revolts against Rome AD 66–135: A Military Analysis*. Jefferson, NC: McFarland.

Blumenkranz, Bernhard (1972a). France. In Cecil Roth and Geoffrey Wigoder (eds.), *Encyclopedia Judaica*, vol. VII, 7–22. Jerusalem: Keter.

(1972b). Paris. In Cecil Roth and Geoffrey Wigoder (eds.), *Encyclopedia Judaica*, vol. VII, 103–9. Jerusalem: Keter.

(1972c). Narbonne. In Cecil Roth and Geoffrey Wigoder (eds.), *Encyclopedia Judaica*, vol. XII, 827–30. Jerusalem: Keter.

Bolton, Kingsley, and Kuteeva, Maria (2012). English as an acdemic language at a Swedish university: parallel language use and the "threat" of English. *Journal of Multingual and Multicultural Development*, 33, 429–47.

Bonfil, Robert (1994). *Jewish Life in Renaissance Italy*. Berkeley: University of California Press.

Botta, Alejandro F. (2009). *The Aramaic and Egyptian Legal Traditions at Elephantine: An Egyptological Approach*. London: Continuum.

Botticini, Maristella, and Eckstein, Zvi (2012). *The Chosen Few: How Education Shaped Jewish History, 70–1492*. Princeton University Press.

Bouganim, Ami, and Roseman, Daniel (2011). France: Jewish education in France. In Helena Miller, Lisa Grant, and Alex Pomson (eds.), *International Handbook of Jewish Education*, 1203–18. Berlin: Springer Science.

Bowersock, Glen W. (2011). The rise and fall of a Jewish kingdom in Arabia. *The Institute Letter*, 8.

  (2013). *The Throne of Adulis: Red Sea Wars on the Eve of Islam*. Oxford University Press.

Bowman, Stephen (2010). Judeo-Greek. In Norman A. Stillman (ed.), *Encyclopedia of Jews in the Islamic World*, vol. III, 60–1. Leiden: Brill.

Boyarin, Daniel (2004). *Border Lines: The Partition of Judaeo-Christianity*. Philadelphia: University of Pennsylvania Press.

Bradley, Henry (1883). *The Goths: From the Earliest Times to the End of the Gothic Dominion in Spain*. London: T. Fisher Unwin.

Bram, Chen (2008a). The Catch-22 of categorization: Soviet Jews, Caucasus Jews, and dilemmas of multicuturalism in Israel. In Zvi Beckerman and Ezra Kopelowitz (eds.), *Cultural Education – Cultural Sustainability: Minority, Diaspora, Indigenous and Ethno-Religious Groups in Multicultural Societies*, 31–50. London: Routledge.

  (2008b). The language of Caucasus Jews: language preservation and sociolinguistic dilemmas before and after the migration to Israel. *Irano-Judaica*, 6, 337–51.

Brann, Ross (2006). Yehudah Halevi. In Maria Rosa Menocal, Raymond P. Scheindlin, and Michael A. Sells (eds.), *The Literature of Al-Andalus*, 265–81. Cambridge University Press.

Bregman, Marc (1982). The Darshan: preacher and teacher of Talmudic times. *Melton Journal*, 14, 3–48.

Bresler, Boris (1999). Harbin's Jewish community, 1898–1958: politics, prosperity and adversity. In Jonathan Goldstein (ed.), *The Jews of China*, vol. I, *Historical and Comparative Perspectives*, 200–15. Armonk, NY: M. E. Sharpe.

Brettler, Marc Zvi (2010). 'The Hebrew Bible and the early history of Israel'. In Judith R. Baskin and Kenneth Seeskin (eds.), *The Cambridge Guide to Jewish History, Religion, and Culture*, 6–33. Cambridge University Press.

Breuer, Yochanan (2006). Aramaic in late antiquity. In Steven T. Katz (ed.), *The Cambridge History of Judaism*, vol. IV, *The Late Roman-Rabbinic Period*, 457–91. Cambridge University Press.

Brink-Danan, Marcy (2012). *Jewish Life in 21st-Century Turkey: The Other Side of Tolerance*. Bloomington: Indiana University Press.

Brisman, Shimeon (2000). *A History and Guide to Judaic Dictionaries and Concordances*, vol. I. Tel Aviv: Ktav Publishing.

Brook, Kevin Alan (2006). *The Jews of Khazaria* (2nd edn). Lanham, MD: Rowman & Littlefield.

Broshi, Magen (2001). *Bread, Wine, Walls and Scrolls*. London: Continuum.

Brown, Peter (2012). The great transition: review of *Byzantium and Islam: Age of Transition*. *New York Review of Books*, 59, 12–15.

Broydé, Isaac (1906). Cologne. In *The Jewish Encyclopedia*, vol. IV, 166–70. New York: Funk & Wagnall.

Bruder, Edith (2012). *The Black Jews of Africa: History, Religion, Identity*. New York: Oxford University Press.

Bunis, David M. (1975). *Problems in Judezmo Linguistics*. New York: American Sephardi Federation.

(2008a). The differential impact of Arabic on Haketía and Turkish on Judezmo. In Tamar Alexander and Yaakov Bentolila (eds.), *La cultura Judeo-Española del Norte de Marruecos*, 177–208. Beersheva: Universidad Ben-Gurion del Negev.

(2008b). The names of Jewish languages: a taxonomy. In Francesco Aspesi, Vermondo Brugnatelli, Anna L. Callow, and Claudia Rosenzweig (eds.), *Il mio cuore è a Oriente: Studi di linguistica storica, filologia e cultura ebraica dedicati a Maria Luisa Mayer Modena*. 415–33. Milan: Cisalpino.

Butler, Alfred J. (1913). *The Treaty of Misr in Tabari: An Essay in Criticism*. Oxford: Clarendon Press.

Byrne, Ryan (2007). The refuge of scribalism in Iron I Palestine. *Bulletin of the American Schools of Oriental Research*, 345, 1–31.

Cabaniss, Allen (1953). Bodo-Eleazar: a famous Jewish convert. *Jewish Quarterly Review*, 43, 313–28.

Cahen, Gilbert (1972). Metz. In Cecil Roth and Geoffrey Wigoder (eds.), *Encyclopedia Judaica*, vol. XI, 1449–52. Jerusalem: Keter.

Calimani, Riccardo (1988). *The Ghetto of Venice*. Milan: Rusconi.

Campbell, Christopher L., Palamara, Pier F., Dubrovsky, Maya, Botigué, Laura R., Fellous, Marc, Atzmon, Gil, Oddoux, Carole, Pearlman, Alexander, Hao, Li, Henn, Brenna M., Burns, Edward, Bustamante, Carlos D., Comas, David, Friedman, Eitan, Pe'er, Itsik, and Ostrer, Harry (2012). North African Jewish and non-Jewish populations form distinctive, orthogonal clusters. *Proceedings of the National Academy of Sciences*, doi:10.1073/pnas.1204840109.

Cappelletti, Syvia (2006). *The Jewish Community of Rome: From the Second Century BC to the Third Century CE*. Leiden: Brill.

Carlebach, Alexander (1972). Cologne. In Cecil Roth and Geoffrey Wigoder (eds.), *Encyclopedia Judaica*, vol. V, 738–44. Jerusalem: Keter.

Central Bureau of Statistics (2013). Selected data from the 2011 "Social survey on mastery of the Hebrew language and usage of languages", www.cbs.gov.il/reader/newhodaot/hodaa_template.html?hodaa=201319017.

Chafets, Zev (2007). The Sy Empire. *New York Times*, October 14.

Charpin, Dominique (2011). *Reading and Writing in Babylon* (trans. Jane Marie Todd). Cambridge, MA: Harvard University Press.

Chazan, Robert (2006). *The Jews of Medieval Western Christendom*. Cambridge University Press.

(2010a). *Reassessing Jewish Life in Medieval Europe*. Cambridge University Press.

(2010b). Jewish life in western Christendom. In Judith R. Baskin and Kenneth Seeskin (eds.), *The Cambridge Guide to Jewish History, Religion, and Culture*, 113–39. Cambridge University Press.

Cherniak, Lawrence (2012). Yiddish resurgence in Winnipeg. *Outlook*, September–October, 38–9.

Chetrit, Joseph (1985). Judeo-Arabic and Judeo-Spanish in Morocco and their socio-linguistic interaction. In Joshua A. Fishman (ed.), *Readings in the Sociology of Jewish Languages*, 260–79. Leiden: Brill.

Chiswick, Barry R. (1993). Hebrew language usage: determinants and effects among immigrants in Israel. Paper presented at conference on immigrant absorption, Technion, Haifa.

Chiswick, Barry R., and Miller, Paul W. (1992). Language in the immigrant labor market. In Barry R. Chiswick (ed.), *Immigration, Language and Ethnicity: Canada and the United States*, 471–6. Washington, DC: American Enterprise Institute.

Chomsky, William (1957). *Hebrew: The Eternal Language*. Philadelphia: Jewish Publication Society of America.

Clifton, John M., Deckinga, Gabriela, Lucht, Laura, and Tiessen, Calvin (2005). Sociolinguistic situation of the Tat and Mountain Jews in Azerbaijan. SIL Electronic Survey Report 2005–017.

Cohen, Israel (1918). *The German Attack on the Hebrew Schools in Palestine*. London: Jewish Chronicle.

Cohen, Menachem (1979). The idea of the sanctity of the biblical text and the science of textual criticism. In Uriel Simon (ed.), *HaMikrah V'anachnu*, 42–69. Tel Aviv: HaMachon L'Yahadut U'Machshava Bat-Z'mananu and Dvir.

Cohn, Jr., Samuel K. (2007). The Black Death and the burning of Jews. *Past and Present*, 196, 3–36.

Collins, Kenneth E. (1990). *Second City Jewry*. Glasgow: Scottish Jewish Archives.

Collins, Roger (1989). *The Arab Conquest of Spain*, 710–797. Oxford: Blackwell.

Conybeare, Frederick (1910). Antiocus Stretegos' account of the sack of Jerusalem in AD 614. *English Historical Review*, 25, 502–17.

Cook, Edward (2010). Aramaic. In John J. Collins and Daniel C. Harlow (eds.), *The Eerdmans Dictionary of Early Judaism*, 360–2). Grand Rapids, MI: William B. Eerdmans Publishing.

Cooper, Robert L. (1982). A framework for the study of language spread. In Robert L. Cooper (ed.), *Language Spread: Studies in Diffusion and Social Change*, 5–36. Bloomington: Indiana University Press.

 (1989). *Language Planning and Social Change*. Cambridge University Press.

Cooper, Robert L., and Carpenter, S. (1976). Language in the market. In M. Lionel Bender, J. Donald Bowen, Robert L. Cooper, and Charles A. Ferguson (eds.), *Language in Ethiopia*, 244–55. Oxford University Press.

Corcos, David (1972a). Algeria. In Cecil Roth and Geoffrey Wigoder (eds.), *Encyclopedia Judaica*, vol. II, 612–16. Jerusalem: Keter.

 (1972b). Tunis, Tunisia. In Cecil Roth and Geoffrey Wigoder (eds.), *Encyclopedia Judaica*, vol. XV, 1430–47. Jerusalem: Keter.

Council of Europe (2001). *Common European Framework of Reference for Languages: Learning, Teaching, Assessment*. Cambridge University Press.

Coverly, Mary C. (2003). *Judeo-Greek: The Language*. New York: Jay Street Publishers.

Crone, Patricia (1980). *Slaves on Horses: The Evolution of the Islamic Polity*. Cambridge University Press.

318   References

(2012). *The Nativist Prophets of Early Islamic Iran: Rural Revolt and Local Zoroastrianism*. Cambridge University Press.

Daniels, Alfonso (2010). Why some Jews would rather live in Siberia than Israel. *Christian Science Monitor*, June 7.

Darmesteter, Arsène, and Blondheim, David Simon (eds.) (1929–1937). *Les gloses françaises dans les commentaires talmudiques de Raschi*, 2 vols. Paris: Champion.

Dauphin, Claudine (1998). *La Palestine Byzantine: Peuplement et Population*. Oxford: Archaeopress.

Davis, Leo Donald (1983). *The First Seven Ecumenical Councils (325–787): Their History and Theology*. Collegeville, MN: Liturgical Press.

De Lange, Nicolas (1996). The Hebrew language in the European Diaspora. In Benjamin Isaac and Aharon Oppenheimer (eds.), *Studies on the Jewish Diaspora in the Hellenistic and Roman Period*, 111–39. Tel Aviv: Ramot Publishing.

(2005). Jews in the age of Justinian. In Michael Maas (ed.), *The Cambridge Companion to the Age of Justinian*, 401–33. Cambridge University Press.

De Vries, John (1990). On coming to our census: a layman's guide to demolinguistics. *Journal of Multilingual and Multicultural Development*, 11, 57–76.

Delitzsch, Friedrich (1914a). *Grundzüge der sumerischen Grammatik*. Leipzig: J. C. Hinrichs.

(1914b). *Sumerisches Glossar*. Leipzig: J. C. Hinrichs.

Delsing, Lars-Olof (2007). Scandinavian intercomprehension today. In Jan D. ten Thije and Ludger Zeevaert (eds.), *Receptive Multilingualism: Linguistic Analyses, Language Policies and Didactic Concepts*, 231–46. Amsterdam: John Benjamins.

Den Heijer, Johannes (2012). Introduction: Middle and Mixed Arabic, a new trend in Arabic studies. In Liesbeth Zack and Arie Schippers (eds.), *Middle Arabic and Mixed Arabic: Diachrony and Synchrony*, 1–50. Leiden: Brill.

Deutsch, Yocheved (2001). English for the legal profession. PhD dissertation, Bar-Ilan University, Ramat-Gan, Israel.

Dines, Jennifer (2004). *The Septuagint*. London: T & T Clark.

Dio, Cassius (1927 [230]). *Roman History*, vol. IX (trans. Earnest Cary and Herbert B. Foster). London: Heineman.

Domnitch, Larry (2003). *The Cantonists: The Jewish Children's Army of the Tsar*. Tel Aviv: Devora Publishing.

Donner, Herbert (1992). *The Mosaic Map of Madaba: An Introductory Guide*. Kampen, Netherlands: Kok Pharos Publishing.

Dothan, Trude, and Dothan, Moshe (1992). *People of the Sea: The Search for the Philistines*. New York: Scribner.

Doughty, Charles M. (1921). *Travels in Arabia Deserta*. London: Jonathan Cape.

Douglas, Mary (1999). *Leviticus as Literature*. Oxford University Press.

Dozier, Edward P. (1966). *Hano: A Tewa Indian Community in Arizona*. New York: Holt, Rinehart and Winston.

Druviete, Ina (1998). Republic of Latvia. In Christina Bratt Paulston and Donald Peckham (eds.), *Linguistic Minorities in Central and Eastern Europe*, 160–83. Clevedon: Multilingual Matters.

Dubnow, Simon (1967). *History of the Jews: From the Beginning to Early Christianity* (trans. Moshe Spiegel). New York: Yoseloff.

Duncan, J. Barrow (1931). *Digging Up Biblical History*. New York: Macmillan.

Dundes, Alan (1991). *The Blood Libel Legend: A Casebook in Anti-Semitic Folklore.* Madison: University of Wisconsin Press.

Dursteler, Eric R. (2012). Speaking in tongues: language and communication in the early modern Mediterranean. *Past and Present*, 217, 48–77.

Eck, Werner (2003). The language of power: Latin in the inscriptions of Iudaea/Syria Palaestina. In Lawrence H. Schiffman (ed.), *Semitic Papyrology in Context: A Climate of Creativity: Papers from a New York University Conference marking the Retirement of Baruch A. Levine*, 123–44. Leiden: Brill.

Editorial staff (1972). Nuremberg. In Cecil Roth and Geoffrey Wigoder (eds.), *Encyclopedia Judaica*, vol. XII, 1274–80. Jerusalem: Keter.

Eggers, Eckhard (1998). *Sprachwandel und Sprachmischung im Jiddischen [Language Change and Language Mixture in Yiddish]*. Frankfurt: Peter Lang.

Elhaik, Eran (2013). The missing link of Jewish European ancestry: contrasting the Rhineland and the Khazarian hypotheses. *Genome Biology and Evolution*, 5, 61–74.

Ellul, Jacques (1985). Preface (trans. David Maisel). In Bat Ye'or (ed.), *The Dhimmi: Jews and Christians under Islam*, 25–33. Rutherford, NJ: Fairleigh Dickinson University Press.

Elyada, Ana (2012). *A Goy Who Speaks Yiddish: Christians and the Jewish Language in Early Modern Germany*. Stanford University Press.

Endelman, Todd M. (1999). *The Jews of Georgian England, 1714–1830: Tradition and Change in a Liberal Society*. Ann Arbor: University of Michigan Press.

(2002). *The Jews of Britain, 1656 to 2000*. Berkeley: University of California Press.

Erdal, Marcel (2007). The Khazar language. In Peter B. Golden, Haggai Ben-Shammai, and András Ròna-Tas (eds.), *The World of the Khazars*, 75–108. Leiden: Brill.

Erder, Yoram (2003). The mourners of Zion: the Karaites in Jerusalem in the tenth and eleventh centuries. In Meira Polliack (ed.), *Karaite Judaism: A Guide to Its History and Literary Sources*, 213–35. Leiden: Brill.

(2010a). Palestine: the first Muslim period (634–1099). In Norman A. Stillman (ed.), *Encyclopedia of Jews in the Islamic World*, vol. IV, 5–17. Leiden: Brill.

(2010b). Yeshiva of Palestine. In Norman A. Stillman (ed.), *Encyclopedia of Jews in the Islamic World*, vol. IV, 639–41. Leiden: Brill.

Evans, Helen C., and Ratliff, Brandie (eds.) (2012). *Byzantium and Islam: Age of Transition*. New Haven, CT: Yale University Press.

Evans, Stephen (2002). Macaulay's Minute revisited: colonial language policy in nineteenth-century India. *Journal of Multilingual and Multicultural Development*, 23, 260–81.

Fader, Ayala (2009). *Mitzvah Girls: Bringing Up the Next Generation of Hasidic Jews in Brooklyn*. Princeton University Press.

Falk, Raphael (2006). *Zionut Vehabiologia Shel Hayehudim [Zionism and Jewish Biology]*. Tel Aviv: Resling.

Fellman, Jack (1973). *The Revival of a Classical Tongue: Eliezer ben Yehuda and the Modern Hebrew Language*. The Hague: Mouton.

(1985). A sociolinguistic perspective on Hebrew. In Joshua A. Fishman (ed.), *Readings in the Sociology of Jewish Languages*, 27–34. Leiden: Brill.

Fenyvesi, Anna (1998). Linguistic minorities in Hungary. In Christina Bratt Paulston and Donald Peckham (eds.), *Linguistic Minorities in Central and Eastern Europe*, 135–59. Clevedon: Multilingual Matters.

Ferguson, Charles A. (1959). Diglossia. *Word*, 15, 325–40.

Fine, Steven (2011). Jewish identity at the Limus: the earliest reception of the Dura Europus Synagogue paintings. In Erich S. Gruen (ed.), *Cultural Identity in the Ancient Mediterranean*, 289–306. Los Angeles: Getty Publications.

(2012). Jews and Judaism between Byzantium and Islam. In Helen C. Evans and Brandie Ratliff (eds.), *Byzantium and Islam: Age of Transition*, 102–16. New Haven, CT: Yale University Press.

Fink, Carole (1998). The minorities question at the Paris Peace Conference: the Polish Minority Treaty, June 28, 1919. In Manfred F. Boemeke, Gerald D. Feldman, and Elisabeth Glaser (eds.), *The Treaty of Versailles: A Reassessment after 75 Years*, 249–74. Cambridge University Press.

Finkelstein, Israel (2007a). Digging for the truth: archaeology and the Bible. In Israel Finkelstein, Amihai Mazar, and Brian B. Schmidt (eds.), *The Quest for the Historical Israel: Debating Archeology and the History of Early Israel*, 9–20. Atlanta: Society for Biblical Literature.

(2007b). A short summary: Bible and archaeology. In Israel Finkelstein, Amihai Mazar, and Brian B. Schmidt (eds.), *The Quest for the Historical Israel: Debating Archeology and the History of Early Israel*, 183–8. Atlanta: Society for Biblical Literature.

Finkelstein, Israel, and Silberman, Neil Asher (2002). *The Bible Unearthed: Archaeology's New Vision of Ancient Israel and the Origin of Its Sacred Texts*. New York: Simon & Schuster.

Finn, James (1878). *Stirring Times, or Records from Jerusalem Consular Chronicles of 1853–1856* (ed. Elizabeth Anne Finn). London: C. K. Paul.

Fishman, David E. (2005). *The Rise of Modern Yiddish Culture*. University of Pittsburgh Press.

Fishman, Joshua A. (ed.) (1966). *Language Loyalty in the United States: The Maintenance and Perpetuation of Non-English Mother Tongues by American Ethnic and Religious Groups*. The Hague: Mouton.

(1976). Yiddish and Loshn-Koydesh in traditional Ashkenaz: problems of societal allocation of macro-functions. In Albert Verdoodt and Rolf Kjolseth (eds.), *Language in Sociology*, 39–48. Louvain: Peeters.

(1980). Attracting a following to high-culture functions for a language of everyday life: the role of the Tshernovits conference in the "rise of Yiddish". *International Journal of the Sociology of Language*, 24, 43–73.

(ed.) (1981a). *Never Say Die! A Thousand Years of Yiddish in Jewish Life and Letters*. The Hague: Mouton.

(1981b). The sociology of Jewish languages from the perspective of the general sociology of language: a preliminary formulation. *International Journal of the Sociology of Language*, 30, 5–16.

(ed.) (1985a). *Readings in the Sociology of Jewish Languages*. Leiden: Brill.

(1985b). The sociology of Jewish languages from a general sociolinguistic point of view. In Joshua A. Fishman (ed.), *Readings in the Sociology of Jewish Languages*, 3–21. Leiden: Brill.

(1991a). The Hebraist response to the Tschernovits conference. In Alan S. Kaye (ed.), *Semitic Studies in Honor of Wolf Leslau on the Occasion of His Eighty-Fifth Birthday*, 437–48. Wiesbaden: Otto Harrassowitz Verlag.

(1991b). *Reversing Language Shift: Theoretical and Empirical Foundations of Assistance to Threatened Languages*. Clevedon: Multilingual Matters.

(1991c). *Yiddish: Turning to Life*. Amsterdam: John Benjamins.

(ed.) (1993a). *The Earliest Stage of Language Planning: The "First Congress" Phenomenon*. Berlin: Mouton de Gruyter.

(1993b). The Tschernovits congress revisited: the First World Congress for Yiddish revisited, 85 years later. In Joshua A. Fishman (ed.), *The Earliest Stage of Language Planning: The "First Congress" Phenomenon*, 321–32. Berlin: Mouton de Gruyter.

(1996). Maintaining languages: what works? What doesn't? In Gina Cantoni (ed.), *Stabilizing Indigenous Languages*, 165–75. Tucson, University of Arizona Press.

(2002). The holiness of Yiddish: who says Yiddish is holy and why? *Language Policy*, 1, 123–41.

Fishman, Joshua A., Cooper, Robert L., and Ma, Roxana (1971). *Bilingualism in the Barrio*. Boston: Walter de Gruyter.

Fishman, Joshua A., and Fishman, David E. (1974). Yiddish in Israel: a case study of efforts to revise a monocentric language policy. *International Journal of the Sociology of Language*, 1, 126–46.

(1978). Yiddish in Israel: a case study of efforts to revise a monocentric language policy. In Joshua A. Fishman (ed.), *Advances in the Study of Societal Monolingualism*, 185–262. The Hague: Mouton.

Fishman, Joshua A., Hayden, Robert G., and Warshauer, Mary E. (1966). The non-English and the ethnic group press 1910–1960. In Joshua A. Fishman (ed.), *Language Loyalty in the United States: The Maintenance and Perpetuation of Non-English Mother Tongues by American Ethnic and Religious Groups*, 51–74. The Hague: Mouton.

Fishman, Joshua A., and Herasimchuk, Eleanor (1969). The multiple prediction of phonological variables in a bilingual speech community. *American Anthropologist*, 70, 648–57.

Fishman, Joshua A., and Hofman, John E. (1966). Mother tongue and nativity in the American population. In Joshua A. Fishman (ed.), *Language Loyalty in the United States: The Maintenance and Perpetuation of non-English Mother Tongues by American Ethnic and Religious Groups*, 34–50. The Hague: Mouton.

Fishman, Joshua A., and Kressel, Rose Helga (1974). The uses of Hebrew loanwords in spoken German in two bilingual communities. *Linguistics*, 139, 69–78.

Fishman, Joshua A., Nahirny, Vladimir C., Hofman, John E., and Hayden, Robert G. (1964). Language loyalty in the United States (mimeographed report). New York: Yeshiva University.

Fortis, Umberto (2006). *La parlata degli ebrei Venezia e le parlate giudeo-italiane*. Florence: La Guintina.

Fraade, Stephen (1992). Rabbinic views on the practice of Targum, and multilingualism in the Jewish Galilee of the third–sixth centuries. In Lee I. Levine (ed.), *The Galilee in Late Antiquity*, 252–86. New York: Jewish Theological Seminary of America.

(2011). Before and after Babel: linguistic exceptionalism and pluralism in early rabbinic literature. *Diné Israel: Studies in Halacha and Jewish Law*, 28, 31–68.

Frey, Jorg (2010). Essenes. In John J. Collins and Daniel C. Harlow (eds.), *The Eerdmans Dictionary of Early Judaism*, 599–602. Grand Rapids, MI: William B. Eerdmans Publishing.

Friedman, Richard Elliot (1997). *Who Wrote the Bible?* New York: HarperOne.

Friedman, Yohanan (2012). Dhimma. In Kate Fleet, Gudrun Krämer, Denis Matringe, John Nawas, and Everett Rowson (eds.), *Encyclopaedia of Islam* (3rd edn), 87–92. Leiden: Brill.

Fudeman, Kirsten (2010). *Vernacular Voices: Language and Identity in Medieval French Jewish Communities*. Philadelphia: University of Pennsylvania Press.

Gar, Joseph (1972). Lithuania. In Cecil Roth and Geoffrey Wigoder (eds.), *Encyclopedia Judaica*, vol. XI, 362–90. Jerusalem: Keter.

Garbell, Irene (1965). *The Jewish Neo-Aramaic Dialect of Persian Azerbaijan*. The Hague: Mouton.

Gerhardsson, Birger (1961). *Memory and Manuscript: Oral Tradition and Written Transmission in Rabbinic Judaism and Early Christianity* (trans. Eric J. Sharpe). Lund, Sweden: C. W. K. Gleerup.

Gerzon, Jacob (1902). *Die judisch–deutsche Sprach*. Cologne: S. Salm.

Gianto, Agustinus (1999). Amarna Akkadian as a contact language. In Karel Van Lerberghe and Gabriela Voet (eds.), Languages and Cultures in Contact: At the Crossroads of Civilizations in the Syro-Mesopotamian Realm: Proceedings of the 42th RAI, 123–32. Louvain: Peeters.

Gil, Moshe (2004). *Jews in Islamic Countries in the Middle Ages* (trans. David Strassler). Leiden: Brill.

Gindin, Thamar E. (2010a). Judeo-Persian language. In Norman A. Stillman (ed.), *Encyclopedia of Jews in the Islamic World*, vol. III, 62–4. Leiden: Brill.

(2010b). Judeo-Persian literature (early period). In Norman A. Stillman (ed.), *Encyclopedia of Jews in the Islamic World*, vol. III, 64–6. Leiden: Brill.

(2012). Judeo-Persian language. In Ehsan Yarshater (ed.), *Encyclopedia Iranica*, vol. XV, fasc. 2, 132–9. New York: Encyclopædia Iranica Foundation.

Ginsburg, Louis (1906). Judah ben Barzillai. In *The Jewish Encyclopedia*, vol. VII, 340–1. New York: Funk & Wagnall.

Glinert, Lewis (1987). Hebrew–Yiddish diglossia: type and stereotype implications of the language of Ganzfried's *Kitzur*. *International Journal of the Sociology of Language*, 67, 39–56.

(1993). The first congress for Hebrew, or when is a congress not a congress? In Joshua A. Fishman (ed.), *The Earliest Stage of Language Planning: The "First Congress" Phenomenon*, 85–115. Berlin: Mouton de Gruyter.

Goitein, Shelomo Dov (1974). *Jews and Arabs: Their Contacts through the Ages*. New York: Schocken Books.

Golb, Norman (1996). *Who Wrote the Dead Sea Scrolls? The Search for the Secret of Qumran*. New York: Scribner.

Gold, David L. (1981). Jewish intralinguistics as a field of study. *International Journal of the Sociology of Language*, 30, 31–48.

Gold, David L. (1989). A sketch of the linguistic situation in Israel today. *Language in Society*, 18, 361–88.

Golden, Peter B., Ben-Shammai, Haggai, and Ròna-Tas, András (eds.) (2007). *The World of the Khazars*. Leiden: Brill.

Goodblatt, David (2010). Population structure and Jewish identity. In Catherine Hezser (ed.), *The Oxford Handbook of Jewish Daily Life in Roman Palestine*, 102–21. Oxford University Press.

Gottreich, Emily (2007). *The Mellah of Marrakesh: Jewish and Muslim Space in Morocco's Red City*. Bloomington: Indiana University Press.

Greenberg, Joseph H. (1950). Studies in African linguistic classification: IV Hamito-Semitic. *Southwestern Journal of Anthropology*, 6, 47–63.

Greenberg, Yosef Alchanan (ed.) (1980). *La'azei Rashi b'Tanakh [Foreign Words in Rashi Te'nach]*. Jerusalem: Greenberg.

Grossman, Jeffrey A. (2000). *The Discourse on Yiddish in Germany: From the Enlightenment to the Second Empire*. Elizabethtown, NY: Camden House.

Gruen, Erich S. (2002). *Heritage and Hellenism: The Reinvention of Jewish Tradition*. Berkeley: University of California Press.

Gruen, Erich S. (2010). Hellenism, Hellenization. In John J. Collins and Daniel C. Harlow (eds.), *The Eerdmans Dictionary of Early Judaism*, 723–6. Grand Rapids, MI: William B. Eerdmans Publishing.

Guanto, Agostinus (2011). Ugaritic. In Holger Gzella (ed.), *Languages from the World of the Bible*, 28–54. Berlin: Walter de Gruyter.

Gumperz, John J. (1968). The speech community. In David L. Sills (ed.), *International Encyclopedia of the Social Sciences*, vol. IX, 381–6. New York: Macmillan.

Gzella, Holger (ed.) (2011a). *Languages from the World of the Bible*. Berlin: Walter de Gruyter.

(2011b). Phoenician. In Holger Gzella (ed.), *Languages from the World of the Bible*, 55–75. Berlin: Walter de Gruyter.

(2011c). Ancient Hebrew. In Holger Gzella (ed.), *Languages from the World of the Bible*, 76–110. Berlin: Walter de Gruyter.

Hacker, Joseph R., and Shear, Adam (2011). Introduction: book history and the Hebrew book in Italy. In Joseph R. Hacker and Adam Shear (eds.), *The Hebrew Book in Early Modern Italy*, 1–17. Philadelphia: University of Pennsylvania Press.

Halevi (Kirtchuk), Pablo-Isaac (2005). The Hebrew language. In Martin Goodman, Jeremy Cohen, and David J. Sorkin (eds.), *The Oxford Handbook of Jewish Studies*, 491–514. Oxford University Press.

Halliday, Michael A. K. (1976). Anti-languages. *American Anthropologist*, 78, 570–84.

Harris, Roy (ed.) (1996). *The Origin of Language*. London: Continuum.

Harris, Tracy K. (1982). Editor's note: the name of the language of the Eastern Sephardim. *International Journal of the Sociology of Language*, 37, 5.

(1994). *Death of a Language: The History of Judeo-Spanish*. Newark: University of Delaware Press.

Harshav, Benjamin (1993). *Language in Time of Revolution*. Berkeley: University of California Press.

Hary, Benjamin (1995). Judeo-Arabic in its sociolinguistic setting. *Israel Oriental Studies*, 15, 73–99.

(2009). *Translating Religion: Linguistic Analysis of Judeo-Arabic Sacred Texts from Egypt*. Leiden: Brill.

(2012). Judeo-Arabic as a mixed language. In Liesbeth Zack and Arie Schippers (eds.), *Middle Arabic and Mixed Arabic: Diachrony and Synchrony*, 125–44. Leiden: Brill.

Haugen, Einar (1971). The ecology of language. *The Linguistic Reporter, Supplement*, 25, 19–26.

(1972a). *The Ecology of Language: Essays* by Einar Haugen, ed. Anwar S. Dil. Stanford University Press.

(1972b). The ecology of language. In *The Ecology of Language: Essays* by Einar Haugen, ed. Anwar S. Dil, 325–39. Stanford University Press.

He Kupenga Hao i te Reo Māori (2000). Māori language conversational ability. In *1966 Census Information*, 17. Wellington: Te Puni Kōkiri (Ministry of Māori Development).

Heather, Peter (1996). *The Goths*. Oxford: Blackwell.

Herman, Jan, and Yahil, Chaim (1972). Prague. In Cecil Roth and Geoffrey Wigoder (eds.), *Encyclopedia Judaica*, vol. XIII, 964–73. Jerusalem: Keter.

Herman, Simon N. (1961). Explorations in the social psychology of language choice. *Human Relations*, 14, 149–64.

Herzog, Marvin, Baviskar, Vera, Kiefer, Ulrike, Neumann, Robert, Putschke, Wolfgang, Sunshine, Andrew, and Weinreich, Uriel (eds.) (1992–2000). *The Language and Culture Atlas of Ashkenazic Jewry*. Tübingen: Max Niemeyer Verlag.

Hess, Richard S. (1993). Early Israel in Canaan: a survey of recent evidence and interpretations. *Palestinian Exploration Quarterly*, 125, 125–42.

Hezser, Catherine (2010a). Correlating literary, epigraphic and archeological sources. In Catherine Hezser (ed.), *The Oxford Handbook of Jewish Daily Life in Roman Palestine*, 9–27. Oxford University Press.

(2010b). Travel and mobility. In Catherine Hezser (ed.), *The Oxford Handbook of Jewish Daily Life in Roman Palestine*, 210–26. Oxford University Press.

(2010c). Private and public education. In Catherine Hezser (ed.), *The Oxford Handbook of Jewish Daily Life in Roman Palestine*, 465–99. Oxford University Press.

Hillgarth, Jocelyn N. (2009). *The Visigoths in History and Legend*. Toronto: Pontifical Institute of Mediaeval Studies.

Hobsbaum, Eric (2005). Benefits of diaspora. *London Review of Books*, 27, 16–19.

Hofman, John E. (1974). Predicting the use of Hebrew terms among Israeli psychologists. *International Journal of the Sociology of Language*, 3, 53–65.

Hohepa, Pat (2000). Towards 2030 AD: Māori language regeneration: examining Māori language health. Paper presented at conference on applied linguistics, Auckland.

Holmes, Urban Tigner (1962). *Daily Living in the Twelfth Century: Based on the Observations of Alexander Neckam in London and Paris*. Madison: University of Wisconsin Press.

Horbury, William, and Noy, David (1992). *Jewish Inscriptions of Graeco-Roman Egypt*. Cambridge University Press.

Hoyland, Robert Gerard (2003). Language and identity: the twin histories of Arabic and Aramaic. *Scripta Israelica Classica*, 23, 183–200.

Hyamson, Albert M. (ed.) (1939). *The British Consulate in Jerusalem in relation to the Jews of Palestine 1838–1914*, vol. I, *1838–1861*. London: Edward Goldston.

Hymes, Dell (1974). *Foundations in Sociolinguistics: An Ethnographic Approach*. Philadelphia: University of Pennsylvania Press.

Israel, Jonathan (1985). *European Jewry in the Age of Mercantilism*. London: Littman Library of Jewish Civilisation.

Jackendoff, Ray (2010a). *Meaning and the Lexicon: The Parallel Architecture 1975–2010*. Oxford University Press.

(2010b). The parallel architecture and its place in cognitive science. In Bernd Heine and Heiko Narrog (eds.), *The Oxford Handbook of Linguistic Analysis*, 583–605. Oxford University Press.

(2012). *Linguistic and sociolinguistic variation from the perspective of the parallel architecture*. Paper presented at the nineteenth Sociolinguistics symposium, Berlin.

Jacobs, Joseph (1892). Notes on the Jews of Angevin England. *Jewish Quarterly Review*, 4, 628–55.

(ed.) (1893). *The Jews of Angevin England: Documents and Records from Latin and Hebrew Sources Printed and Manuscript for the First Time Collected and Translated*. London: David Nutt.

(1906). Typography. In *The Jewish Encyclopedia*, vol. XII, 295–335. New York: Funk & Wagnall.

Jacobs, Neil G. (2005). *Yiddish: A Linguistic Introduction*. Cambridge University Press.

Jaffee, Martin S. (2001). *Torah in the Mouth: Writing and Oral Tradition in Palestinian Judaism, 200 BCE–400 CE*. Oxford University Press.

Janton, Pierre (1993). *Esperanto: Language, Literature, and Community* (trans. Humphrey Tonkin). Albany: State University of New York Press.

Jeffers, James S. (1998). Jewish and Christian families in first-century Rome. In Karl P. Donfried and Peter Richardson (eds.), *Judaism and Christianity in First-Century Rome*, 128–50. Grand Rapids, MI: William B. Eerdmans Publishing.

Jewish Publication Society (1982). *The Writings: A New Translation of the Holy Scriptures according to the Masoretic Text*. Philadelphia: Jewish Publication Society.

Jochnowitz, George (1981). Religion and taboo in Lason Akodesh (Judeo-Piedmontese). *International Journal of the Sociology of Language*, 30, 107–17.

(1985). Had-Gadya in Judeo-Italian and Chuadit (Judeo-Provençal). In Joshua A. Fishman (ed.), *Readings in the Sociology of Jewish Languages*, 241–5. Leiden: Brill.

Johansson, Sverker (2005). *Origins of Language: Constraints on Hypotheses*. Amsterdam: John Benjamins.

Johnson, Paul (1987). *The History of the Jews*. New York: Harper & Row.

Jones, Mari C. (1998a). Death of a language, birth of an identity: Brittany and the Bretons. *Language Problems and Language Planning*, 22, 129–42.

(1998b). *Language Obsolescence and Revitalization: Linguistic Change in Two Sociolinguistically Contrasting Welsh Communities*. Oxford: Clarendon Press.

Josephus, Flavius (1737 [78]). *Wars of the Jews* (trans. William Whiston). London: Bowyer.

Kachru, Braj B. (1986). *The Alchemy of English: The Spread, Functions, and Models of Non-Native Englishes*. Oxford: Pergamon Press.

Kahneman, Daniel (2011). *Thinking, Fast and Slow*. New York: Farrar, Straus & Giroux.

Kalisch, Sven Muhammad (2008a). Islamic theology without the historic Muhammad: comments on the challenges of the historical-critical method for Islamic thinking. *Wall Street Journal*, November 15.

(2008b). Islamische Theologie ohne historichen Muhammad: Anmerkungen zu den Herausforderungen der historisch-kritischen Methode für das islamische Denken. *Newsletter der Giordano-Bruno-Stiftung*, November 20.

Kaplan, Steven (1992). *The Beta Israel (Falasha) in Ethiopia: From Earliest Times to the Twentieth Century*. New York University Press.

Kassow, Samuel (2007). Introduction. In Steven Katz (ed.), *The Shtetl: New Evaluations*, 1–28. New York University Press.

Katz, Dovid (1985). Hebrew, Aramaic and the rise of Yiddish. In Joshua A. Fishman (ed.), *Readings in the Sociology of Jewish Languages*, 85–103. Leiden: Brill.

(1991). A late twentieth century case of *katoves*. In Dov-Ber Kerler (ed.), *History of Yiddish Studies*, 141–63. Chur, Switzerland: Harwood Academic Publishers.

(1993). East and West, khes and shin and the origin of Yiddish. In Israel Bartal, Ezra Mendelsohn, and Chava Turniansky (eds.), *Studies in Jewish Culture in Honour of Chone Shmeruk*, 9–38. Jerusalem: Zalman Center for Jewish History.

(2004). *Words on Fire: The Unfinished Story of Yiddish*. New York: Basic Books.

Katz, Steven (ed.) (2007). *The Shtetl: New Evaluations*. New York University Press.

Katzburg, Nathaniel (1972). Hungary. In Cecil Roth and Geoffrey Wigoder (eds.), *Encyclopedia Judaica*, vol. VIII, 1088–110. Jerusalem: Keter.

Kayserling, Moritz (Meyer) (1906). Moses ben Enoch. In *The Jewish Encyclopedia*, vol. IX, 65. New York: Funk & Wagnall.

Kennedy, Hugh (2007). *The Great Arab Conquests: How the Spread of Islam Changed the World We Live In*. Philadelphia: Da Capo Press.

Kerkeslager, Allen (2010). Cyrenaica. In John J. Collins and Daniel C. Harlow (eds.), *The Eerdmans Dictionary of Early Judaism*, 503–4. Grand Rapids, MI: William B. Eerdmans Publishing.

Kheimets, Nina G., and Epstein, Alek D. (2005). Languages of science in the era of nation-state formation: the Israeli universities and their (non)participation in the revival of Hebrew. *Journal of Multilingual and Multicultural Development*, 26, 12–36.

Killebrew, Anne (2010). Village and countryside. In Catherine Hezser (ed.), *The Oxford Handbook of Jewish Daily Life in Roman Palestine*, 189–209. Oxford University Press.

King, Robert D. (2012). Were Polish Jews displaced Germans? *Historical Methods: A Journal of Quantitative and Interdisciplinary History*, 45, 161–4.

King, Robert D., and Faber, Alice (1984). Yiddish and the settlement history of Ashkenazic Jews. In David R. Blumenthal (ed.), *Approaches to Judaism in Medieval Times*, vol. I, 393–425. Chico, CA: Scholars Press.

Kisch, Guido (1949). *The Jews in Medieval Germany: A Study of Their Legal and Social Status*. University of Chicago Press.

Kister, Meir J. (1986). The massacre of the Banū Qurayẓa: a re-examination of a tradition. *Jerusalem Studies in Arabic and Islam*, 8, 61–96.

Kiwitt, Marc (2011). Judeo-French. Jewish Language Research Website, www.jewish-languages.org/judeo-french.html.

Klein, Elka (2006). *Jews, Christian Society, and Royal Power in Medieval Barcelona*. Ann Arbor: University of Michigan Press.

Kleineidam, Hartmut (1992). Politique de diffusion linguistique et francophonie: l'action linguistique menée par la France. *International Journal of the Sociology of Language*, 95, 11–31.

Klijnsmit, Anthony J. (1986). *Spinoza and Grammatical Tradition*. Leiden: Brill.

Kloss, Heinz (1966). German-American language maintenance efforts. In Joshua A. Fishman (ed.), *Language Loyalty in the United States: The Maintenance and Perpetuation of Non-English Mother Tongues by American Ethnic and Religious Groups*, 206–52. The Hague: Mouton.

Koester, Helmut (2000). *Introduction to the New Testament: History and Literature of Early Christianity* (2nd edn). Berlin: Walter de Gruyter.

Koestler, Arthur (1976). *The Thirteenth Tribe: The Khazar Empire and Its Heritage.* New York: Random House

Kopeliovich, Shulamit (2009). *Reversing Language Shift in the Immigrant Family: A Case Study of a Russian-Speaking Community in Israel.* Saarbrücken: Verlag Dr Müller.

(2011). Family language policy: a case study of a Russian-Hebrew bilingual family: toward a theoretical framework. *Diaspora, Indigenous, and Minority Education,* 4, 162–78.

Kosover, Mordecai (1966). *Arabic Elements in Palestinian Yiddish: The Old Ashkenazic Jewish Community in Palestine, Its History and Its Language.* Jerusalem: Rubin Mass.

Kottsieper, Ingo (2007). "And they did not care to speak Yehudit": on linguistic change in Judah during the late Persian era. In Oded Lipschits, Gary N. Knoppers, and Rainer Albertz (eds.), *Judah and the Judeans in the Fourth Century BCE,* 95–124. Winona Lake, IN: Eisenbrauns.

Kovács, András, and Forrás-Biró, Aletta (2011). *Jewish Life in Hungary: Achievements, Challenges and Priorities since the Collapse of Communism.* London: Institute for Jewish Policy Research.

Kraemer, Roberta, Zisenwine, David, Keren, Michal Levy, and Schers, David (1995). A study of Jewish adolescent Russian immigrants to Israel: language and identity. *International Journal of the Sociology of Language,* 116, 153–9.

Krämer, Gudrun (1989). *The Jews of Modern Egypt 1914–1952.* London: I. B. Tauris.

Krauss, Michael (1998). The condition of Native North American languages: the need for realistic assessment and action. *International Journal of the Sociology of Language,* 132, 9–21.

Kreindler, Isabelle, Bensoussan, Marsha, Avinor, Eleanor, and Bram, Chen (1995). Circassian Israelis: multilingualism as a way of life. *Language, Culture and Curriculum,* 8, 149–62.

Kugel, James L. (2008). *How to Read the Bible: A Guide to Scripture, Then and Now.* New York: Simon & Schuster.

Kugel, James L., and Greer, Rowan A. (1986). *Early Biblical Interpretation.* Philadelphia: Westminster Press.

Kulick, Don (1992). *Language Shift and Cultural Reproduction: Socialization, Self and Syncretism in a Papua New Guinean Village.* Cambridge University Press.

Kushner, David (1986). *Palestine in the Late Ottoman Period: Political, Social, and Economic Transformation.* Leiden: Brill.

Kutscher, Edward Y. (1974). *The Language and Linguistic Background of the Isaiah Scroll (I Q Isaa).* Leiden: Brill.

Kuzar, Ron (2001). *Hebrew and Zionism: A Discourse Analytic Cultural Study.* Berlin: Mouton de Gruyter.

Labov, William (1966). *The Social Stratification of English in New York City.* Washington, DC: Center for Applied Linguistics.

(2008). Unendangered dialects, endangered people. In Kendall A. King, Natalie Schilling-Estes, Lyn Fogle, Jackie Lou Lia, and Barbara Soukup (eds.), *Sustaining Linguistic Diversity: Endangered and Minority Languages and Language Varieties,* 219–38. Washington, DC: Georgetown University Press.

Lamy, Paul (ed.) (1977). *Language Maintenance and Language Shift in Canada: New Dimensions in the Use of Census Language Data*. University of Ottawa Press.

Lapin, Hayim (2010). The rabbinic movement. In Judith R. Baskin and Kenneth Seeskin (eds.), *The Cambridge Guide to Jewish History, Religion, and Culture*, 58–84. Cambridge University Press.

Lasker, Daniel J. (2010). Karaism. In Norman A. Stillman (ed.), *Encyclopedia of Jews in the Islamic World*, vol. III, 104–14. Leiden: Brill.

Laskier, Michael M. (1995). Egyptian Jewry under the Nasser regime, 1956–70. *Middle Eastern Studies*, 31, 573–620.

Lass, Roger (1997). *Historical Linguistics and Language Change*. Cambridge University Press.

Lassner, Jacob (1993). *Demonizing the Queen of Sheba: Boundaries of Gender and Culture in Postbiblical Judaism and Medieval Islam*. University of Chicago Press.

Lecker, Michael (1995). Judaism among Kinda and the ridda of Kinda. *Journal of the American Oriental Society*, 115, 625–50.

Lefebvre, Claire (1986). Relexification in creole linguistics revisited: the case of Haitian creole. In Pieter Muysken and Norval Smith (eds.), *Substrata versus Universals in Creole Genesis*, 279–301. Philadelphia: John Benjamins.

Lentin, Jérôme, and Grand'Henry, Jacques (eds.) (2008). *Moyen arabe et variétés mixtes de l'arabe à travers l'histoire*. Institut Orientaliste de Louvain.

Lesser, Jeff (1995). *Welcoming the Undesirables: Brazil and the Jewish Question*. Berkeley: University of California Press.

Lesser, Jeff, and Rein, Ranan (eds.) (2008). *Rethinking Jewish-Latin Americans*. Albuquerque: University of New Mexico Press.

Levi, John S., and Bergman, George (1974). *Australian Genesis: Jewish Convicts and Settlers 1788–1850*. Adelaide: Rigby.

Levin, Tamar, Shohamy, Elana, and Spolsky, Bernard (2003). Academic achievements of immigrants in schools: report to the Ministry of Education. University of Tel Aviv.

Levine, Irene (2009). Jews in Norway. In M. Avrum Ehrlich (ed.), *Encyclopedia of the Jewish Diaspora: Origins, Experiences, and Culture*, vol. III, 1082–6. Santa Barbara, CA: ABC-CLIO.

Levine, Lee I. (2000). *The Ancient Synagogue: The First Thousand Years*. New Haven, CT: Yale University Press.

Levinsohn, Isaac Baer (1828). *Teudah beyisrael*. Vilna: Grodno.

Levy, Raphael (1941). Rashi's contribution to the French language. *Jewish Quarterly Review*, 23, 71–8.

    (1964). *Trésor de la langue des juifs français au moyen âge*. Austin: University of Texas Press.

Lewis, Geoffrey (1999). *The Turkish Language Reform: A Catastrophic Success*. Oxford University Press.

Lewis, M. Paul (ed.) (2009). *Ethnologue: Languages of the World* (16th edn). Dallas: SIL International.

Lewis, M. Paul, Simons, Gary F., and Fennig, Charles D. (eds.) (2013). *Ethnologue: Languages of the World* (17th edn). Dallas: SIL International.

Lewontin, Richard C. (2012). Is there a Jewish gene? *New York Review of Books*, December 6.

Lewy, Hans (1938). Aristotle and the Jewish sage according to Clearchus of Soli. *Harvard Theological Review*, 31, 205–35.

Lieberman, Saul (1942). *Greek in Jewish Palestine*. New York: Jewish Theological Seminary.

Lim, Timothy H. (2010). Multilingualism. In John J. Collins and Daniel C. Harlow (eds.), *The Eerdmans Dictionary of Early Judaism*, 973–5. Grand Rapids, MI: William B. Eerdmans Publishing.

Lipman, Vivian David (1972). England. In Cecil Roth and Geoffrey Wigoder (eds.), *Encyclopedia Judaica*, vol. VI, 758–67. Jerusalem: Keter.

Loewe, Louis (ed.) (1890). *Diaries of Sir Moses and Lady Montefiore*. London: Griffith, Farran & Co.

Loftus, Elizabeth F. (1996). *Eyewitness Testimony*. Cambridge, MA: Harvard University Press.

López-Moorillas, Consuelo (2006). Language. In Maria Rosa Menocal, Raymond P. Scheindlin, and Michael A. Sells (eds.), *The Literature of Al-Andalus*, 33–59. Cambridge University Press.

Lord, Albert B. (1981). *The Singer of Tales*. Cambridge, MA: Harvard University Press.

Lowenstein, Stephen M. (1989). *Frankfurt on the Hudson: The German–Jewish Community of Washington Heights*. Detroit: Wayne State University Press.

Lumpkin, Joseph B. (ed.) (2009). *The Books of Enoch: The Complete Volume Containing: 1 Enoch (The Ethiopic Book of Enoch), 2 Enoch (The Slavonic Secrets of Enoch), 3 Enoch (The Hebrew Book of Enoch)*. Blountsville, AL: Fifth Estate Publishers.

Luncz, Abraham Moses (1882–1919). *Jerusalem Year-Book for the Diffusion of an Accurate Knowledge of Ancient and Modern Palestine*. Jerusalem: A. M. Luncz.

Lundgren, Svante (2009). Jews in Finland. In M. Avrum Ehrlich (ed.), *Encyclopedia of the Jewish Diaspora: Origins, Experiences, and Culture*, vol. III, 1071–6. Santa Barbara, CA: ABC-CLIO.

Malinowski, Arlese (1985). Judezmo in the US today. In Joshua A. Fishman (ed.), *Readings in the Sociology of Jewish Languages*, 212–24. Leiden: Brill.

Mandel, George (1993). Why did Ben-Yehuda suggest the revival of spoken Hebrew? In Lewis Glinert (ed.), *Hebrew in Ashkenaz: A Language in Exile*, 193–207. Oxford University Press.

Marcus, Simon (1972). Corfu. In Cecil Roth and Geoffrey Wigoder (eds.), *Encyclopedia Judaica*, vol. V, 970–2. Jerusalem: Keter.

Margolis, Rebecca (2010). Le Montréal yiddish: un siècle d'évolution. In Pierre Anctil and Ira Robinson (eds.), *Les communautés juives de Montréal: Histoire et enjeux contemporains*, 92–115. Sillery, CA: Editions du Septentrion.

McNeill, David (2012). *How Language Began: Gesture and Speech in Human Evolution*. Cambridge University Press.

Medres, Israel (2003). *Between the Wars: Canadian Jews in Transition* (trans. Vivian Felsen). Montreal: Véhicule Press.

Meir, Iris, and Sandler, Wendy (2008). *A Language in Space: The Story of Israeli Sign Language*. New York: Lawrence Erlbaum.

Meir-Glitzenstein, Esther (2011). Operation Magic Carpet: constructing the myth of the magical immigration of Yemenite Jews to Israel. *Israel Studies*, 16, 149–73.

Mendelsohn, Ezra (1987). *The Jews of East Central Europe between the World Wars.* Bloomington: Indiana University Press.

Meroz, Yohanan (1972). Netherlands. In Cecil Roth and Geoffrey Wigoder (eds.), *Encyclopedia Judaica*, vol. XII, 973–93. Jerusalem: Keter.

Mieses, Matthias (1915). *Die Entstehungsursache der jüdeschen Dialekte.* Vienna: R. Löwit.

(1924). *Die jiddische Sprache: Eine historische Grammatik des Idioms der integtralen Juden Ost- und Mitteleuropas.* Berlin: Benjamin Harz.

Milano, Attilio (1972a). Italy. In Cecil Roth and Geoffrey Wigoder (eds.), *Encyclopedia Judaica*, vol. IX, 1115–32. Jerusalem: Keter.

(1972b). Milan. In Cecil Roth and Geoffrey Wigoder (eds.), *Encyclopedia Judaica*, vol. XI, 1545. Jerusalem: Keter.

Miles, Wlilliam E. S. (2012). *Jews of Nigeria: An Afro-Judaic Odyssey.* Princeton, NJ: Marcus Wiener Publishers.

Mintz, Alan (ed.) (1993a). *Hebrew in America: Perspectives and Prospects.* Detroit: Wayne State University Press.

(1993b). A sanctuary in the wilderness: the beginnings of the Hebrew movement in America in Hatoren. In Alan Mintz (ed.), *Hebrew in America: Perspectives and Prospects*, 29–67. Detroit: Wayne State University Press.

Montefiore, Simon Sebag (2011). *Jerusalem: The Biography.* London: Weidenfeld & Nicolson.

Moore, Robert Ian (2012). *The War on Heresy.* Cambridge, MA: Harvard University Press.

Morag, Shlomo (1972). Pronunciations of Hebrew. In Cecil Roth and Geoffrey Wigoder (eds.), *Encyclopedia Judaica*, vol. XIII, 1120–45. Jerusalem: Keter.

(1993). The emergence of Modern Hebrew. In Lewis Glinert (ed.), *Hebrew in Ashkenaz: A Language in Exile*, 208–21. Oxford University Press.

Moreen, Vera B. (2010a). Judeo-Persian literature (medieval period). In Norman A. Stillman (ed.), *Encyclopedia of Jews in the Islamic World*, vol. III, 65–9. Leiden: Brill.

(2010b). Iran/Persia. In Norman A. Stillman (ed.), *Encyclopedia of Jews in the Islamic World*, vol. III, 581–6 Leiden: Brill.

Muysken, Pieter (1981). Halfway between Quechua and Spanish: the case for relexification. In Arnold Highfield and Albert Valdman (eds.), *Historicity and Variation in Creole Studies*, 52–78. Ann Arbor, MI: Karoma.

Myhill, John (2004). *Language in Jewish Society: Towards a New Understanding.* Clevedon: Multilingual Matters.

Nadel, Elizabeth, and Fishman, Joshua A. (1977). English in Israel. In Joshua A. Fishman, Robert L. Cooper, and Andrew W. Conrad (eds.), *The Spread of English*, 137–67. Rowley, MA: Newbury House Publishers.

Nadler, Steven (2001). *Spinoza: A Life.* Cambridge University Press.

Nahir, Moshe (1974). A study on the acceptance of the lexical work of the Hebrew Language Academy. *Hebrew Abstracts*, 15, 50–2.

(1988). Language planning and language acquisition: the "Great Leap" in the Hebrew revival. In Christina Bratt Paulston (ed.), *International Handbook of Bilingualism and Bilingual Education*, 275–95. New York: Greenwood Press.

Nebes, Norbert, and Stein, Peter (2008). Ancient South Arabian. In Roger D. Woodard (ed.), *The Ancient Languages of Syria-Palestine and Arabia*, 145–78. Cambridge University Press.

Nekvapil, Jiří, and Neustupný, Jiří V. (1998). Linguistic minorities in the Czech Republic. In Christina Bratt Paulston and Donald Peckham (eds.), *Linguistic Minorities in Central and Eastern Europe*, 116–35. Clevedon: Multilingual Matters.

Newby, Gordon Daniel (1971). Observations about an early Judaeo-Arabic. *Jewish Quarterly Review*, 61, 212–21.

(2010). Arabian Peninsula. In John J. Collins and Daniel C. Harlow (eds.), *The Eerdmans Dictionary of Early Judaism*, 358–60. Grand Rapids, MI: William B. Eerdmans Publishing.

Niborski, Yitskhok, and Neuberg, Simon (eds.) (2012). *Dictionnaire des mots d'origine hébraïque et araméenne en usage dans la langue yiddish* (3rd edn). Paris: Bibliothèque Medem.

Nirenberg, David (2013). *Anti-Judaism: The Western Tradition*. New York: W. W. Norton.

Noy, David (1997). Writing in tongues: the use of Greek, Latin and Hebrew in Jewish inscriptions from Roman Italy. *Journal of Jewish Studies*, 48, 300–11.

(2005a). *Jewish Inscriptions of Western Europe*, vol. I, *Italy (excluding the City of Rome), Spain and Gaul*. Cambridge University Press.

(2005b). *Jewish Inscriptions of Western Europe*, vol. II, Rome. Cambridge University Press.

Olshtain, Elite, and Blum-Kulka, Shoshana (1989). Happy Hebrish: mixing and switching in American–Israeli family interactions. In Susan Gass, Carolyn Madden, Dennis Preston, and Larry Selinker (eds.), *Variation in Second Language Acquisition: Discourse and Pragmatics*, 37–59. Clevedon: Multilingual Matters.

Orleck, Annelise (2001). Soviet Jews: the city's newest immigrants. In Nancy Foner (ed.), *New Immigrants in New York* (rev. edn), 111–41. New York: Columbia University Press.

Ornan, Uzzi (1985). Hebrew is not a Jewish language. In Joshua A. Fishman (ed.), *Readings in the Sociology of Jewish Languages*, 22–6. Leiden: Brill.

Ostrer, Harry (2012). *Legacy: A Genetic History of the Jewish People*. Oxford University Press.

Outhwaite, Ben (2010). Hebrew letters in the Geniza. In Norman A. Stillman (ed.), *Encyclopedia of Jews in the Islamic World*, vol. I, 550–1. Leiden: Brill.

Paper, Herbert H. (1982). Language spread: the ancient Near Eastern world. In Robert L. Cooper (ed.), *Language Spread: Studies in Diffusion and Social Change*, 107–17. Bloomington: Indiana University Press.

(1995). Review of Wexler. *Jewish Quarterly Review*, 85, 451–2.

Parfitt, Tudor (2013). *Black Jews in Africa and the Americas*. Cambridge, MA: Harvard University Press.

Parfitt, Tudor, and Egorova, Yulia (2006). *Genetics, Mass Media and Identity: A Case Study of the Genetic Research on Lemba and Bene Israel*. London: Routledge.

Parker, Sandra (1978). Yiddish schools in North America. In Bernard Spolsky and Robert L. Cooper (eds.), *Case Studies in Bilingual Education*, 312–30. Rowley, MA: Newbury House Publishers.

Patai, Raphael (1977). *The Jewish Mind*. New York: Scribner.

Penny, Ralph John (1991). *A History of the Spanish Language*. Cambridge University Press.

Perez Fernandez, Miguel (1997). *An Introductory Grammar of Rabbinic Hebrew* (trans. John Elwode). Leiden: Brill.

Person, Jr., Raymond E. (2010). *The Deuteronomic History and the Book of Chronicles: Scribal Works in an Oral World*. Atlanta: Society of Biblical Literature.

Petrie, Sir William Matthew Flinders, and Spiegelberg, Wilhelm (1896). *Six Temples at Thebes*. London: B. Quaritch.

Philo (1854 [40]). Legatio ad Gaium. In Charles D. Yonge (ed., trans.), *The Works of Philo: Complete and Unabridged*, 757–90. London: H. G. Bohn.

Pirnazar, Nahid (2005). The rainbow of Jewish ethnicity. *Jewish Chronicle*, 124, 34–7.

Polotsky, Hans Jacob (1964). Aramaic, Syriac, and Ge'ez. *Journal of Semitic Studies*, 9, 1–10.

Porten, Bezalel (1968). The Aramaic texts. In Bezalel Porten (ed.), *The Elephantine Papyri in English: Three Millennia of Cross-Cultural Continuity and Change*, 75–276. Leiden: Brill.

Preston, Dennis R. (ed.) (1999). *Handbook of Perceptual Dialectology*. Amsterdam: John Benjamins.

Prince-Gibson, Bella (2012). "Lost" Indian Jews come home. *Haaretz*, December 27.

Quirin, James (1992). *The Evolution of the Ethiopian Jews: A History of the Beta Israel (Falasha) to 1920*. Philadelphia: University of Pennsylvania Press.

Rabin, Chaim (1958). *A Short History of the Hebrew Language*. Jerusalem: Jewish Agency.

(1968). The translation process and the nature of the Septuagint. *Textus*, 6, 1–26.

(1981). What constitutes a Jewish language? *International Journal of the Sociology of Language*, 30, 19–28.

Rajak, Tessa (2011). Surviving by the book: the language of the Greek Bible and Jewish identity. In Erich S. Gruen (ed.), *Cultural Identity in the Ancient Mediterranean*, 273–88. Los Angeles: Getty Publications.

Ram, Drorit (2006). *Hebrew and English as medium of instruction in Israeli tertiaty education: linguistic ideology and practice*. PhD dissertation, Bar-Ilan University, Ramat-Gan, Israel.

Raphael, Fredric (2013). *A Jew among Romans: The Life and Legacy of Flavius Josephus*. New York: Pantheon Books.

Reif, Stefan C. (2010). Prayer and liturgy. In Catherine Hezser (ed.), *The Oxford Handbook of Jewish Daily Life in Roman Palestine*, 545–65. Oxford University Press.

Remmenick, Larissa (2012). *Russian Jews on Three Continents: Identity, Integration, and Conflict*. New Brunswick, NJ: Transaction Publishers.

Renauld, Georges (2002). *Adolphe Crémieux: Homme d'Etat français, Juif et franc-maçon: Le combat pour la République*. Paris: Detrad.

Richey, Matthew (2012). The use of Greek at Qumran: manuscript and epigraphic evidence for a marginalized language. *Dead Sea Discoveries*, 19, 177–97.

Robin, Christian Julien (2003). Le judaïsme de Himyar. *Arabia*, 1, 97–172.

Roland, Joan G. (1998). *The Jewish Communities of India: Identity in a Colonial Era*. New Brunswick, NJ: Transaction Publishers.

Rollston, Christopher A. (2006). Scribal education in ancient Israel: the Old Hebrew epigraphic evidence. *Bulletin of the American Schools of Oriental Research*, 344, 47–73.

Rosenbaum, Yehudit, Nadel, Elizabeth, Cooper, Robert L., and Fishman, Joshua A. (1977). English on Keren Kayemet Street. In Joshua A. Fishman, Robert L. Cooper, and Andrew W. Conrad (eds.), *The Spread of English*, 179–96. Rowley, MA: Newbury House Publishers.

Rosenberg, Stephen G. (2004). The Jewish temple at Elephantine. *Near Eastern Archeology*, 67, 4–13.

Roskies, Diane K., and Roskies, David G. (1975). *The Shtetl Book: An Introduction to East European Jewish Life and Lore*. New York: Workman's Circle.

Rosman, Moshe (2007). *How Jewish Is Jewish History?* Portland, OR: Littman Library of Jewish Civilization.

Roth, Cecil (1941). *The French Connection: A History of the Jews in England*. Oxford University Press.

Roumani, Maurice M. (2008). *The Jews of Libya: Coexistence, Persecution, Resettlement*. Eastbourne: Sussex Academic Press.

Rozenblit, Marsha L. (2010). European Jewry: 1800–1933. In Judith R. Baskin and Kenneth Seeskin (eds.), *The Cambridge Guide to Jewish History, Religion, and Culture*, 169–207. Cambridge University Press.

Ruderman, David B. (2010). *Early Modern Jewry: A New Cultural History*. Princeton University Press.

Rutgers, Leonard V. (2002). Justinian's Novella 146 between Jews and Christians. In Richard L. Kalmin and Seth Schwartz (eds.), *Jewish Culture and Society under the Christian Roman Empire*, 385–407. Leiden: Peeters.

Rutland, Suzanne (2005). *The Jews in Australia*. Cambridge University Press.

Sáenz-Badillos, Angel (1996). *A History of the Hebrew Language* (trans. John Elwode). Cambridge University Press.

Safrai, Ze'ev (1994). *The Economy of Roman Palestine*. London: Routledge.

Safran, Linda (2011). Public textual cultures: a case study in southern Italy. In William Robins (ed.), *Textual Cultures of Medieval Italy*, 115–44. University of Toronto Press.

Salminen, Tapani (1999). UNESCO red book on endangered languages: Europe. Helsinki University, www.helsinki.fi/~tasalmin/europe_index.html.

(2007). Europe and north Asia. In Christopher Moseley (ed.), *Encyclopedia of the World's Endangered Languages*, 211–82. London: Routledge.

Sand, Shlomo (2009). *The Invention of the Jewish People* (trans. Yael Lotan). London: Verso.

Saulson, Scott B. (ed.) (1979). *Institutionalized Language Planning: Documents and Analysis of the Revival of Hebrew*. The Hague: Mouton.

Scheiber, Alexander (1955). Jews at Intercisa in Pannonia. *Jewish Quarterly Review*, 45, 189–97.

Scheindlin, Raymond P. (2006). Moses ibn Ezra. In Maria Rosa Menocal, Raymond P. Scheindlin, and Michael A. Sells (eds.), *The Literature of Al-Andalus*, 252–64. Cambridge University Press.

Schenker, Adrian (2008). From the first printed Hebrew, Greek and Latin Bibles to the first polyglot Bible, the Complutensian Polyglot Bible: 1477–1517. In Magne Saebø (ed.), *Hebrew Bible/Old Testament: The History of Its Interpretation, from the Renaissance to the Enlightenment*, 276–94. Göttingen: Vandenhoeck & Ruprecht.

Schniedewind, William M. (1999). Qumran Hebrew as an antilanguage. *Journal of Biblical Hebrew*, 118, 235–52.

Schniedewind, William M., and Hunt, Joel H. (2007). *A Primer on Ugaritic: Language, Culture, and Literature*. Cambridge University Press.

Schor, Esther (2009). Esperanto: a Jewish story. *Pakn Treger*, 60, 2–7.

Schreier, Joshua (2010). *Arabs of the Jewish Faith: The Civilizing Mission in Colonial Algeria*. Piscataway, NJ: Rutgers University Press.

Schwartz, Mila, and Katzir, Tami (2012). Depth of lexical knowledge among bilingual children: the impact of schooling. *Reading and Writing*, 25, 1947–71.

Schwartz, Mila, Kozminsky, Eli, and Leiken, Mark (2009). Socio-linguistic factors in second language lexical knowledge: the case of second-generation children of Russian-Jewish immigrants in Israel. *Language, Culture and Curriculum*, 21, 14–27.

Schwartz, Seth (1995). Language, power and identity in ancient Palestine. *Past and Present*, 148, 3–47.

Schwarzfuchs, Lyse (2011). *L'Hébreu dans le livre à Genève au XVIe siècle*. Geneva: Librairie Droz.

Schwarzfuchs, Simon (1972a). Crusades. In Cecil Roth and Geoffrey Wigoder (eds.), *Encyclopedia Judaica*, vol. V, 1134–45. Jerusalem: Keter.

(1972b). France. In Cecil Roth and Geoffrey Wigoder (eds.), *Encyclopedia Judaica*, vol. VII, 22–32. Jerusalem: Keter.

(1972c). Spain. In Cecil Roth and Geoffrey Wigoder (eds.), *Encyclopedia Judaica*, vol. XV, 220–2, 226–44. Jerusalem: Keter.

Seckbach, Fern, and Cooper, Robert L. (1977). The maintenance of English in Ramat Eshkol. In Joshua A. Fishman, Robert L. Cooper, and Andrew W. Conrad (eds.), *The Spread of English*, 168–78. Rowley, MA: Newbury House Publishers.

Segal, Moses Hirsch (1927). *A Grammar of Mishnaic Hebrew*. Oxford: Clarendon Press.

Sephiha, Haim Vidal (1985). "Christianisms" in Judeo-Spanish (calque and vernacular). In Joshua A. Fishman (ed.), *Readings in the Sociology of Jewish Languages*, 179–94. Leiden: Brill.

(1992). Ladino and Djudezmo. In Gilles Veinstein (ed.), *Salonique, 1850–1918: La "ville des Juifs" et le réveil des Balkans*, 79–92. Paris: Editions Autrement.

Shandler, Jeffrey (2006). *Adventures in Yiddishland: Postvernacular Language and Culture*. Berkeley: University of California Press.

Shapiro, Daniel (2010). Juhuri. In Norman A. Stillman (ed.), *Encyclopedia of Jews in the Islamic World*, vol. III, 80–1. Leiden: Brill.

Shear, Adam (2010). Jews and Judaism in early modern Europe. In Judith R. Baskin and Kenneth Seeskin (eds.), *The Cambridge Guide to Jewish History, Religion, and Culture*, 140–68. Cambridge University Press.

Shinan, Avigdor (1987). Sermons, Targums and reading from Scriptures in the ancient synagogue. In Lee I. Levine (ed.), *The Synagogue in Late Antiquity*, 97–102. Philadelphia: Jewish Theological Seminary.

Shohamy, Elana (2007). At what cost? Methods of language revival and protection: examples from Hebrew. In Kendall A. King, Natalie Schilling-Estes, Lyn Fogle, Jia Jackie Lou, and Barbara Soukup (eds.), *Sustaining Linguistic Diversity: Endangered and Minority Languages and Language Varieties*, 205–18. Washington, DC: Georgetown University Press.

Sivan, Daniel (2001). *A Grammar of the Ugaritic Language.* Leiden: Brill.

Slutsky, Yehuda (1972a). Idelovitch, David. In Cecil Roth and Geoffrey Wigoder (eds.), *Encyclopedia Judaica,* vol. VIII, 1223–4. Jerusalem: Keter.

(1972b). Russia. In Cecil Roth and Geoffrey Wigoder (eds.), *Encyclopedia Judaica,* vol. XIV, 433–93. Jerusalem: Keter.

Smelik, Willem (2010). The languages of Roman Palestine. In Catherine Hezser (ed.), *The Oxford Handbook of Jewish Daily Life in Roman Palestine,* 122–44. Oxford University Press.

Sokoloff, Michael (ed.) (2002a). *A Dictionary of Jewish Palestinian Aramaic of the Byzantine Period.* Ramat Gan, Israel: Bar-Ilan University Press.

(2002b). *A Dictionary of Jewish Babylonian Aramaic of the Talmudic and Geonic Periods.* Ramat-Gan, Israel: Bar-Ilan University Press.

Sokoloff, Michael, and Yahalom, Joseph (1985). Aramaic piyyutim from the Byzantine period. *Jewish Quarterly Review,* 75, 309–21.

Southwood, Katherine E. (2011). "And they could not understand Jewish speech": language, ethnicity, and Nehemiah's intermarriage crisis. *Journal of Theological Studies,* 62, 1–19.

Spector, Graciela (1998). On being non-native: language and national identity among Argentinian immigrants to Israel. PhD dissertation, Hebrew University, Jerusalem.

Sperber, Daniel (2012). *Greek in Talmudic Palestine.* Ramat-Gan, Israel: Bar-Ilan University Press.

Spitzer, Leo (1942). Milieu and ambiance: an essay in historical semantics. *Philosophy and Phenomenological Research,* 3, 1–42, 169–218.

Spolsky, Bernard (1974). Navajo language maintenance: six-year-olds in 1969. In Frank Pialorsi (ed.), *Teaching the Bilingual,* 138–49. Tucson: University of Arizona Press.

(1983). Triglossia and literacy in Jewish Palestine of the first century. *International Journal of the Sociology of Language,* 42, 95–110.

(1985). Jewish multilingualism in the first century: an essay in historical sociolinguistics. In Joshua A. Fishman (ed.), *Readings in the Sociology of Jewish Languages,* 35–50. Leiden: Brill.

(1989). Māori bilingual education and language revitalization. *Journal of Multilingual and Multicultural Development,* 9, 1–18.

(1995). Two Wellington families: Green and Spolsky. In Stephen Levine (ed.), *A Standard for the People: The 150th Anniversary of the Wellington Hebrew Congregation 1843–1993,* 271–8. Wellington: Hazard Press.

(2002). Norms, native speakers and reversing language shift. In Susan M. Gass, Kathleen Bardovi-Harlig, Sally Sieloff Magnan, and Joel Walz (eds.), *Pedagogical Norms for Second and Foreign Language and Teaching: Studies in Honour of Albert Valdman,* 41–58. Amsterdam: John Benjamins.

(2004). *Language Policy.* Cambridge University Press.

(2009a). *Language Management.* Cambridge University Press.

(2009b). Rescuing Māori: the last 40 years. In Peter K. Austin (ed.), *Language Documentation and Description,* vol. VI, 11–36. London: School of Oriental and African Studies.

(2011). Ferguson and Fishman: sociolinguistics and the sociology of language. In Ruth Wodak, Barbara Johnstone, and Paul Kerswill (eds.), *The Sage Handbook of Sociolinguistics*, 11–23. London: Sage.

(ed.) (2012). *The Cambridge Handbook of Language Policy*. Cambridge University Press.

Spolsky, Bernard, and Amara, Muhammad Hasan (1986). The diffusion and integration of Hebrew and English lexical items in the spoken Arabic of an Israeli village. *Anthropological Linguistics*, 28, 43–54.

Spolsky, Bernard, and Cooper, Robert L. (1991). *The Languages of Jerusalem*. Oxford: Clarendon Press.

Spolsky, Bernard, and Shohamy, Elana (1999). *The Languages of Israel: Policy, Ideology and Practice*. Clevedon: Multilingual Matters.

(2001a). Hebrew after a century of RLS efforts. In Joshua A. Fishman (ed.), *Can Threatened Languages Be Saved?*, 349–62. Clevedon: Multilingual Matters.

(2001b). The penetration of English as language of science and technology into the Israeli linguistic repertoire: a preliminary enquiry. In Ulrich Ammon (ed.), *The Dominance of English as a Language of Science: Effects on Other Languages and Language Communities*, 167–76. Berlin: Mouton de Gruyter.

Stampfer, Shaul (1993). What did "knowing Hebrew" mean in eastern Europe? In Lewis Glinert (ed.), *Hebrew in Ashkenaz: A Language in Exile*, 129–40. Oxford University Press.

Statistics New Zealand (1997). *1996 Census of Population and Dwellings*. Wellington: Statistics New Zealand.

Stavans, Anat, Olshtain, Elite, and Goldzweig, Gil (2009). Parental perceptions of children's literacy and bilingualism: the case of Ethiopian immigrants in Israel. *Journal of Multilingual and Multicultural Development*, 30, 111–26.

Stavans, Ilan (2008). *Resurrecting Hebrew*. New York: Schocken Books.

Steinhardt, Nancy Schatzman (1999). The synagogue at Kaifeng: Sino-Judaic architecture of the diaspora. In Jonathan Goldstein (ed.), *The Jews of China*, vol. I, *Historical and Comparative Perspectives*, 3–21. Armonk, NY: M. E. Sharpe.

Stern, David (1986). Midrash and the language of exegesis: an analysis of Vayikra Rabbah, chap. 1. In Geoffrey H. Hartman and Sanford Budick (eds.), *Midrash and Literature*, 105–24. New Haven, CT: Yale University Press.

(1996). *Midrash and Theory: Ancient Jewish Exegesis and Contempory Literary Studies*. Evanston, IL: Northwestern University Press.

Stewart, William (1968). A sociolinguistic typology for describing national multilingualism. In Joshua A. Fishman (ed.), *Readings in the Sociology of Language*, 531–45. The Hague: Mouton.

Stillman, Norman A. (ed.) (1979). *The Jews of Arab Lands: A History and Source Book*. Philadelphia: Jewish Publication Society of America.

(2010a). Al-Andalus. In Norman A. Stillman (ed.), *Encyclopedia of Jews in the Islamic World*, vol. I, 100–15. Leiden: Brill.

(2010b). The Jewish experience in the Muslim world. In Judith R. Baskin and Kenneth Seeskin (eds.), *The Cambridge Guide to Jewish History, Religion, and Culture*, 85–112. Cambridge University Press.

Stone, Michael (2011). *Ancient Judaism: New Visions and Views*. Grand Rapids, MI: William B. Eerdmans Publishing.

Straten, Jits van (2011). *The Origin of Ashkenazi Jewry: The Controversy Unraveled.* Berlin: Walter de Gruyter.

Suleiman, Camelia (2011). *Language and Identity in the Israel–Palestine Conflict: The Politics of Self-Perception in the Middle East.* London: I. B. Tauris.

Szajkowski, Zosa (1970). *Jews and the French Revolutions of 1789, 1830 and 1848.* Tel Aviv: Ktav.

Taitz, Emily (1994). *The Jews of Medieval France: The Community of Champagne.* Westport, CT: Greenwood Press.

Tallerman, Maggie, and Gibson, Kathleen (eds.) (2011). *The Oxford Handbook of Language Evolution.* Oxford University Press.

Talmon, Shemaryahu (1975). The textual study of the Bible: a new outlook. In Frank Moore Cross and Shemaryahu Talmon (eds.), *Qumran and the History of the Biblical Text*, 321–400. Cambridge, MA: Harvard University Press.

Taylor, Douglas (1961). New languages for old in the West Indies. *Comparative Studies in Society and History*, 3, 277–88.

Taylor, Joan E. (2012). *The Essenes, the Scrolls, and the Dead Sea.* Oxford University Press.

Teeter, D. Andrew (2010). Scribes and scribalism. In John J. Collins and Daniel C. Harlow (eds.), *The Eerdmans Dictionary of Early Judaism*, 1201–4. Grand Rapids, MI: William B. Eerdmans Publishing.

Thompson, R. W. (1961). A note on some possible affinities between the creole dialects of the Old World and those of the New. In Robert P. Le Page (ed.), *Proceedings of the Conference on Creole Language Studies*, vol. II, 107–13. London: Macmillan.

Thompson, Roger M. (1974). Mexican American language loyalty and the validity of the 1970 census. *International Journal of the Sociology of Language*, 2, 7–18.

Tigchelaar, Eibert (2010). The Dead Sea Scrolls. In John J. Collins and Daniel C. Harlow (eds.), *The Eerdmans Dictionary of Early Judaism*, 163–80. Grand Rapids, MI: William B. Eerdmans Publishing.

Timm, Erika, and Beckerman, Gustav Adolf (2006). *Etymologische Studien zum Jiddischen: Zugleich ein Beitrag zur Problematik der jiddischen Südost- und Ostflanke.* Hamburg: Helmut Buske Verlag.

Toaff, Ariel (1972). Naples. In Cecil Roth and Geoffrey Wigoder (eds.), *Encyclopedia Judaica*, vol. XII, 822. Jerusalem: Keter.

Tobi, Joseph (1999). *The Jews of Yemen: Studies in Their History and Culture.* Leiden: Brill.

Tobias, Henry J. (1969). The Jews in tsarist Russia: the political education of a minority. In Henry J. Tobias and Charles E. Woodhouse (eds.), *Minorities and Politics*, 19–38. Albuquerque: University of New Mexico Press.

Tossavainen, Mikael (2009a). Scandinavia. In M. Avrum Ehrlich (ed.), *Encyclopedia of the Jewish Diaspora: Origins, Experiences, and Culture*, vol. III, 1050–7. Santa Barbara, CA: ABC-CLIO.

(2009b). Jews in Sweden. In M. Avrum Ehrlich (ed.), *Encyclopedia of the Jewish Diaspora: Origins, Experiences, and Culture*, vol. III, 1087–92. Santa Barbara, CA: ABC-CLIO.

Trumper-Hecht, Nira (2009). Constructing national identity in mixed cities in Israel: Arabic on signs in the public space of Upper Nazareth. In Elana Shohamy and

Durk Gorter (eds.), *Linguistic Landscape: Expanding the Scenery*, 238–52. London: Routledge.

Tsiliyianni, Constantinos A. (2004). The Jews of Arta (trans. Marcia H. Ikonomopoulos). *Chronika*, 192; available at www.kkjsm.org/archives/Jews%20of%20Arta%20Chronika%202004.pdf.

Tulchinsky, Gerald (1993). *Taking Root: The Origins of the Canadian Jewish Community*. Hanover, NH: Brandeis University Press.

(2008). *Canada's Jews: A People's Journey*. University of Toronto Press.

Ulrich, Eugene (1992). The canonical process, textual study, and later stages in the composition of the Bible. In Shemaryahu Talmon, Michael A. Fishbane, Emanuel Tov, and Weston W. Fields (eds.), *"Sha'arei Talmon": Studies in the Bible, Qumran, and the Ancient Near East presented to Shemaryahu Talmon*, 267–91. Winona Lake, IN: Eisenbrauns.

Ury, Adolphe (1906). Metz. In *The Jewish Encyclopedia*, vol. VIII, 522–4. New York: Funk & Wagnall.

Van der Horst, Pieter W. (2010). Greek. In John J. Collins and Daniel C. Harlow (eds.), *The Eerdmans Dictionary of Early Judaism*, 690–2. Grand Rapids, MI: William B. Eerdmans Publishing.

Van Seters, John (1999). In the Babylonian exile with J: between judgement in Ezekiel and salvation in Second Isaiah. In Bob Becking and Marjo C. A. Korpel (eds.), *The Crisis of Israelite Religion: Transformation of Religious Tradition in Exilic and Post-Exilic Times*, 71–89. Leiden: Brill.

Vanderkam, James C. (2010). *The Dead Sea Scrolls Today* (2nd edn). Grand Rapids, MI: William B. Eerdmans Publishing.

Verschik, Anna (1999). The Yiddish language in Estonia: past and present. *Journal of Baltic Studies*, 30, 117–28.

(2007). Jewish Russian and the field of ethnolect study. *Language in Society*, 36, 213–32.

(2010a). Ethnolect debate: evidence from Jewish Lithuanian. *International Journal of Multilingualism*, 7, 285–305.

(2010b). The Jewish Lithuanian periodical *Apžvalga* (1935–1940): towards a new cultural polysystem. *Central and East European Review*, 4, 1–17.

Versteegh, Kees (1997). *The Arabic Language*. New York: Columbia University Press.

Vilhjálmsson, Vilhjálmur Örn (2004). Iceland, the Jews, and anti-Semitism, 1625–2004. *Jewish Political Studies Review*, 16, 131–56.

Von Falkenhausen, Vera. The Jews of Byzantine south Italy. In Robert Bonfil (ed.), *Jews in Byzantium: Dialectics of Minority and Majority Cultures*, 271–96. Leiden: Brill.

Wacholder, Ben Zion (1956). The proselytizing of slaves during the Gaonic era. *Historia Judaica*, 18, 89–106.

Wallet, Bart T. (2006). "End of the jargon-scandal": the decline and fall of Yiddish in the Netherlands (1796–1886). *Jewish History*, 20, 333–48.

(2012). Links in a chain: early modern Yiddish historiography in the northern Netherlands (1743–1812). PhD dissertation, University of Amsterdam.

Walter, Stephen L. (2003). Does language of instruction matter in education? In Mary Ruth Wise, Thomas N. Headland, and Ruth M. Brend (eds.), *Language and Life: Essays in Memory of Kenneth L. Pike*, 611–35. Dallas: SIL International.

(2008). The language of instruction issue: framing an empirical perspective. In Bernard Spolsky and Francis M. Hult (eds.), *Handbook of Educational Linguistics*, 129–46. Malden, MA: Blackwell.

Walters, Keith (2011). Education for Jewish girls in late nineteenth- and early twentieth-century Tunis and the spread of French in Tunisia. In Emily Benichou Gottreich and Daniel J. Schroeter (eds.), *Jewish Culture and Society in North Africa*, 257–81. Bloomington: Indiana University Press.

Walzer, Michael (2012). *In God's Shadow: Politics in the Hebrew Bible*. New Haven, CT: Yale University Press.

Warren, Charles (1876). *Underground Jerusalem: An Account of Some of the Principal Difficulties Encountered in Its Exploration and the Results Obtained*. London: Richard Bentley & Son.

Wasserman, Henry (1972). Regensburg. In Cecil Roth and Geoffrey Wigoder (eds.), *Encyclopedia Judaica*, vol. XIV, 35–7. Jerusalem: Keter.

Wasserstein, Bernard (2012). *On the Eve: The Jews of Europe before the Second World War*. New York: Simon & Schuster.

Watts, James W. (ed.) (2001). *Persia and Torah: The Theory of Imperial Authorization of the Pentateuch*. Atlanta: Society of Biblical Literature.

Weil, Shalva (2001). Bene Israel of Mumbai, India. Beit Hatfutsot, www.bh.org.il/database-article.aspx?48701.

Weinreich, Max (1956). Yiddish, Knaanic, Slavic: the basic relationships. In Morris Halle, Horace G. Lunt, Hugh McLean, and Cornelis H. van Schooneveld (eds.), *For Roman Jakobson: Essays on the Occasion of His Sixtieth Birthday, 11 October 1956*, 622–32. The Hague: Mouton.

(1980). *History of the Yiddish Language* (trans. Joshua A. Fishman and Shlomo Noble). University of Chicago Press.

(2008). *History of the Yiddish Language* (rev. 2-vol. edn, trans. Shlomo Noble). New Haven, CT: Yale University Press.

Weinreich, Uriel (1949). *College Yiddish: An Introduction to the Yiddish Language and to Jewish Life and Culture*. New York: Yiddish Scientific Institute.

(1953). *Languages in Contact: Findings and Problems*. Linguistic Circle of New York.

(ed.) (1968). *Modern English–Yiddish Yiddish–English Dictionary*. New York: YIVO Institute for Jewish Research.

Weinryb, Bernard Dov Sucher (1972). Mainz. In Cecil Roth and Geoffrey Wigoder (eds.), *Encyclopedia Judaica*, vol. XI, 788–91. Jerusalem: Keter.

Weiser, Chaim M. (1995). *Frumspeak: The First Dictionary of Yeshivish*. Lanham, MD: Rowman & Littlefield.

Weitzman, Steve (1989). Why did the Qumran community write in Hebrew? *Journal of the American Oriental Society*, 119, 35–45.

Wellhausen, Julius (1878). *Prolegomena to the History of Israel* (trans. J. Sutherland Black and Allan Menzies). Edinburgh: A. C. Black.

Weltsch, Robert (1972). Germany. In Cecil Roth and Geoffrey Wigoder (eds.), *Encyclopedia Judaica*, vol. VII, 483–95. Jerusalem: Keter.

Wexler, Paul (1987). *Explorations in Judeo-Slavic Linguistics*. Leiden: Brill.

(1991). Yiddish – the fifteenth Slavic language: a study of partial language shift from Judeo-Sorbian to German. *International Journal of the Sociology of Language*, 91, 9–150.

(1996). *The Non-Jewish Origins of the Sephardic Jews*. Albany: State University of New York Press.

(1997). The case for the relexification hypothesis in Rumanian. In Julia Horvath and Paul Wexler (eds.), *Relexification in Creole and Non-Creole Languages, with special attention to Haitian Creole, Modern Hebrew, Romani, and Rumanian*, 162–88. Wiesbaden: Otto Harrassowitz Verlag.

(2002). *Two-Tiered Relexification in Yiddish: Jews, Sorbs, Khazars and the Kiev-Polessian Dialect*. Berlin: Mouton de Gruyter.

(ed.) (2006). *Jewish and Non-Jewish Creators of "Jewish" Languages, with special attention to Judaized Arabic, Chinese, German, Greek, Persian, Portuguese, Slavic (Modern Hebrew/Yiddish), Spanish, and Karaite, and Semitic Hebrew/Ladino: A Collection of Reprinted Articles from across Four Decades with a Reassessment*. Wiesbaden: Otto Harrassowitz Verlag.

Wickham, Chris (2009). *The Inheritance of Rome: Illuminating the Dark Ages*. London: Penguin Books.

Wirth, Louis (1998 [1928]). *The Ghetto: with a New Introduction by Hasia R. Diner*. New Brunswick, NJ: Transaction Publishers.

Wojciehowski, Hanna Chapelle (2011). *Group Identity in the Renaissance World*. Cambridge University Press.

Woodworth, Cherie (2010). Where did the east European Jews come from? An explosive debate erupts from old footnotes. *Kritika*, 11, 105–23.

Xin, Xu (2003). *The Jews of Kaifeng, China: History, Culture, and Religion*. Jersey City, NJ: Ktav.

Xu, Daming (2004). The speech community theory. *Journal of Chinese Sociolinguistics*, 2, 18–28.

Yadin, Yigael, and Naveh, Joseph (1989). *Masada I: The Yigael Yadin Excavations 1963–1965 Final Reports*. Jerusalem: Israel Exploration Society.

Yahil, Chaim (1972). Czechoslovakia. In Cecil Roth and Geoffrey Wigoder (eds.), *Encyclopedia Judaica*, vol. V, 1188–94. Jerusalem: Keter.

Ye'or, Bat (ed.) (1985). *The Dhimmi: Jews and Christians under Islam*. Rutherford, NJ: Fairleigh Dickinson University Press.

Yehoshua, Abraham B. (1999). *A Journey to the End of the Millennium: A Novel of the Middle Ages* (trans. Nicholas de Lange). London: Peter Halban.

Young, Ian, Rezetko, Robert, and Ehrenvard, Martin (2008). *Linguistic Dating of Biblical Texts: An Introduction to Approaches and Problems*. London: Equinox.

Young, Robert W. (1977). Written Navajo: a brief history. In Joshua A. Fishman (ed.), *Advances in the Creation and Revision of Writing Systems*, 459–70. The Hague: Mouton.

Zacharia, Scaria (2012). Jewish Malayalam. Jewish Language Research Website, www.jewish-languages.org/jewish-malayalam.html.

Zack, Liesbeth, and Schippers, Arie (eds.) (2012). *Middle Arabic and Mixed Arabic: Diachrony and Synchrony*. Leiden: Brill.

Zamenhof, Ludwig (1982). *Provo de gramatiko de novjuda lingvo kaj Alvoko al la juda intelektularo* (ed. Adolf Holzhaus). Espoo, Finland: Esperantosäätiö.

Zangenberg, Jürgen K., and van de Zande, Dianne (2010). Urbanization. In Catherine Hezser (ed.), *The Oxford Handbook of Jewish Daily Life in Roman Palestine*, 165–87. Oxford University Press.

Zenner, Walter P. (2000). *A Global Community: The Jews from Aleppo*. Detroit: Wayne State University Press.

Zfatman, Sarah (2010). *From Talmud Times to the Middle Ages*. Jerusalem: Magnes Press.

Zuckermann, Ghil'ad (2006). *Israelit Safa Yafa [Israeli – a Beautiful Language]*. Tel Aviv: Am Oved.

Index